A NATION *of* SPEECHIFIERS

A NATION OF SPEECHIFIERS

Making an American Public after the Revolution

CAROLYN EASTMAN

THE UNIVERSITY OF CHICAGO PRESS × CHICAGO AND LONDON

CAROLYN EASTMAN was born in Reedley, California, and received her doctorate at Johns Hopkins University. She is now assistant professor of history at the University of Texas and lives in Austin. Her essays have appeared in *Gender and History*, the *William and Mary Quarterly*, and *American Nineteenth-Century History*.

The University of Chicago Press, Chicago 60637
The University of Chicago Press, Ltd., London
© 2009 by The University of Chicago
All rights reserved. Published 2009
Printed in the United States of America

18 17 16 15 14 13 12 11 10 09   1 2 3 4 5

ISBN-13: 978-0-226-18019-9 (cloth)
ISBN-10: 0-226-18019-0 (cloth)

Library of Congress Cataloging-in-Publication Data
Eastman, Carolyn.
 A nation of speechifiers: making an American public after the Revolution / Carolyn Eastman.
  p. cm.
 Includes bibliographical references and index.
 ISBN-13: 978-0-226-18019-9 (cloth : alk. paper)
 ISBN-10: 0-226-18019-0 (cloth : alk. paper)
  1. Oratory—Social aspects—United States—History—18th century. 2. Oratory—Social aspects—United States—History—19th century. 3. Nationalism—United States—History—18th century. 4. Nationalism—United States—History—19th century. I. Title.
 PN4055.U5E27 2010
 808.5'1097309034—dc22
                                         2009010515

♾ The paper used in this publication meets the minimum requirements of the American National Standard for Information Sciences—Permanence of Paper for Printed Library Materials, ANSI Z39.48-1992.

FOR *Jennifer, Jeannie, and Roger Eastman,*

AND FOR *Ella Coghlan Eastman (1903–2003), who knew about history*

Contents

ACKNOWLEDGMENTS {ix}

Introduction: Messy Beginnings {1}

PART I Making an American Public: Overviews {15}

1 Demosthenes in America {17}
FROM SENSIBILITY TO NATIONALISM IN ELOCUTIONARY EDUCATION

2 Vindicating Female Eloquence {53}
GIRLS' ORATORY AND THE RISE AND FALL OF A FEMALE COUNTERPUBLIC

3 Mourning for Logan {83}
"INDIAN ELOQUENCE" AND THE MAKING OF AN AMERICAN PUBLIC

PART II Contesting Public Participation: Debating "the Public" {113}

4 "A Club Is a Nation in Miniature" {115}
YOUNG MEN ON THE MAKE AND THEIR DEBATING SOCIETIES

5 Saint Franklin {145}
JOURNEYMEN PRINTERS AND THE MEDIUM OF DEMOCRATIC VIRTUE

6 "Who's Afraid" of Frances Wright? {179}
MEDIA DEBATES ABOUT THE PUBLIC AND ITS SPOKESMEN

Conclusion: The Ongoing Process of Making an American Public {211}

ABBREVIATIONS {219}   NOTES {221}   INDEX {283}

Acknowledgments

From the beginning of this project I have been lucky to gain support and advice from brilliant scholars, friends, and institutions. Among the latter I offer special thanks to the American Antiquarian Society and the Massachusetts Historical Society, which offered me short-term fellowships early in my research, experiences that proved invaluable for learning how to find materials and think about a large-scale project.

In addition the Library Company of Philadelphia, the Frederick Jackson Turner Fund from the Johns Hopkins University History Department, the New-York Historical Society, the Gilder Lehrman Institute of American History, the Kluge Center at the Library of Congress, the American Historical Association, and the University of Texas offered research time and financial support to visit remote archival and rare books collections.

I also wish to thank the archivists and librarians at the Boston Athenaeum, the Historical Society of Pennsylvania, the Library of Congress, the Maryland Historical Society, and the New York Public Library for providing assistance with their special collections.

I began this work at Johns Hopkins University, where the exchanges among disciplines and the generosity of many scholars helped me develop and refine the project. For their help I thank Nancy Berlage, Dirk Bönker, François Furstenberg, Jack Greene, Michael Henderson, Michael Moon, Dorothy Ross, Judy Walkowitz, Larzer Ziff, and the members of Toby Ditz's Early American Research Seminar, Jack Greene's Early Modern British American Research Seminar, and the General Seminar of the Program for the Study of Women, Gender, and Sexuality. Ron Walters in particular offered advice and insights on the whole manuscript that often fundamentally shifted my views, and did so with such gentleness and grace that I often only recognized the full extent of his critique days later.

It was at Hopkins that I met Frances Clarke, Thomas Foster, and Rebecca Plant, whose friendships have been the most important of my life. During grad school CRAFT met weekly for dinner, mutual support, and rigorous criticism of one another's work. They read every word of each draft of my chapters, no matter how awful; this experience was so formative that I still feel more enthusiastic about their books than I do about my own. I continue to rely on them today and deeply miss the food and drink that fueled our conversations when we all lived within blocks of one another. For a short-term and shorthanded version of CRAFT, I am ever grateful to Rebecca Plant and Rand Steiger for offering me a semester at the Torrey Pines Institute of Advanced Study, and to Sam Steiger, who exchanged ideas with me when we went to the Thoughtful Place.

At two junctures this project was deeply improved as a result of residential fellowships, each of which allowed me to dedicate a year to writing and exchanging ideas with experts in all facets of early American and early modern history. A dissertation fellowship from the McNeil Center for Early American Studies—just at the point when I began writing chapters—left me indebted to the Center's director, Richard Dunn, as well as to Roger Abrahams, Seth Cotlar, Konstantin Dierks, Rodney Hessinger, Albrecht Koschnik, Trish Loughran, Karim Tiro, and Mike Zuckerman, and the rest of the members of the Center Seminar. Later, a Lloyd Lewis fellowship from the Newberry Library gave me the opportunity to revise the manuscript while working alongside Jason Frank, Jim Grossman, Jen Koslow, Ruth MacKay, Jeff Sklansky, Eric Slauter, Frank Valadez, Dror Wahrman, Liz Wingrove, Al Young, and other fellows and Chicago-area scholars. The Newberry was an ideal place for writing and reflecting when I was at a crucial stage in rethinking the project. For ongoing conversations with scholars in the broader field of early American studies, I thank Pat Crain, Sandra Gustafson, Cathy Kelly, David Shields, Michael Warner, and Caroline Winterer, each of whom provided critical advice at crucial stages. At the University of Chicago Press, I thank Robert Devens, Alice Bennett, and Anne Summers Goldberg.

I found at the University of Texas an extraordinary community of scholars in my field who are unparalleled in their engagement and generosity: Jorge Cañizares-Esguerra, Judy Coffin, Julie Hardwick, Neil Kamil, Lisa Moore, Bob Olwell, and Jim Sidbury, whose conversations about Atlantic histories have changed how I think. I cannot thank enough my Austin friends, colleagues, and grad students: Bob Abzug, Samer Ali, Kim Alidio,

Shana Bernstein, Lissa Bollettino, Erika Bsumek, Janet Davis, George Forgie, Claire Gherini, Jessica Luther, Al Martinez, Anne Martínez, Tracie Matysik, Holly and Shane Melear, the fierce Chloe Melear, Julia Mickenberg, Howard Miller, Amy Hagstrom Miller, Karl Hagstrom Miller, Sharmila Rudrappa, Mike Stoff, Susan Stolar, and Shirley Thompson. Early in my tenure here, friendships with Ethan Blue, Ryan Carey, Steve Galpern, and Jimmy McWilliams helped me get acclimated. Later on Kenny Aslakson shared his voracious appetite for discussing all things: politics, the contradictions of life in Texas, gender trouble, and early American history—conversations that meant more to me than he knows.

Finally, throughout these years Susan Boettcher and Jolie Olcott have been my friends and interlocutors: suffice it to say that these are righteous women.

My deepest debt goes to Toby Ditz, who has provided clearheaded advice and energy at every stage of my career. Every scholar should have an adviser who so insistently holds her to high standards. I told Toby once that I was trying to channel her presence when I worked with graduate students, but I am a sorry imitation.

Last of all I thank my beloved family, Jeannie, Jennifer, and Roger Eastman, and Kevin Shupe, who is true blue.

INTRODUCTION

Messy Beginnings

Few phrases in American history are as evocative as the one that opens the Preamble to the United States Constitution: "We, the People of the United States." With that introduction, the framers summoned a "we" responsible for, and constitutive of, "a more perfect union." The Constitution gained much of its authority through this invocation of a unified "people" who shared a singleness of mind and purpose.[1] The phrase would also come to commemorate a particular story of the ratification of the Constitution as an orderly procedure in which communities gathered together to hear it read aloud and to consider the merits of a strong federal government. A satisfying opening to be sure, it has long spurred Americans to look back to this moment and imagine that a unified "we" existed from the beginning and that becoming the subjects of a new nation entailed an obvious and easy shifting of allegiance from Britain to the new United States.

But in 1787 that notion of "we" obfuscated more than it described, for it cloaked vast disagreements over politics, culture, and the Constitution itself. And it left many questions unresolved during the fifty years after the Revolution. Who, exactly, counted within it, given that such disenfranchised groups as women, Indians, white men without property, and enslaved and indentured peoples easily constituted a majority of the population? Did inclusion imply other privileges or rights, such as citizenship or the right to vote? Even by the early 1830s, the end of the period under review here, these questions remained in flux.

The new United States had few institutional resources to stimulate a shared national identity among the populace. It lacked a system of public education, a canon of patriotic literature, and a postal system. Boats were the most efficient form of transportation, since horse-drawn carriages could travel only intermittently during wet and icy seasons; even in good weather, it took up to two weeks to traverse the myriad dirt roads from Philadelphia to Pittsburgh. Patriotic symbols remained notoriously in flux as well. The official design of the American flag changed several times by 1818, as legislators vacillated on whether the total number of stripes as well as stars should match the number of states. Even the Indian princess, the iconic female figure used to symbolize America in popular visual imagery, was gradually being supplanted by the white Columbia. The one exception to this chaotic state of patriotic symbols was the figure of George Washington, who, upon his election to the presidency in 1788 (and even more so after his death in 1799), quickly came to exemplify leadership and virtue in numerous paintings, speeches, and Fourth of July toasts. Yet some feared that Americans venerated Washington as the British did their king, exposing a dangerous tendency toward idolatry. The one identity that most white Americans had previously shared—their Britishness—was now precisely what they were *not*.

In the years after the Revolution, Americans had surprisingly vague understandings of themselves as national subjects. This had not been true before the war. For generations, and especially during the eighteenth century, most colonists had identified as subjects of Great Britain, an empire that reinforced national identity through a set of well-defined characteristics and institutions—a unique language, a long history, a strong tradition of the law, clear definitions of the rights of its subjects and citizens, Protestantism, and superior arts and sciences, to name a few. All these qualities had gained heightened meaning as eighteenth-century Britons (including the British colonists in America) contrasted themselves with the French; not being French brought a vast, heterogeneous population together in a powerful sense of shared Britishness.[2] In addition, the former colonists had only recently ceased to think of "American" as an alternative designation for Indians, or even as a synonym for "hick." Therefore the establishment of new governments and constitutions in the United States was only one part of a larger project to foster unification and civic engagement by men and women. They had to *learn* to be American.

It is difficult at our remove to recapture the messiness surrounding these identities. By the twentieth century, Americans would take for granted and even celebrate the vast differences in culture and sensibility between residents of Miami, Anchorage, rural Utah, and Manhattan while also finding those differences consonant with a shared American identity. Modern-day men and women see their national identity as one among many identities they embrace, including religious, ethnic, regional, and familial. But in postrevolutionary America such heterogeneity provoked deep anxieties. Delegates to the Continental Congress during the war, for example, wrote home of their fascination with far-flung fellow delegates, who spoke with unintelligible accents and maintained bizarre personal habits and modes of dress. To delegates such as Joseph Galloway of Pennsylvania, it appeared that the colonists' "different forms of Government—Productions of the Soil—and Views of Commerce, their different Religions—Tempers and private Interest—their Prejudices against, and Jealousies of, each other" were so pronounced that "they never can unite together even for their own Protection."[3] If delegates from urban Boston and rural South Carolina appeared so foreign to one another despite their shared elite status, what might this mean for the even more diverse populations they sought to represent?

Compounding regional differences was the resolute localism of virtually all American communities aside from a few port-based coastal cities. Most men and women maintained attachments that were overwhelmingly local, extending only intermittently to state or regional affiliations.[4] Moreover, no coherent media network, such as a national newspaper or publishing system, fostered national feeling or tied these local communities together into a national rubric.[5] Print shops operated on the smallest scale, usually run by a single owner and a tiny group of hired press hands. Printers in the postrevolutionary era served small locales and were technologically incapable of producing more than about four thousand copies of any given edition; most books, newspapers, and magazines emerged in editions of one thousand copies or fewer, even from the most prosperous urban printers.[6] Considering the exorbitant costs of paper and labor and slim profit margin, printers took the risk of printing large editions only with surefire items, usually popular British books; an estimated 75 percent of all American imprints before 1820 were reprints of European texts, mostly British—and some of these were reproduced so faithfully that they appeared in American editions with their paeans to British superiority intact.[7] For these reasons we cannot assume that any particular nationalistic text, no matter how popular, circulated widely enough to reach most of the reading public.

Neither did Americans coalesce around a clear notion of citizenship. In part because each state had established its own constitution with different definitions of citizenship, residency, and the right to vote. Americans seldom looked to citizenship per se to provide a common identity. Even after the ratification of the Constitution, political and judicial leaders did little to resolve issues concerning citizenship and naturalization, and in fact these matters quickly became fodder for battles between the Federalists and the Republicans. For generations, postrevolutionary society remained "shot through with forms of second-class citizenship, denying personal liberties and opportunities for political participation to most of the adult population on the basis of race, ethnicity, gender, and even religion," as Rogers Smith has shown.[8] Most people lacked both local and federal voting rights owing to age, sex, race, or property restrictions—moreover, many individuals did not know what federal citizenship rights they possessed.

Clearly, the fostering of national sentiment was not an inevitable or natural result of American independence. The diverse, localized, and largely disconnected material and institutional conditions of the new United States created serious impediments to national identification by nonelite Americans. And yet in a gradual, uneven manner, far-flung peoples gradually learned to see themselves as participants in a community that stretched well beyond their immediate locales. They learned to grant new civic and political valences to older forms of community affiliation. This book argues that they did so by engaging with the media of the day, as both consumers and producers of writing and oratory. In other words, here I explore not how Americans imagined their nation but rather the means by which they learned to conceive of *themselves* as members of a public and eventually to identify as national citizens.

"The public" is, to be sure, a vague descriptor for a community that was broader and more abstract than one's local or regional home. But orations and printed writings had long used this term to refer to both abstract and literal audiences, and during the early republic its use accelerated rapidly. Newspapers made announcements "To the Public!" and orators begged the public's indulgence as they opened their speeches. This designation predated the Revolution and American nationalism and was related to the newly positive appraisal of public opinion that spread throughout much of the Euro-American world during the mid-eighteenth century.[9] (It was not always used on Jürgen Habermas's terms, however, as I describe in more detail below.) In the pages that follow, I trace numerous means by which nonelite men and women identified themselves as belonging to the abstract social body of "the public." This identification at times overlapped with nationalistic sentiment, yet the two were not always equivalent. Print and oral media helped lay Americans think of themselves as members of a unified body before nationalism had cohered and could be buttressed by institutions. Any given speech or printed item did not have to reach a large number of auditors or readers to ask them to think of themselves as part of a larger community.

Men and women interacted with public speaking and print on two levels: as readers and listeners, of course, but also as writers and orators. Indeed, the title *A Nation of Speechifiers* is meant to emphasize that many nonelites were fully engaged in producing ideas about politics, manners, gender relations, and a host of other topics—and they did so to an extent heretofore unrecognized in historical scholarship. Each chapter analyzes a different site where men and women learned how to comport themselves in speech and writing and to engage in public conversation. Some chapters deal with specific groups or categories of individuals who learned to engage as public actors in particular ways; other chapters take a slightly different view, focusing on how formal writers and orators learned to address their reading and listening audiences in innovative and effective ways. Thus I explore how print and oratory were thoroughly interdependent and mutually constitutive in this era. Throughout, I seek to connect the experiences of lay citizens to broader changes in oral and print media as well as American political culture to demonstrate that Americans gradually came to imagine a national "people," tied together by shared manners and opinions as well as civic values.

As such, this book is situated at the intersection of two scholarly literatures, both of which have drawn on Habermas's powerful, if idealized, conceptions of an "authentic public sphere" in which individuals discussed and considered politics.[10] The first body of literature has sought to go "beyond the founders" to illustrate nonelites' and women's active engagement with politics. Scholars including Dena Goodman, Mary Kelley, Lawrence Klein, Joan Scott, and David Waldstreicher have refined Habermas's portrait of a clear distinction between public and private to show that a broad range of activities by men and women contributed substantially to the ongoing definitions of the state and to debates about it. These activities encompassed both formal political action, such as signing petitions and voting, and other forms of social behavior that had political import, such as discussions of manners or behavior, social reform, and the reading of fiction.[11] The second set of research has explored the crucial role of print and oral media in forming political relevant publics. This interdisciplinary group, including Kenneth Cmiel, Jay Fliegelman, Sandra Gustafson, Trish Loughran, and Michael Warner, has reinterpreted and historicized Habermas's understanding of the roles of print and oratory in the American public sphere.[12] But rather than focusing on canonical texts or prominent authors, *A Nation of Speechifiers* examines a profusion of writing and oratory by nonelites and their active uses of the media. It thus does more than bridge these rich historiographical literatures; it sketches a highly dynamic picture of Americans' engagement with oral and written media. I seek to demonstrate the broad political import of speeches and writings by ordinary people within the context of constructing an American public.

My ultimate goal is to consider the ways "the public" functioned as a vital concept during this era. I argue that an essential element of the political culture after the Revolution was an ongoing debate over the makeup of the public and a properly constituted public sphere. To do so, this book returns to three key questions: How did nonelite men and women learn to think of themselves as members of the public? How did the media play a role in that identification? And how did ideas of "the public" get reimagined and debated during this era? In their speeches and writings, political leaders and nonelites alike called forth new and varying iterations of the public. In doing so, a writer or speaker might position herself at the center of a unified body or, alternatively, speak as an outsider in order to redress perceived wrongs or inequities. Print and oral media mattered so much not only because they disseminated important public information, but because they provided sites for modeling exemplary public interactions, debates, and behavior. The significance of my work rests on its analysis of the production of new gender, class, and citizenship roles as they developed mutually between cultural leaders, the two mediums of print and oratory, and the reading and listening audiences at the center of an emerging national public. By the early 1830s, major changes had taken place in the ways men and women discussed their public participation, reflecting how contested and fraught the concept was throughout this era. Overall, then, my goal is less to argue that a public had been "made" by the 1830s than to illustrate the impact of lay individuals in debating the nature of the American public—jockeying for position and authority in the public sphere.

A very wide spectrum of white men and women in the Northeast (between the District of Columbia and Maine) learned at least rudimentary skills in composition and public speaking, whether in schools, in self-education societies, or on their own; these skills led them to read and listen critically to public debate in speech and print and to anchor that critical sensibility to an understanding of an idealized public. This was not unique to the Northeast; similar processes and circulations occurred in the South and West, although here I have taken advantage of the high concentration of literacy and communication pathways in the Northeast. Texts, schools, and literary societies strongly emphasized that writing or voicing one's own ideas prompted active learning and reasoning.[13] Focusing on interactions between people and the media reveals how far lay men and women shaped the meanings of nation and national belonging.

Print and oratory stand at the center of this project, for they were deeply implicated in the formation of national identity. These media called forth engagement from their reading and listening audiences. Writers and orators understood print and oratory to be not simply mediums for transmitting information but important institutions in themselves that pointed to the special nature of the United States and its place in the history of republics. Public speakers, for example, often reminded their audiences that oratory had galvanized the publics of ancient Greece and Rome; considering the enormous geographical terrain of the new United States, they speculated, print would provide the modern means of unifying an American public. Likewise, writers reminded Americans that their unusually high rate of literacy offered the republic a singular opportunity to realize the ideal of an informed citizenry.[14] With such invocations of print and oral media, authors continually reminded readers of their vital role in the republic. Idealized portrayals of literate, discerning audiences inspired actual men and women to see themselves in those roles. Print and oral media elicited the engaged national subjects they imagined already to be present. To be clear: I am concerned with how the media helped to create an imagined American public—a fantasy of an educated, understanding, discerning public that was so powerful that nonelite men and women contributed to it.

The dynamics of imagining a public in this era are exemplified in an 1834 speech given before a club at Harvard by a young lawyer named William Howard Gardiner. He explained: "We are indeed a nation of speechifiers. The pulpit speaks how copiously! The bar how interminably! Every public event of festivity, or condolence, is the occasion of meetings throughout the Union, and every meeting the occasion of a speech. . . . What millions of speeches are produced annually by these thirteen millions of people, [making us wonder] what in America is the daily average consumption of speech."[15] Gardiner was striking a humorous note: his hyperbolic portrayal of a "nation of speechifiers," and even more so the jab at his "interminably" verbose fellow lawyers, was doubtless designed for the ears of his classically trained auditors. Still, he reiterated a theme prevalent in the previous fifty years of speechifying when he imagined a public actively engaged in creating and sustaining its national ties by eloquence—and by print as well, since his speech was subsequently published. This was no image of a top-down culture orchestrated by powerful elites; it reflected a public that flocked to deliver and to enjoy public oratory. It did not matter whether a given individual was an auditor, an orator, or both, since Gardiner's point that any American might give a speech one day and listen to one the next augmented the ideal of an engaged public, animated and brought together by "eloquence, written and spoken" that served as "the great engine of this government."[16] In articulating such a fantasy of a unified and activist American public, Gardiner brought out that public from his listeners and readers. Textual and oratorical moments like this one prompted their audiences to imagine themselves as constituting a model public; they provided what the philosopher Charles Taylor calls the "webs of interlocution" that helped Americans feel they were engaged in a national conversation in which each of them had a part.[17]

Educational practices constituted the most common attempts to disseminate and democratize Americans' understandings of civic engagement, and as such they form important sites of study in the first half of this book. Schools existed everywhere in the states even during the colonial period, but they were unconnected and unregulated, almost always organized and funded at the local level, and sometimes lasted only eight weeks at a time. Moreover, schools were often led by untrained, poorly paid, and very young teachers who usually left their jobs quickly for more attractive employment.[18] Yet while schools in the new republic were in no way uniform or systematic, my analysis shows that they shared important practices—most notably the school "exhibition" at which the students performed speeches and theatrical scenes before their parents and other community members to demonstrate their educational progress, as described in chapter 1. These practices spread common understandings about individuals' relation to a larger society by demonstrating the critical role of writing and speech.

Schoolbooks, one of the main sources used here, illustrate well the nexus between a dispersed populace, a locally based print industry, and a cohering public culture. Although Americans had access to very different books depending on their region, schoolbooks in general shared themes, selections, and pedagogical uses such that they provided far-flung readers with common understandings of education and literary culture. Americans had long purchased these inexpensive books in record numbers. They became so ubiquitous during the early republic that they constituted a significant part of a typical printer's bread-and-butter income. Even in the most hardscrabble areas of the rural Northeast, stores offered schoolbooks for sale alongside the Bible, devotional works, and almanacs, and estate records demonstrate that even poor families were likely to own them.[19] Although some titles became best sellers that sold in the millions, hundreds of other titles appeared in only one or two editions, almost always edited by little-known schoolteachers or small-town printers who cribbed most of their material from other schoolbooks, magazines, or newspapers.[20] That most editors borrowed content from one another meant these texts transmitted a shared set of rules for pronunciation and recitation, moral lessons about gender roles and self-improvement, speeches, and literary texts. The diaries of boys and girls confirm that they used these books intensively, memorizing individual passages for schoolroom recitation and for entertaining their families at night; the records of literary clubs and debating societies show that their members used these schoolbook "pieces" in their meetings as examples of fine literature and oratory.[21] In other words, despite the diversity of titles that appeared and the scattershot nature of schools, a vast majority of Americans in the greater Northeast shared the experience of learning to read and speak aloud from schoolbooks. Taken together, the popular sites and practices examined in this book illustrate some of the key mechanisms by which men and women came to share a public culture.

Throughout this book, I depict the gradual expansion of public culture while also drawing attention to the limits and boundaries of that expansion. No matter how optimistically inclusive were popular depictions of the American public, they always reflected the conditions of power and the social hierarchy of politics during this era. Images of the public especially tended to exclude, in varying degrees, such individuals and groups as racial minorities, poor whites, and women. Spoken and written eloquence could help demarcate class, racial, and gender boundaries when it was delivered by a privileged member of society who assumed that his audience shared the knowledge and position required to join an informed public.[22] Some of those individuals who felt marginalized countered those assumptions and asserted that they deserved to be included as public actors, as we shall see in the case of young female orators in chapter 2. These girls articulated a counterpublic that celebrated the public contributions of women and, in turn, called on their peers to improve their oratory, writing, and behavior. At times, as other scholars have shown, African American and Indian writers or speakers employed similar rhetorical tactics.[23] But this was not the only strategy for improving one's position, as we shall see in the cases of teenage members of a young men's debating society and the journeymen printers of chapters 4 and 5 who, in their speeches and writings, figured themselves already at the center of an American public even though they had not yet established themselves. The book's sustained attention to the gendered and classed aspects of public participation signals my wider concern with the patterns of inclusion and exclusion that obtained in the early American public sphere.

In addition, imagining an *American* public during this era required strong contrasts to other publics—and rejection of them. Americans cultivated a complex triangular relationship with European societies and American Indians that, as Philip Deloria has noted, "prevented its creators from ever effectively developing a positive, stand-alone identity that did not rely heavily on either a British or an Indian foil."[24] American media frequently vacillated between admiring Indian or British eloquence and dismissing those peoples' inadequate commitment to civilization (Indians) or to democracy (Britain). Thus those foils helped create a clearer sense of American identity by means of both envy and exclusion. White Americans could display a sympathetic identification with the Indians (as in their fascination with Indian oratory, as analyzed in chapter 3) yet do so in a way that enhanced national identification and confidence.

A Nation of Speechifiers returns throughout to three themes: the symbiotic relationship between print and oratory, the role of gender categories in men's and women's civic lives, and the concept of the "public" and its complicated relation to the "private." Focusing on these themes allows me to challenge the tendency to frame each as a dichotomy—print versus oral culture, the male citizen versus the female subject, public versus private. In the political culture of the early republic, each was integrated with its opposite in intense and meaningful ways; each set of concepts was related reciprocally to the others; and none held static meanings.

I examine print and oratory together to underscore the interdependence of these mediums.[25] Viewing them in interaction rather than as artificially distinct (or even in opposition) allows us to see the specific ways men and women interacted with the media of their day. There are countless ways that the mediums of print and oratory were mutually constitutive. Schoolbooks, for example, frequently defined "reading" as an oral exercise, as when Montgomery Bartlett's *Practical Reader* (1822) stated that "reading implies, generally, the oral delivery or audible pronunciation of written composition."[26] Some Americans virtually never read silently. As Abraham Lincoln explained, "When I read aloud, two senses catch the idea: first, I see what I read, second, I hear it, and therefore can remember it better."[27] Children learned to read by reading aloud; they learned public speaking skills by reading books on oratory; they polished their epistolary skills to make letters more "conversational." Magazine editors read submissions aloud to gauge their suitability for publication, and public speakers submitted their speeches to newspapers and magazines to gain larger audiences for their ideas. George Washington's 1796 Farewell Address was *never* delivered orally, even though it became one of the earliest canonic American "speeches" used for elocutionary memorization and recitation during this era.

My focus on the complex reciprocity between print and oratory joins the most recent scholarship to revise earlier tendencies to position these mediums in opposition or to stress the ascendance of print culture in the eighteenth and nineteenth centuries at the expense of orality. Earlier scholars often characterized oral culture as a static, "traditional" medium in contrast to the modern and individuating nature of print culture and literacy, a dualism that persists in some current literature.[28] Until recently, histories of the public sphere have also tended to uphold a dualism between the mediums, associating print with abstract critical reasoning and the formation of publics. Foregrounding the reciprocal development of the two allows me to historicize their relationship within a complex cultural system.

Women and gender played important roles in evolving conceptions of public participation and civic orders during the early republic and appear as central topics in three of the six chapters in this book. Men and women experienced public culture in different ways, of course, but public and private worlds in this era were far from being sharply divided along gender lines. Some elite women in the Atlantic world had long held prominent public positions as writers, *salonistes*, and political brokers, and they continued to do so in America long after the war. During the Revolution and for several decades thereafter, new possibilities opened for rural and middling women beyond the realm of family and household—as speakers and writers as well as members of audiences. Virtually all girls who attended common schools were educated in composition and declamation in the same manner as boys and spoke before public audiences at school exhibitions. In addition, the postrevolutionary expansion of female education had wide-ranging implications for women's role in American society. Girls learned to couch their public speech in a feminine style, to be sure; but early republican public culture had much more room for women's participation than previous scholarship has assumed.

In addition, gender was an integral topic in a larger conversation about the nature and composition of a properly constituted American public sphere.[29] On a wide scale, men and women debated such subjects as appropriate gender relations, masculinity and femininity, the politics of bachelorhood and marriage, and the merits of women's public writing and speech—all germane to larger elements of political culture. The sometimes heated nature of these discussions suggests that they connoted much about the broader nature of American society. Analyzing the interactions between men and women regarding constructions of gender in society adds to my overall portrayal of the complex and mutual production of public life. These also demonstrate the relative agency of lay individuals while depicting the shape and hierarchies of power within political culture overall.

I likewise examine the notion of "public" on two levels—as a noun to describe an entity more all-encompassing than the juridical term "citizenry" and as an adjective that indicated a quality of activity or discourse within civil society, as in "public speech." In its description of the populace, the notion of "the public" did not rest on an opposition to private: this concept was deceptively plastic. Referring to the public allowed any writer or speaker to appear to speak to a wide "people" yet to also elicit a specific community of right-thinking individuals that was both inclusive and intimate.[30] In its vagueness, the term "the public" could evoke an imagined national unity by declaring that it already existed. But American culture was also rife with sharply divergent and conflicting definitions of the public, as we shall see in the case of Frances Wright and newspaper editors in chapter 6.

Examining the use of "public" as an adjective in this era allows me to contribute to a broader scholarly effort to disaggregate the conceptual categories of public and private from a strict Habermasian notion, which portrays the eighteenth-century public sphere as a realm of purely rational, deliberative debate. In doing so, I examine an in-between realm of experience that scholars have termed "civil society," encompassing a wide range of social action and behavior centered on shared interests, purposes, and values—endeavors that might have political import but that blurred the lines between state, family, market, and culture. This concept has allowed scholars to examine a great diversity of historical spaces, actors, and civil institutions that do not fit within a public/private dichotomy, subjects that explicitly demonstrate the absence of stable boundaries between public and private.[31] As Lawrence Klein has argued, "What people in the eighteenth century most often meant by 'public' was sociable as opposed to solitary (which was 'private')." Such insights have powerful implications, particularly for the analysis of women and gender in the constitution of American culture, as scholars have drawn new attention to shared-sex activities and heterosociability: "[Even if] women spent more time at home, they were not necessarily spending more time in private."[32] When Americans brought these terms into play, they rarely conceived of public and private as specifically oppositional terms. This becomes especially clear when we examine specific sites where men and women articulated their positions as legitimate members of a public culture. In these moments they offered rationales for their inclusion, requested public recognition, and sought to shape the opinions and feelings of their peers in ways that created ligatures between their public words and actions and their positions as private subjects.

The first three chapters of *A Nation of Speechifiers* take a broad view of the fifty-year span after the Revolution, focusing thematically on educational prints and sites that enhanced children's sense of themselves as belonging to a public. The first chapter, "Demosthenes in America," inspects the ways educational practices gradually gained civic and nationalistic power. Elocutionary schoolbooks and children's schoolroom performances are ideal sources for understanding new civic roles, since they explicitly linked graceful speech and proper conduct to the cultivation of character and, eventually, to the expression of patriotic belonging. The second chapter, "Vindicating Female Eloquence," closely follows the first by focusing on the gendered qualities of girls' elocution. Not only did girls speak regularly at their schools' public exhibitions, but they also learned elocution in virtually the same way as boys, and the knowledge was considered highly relevant to their comportment in everyday life. These themes emerged powerfully in the speeches by real girls written, delivered in front of their schools, and published, speeches that sometimes made broad claims about the possibilities of women's active participation in civic matters. The third chapter, "Mourning for Logan," analyzes Americans' fascination with Indian speeches by examining their place in schoolroom declamation and as reprinted in magazines. The specific uses print media made of this oratory taught readers that their singular capacity for remorse promised a new beginning for the United States. But changes in literary portrayals of Indians gradually permitted white readers to believe they might supersede the Indians and even make them obsolete. Each of these chapters locates a significant shift in American culture during the 1810s—in educational practices, in views of women in public, or in ways of speaking about whites' crimes against the Indians—that illuminates important changes in American identity and society cohering in that era.

In part 2, three case studies examine debates over public inclusion and the efforts by specific groups and individuals to make a place for themselves in public discourse. Chapter 4, "A Club Is a Nation in Miniature," studies a young men's debating society designed to assist its middling, upwardly mobile members at a formative period in their lives by helping them cultivate skills in speech and social engagement and providing the social connections useful to success in business. As writers and editors of a column for a literary magazine, these men embraced the elegant and witty literary styles of cultural elites—and the frequent subjects of gender behavior and courtships—to assert themselves as worthy commentators and mediators to the public. The fifth chapter, "Saint Franklin," analyzes journeymen printers' societies in several northeastern cities to show how these wage laborers helped promote print as a uniquely democratic and *American* medium for transmitting information. They did so in large part by portraying themselves as exemplars of print's magical and democratizing power: in their published speeches and anniversary toasts, "typographical" societies showed that their daily work in the print shop conferred the political knowledge and even eloquence that granted them full admittance to an educated public. But they also found that such self-representations became fragile during extended labor disputes and the ensuing battle for public opinion. The final chapter, "Who's Afraid of Frances Wright," examines the furor in the newspapers over the 1829 public lecture tour of Frances Wright, a radical English reformer, whom editors sought to discredit with a vehement gendered critique and sarcastic, dismissive portrayals of those who flocked to lecture halls to hear her. They produced a sense of conflict between right-thinking, refined newspaper readers who avoided the heterodoxies of lecturers like Wright and the promiscuous, heterogeneous audiences who, according to the editors, displayed their incapacity to be reasoning members of a republic. Each of the chapters in part 2 displays the relative agency of lay individuals while also depicting the social hierarchies and the shape of power within political culture overall. Together, these two sections of *A Nation of Speechifiers* scrutinize some of the means by which ordinary men and women articulated their place in a postrevolutionary culture, both as audiences for formal oratory or published writing and as speakers and writers. In the book as a whole, we see the development of the meaning of "the public"—from the efforts by some individuals to expand their role to the widespread debates and discussions over the nature of a properly constituted public sphere.

PART 1
Making an American Public: Overviews

CHAPTER 1

Demosthenes in America
FROM SENSIBILITY TO NATIONALISM IN ELOCUTIONARY EDUCATION

American schoolbooks routinely presented the Greek orator Demosthenes as a model for children to admire and emulate. In their stories, Demosthenes appears as a youth eager to display his civic virtue by speaking before the assembly but stymied by crippling speech impediments. As one early nineteenth-century schoolbook told the tale, he was "hissed by the whole audience" in his earliest attempts at public speaking, yet he triumphed over his humiliation through sheer will. He "went to the sea shore; and whilst the waves were in the most violent agitation, he pronounced harangues, to accustom himself by the confused noise of the waters, to the roar of the people, and the tumultuous cries of public assemblies." He placed pebbles in his mouth to overcome his "thick mumbling way of speaking," and to correct his chronic shortness of breath, he declaimed while marching uphill.[1] These legends of his perseverance raised him to the status of an elocutionary saint in early national schoolbooks. By learning to invest his speech with power and eloquence, Demosthenes went on to champion some of his country's most important causes, earning fame for both Greece and the art of oratory.

Demosthenes was the perfect model for American schoolchildren—and not just because his life epitomized the benefits of hard work and self-improvement. He symbolized the ideal civic orator, the "good man" whose selfless passion for virtue infused his speech with conviction and moved others to public action. The new United States decidedly lacked such a leader. American schoolbooks were replete with eloquent speeches on liberty and truth, but most had been delivered by contemporary British leaders such as William Pitt and Edmund Burke. The Revolution had produced a few memorable speakers—most notably Patrick Henry, whose "give me liberty or give me death" speech remained legendary (and apocryphal) — but none had assumed prominent positions in the postwar federal government; some of them, including Henry, had even become vocal Anti-Federalists. In fact, the most prominent American political figures of the late eighteenth century were notoriously weak speakers. When George Washington read a prepared speech for his inauguration in 1789 from handwritten notes, many in attendance cringed at his clumsy attempts to gesture while shifting the pages from hand to hand.[2] Schoolbook editors did not hesitate to address this gap in oratorical leadership. Trying to put the best face on the problem, Increase Cooke's *American Orator* (1811) explained that "the public speakers of this country have been celebrated as excellent reasoners; while their orators have been few." Cooke attributed these leaders' oratorical failings to "indolence with regard to the requisite labour, and inattention to the high value of eloquence."[3] Acknowledgments like this, alongside the story of Demosthenes, allowed schoolbooks to up the ante when they asked children to improve their speech. The future of the republic depended on it — or so they implied.

Apparently the republic depended more on children's good speech habits than on what came to be called "civics," since information about the nation's history, its founding texts, or the people's shared characteristics was almost entirely absent from American schoolbooks and children's reports of school curricula before the 1810s. Instead, teachers and schoolbooks alike concentrated on refining children's characters, deportment, and speech as important elements of preparing them to participate in society. Learning "genteel address" via the methods circulated by the transatlantic elocution movement was crucial to all walks of life, educators insisted. "Knowledge adorned by manners, and polished by refinement, will infallibly procure" a good reputation and success in business, the *Universal Asylum* told its readers in 1791.[4] As much as this philosophy differed from later notions of civics instruction, however, contemporaries would have argued that it did teach children that they had important roles as members of the public. As they improved themselves, they improved the nation as a whole. Educational practices forwarded an understanding of belonging to the public that prompted highly engaged participation by nonelite men and women.

This chapter establishes a conceptual foundation for the book as a whole by showing that elocutionary education taught lay Americans to share views of public engagement long before such participation was defined solely in patriotic terms. My close examination of the ideals and practices of this ubiquitous form of learning demonstrates that its early emphasis on cultivating sensibility transmitted a powerful sense of children's responsibilities as members of the public. Nor were those prescriptive messages limited to printed schoolbooks; they were evident at the "exhibition days" when schoolchildren displayed their knowledge by declaiming short speeches and scenes before large audiences of parents and community members, performances that gave enormous numbers of boys and girls throughout the Northeast similar experiences in public speaking. Not until the 1810s did schoolbooks begin to engage their readers explicitly as national subjects and to cultivate patriotism—and even then they emphasized the central significance of oratory. As schoolbooks heralded new congressional orators such as Daniel Webster, John Randolph, and Henry Clay as exemplifying political virtue, they claimed that the United States had now realized its potential to create civic leaders who might fulfill the role of Demosthenes in America. In sum, the focus on oratory in early republican education established conceptions of public engagement that were widely shared across regions and in urban and rural settings alike and played an important role in offering a range of definitions of the American public overall. The cross-fertilization of education, public speech, and nationalism created new ways of understanding the public and its leaders in the early American republic.

EDUCATION AND ELOCUTION IN THE EARLY REPUBLIC

By the twentieth century, American public education had become such a powerful institution, and so integral to fostering patriotic identification and civic education among the young, that scholars often struggled to describe earlier educational practices and theories outside those terms.[5] To be sure, it proved easy to find late eighteenth-century writings that advocated education as the best means of promoting national identification in youth, as if it were only a matter of time before Americans would arrive at a uniform, publicly financed system for educating the masses (it would take a century). Benjamin Rush, for example, wrote that Americans must "adapt our modes of teaching to the peculiar form of our government." He famously theorized that a systematic education could "convert men into republican machines. This must be done, if we expect them to perform their parts properly, in the great machine of the government of state."[6] Rush's enthusiasm for an orderly system by which citizens learned "a regard for their country" was matched by that of Noah Webster, who also advocated educating Americans *as* Americans, by seeking to "implant . . . the principles of virtue and of liberty; and inspire them with just and liberal ideas of government, and with an inviolable attachment to their own country."[7] In 1795 the American Philosophical Society sponsored a contest for the best essay on a national system of education, promising a prize of one hundred dollars. When the society emerged with two winners to share the prize (one a prominent minister, the other a newspaper editor), it arranged for the publication of both essays.[8] Writings by prominent cultural leaders were supplemented by hundreds of additional published writings by lay citizens similarly recommending educational reform.[9] The frequent appearance of such writings demonstrates how thoroughly some of the most visible cultural leaders of this era imagined education as a primary means of prompting national identification among the public. As the historian Lawrence Cremin has noted, no other topic was so thoroughly discussed in the early republic as the need for universal education.[10]

But if these writers agreed that education was essential to the flourishing of the republic, they differed on nearly all the specifics. Foremost were disagreements over the appropriate aims of such a national system. Whereas some advocates of egalitarianism saw education as a tool for creating a more democratic society and preparing large numbers of the people (even women and racial minorities) for political participation, most Americans—Federalist and Republican alike—did not agree. They maintained more conventional views that education was not necessary for the poor beyond learning to read and cipher. Neither did citizens believe that tuition should be free, particularly for older children who required more advanced or specialized topics. Some of the most aristocratic thinkers saw education more as a means of fostering social obedience than enhancing intellects; a few went so far as to oppose educating the poor.[11] Others disregarded elementary-level schooling altogether, instead promoting improvements in advanced academies and colleges; one popular conversation concerned establishing a single national university. A significant subset of magazine writers were preoccupied with whether schools should teach "practical" subjects to boys and eschew Latin and Greek—a topic laden with class assumptions, since only a tiny number of the most privileged boys would find use for those languages. Virtually no one discussed the prospect of national oversight of schools or uniformity of curricula—most likely because such ideas were unimaginable, but also because they would have been anathema to a population accustomed to local control.

Virtually none of these proposals was implemented—and not for lack of trying. Several times between 1779 and 1817, Thomas Jefferson backed plans for Virginia to establish a state-administered system of free local "reading" schools and advanced regional academies for especially talented boys, the neediest of whom would receive free tuition at the College of William and Mary. Each time, however, his plan failed to win approval, as did similar legislation designed by Benjamin Rush for the state of Pennsylvania. Georgia passed a bill in 1785 modeled on Jefferson's ideas but did almost nothing to enact it except at the college and academy levels—efforts that were delayed by decades. Massachusetts passed a law in 1789 requiring towns of a certain size to provide schools for local children but neither funded nor enforced the measure. Considering the relative prevalence of common schools in that state, the law probably did little more than codify existing practices. New York and Connecticut established state-based endowments to fund local schools in 1795, but the New York legislature repealed its law after only five years, unwilling to continue exacting property taxes to pay for schools.[12]

In each of these cases, the costs of instituting state-funded schools at any level may have been prohibitive, but expense was not the primary reason for the bills' demise. Most Americans in this era had little reason to view centralization as feasible, much less as a measurable improvement over existing schools, which were organized at the local level and funded by a combination of state assistance, taxes, and parents' tuition payments. This rule held true as much for funding colleges and upper-level academies as for elementary or reading schools. The later nineteenth-century distinction between "public" and "private" schools would have been meaningless in this era, when most Americans saw all schools, even those reserved for the elite, as serving the public good.[13] Even those who argued most strongly for educational reform objected to losing local control, on both practical and philosophical grounds.

The disconnected and locally organized nature of schools is best exemplified in their use of schoolbooks. By the time of the Revolution it had become common for most schools to expect children to bring their own books—whatever titles they happened to own. "The spelling-lesson of a class would be heard one morning from one kind of book and on the next from a different kind," one memoirist remembered of his New York City childhood in the 1820s. "That boy was accounted lucky whose book chanced to be selected for any single occasion, as he, therefore, was more likely to be posted in the lesson than the rest of the class."[14] Children transcribed lines from classmates' books into their own copybooks—a task that teachers viewed as doubly useful since it allowed them to improve their handwriting at the same time as they learned lessons.

To add to the lack of uniformity, families enjoyed a surprising choice in schoolbooks. Hundreds of titles appeared in the early republic, compiled by teachers, printers, college students, and ministers, most known only within their local communities.[15] A few of these titles became extraordinary best sellers, far beyond the sales of other titles in this era aside from the Bible and psalters. The most prominent of these, Lindley Murray's *English Reader* (1799), went through 327 editions throughout the states by 1840 and, together with Murray's two other literacy textbooks, sold more than 12.5 million copies. Not far behind was Noah Webster's three-volume *Grammatical Institute*, which sold an estimated 10.6 million copies in the same period.[16] These books were extraordinary sellers, but others achieved more localized success. John Hubbard's *American Reader* appeared in ten editions in rural areas of western New Hampshire, Vermont, and upstate New York, probably selling between 10,000 and 30,000 copies.[17] But since dozens of other titles existed alongside these volumes in both the retail and used-book markets, classrooms always featured a wide variety of books.[18]

Between the plethora of titles available to students and disagreements about the means and ends of education, Americans evinced little desire to make education more regular or uniform, even within a single state. Schools in the early republic remained locally run, decentralized, and subject to community-based educational standards, as they had during the colonial era. The uneven nature of formal schooling thus makes it impossible to gauge how many Americans in the Northeast attended school in the early days of the republic, particularly considering the vast differences in status, wealth, locale, and region.[19] Most states required parents and guardians to arrange for their children's education, but some taught reading and ciphering within the family circle while others sent their children to school for as little as a single session. Moreover, while some areas featured established schools with regular schedules, other locales had "moving" schools (in which a single teacher traveled between several remote rural communities to teach brief sessions) or hired temporary teachers for periods as short as eight weeks.

Yet despite the apparently chaotic nature of early American schools, they shared important practices—primarily their reliance on oral performance. Their views of orality were grounded in theories derived from the Anglo-American elocution movement that began in the mid-eighteenth century and held sway long into the nineteenth. "If we add *cadence, emphasis*, together with *suitable modulations of the voice*, we shall then have included every thing necessary to [teach] children to read," explained Daniel Adams in his 1803 schoolbook, *The Understanding Reader*.[20] As Adams and virtually all his contemporaries would have it, learning to *read* necessarily meant reading *aloud* and using "suitable modulations of the voice" to convey a text's meaning clearly. Educational theories and practices repeatedly stressed that written texts were directly related to spoken words, vocal emphasis, and inflection—practices believed to be useful for students at all levels, and outside the classroom as well as within.

Elocution earned so much popularity because it tied long-standing methods for teaching children to read and pronounce their words to a new emphasis on refined self-presentation. As a movement, it sought to change how people spoke by providing specific instruction on how to successfully convey ideas and feeling tones.[21] In contrast to seventeenth-century American rhetorical styles, which disdained the performative aspects of oratory,[22] elocution viewed persuasion and the stylistic components of public speaking as crucial.[23] This movement placed a new premium on approachable compositional style and graceful vocal and physical delivery. Elocutionists believed this new emphasis on manner would invigorate both secular and religious public speech by eliminating dry, logical argument. "That the *manner*, or *address* of a speaker, is of the utmost *importance*, and that a *just* and *pleasing* manner in delivering one's own compositions, [is] too much *neglected* amongst us, seems unquestionable from the *deficiencies* we so commonly observe in the *address* of our public speakers ... and from the little *effect* produced by their labours," wrote the British elocution theorist James Burgh in his influential and much-reprinted *Art of Speaking* (1761).[24] In calling for a reform of speaking styles, Burgh joined many British and American elocutionists, including Hugh Blair, George Campbell, and Joseph Priestley, who encouraged speakers to woo their auditors with animated and emotionally driven speech. This movement arose during a period of strong parliamentary government, a reassessment of public opinion and new respect for it, and an upsurge in evangelical religion, all emphasizing the central importance of persuasive speakers.[25] Elocution taught its adherents that persuasion rested on close attention to listeners and that good speakers altered their approach if their audiences seemed to require it. Above all, it sought to reform the relationship between speakers and auditors and to create a more engaged bond between them.

The "elocution revolution" sought to transform the speech of all citizens, not merely the elite. James Burgh, who served as the headmaster of a British boys' school, argued that proper speaking was necessary for men of many trades and professions whose livelihoods relied on the estimation of their peers; others saw it as a model of public deliberation translatable to informal settings, even mundane conversations. Indeed, schoolbooks overlapped significantly with the genre of conduct manuals and "courtesy books" that since the early part of the century had taught status-conscious colonists to develop their sensibility.[26] Popular American media such as newspapers and magazines disseminated the ideas of elocution theorists as well. "Grace in eloquence,—in the pulpit, at the bar,—cannot be separated from grace in ordinary manners, in private life, in the social circle, in the family," the *Norwich Courier* told its readers, insisting that elocution was consonant with "good breeding."[27] A Mr. Turner, who posted broadside advertisements in Boston in 1821 announcing his availability as a tutor of "Elocution and Belles-Lettres, "pronounced that "in every walk of life elocution is proportionably useful" since ordinary conversation was sometimes the sole means by which others gauged one's character and reputation.[28] One must not expect graceful outward appearance and conduct to emerge naturally, guidebooks warned; these skills required work, training, and constant criticism.

By the 1780s, schoolbooks had become the primary venue for transmitting elocutionary exercises. In fact, virtually all of the many schoolbooks published in this era disseminated that information in the same way. By far the most prevalent type of book used in American schools can be termed an "elocutionary schoolbook" (or "speaker" in eighteenth-century terms): these books provided suitable passages to be read aloud and sought to instruct children in the tenets of elocution, punctuation, and grammar. Contemporaries sometimes called them "piece books" because they contained short "pieces" to be memorized and recited.[29] Nathaniel Heaton Jr.'s *Columbian Preceptor* (1801) is representative of these. Heaton, a small-town printer, opened his book with excerpts from the British rhetorician Hugh Blair, describing basic elocutionary rules. These were followed by sections titled "Select Sentences" and "Select Paragraphs," intended to introduce children to memorization and recitation in a series of progressively longer lessons. The "Sentences" themselves were tirelessly didactic and often reiterated the importance of education or good speech: "The acquisition of knowledge is one of the most honorable occupations of youth" or "To read with propriety is a pleasing and important attainment; productive of improvement both to the understanding and the heart."[30] The remaining text contained anthologized poetry, oratory, prose, and plays by "the most approved" British, European, classical, and to a lesser extent American authors, texts often lifted from other schoolbooks and literary miscellanies.[31] By gradually increasing the difficulty of the selections, a single book could appeal to readers of all levels of proficiency, whether or not they attended a formal school (thereby allowing printers to sell more copies).

The details of schoolbooks' advice followed the same pattern. To start children on the path to graceful and persuasive speech, elocutionists prescribed specific modes of expression, gesture, and rhythm. A central component was the dictum that children internalize the meaning and emotion of the text they read aloud, which ideally involved a high degree of sympathetic apprehension. A student must "minutely perceive the ideas, and enter into the feelings of the author, whose sentiments he professes to repeat: for how is it possible to represent clearly to others, what we have but faint or inaccurate conceptions of ourselves?" asked one 1811 schoolbook.[32] To convey ideas properly, one must not only understand them but enter into the "sentiments" that motivated them. Speakers who failed risked transmitting a "counterfeit resemblance of feeling" that would be "immediately seen through" by the audience, draining them of authority and persuasive power.[33] In this regard, elocution complemented contemporary acting theory and psychobiological science, disciplines that also postulated an important correspondence between body, emotions, and understanding.[34] Above all, guidelines for reading aloud urged that the speaker actively emulate the author in order to present those words with appropriate effect.

Children also learned to pattern their vocal delivery and bodily comportment "after nature," since writers argued that "civilized" peoples had lost the ability to express their natural feelings outwardly. According to these theories, the advancement of civilization had transformed language and expression among Europeans (and by extension Anglo-Americans), making it highly detailed and precise but lacking the vigor and passion that persisted in the eloquence of more "primitive" societies. This had produced an artificial divide between words and feelings that it took training to overcome. Thus schoolbooks provided an elaborately detailed "choreography" of the facial expressions and gestures that ought to accompany passionate speech. "Whenever you have occasion to speak of your conscience, your mind, your feelings or your heart, let your right hand be laid gently on your left breast, and your eyes be gently cast down," explained *The Virginian Orator* in 1808. "When you would express desire or affection, both hands must be spread forth, and the same when inviting. When threatening, the right hand clenched, and the arm brandished, with a stamp of the foot."[35] Even books intended for beginning readers included instructions for facial expression and gesture, since authors believed that gesture was "a collateral consequence of thought" and that "the mind and the body [must] improve together."[36] *The Elements of Gesture* (1790) taught its readers to begin a speech with their weight on the right leg and the right hand "held out, with the palm open, the fingers straight and close, the thumb almost as distant from them as it will go, and the flat of the hand neither horizontal nor vertical, but exactly between both" (fig. 1). When finishing the first

FIGURE 1. The proper postures for delivering a recitation. These images originally appeared in *The Elements of Gesture* (Philadelphia, 1790) and were reprinted in the *Columbian Magazine* 1 (1790): 1. Image courtesy of the American Antiquarian Society.

FIGURE 2. A nearly identical illustration demonstrating the proper postures for elocution, taken from Seth Leonard's *American Grammar* (New York, 1819); clearly, the rules have not changed. Courtesy of the American Antiquarian Society.

sentence and beginning the second, the speaker should smoothly shift this posture from the right side of the body to the left, "and so on, from right to left, and from left to right, alternately, till the speech is ended."[37] The author promised that this simple, mechanistic pattern would instill the habit of always accompanying one's speech with graceful gesture. It also assured readers that these were merely the first steps in an ongoing process of learning natural vocal delivery; older and more advanced students would learn progressively more complex movements and facial expressions, which they might eventually personalize with innovations of their own. These methods for teaching the integration of voice and gesture remained virtually unchanged during the early republic, as demonstrated by figure 2, which illustrates the identical postures from a volume printed thirty years later.

Elocution fostered an intensely symbiotic relationship between text and speech: children learned to speak by reading *printed* instructions. Rules for punctuation made those interrelations all the more vivid, for they guided children to "mind the stops" and make the appropriately dramatic pauses that affected the tone and meaning of a text. All writings of the period, whether print or manuscript (and especially self-consciously literary writing), took these rules so seriously that they contained a profusion of punctuation, assiduously marking time and emphasis—highlighting the way print and oratory intersected on many levels. A comma required a pause of one beat, for example, whereas a semicolon took two beats and dashes, colons, and periods required successively longer pauses. Such rules required students to read their own writing aloud to ensure that they had conveyed their meaning and emotion perfectly. "Sentences are divided by stops to make the sense and grammatical construction more clear, and to assist the reader or speaker in pronouncing with propriety and elegance," explained Joseph Richardson in an 1810 schoolbook.[38] Authors' promise that rules for punctuation made it easier for readers to ascertain a writer's true sentiments illustrated the belief that meaning could be transparently revealed: the meaning of a properly written text or well-delivered speech was clear, not obscure. Students thus learned a double message: that they could attune themselves to an author's intentions and emotions and that one's own passions should be finely honed in order to convey them to one's readers or auditors.

Even though the books portrayed graceful public speech and self-presentation as "natural," the elaborate rules belied the artfulness and exertion required to achieve "true feeling." Given the detailed instructions for perfecting the correspondence between inner emotion and outward expression, what prevented the unscrupulous from simply faking the appearance of virtue? Indeed, schoolbooks might even be seen as training guides for would-be confidence men.[39] Schoolbooks somewhat defensively insisted that emotional deception was difficult to pull off, since the speaker's true nature was bound to betray him. "It is many times as troublesome to make good the pretence of a good quality, as to have it; ... for where truth is not at the bottom, nature will always be endeavouring to return, and will peep out and betray herself," wrote the editor of *Lessons for Youth* in 1799, warning his readers not to attempt so flimsy a disguise.[40] But rather than focusing on children's potential duplicity, most editors sought to resolve this danger by teaching them how to discern it in others. "Observe and mark as well as you may, what is the temper and disposition of those persons, whose speeches you hear, whether they be grave, serious, sober, wise discreet persons," instructed *The American Preceptor Improved*. Evidence of "craft and ingenuity" in speech, the editor explained, signaled to the child the speaker's "artifice" or "trick."[41] Training their readers to be extraordinarily sensitive to duplicity in others accomplished more than reassurance that schoolbooks' aims were virtuous and reinforcement of the boundary between the sincere and the deceptive. It also anchored education to a vision of the public as consisting of "grave, serious, sober, wise" individuals, monitored by highly skeptical, critical persons who carefully observed the behavior of their peers.

Reports of classroom practices confirm that not only were elocutionary techniques taught extensively, but children learned "right" and "wrong" ways of delivering their lessons aloud. Some schools asked the children to help check the delivery of their peers. One New Jersey memoirist remembered that his teacher, who believed that reading aloud was "one of the most indispensable accomplishments of a gentleman or gentlewoman," turned his students' daily recitations into a competitive sport in the 1820s. As the children stood to recite their pieces, they took special care to perform well lest they be "challenged" by other children, including younger ones, who raised a hand to get the teacher's attention:

> Mr. Spalding would ask, "What is the challenge?" The challenger would reply, designating the error of accent, emphasis, inflection, modulation, articulation, pronunciation, or whatever mistake it might be.... If the challenger made out a case which Mr. Spalding considered valid, he bowed his head in assent, whereupon the challenger and the challenged exchanged places.... Then the pupil, whether boy or girl, who had maintained the highest standing in the reading class during the previous week would take a stand on a moveable platform ... in full view of every scholar in the entire school.

In Mr. Spalding's classroom, a single sloppy recitation could bring a dramatic drop in status at the hands of an alert peer. In contrast, an accomplished speaker who also knew how to deploy elocutionary criticism could earn a high classroom position and Mr. Spalding's respect. He rewarded his best students with "a pronounced deference of manner and a degree of consideration and trust which was more highly valued than medals or prizes could possibly have been," the writer remembered as an old man.[42] The teacher's praise and manner promised that one might attain esteem via good speech and proper conduct outside the classroom as well.

The Anglo-American elocution movement had a profound effect on the postrevolutionary United States by helping to create an element of uniformity in a radically decentralized educational environment. Whereas colonial schools had merely taught children to read and cipher, the postwar emphasis on elocution turned reading into a skill that reflected one's character. It provided an extensive vocabulary for describing modulations of voice, face, and body and equated those skills with social elegance and proper conduct that would be carefully judged by other members of society. Thus even the most remote rural men and women who had access to print could have grown familiar with elocutionary views of speech and conduct. Elocutionary education thus helped to create a postrevolutionary society deeply oriented to a particular mode of oral culture. And as we shall see, educational practices granted children extraordinarily frequent opportunities to become formal speakers in far more public settings than their daily classroom exercises—ceremonial exhibitions that underscored the public importance of their speech and conduct.

SPEAKING IN PUBLIC: EXHIBITION DAYS AND PUBLIC CRITICISM

When the students at Atkinson Academy in rural New Hampshire performed their first exhibition before the community in 1787, the town had only eighty-seven men eligible to vote, nearly all farmers. A group of them had dedicated most of the previous fall and winter to erecting the school building and completing the masonry on its chimney—an essential addition, since many schools in New Hampshire used unheated barns. The school's self-appointed trustees believed this luxury was necessary if they expected parents to pay the controversial one dollar a quarter tuition to cover the teacher's board and school expenses. They also saw that having a neat, framed building allowed them to hold exhibitions in the schoolhouse itself rather than at the town's meetinghouse as other schools did.[43]

The school's October exhibition mixed formality with "diversions" for the enjoyment of the audience, as the local minister noted in his diary. Early in the afternoon the "scholars" sat down, with the audience of community members behind them, while they waited for the ceremonial arrival of the trustees and examiners, who sat in front. The minister's young son rose first to deliver a Latin oration ("and spoke it well," his father noted), which opened the day's slate of "a number of diverting scenes with singing interspersed till it grew dark." After a long intermission of nearly an hour for dinner and drinking, the audience settled back into the schoolhouse for the remainder of the students' performances of oratory, theatrical scenes, and song. "There were some pieces improperly introduced which gave umbrage," Rev. Stephen Peabody noted: the students' choice of off-color scenes from Molière's satirical "The Doctor in Spite of Himself" particularly alarmed one of the visiting ministers. "But the actors really did themselves honor," he concluded. After the performance a number of audience members "filled my house" once more for additional drink.[44] For a small agricultural town, the school's exhibition—involving hours of performance, dining, and "diversions" that lasted long into the evening—constituted a major community event.

Virtually every school throughout the Northeast used exhibitions as a means of assessing children's educational progress and teachers' achievements.[45] Yet despite the ubiquity of these practices, they have received only glancing attention from scholars. Without a system of testing or grades or even a clear understanding between parents and teachers as to what constituted appropriate advancement, communities relied on periodic exhibitions as the sole measure of evaluation. Their format adhered to a standard scheme. A small number of trustees or school visitors "examined" the children by having them answer questions in mathematics, spelling, geography, history, and other subjects. Afterward the students "exhibited" their knowledge and elocutionary polish by performing a variety of memorized texts (plays or short theatrical scenes, poems, and oratory gleaned from their schoolbooks, as well as compositions by the most advanced students) before large audiences of parents and community members. Thus these events constituted an important element of uniformity in American educational practices. Rich and poor, rural and urban, North, South and West—across the board, Americans clearly believed that children's oral declamation revealed whether educational standards had been met. Elocutionary experience in such public settings taught children skills they could not glean otherwise.

Individual exhibitions varied widely in length and frequency, but they all drew a broad cross section of the community as audience. The "visiting committee" of examiners usually consisted of prominent men from the area, often ministers or, if possible, college-educated figures. William Sewell's school in Hallowell, Maine, for example, was examined by a local minister, a merchant, and an attorney; other schools invited college professors or town selectmen. Teachers who hoped to enroll the children of elites took care to invite examiners or audiences who might be influential in bringing in new students. When Sewell assumed a teaching position in rural Culpeper County, Virginia, for example, he issued invitations for his school's exhibition to "a considerable number of gentlemen and ladies" with the hope of adding more "scholars."[46] Most teachers' exhibitions tended to be long. Bathsheba Whitman's school in rural Sandwich, Rhode Island, featured daylong public ceremonies at the town meetinghouse, beginning with a sermon in the morning by the minister. Other teachers extended the exhibition over the course of two days or, as at Atkinson Academy, held the formal examination by the committee and the public exhibition on separate days. One schoolbook author recommended that exhibitions run no more than four and a half to five hours, but there is anecdotal evidence that many were longer.[47] And whereas some schools held exhibitions quarterly or even more frequently, others had as few as two a year.

These were not pro forma exercises; participants and teachers placed great weight on the community's evaluation. Teachers depended on a good assessment for continued employment. Schools with disposable income even had playbills printed that listed the students' parts and pieces (fig. 3). One man remembered of his turn-of-the-century Boston boyhood that as soon as the teacher received six weeks' notice of the event, "pieces were selected for reading, and lessons set to be recited, every child knew his piece & his answer, reciting or reading every day till exhibition."[48] A Connecticut student also recalled constant preparation. "The anticipation of them kept up an interest all winter, and stimulated teachers and scholars to do their best in the way of preparation. As the time approached, we had evening schools for reading and rehearsing the dialogues."[49] The intensive preparation reflected anxieties felt by both teachers and students. "I think of it only with anxiety, dread, and fear," wrote Bathsheba Whitman about her students' upcoming performance in 1806, "but these sensations I mention to no one, as all appear to anticipate them with pleasure I hope they may not be disappointed."[50]

Such anxiety was warranted, for observers did not hesitate to criticize the students' performances when disappointed. In western Massachusetts

Order of the Exercises,
OF COMMENCEMENT AT
KINGSTON ACADEMY
ON THE 4TH OCTOBER, 1808.

Salutatory Oration	by	*William S. Dezeng.*
Hope,	by	*William Bailey.*
Frailty of human life,	by	*Lewis Tucker.*
The praises of a long and heavy purse,	by	*Samuel Van Orden*,

A scene from the comedy " Mother of a Family."
 Latitia by Blandina V. Gaasbeek ; Nelly by Eliza Beekman.

The Seasons	by	*Moses C. Cantine.*
The Fop, a Poem	by	*Cornelius C. Eltinge.*
Captain Bobadil	by	*Henry Tappen*
Extract from Emmett,	by	*David L: Grier*

My Grandmother;
A FARCE.

MEN.	Vapour,	:	*Lewis Tucker.*		Souffrance,	.	*Robert L. Wilson.*
	Sir Matthew,	.	*Moses C. Cantine.*		Tom,	.	*Cornelius C. Eltinge.*
	Woodley,	.	*William S. Dezeng.*	WOMEN.	Florella,	:	*Sarah Elmendorf.*
	Gossip,	.	*Solomon E. Eltinge.*		Charlotte,	,	*Maria Hasbrouck.*

Extract from Curran, by Samuel J. Wilkin.
Conference on the question—" Do the Anglo-Americans possess mental powers equal to the Europeans ?" between Gurdon Hewitt, jun. Solomon E. Eltinge and Cornelius E. Depuy.

A COMEDY,
" Who's the Dupe ?"

MEN.	Doiley,	:	*Samuel J. Wilkin.*		Servant,	.	*David L. Grier.*
	Sandford,	.	*William S. Dezeng.*				
	Granger,	.	*Gurdon Hewitt, jun.*	WOMEN.	Elizabeth,	,	*Ann M. Wells.*
	Gradus,	.	*William Bailey.*		Charlotte,	.	*Eliza Cantine.*

J. BUEL'S PRINT.

FIGURE 3. Broadside/playbill for the school exhibition at Kingston Academy in Kingston, New York, in 1808. Note the bold headlines advertising the two plays performed. Courtesy of the William L. Clements Library, University of Michigan.

in 1800, the fifteen-year-old Sally Ripley recorded the local minister's stern words in her diary. Although "many of us pronounced our words well & read loud &c. . . . we did not read intelligibly but blended our words together," she reported, adding, "I hope I shall correct this fault before another examination takes place."[51] Ordinary members of the audience commonly critiqued the performances, as when one woman described in her diary the girls' presentations as "very good" and the boys' oratory as only "tolerable."[52] After observing an exhibition at one of Philadelphia's schools "for coloured boys," a teacher noted in her diary that she was "much pleased." "I believe their understandings are nearly, if not quite equal to the whites."[53] These criticisms gained a new degree of visibility when local newspapers began reporting on exhibitions in the early nineteenth century. *The Pastime*, a literary weekly based in Schenectady, New York, struggled to "speak charitably" of the local grammar school's performance of the "Tragedy of Abaellino" at its exhibition in 1808. The students had "acquitted themselves with respectable success," the writer granted, but a Mr. Blain in the lead role had left much to be desired. "We wish . . . that he would correct a graceless habit of bending his knees at every emphatic word," the paper said sternly, comparing him unfavorably to another student whose speech "was witty and appropriate, and performed with much taste and judgement."[54] Likewise, when one Massachusetts youth anticipated his upcoming school exhibition, his father wrote to promise to "hear & see you rehearse your part several times; that every attitude, every jesture & modulation may be observed & corrected."[55] The very real possibility of public embarrassment and even humiliation led students, teachers, and protective parents to lend enormous weight to the exhibition during each school session.

Given the importance placed on "natural" emotions and the public display of self, it is not surprising that some observers found plays dangerously theatrical. Even though the plays often proved the most popular parts of the exhibition—especially judging by the bold headlines they earned in schools' exhibition broadsides—several commentators felt they taught children false emotional expression. As a result, schoolbook editors frequently found themselves defending the use of theatrical scenes and dialogues by drawing a distinction between appropriate speaking skills and "the finesses of acting." Children should "be accustomed to speak such speeches, as require a full, open, animated pronunciation," claimed one volume, which recommended that teachers confine their selections to "orations, odes, and such single speeches of plays, as are in the declamatory and vehement style."[56] Other essays condemned the "dangerous tendency" of exhibitions to "seduce the active powers of the mind into a state of frivolity" by teaching children that entertaining one's audience was more important than acquiring more substantial knowledge. Still other writers worried about the boy who "acquires the greatest applause" at an exhibition. "For the sake of gratifying his own, or his parent's vanity, he is invited to all their little *parties*, and at each of these, is requested to *speak* his *piece*. Highly honoured, as he imagines, the unfortunate boy conceits that he has completed his education, and can never after be persuaded to direct his attention to serious and rational study."[57]

Considering the "dangerous tendencies" of public exhibitions—the false emotion, self-aggrandizement, and risk of public humiliation—why did schools place so much emphasis on these performances, particularly for those children with no hope for a career that required public speaking? Because, as many volumes stated, the practice of public performance taught children a refined bearing and manner of speech important to all aspects of everyday life. Concerned that other nations viewed them as rustic and provincial, Americans placed enormous stress on cultivating good speech and manners, believing that practice in declamation, particularly with the added pressure of public performance, was the best means of achieving it. Even "the rudest nymphs or swains by practicing on rhetoric will soon acquire polite manners, for they will often personate the most polite characters," explained Charles Stearns in his *Dramatic Dialogues for the Use of Schools*.[58] In other words, elocution could make fine manners and graceful speech second nature for children; the regular practice of outward habits could improve the inner self.

Emphasizing that children's speech would be judged by their families and friends in all settings, schoolbooks filled their pages with theatrical scenes that took place in informal domestic and social settings where characters debated the virtues of polished speech and refined comportment. In fact, good speech was a primary *topic* of the pieces that children memorized and recited. *The Juvenile Reader*, for example, contained a dialogue in which two schoolboys discuss the skills of their peers as each is called to "speak a piece" before a parlor gathering of adults. The first boy fails miserably. "No sooner had he spoke the first sentence, than the surprise and disappointment of the company were apparent; for you never heard such a disagreeable, *unnatural* tone," one boy says to the other, reiterating the adults' disapproval. In contrast, little Henry impresses everyone with his natural delivery and "graceful manner." "Every person was silent and attentive; for not one of them spoke, except in a low voice you might hear them say, sweet fellow! charming boy! dear little creature! And they all seemed to be delighted with him," gushes one of the boys admiringly.[59] Henry's triumph lay not only in enchanting the adults in the room with his gift of eloquence, but also in gaining distinction among his schoolmates. The countless schoolbook scenes that contrasted the rustic or ungrammatical speech of comic or crude characters with that of their respectable friends reiterated time and again the message that good speech deeply influenced one's social standing and reputation. These lessons were not incidental;

they were essential to the educational process, displaying how greatly the prevailing ethic in schools focused on cultivating sensibility in children.

Schoolbook dialogues like this—used for both classroom declamation and exhibition performances—*publicized* conversational speech. Even at the most quotidian social gatherings, the stories suggested, one might gain or lose status by the quality of one's speech. To drive the point home, schoolbooks situated those dialogues in parlors. When children recited such dialogues before their classmates or at exhibitions, they forwarded the notion that all kinds of conversational speech were "public." Moreover, that schools focused so fixedly on oral performance and self-presentation for teaching respectability conveyed the expectation that children required these characteristics to assume their place as members of the public. If the theorists of the elocution movement had imagined that eloquent, effective speech would produce a highly engaged bond between the public and its leaders, the popularizers of those techniques taught children to uphold their end of the bargain. Through a combination of carrot and stick—the esteem of one's friends, the threat of public humiliation—education in elocution prepared children to expect criticism as they progressed. Beyond that, it taught them to be critics, demanding the same high standards from the public speakers that they in turn observed. Taken together, the combination of elocutionary rules, school exhibitions, and schoolbook lessons transmitted an understanding of belonging to the public that fostered engaged behavior by ordinary people. The ideal of an educated citizenry thus dovetailed with apolitical understandings of public comportment.

And indeed, ordinary American youths scrutinized the performances of public orators, from ministers' sermons to Fourth of July speeches; letters and diaries are replete with careful analyses of the speakers they observed, detailed analyses that used extensive elocutionary vocabularies. One thirteen-year-old Baltimore clerk, for example, described in his diary the debates he observed in the United States Congress in Philadelphia in 1796. "Mr. Harper's a good Speaker, but some particular motions of the Body he has such as rising on his Toes renders him disagreeable. Mr. Gallatin is no Orator but understands what he's about in an argument very well."[60] Another clerk from Lynn, Massachusetts, complained of his local minister, "I think he has too much saw in the air and a great deal of Gesticulation which is unnecessary."[61] Expressing such criticism of public speakers was no idle pursuit; it reflected the writers' own critical talents and refined sensibilities—even their characters. Some youths admired the finely wrought criticism composed by others, as when Anna Eliza Heath copied into her commonplace book: "He had no brilliancy of address, but he had what is still more rare, that perfect simplicity of manner, which borrows nothing from imitation; and as some one has well remarked, few peculiarities are more striking than a total absence of all affectation"—a sentiment that, like the others she copied, expressed with succinct elegance an insight she found valuable.[62] When discussing dull or effective speakers, these youth drew heavily on elocutionary terms to discuss and rate the niceties of gesture, voice, and emphasis in ways that revealed their own skills in critical appraisal.

Youths of both sexes frequently expressed fear of public embarrassment in exhibitions, anxieties that were even greater for slightly older youths—usually young men—who hoped to assume public roles that demanded regular oral address and argument. The more these men attempted to ratchet up their oral skills, the more they felt stymied by the expectations of the job. Elocution taught them a contradictory set of rules—to "please yet persuade, to control oneself but stimulate passions in others, to reveal oneself and yet efface oneself," as Jay Fliegelman summarized it—requiring would-be lawyers and ministers to walk a tightrope between modulating every gesture and appearing "natural."[63] Their writings often revealed that youths felt an acute sense of failure. In an extended diary entry, the twenty-two-year-old Thomas Amory despaired of achieving these conflicting goals of oratorical training:

> How am I to make myself this intellectual & highly cultivated being—this prompt & fluid orator—this elegant yet correct writer, this clear reasoner.... Where is the ambrosia that is to feed this miracle where are the books—what are the studies—What should be the system—what the regimen of this paragon of perfection—How many years or rather generations are to bring him to maturity—What supernatural agency is to round the angular motions—to polish the uncouth phrases—to modulate the thickened voice.[64]

Amory's quest for a magical "ambrosia" or "miracle" reveals how a purportedly orderly "system" or "regimen" failed to teach one the impossible expectations of formal oratory. Nor were these fears limited to youth. Even John Quincy Adams, one of the most celebrated orators in the nation, confessed profound embarrassment following a public appearance. "I should have done better to remain silent," he wrote in his diary. "My defects of elocution are incurable, and amidst so many better speakers . . . I never speak without mortification."[65] It is worth noting that Adams recorded this entry shortly after he had been granted a prestigious chair as professor of rhetoric at Harvard.

These diary entries reveal that the greater one's expectations for public performances, the more withering was one's critical eye for the speakers one observed. The diaries of would-be ministers and lawyers became testaments to both the mystical promise of oratorical achievement and the ever-present doubt that accompanied the pursuit. One of the most assiduous commentators was John Gallison, a twenty-year-old law clerk, who rarely praised a speaker without also detailing the weaknesses in his delivery. In 1809, for example, he admired a speech by James Ogilvie, an orator in the midst of a commercial lecture tour, as "an ingenious performance, abounding in strong description," but adjudged the man "rather an actor than an orator": "He has fancy, imagination, & a powerful command of language. His action is spirited & graceful. His voice has great compass & is ever well-modulated. It is particularly adapted for the expression of terror. All these pleasing qualities he possesses in a high degree. But he does not speak like one warmed with the vehement desire to impress some opinion upon the minds of his hearers, or to persuade them to some action."

Despite Ogilvie's obvious talents, Gallison still found fault. For him, admirable oratory was more than the sum of accomplished parts. Likewise, he concluded that a local minister "exhibited some of the qualities of an orator. His voice was strong & flexible, and . . . his gestures were occasionally appropriate & impressive.—But this is the sum of his praises." But what makes Gallison's highly critical perspective so striking is that he applied it with equal vigor to himself, often within the same diary entry, as he struggled to improve his own delivery for use in the courtroom. He and another student met in the Salem meetinghouse on weekday mornings "for the purpose of exercising ourselves in speaking, & of delivering"—sessions that frequently produced despair. "My success in this exercise was indeed little," he confessed. A week later it was no better. "I had meditated the subject & thought it a very copious one, but I found myself unequal to the discussion. I could produce nothing but stammering & hesitation. . . . I experienced a most discouraging paucity of ideas & of words."[66]

Of course, the ideal that motivated Gallison, Thomas Amory, and John Quincy Adams—the "prompt & fluid" brilliancy of address that created a magical experience for auditors—was far more rigorous and unforgiving than schoolchildren's quarterly exhibitions. Not only did they envision themselves in far more formal settings that entailed greater risk of reputation, they saw themselves in a different relationship with the public, with greater responsibilities. And yet their preparation, anxieties, and impulse to study the performances of others all reveal the ways their work simply extended the exhibition training of younger children. The dialogues they memorized and performed before local audiences evinced a view of the public that traced close connections between formal public forums or political settings and the more intimate interactions between families and neighbors. Children learned at every turn that their words, their gestures, and even their capacity for critical discernment would be an index of their characters, whether in an exhibition or in a neighbor's parlor.

The intense focus on oral delivery and graceful comportment taught children and young adults that their entry into adulthood rested on their mastery of specific standards for public behavior. These practices evoked a particular vision of the public as a whole—one made up of individuals who understood a particular language or dialect for speaking properly to one another and who could be highly critical as they demanded that others likewise adhere to those standards. Moreover, the numerous reports by nonelite men and women of their efforts to acquire these skills show how pervasive were such ideas of public speech and social engagement. Thus, despite the disconnected nature of education in general, a vast majority of the white population of the Northeast gleaned very similar messages about the ways that cultivating one's character helped unite an American public in sensibility. By the 1810s, these shared practices began to integrate new messages of civic ideals and nationalistic sentiments. Methods of cultivating patriotism in children created new ways of envisioning their roles as citizens and members of the public, even as the older emphasis on sensibility remained intact.

PROMOTING NATIONALISM: EDUCATION AFTER 1810

Although it took decades for Americans to enlist education in a project to cultivate civic behavior in children, communities gathered to observe speaking talent in civic settings other than school exhibitions throughout the eighteenth century. Locals flocked to monthly court days to watch their litigious neighbors contest such matters as slander, property disputes, or petty brawling, and on occasion to hear lawyers debate dramatic cases of murder or other criminal trials. Increasingly after midcentury, citizens also attended the proceedings of colonial legislatures, particularly after word spread that colonial leaders were debating solutions to the colonies' escalating tensions with Britain—and they did so from new auditors' galleries or public seating areas, architectural innovations that spread rapidly in courthouses and legislative buildings throughout the country.[67] By the Revolution, Americans felt it was their prerogative to observe many forms of legal debate, which "served not only to make the community a witness to important decisions and transactions but also to teach men the very nature and forms of government," as Rhys Isaac has recognized.[68] In this regard, the Constitutional Convention's rule of strict privacy for its proceedings in 1787 was a highly unusual exception to the new open-door policy.

Attendees at court days or even congressional debates doubtless gleaned a spotty education in the law and representative government, but it was more than they learned from schoolbooks at the time. Before the 1810s, schoolbooks seldom attempted to instruct their readers in civics or government: they did not include a copy of the Constitution or the Declaration of Independence, nor did they summarize those texts. During the first thirty years of nationhood, these volumes remained oriented to teaching children to be gentlemen and gentlewomen and expressed only passing concern with what would later be termed civic or national values. This analysis contrasts sharply with earlier scholars' assertions that schoolbooks in this era constituted "civic texts" oriented to teaching republican values—assessments that refer solely to two exceptionally nationalistic books, by Caleb Bingham and by Noah Webster. Each of these authors dedicated up to a third of his volume to pieces by American writers or to nationalistic topics, such as William Pitt's defense of the colonies during the Stamp Act crisis or a eulogy of Benjamin Franklin by a prominent European.[69] Other than these two books, the scores of texts published in this era displayed virtually no concern with civic matters until after the War of 1812. On occasion, students' writings reveal that they had learned about matters of civic importance in school, but these moments were rare. In the diary she kept for nearly eight years describing her school lessons, for example, Sally Ripley had only one such entry. "The American Republic is composed of almost all nations, languages, character & religion which Europe can furnish, The English language is universally spoken in the United States it is spoken with great purity, untill the 4th July 1776 the present sixteen United States were British colonies, On that ever memorable day the representatives of the United States in Congress assembled made a solemn declaration of Independence," she wrote in 1799.[70]

In this respect the books' bold, patriotic titles contrasted strikingly with their lack of writings by Americans or about the nation. Approximately one-third of the schoolbooks issued by American presses between 1780 and 1810 boasted titles such as *The American Reader* or *The Columbian Preceptor* yet contained almost exclusively texts by British authors. (About

12 percent of the schoolbook titles emphasized refinement, such as *The Young Gentlemen and Ladies' Instructor*; the rest—slightly more than half of all American schoolbook titles—stressed the books' educational content, such as *An Introduction to the Art of Reading* or *The Student's Companion*.[71]) At times, editors paired a nationalistic title with similar sentiments in a prologue, as when the *Columbian Monitor* promised to teach "*American* readers" to "lead the youth of these rising states to *usefulness* and *honor*."[72] Others implied that such ideals as freedom and virtue constituted core American values, as when *The School of Wisdom, or American Monitor* sought to convince readers of "the advantages of liberty, of peace, of good order"—yet they remained vague on how such values differed from those of other nations.[73] These statements were almost always the sum of the books' patriotic message. The vast majority of schoolbooks staked their claim to Americanness solely on being compiled and printed in the United States, as Michael Warner has shown; editors used such titles to distinguish their publications from the dozens of reprinted British schoolbooks that still dominated the market rather than to indicate their advocacy of American writings or values.[74]

By the end of the eighteenth century, some editors were beginning to include American writers, but this incorporation was slow. Schoolbooks remained indebted to the British and European schoolbooks and conduct manuals from which they drew their material. Murray's *English Reader*, the most popular schoolbook of the era, contained no American authors at all. Nearly half of all schoolbooks contained at least one American piece, but there were seldom more than three out of sixty to two hundred items. Joseph Dana's *New American Selection of Lessons* was representative of this trend: while dominated by British orations, extracts from Hugh Blair's writings on elocution, and dialogues on manners, it also contained George Washington's speech to Congress on resigning his military commission and a description of the first American Congress.[75] Even books published by ardent nationalists never featured a majority of pieces relating to the United States. Given the relative dearth of well-known or canonical American writings in the postrevolutionary era, it is hardly surprising that most schoolbooks had just begun to insert the writings of American authors and orators alongside those of British luminaries.

Beginning in the early nineteenth century, the content of schoolbooks shifted to reveal a growing preoccupation with national identification and civic engagement. This shift notably occurred in the wake of the partisan rancor of the 1790s between Federalists and Republicans that had resulted in a particularly bitter presidential campaign of 1800. Within approximately one year, Jefferson had been elected, promising to usher in a new conciliation between the parties; Congress had moved from Philadelphia to buildings in the new city of Washington, DC; and George Washington had died, leading to an abundance of tributes by Americans at all levels of society. Each event produced a profusion of publications calling on the public to focus on the social changes and powerful symbols that united them—an end to partisan conflict, an elegant new federal city, and an uncomplicatedly heroic national leader.

By the 1810s schoolbook compilers increasingly defined their collections as "American" by virtue of a new emphasis on native literature. *The American Reader* (1810), probably the earliest text to feature exclusively writings of American authors, expressed the editor's belief that national pride was tied to native literature. Joseph Richardson announced that his selection of pieces illustrated "the true language of our country; it is principally taken from those authors to whom we look for our most important information. Of whom shall our youth learn this language? of whom in preference to the best speakers and writers our country can boast?"[76] Following in Richardson's footsteps, the editor of *The American Lady's Preceptor* (1811) put an even finer point on the problem. "Young persons being accustomed to regard *English* literature as exclusively deserving their applause and imitation, acquire a disrelish and disrespect for the productions of their own country," he stated, and called on his fellow editors to "exert themselves to vindicate their national character . . . [and] convince youth, that American productions exist, which they may admire and imitate."[77] No matter how convincing this sounds, most schoolbooks published during the early republic continued to combine English and American authors, granting more space to the latter. Still, the swing toward nationalism was decisive; by the time of the Boston Latin School's July 1825 exhibition, only five of the twenty-five pieces performed had nothing to do with American writers or themes (fig. 4).

As their content shifted, schoolbooks retained a primary concern for developing their readers' sensibilities and characters, revealing that their compilers still believed this was education's primary goal. In fact, at times they simply appeared to ask children to emulate the virtues and manners of a different list of individuals. Especially after his death, Washington proved the most popular choice for illustrating good character. One 1800 schoolbook, for example, neglected virtually all of his public accomplishments and focused instead on his manners:

> No person appears to have had a higher sense of decorum, and universal propriety. The eye, following his public and private life, traces

ORDER OF DECLAMATION.
JULY 2, 1825. [Boston Latin Sch]

1. Extract from Mr. Webster's speech on the Greek Question, - - G. F. Simmons.
2. Extract from Dr. Ramsay's eulogy on Washington - - - - S. P. Shaw.
3. Ode for the celebration of the Battle of Bunker Hill - - - - W. A. Pierpont.
4. Extract from Prof. Everett's Oration before the Phi Beta Kappa A. O. Spooner.
5. Extract from President Nott's address - - - - - - - - E. Smith.
6. Extract from Mr. Canning's speech in answer to Mr. Brougham J. S. B. Thacher.
7. Extract from Prof. Everett's oration at Concord - - - - - J. Bradford.
8. Antony's speech over the body of Cæsar - - - - - - - C. M. Winship.
9. Extract from Lord Chatham's speech on the privilege of Parliament T. O. Thacher.
10. Extract from Curran's speech on the trial of Justice Johnson - J. O. Sargent.
11. Extract from Mr. Webster's address on Bunker Hill - - - - G. J. Foster.
12. 'Pedantry,' a Dialogue, C. M. Winship, A. C. Patterson, C. B. Trott, J. M. Warren.
13. Extract from Sheridan's invective against Hastings - - - - J. Q. Loring.
14. Extract from Mr. Morris' speech on the Judiciary - - - - G. Gardner.
15. "Dirge of Alaric" by Prof. Everett - - - - - - - - - F. H. Gray.
16. Extract from R. T. Paine's oration - - - - - - - - - E. Cruft.
17. Extract from Patrick Henry's speech - - - - - - - - W. Phillips.
18. Extract from Prof. Everett's oration at Plymouth - - - - - A. C. Patterson.
19. Speech of Catiline before the Roman senate—'Croly's Catiline' F. A. Williams.
20. Extract from Byron - - - - - - - - - - - - - - S. Wigglesworth.
21. Extract from Fisher Ames, on American Literature - - - - A. D. Hall.
22. 'Amateurs,' from the Monthly Anthology—Dr. Bigelow - - R. E. Apthorp.
23. Extract from Mr. Webster's oration at Plymouth - - - - - S. May.
24. Extract from Prof. Everett's oration at Plymouth - - - - - W. Gray.
25. Extract from Burke's speech on the conciliation with America - W. H. Channing.

FIGURE 4. Broadside/playbill for the 1825 exhibition of the Boston Latin School, displaying the new tendency to emphasize patriotic texts and orations by American speakers, now outweighing the familiar slate of classical and British texts. Courtesy of the American Antiquarian Society.

an unexceptionable propriety, an exact decorum, in every action; in every word; in his demeanour to men of every class; in his public communications; in his convivial entertainments; in his letters; and in his familiar conversation; from which bluntness, flattery, witticism, indelicacy, negligence, passion, and overaction, were alike excluded.[78]

In like fashion, *The American Reader* described Washington's speech and comportment in a manner almost unconnected to his civic or military actions. "His manners were rather reserved than free. His person and whole deportment exhibited an unaffected and indescribable dignity, unmingled with haughtiness, of which all, who approached him, were sensible."[79] According to these passages, manners mattered as much as actions in the public sphere. In other words, schoolbooks superimposed an emergent nationalist impulse on their ongoing preoccupation with character and respectability by finding patriotic models for that behavior.

Washington especially served as a useful model because Americans saw him as a national figure who transcended the pernicious regional and partisan divisions of the 1790s.[80] His Farewell Address cemented that perception by addressing those divisions directly and calling on members of the public to see themselves as "an indissoluble community of Interest as *one Nation*." Thereafter, editors went in search of similar pieces asserting that the United States possessed a uniformity of mind and manners across the different states. "Providence has been pleased to give this one connected country to one united people; a people descended from the same ancestors, speaking the same language, professing the same religion, attached to the same principles of government, [and] very similar in their manners and customs," announced an excerpt from *The Federalist #2* in the *American Orator*.[81] Taken together, these documents drew the public's attention to the central leaders it shared and faced off against the rancor that had prevailed in the earlier decade.

Considering education's emphasis on orality, finding leaders who also fit the bill as good orators quickly became a concern for schoolbook editors. One of the first to satisfy this need was John Quincy Adams, whose speech upon his inauguration as Boylston Professor of Rhetorick and Oratory at Harvard in 1806 was widely circulated. In it Adams narrated a historical trajectory in which the cultivation of oratory in society ensured progress and social virtue. "Eloquence was POWER" in the Greek and Roman republics, he began. "The whole duty of man consisted in making himself an accomplished publick speaker," and eloquence ensured social virtue because the orator was dedicated to public life and civic engagement: "None but a good man could be an orator." Political corruption diminished both the republic and the art of oratory in Rome, he continued, for "eloquence was perverted from persuasion to panegyrick." Even with the revival of eloquence in modern Europe, Adams claimed, it had never regained the grandeur of the classical republics. With this narrative he was poised for the speech's true goal: the call for American youth to assume the mantle of oratorical heroism. "Is there among you a youth, whose bosom burns with the fires of honourable ambition; who aspires to immortalize his name by the extent and importance of his services to his country; whose visions of futurity glow with the hope of presiding in her councils, of directing her affairs, or appearing to future ages on the rolls of fame, as her ornament and pride?" Adams asked with a riveting appeal to his Harvard auditors' ambition. In the United States, he promised, the eloquent glory of the classical past might be revived by young Americans who felt strongly their republican duty to inspire their fellow citizens.[82] This indeed would be a promising future for the new nation, one in which debate and oratory bound the public and its leaders in dynamic exchange.

Judging by the frequency with which his speech was reprinted or excerpted in schoolbooks, magazines, and other collections, Adams clearly did more than inspire a new generation of orators; he established *himself* as the kind of civic leader he claimed was necessary to the republic's survival. Though he modestly deflected attention from himself—as Cicero had taught was necessary to the orator's appeal—to assume the part of the teacher who drew out the best talents of his students, his eloquent appeal to youth could not help but draw attention to his own oratorical mastery. "They must have been wrapt in ecstasy," wrote a reviewer of the printed text in the *Emerald*, who imagined attending the speech's delivery. Adams's erudition "must have struck the audience at the time with the force of one living example" of the orator-hero he had described.[83]

Following the lead of the *Emerald*'s delighted reviewer, in the 1810s schoolbooks began to endow American speeches with a new grandeur at the same time that they devoted more space to them. This habit dovetailed with the culture's overall appreciation for oratory, but it also created a new body of oratorical heroes for schoolchildren to admire. For the first time, schoolbooks often paired a transcribed speech with an elaborate description of the oratorical style of the man who had delivered it. Such depictions stressed a speech's importance by asking readers to consider the text and the orator's manner together as integrated parts of the whole. By helping readers imagine these men in action, the books created a growing hagiography of national oratorical giants. Devoting three pages to a description of Fisher Ames, for example, *The Columbian Reader* (1818) explained that "his attitude was erect and easy, his gestures manly and forcible, his intonations varied and expressive, his articulation direct, and his whole manner animated and natural." Even though he had never formally studied oratory or attended an elite college, the author noted, Ames had learned on his own "the power to enlighten and persuade, to move, to please, to charm, to astonish."[84] Like the story of Demosthenes overcoming his speech handicaps, such a biography could inspire children to value perseverance in learning any skill, not just elocution. Yet as detailed as these descriptions were, they hardly constituted a clear set of instructions for truly emulating Ames's style; the effect was less to urge children to imitate the nuances of delivery than to foster admiration. Above all, these depictions contributed to the sense that the United States had begun to fulfill its promise of producing brilliant orators whose words galvanized their fellow citizens.

Through lessons like these, civic ideals for the first time became tied to the task of learning to read, and schoolrooms became sites for instilling and performing nationalism. On top of learning to emulate virtuous models, children now learned to admire *in particular* their own national leaders—and perhaps by extension to view more skeptically the prominent English orators they had previously emulated. Some schoolbooks went one step further and described not just an orator's style but the specific drama of the setting where the speech was delivered. Such detailed depictions suggested that when students recited the words of a legislator, they engaged in a ritualistic re-creation of an important moment in American history. Duplicating the eloquent words of an Ames or a Washington therefore had patriotic ends over and above the task of learning elocutionary style. These lessons implied that students should memorize American speeches as part of their *political* education as well as their elocutionary education.

Schoolbook depictions of national oratory presented an altered view of students' responsibilities in the classroom and by extension changed their portrayal of the American public at large. They especially did so by including enthusiastic descriptions of orators that cast readers as "spectators" at these momentous speeches, not necessarily emulators of the speakers. "How is it possible, that such a man can hold the attention of an audience enchained, through a speech of even ordinary length?" one author asked rhetorically about the powerful eloquence of John Marshall. "The audience are never permitted to pause for a moment. . . . Every sentence is progressive—every idea sheds new lights on the subjects—the listener is kept perpetually in that sweetly pleasurable vibration, with which the mind of man always receives new truths . . . until, rising, in high relief, in all its native colors and proportions, the argument is consummated, by the conviction of the delighted hearer."[85] Even more than the description of Ames from the same volume, this passage asked readers to be the "delighted hearers," rather than the imitators, of Marshall's brilliance. The erotic overtones of the writer's language (the auditors' "sweetly pleasurable vibration"; a "rising" and gradually "consummated" argument) only underscored this perspective. Passages like these drew readers' attention to the pleasure of listening, of submitting, to a magical speech, even of being ravished by it. They created an image of the auditor as an uncritical, passive observer of an unfolding national drama.

Even stories about Demosthenes changed in the 1810s and 1820s to imagine readers as awestruck spectators of the man's gifts rather than as emulators of his example—and to do so required a significant leap of the imagination. *The American Orator* contained a first-person, present-tense reverie on the experience of hearing one of his orations. "I transport myself to old Athens. I mingle with the popular assembly, I behold the lightning, I listen to the thunder of Demosthenes. I feel my blood thrilled, I see the auditory tost and shaken like some deep forest by a mighty storm."[86] Schoolbook descriptions of fine oratory thus differed markedly from those by lay observers in their letters and diaries. Whereas ordinary men and women used such reports to display their critical acumen and deploy their elocutionary knowledge, schoolbooks instead presented a happily uncritical view of spectatorship; they imagined an American public distinguished by its unflinching loyalty to legislative leaders.

There is no single reason such portrayals of a more uncritical, awestruck public appeared in increasing numbers in schoolbooks during the early nineteenth century. Certainly the trend reflected new patterns in the practices of patriotism and changed perspectives on joining in crowds. But for my purposes here, it corresponded to educational changes after 1810 that reflected cultural anxieties about the growth of urban underclasses of impoverished Americans. At the same time that schools were becoming sites for the performance of nationalism, urban educators sought economical means of expanding schooling for poor children (and to some extent for African American and Indian children). These moves toward universal education shifted the earlier purpose of teaching children refinement and instead urged them to be loyal citizens—with profound implications for their conception of themselves as members of the public and future adults.

The notion that states ought to provide widespread education to the poor was new in the early nineteenth century and resulted from fitful discussions about how to provide social stability to urban areas with growing numbers of the poor. On the whole they were not motivated by a drive to democratize society. "The more anxious they became about the security of their world, the more they favored mass education," Carl Kaestle has noted.[87] Leaders suggested that schools might reduce urban crime by teaching morality, moderate ambition, and responsibility to a young generation. To achieve such stability, existing schools for poor children needed to be greatly expanded. Denominational charity schools had long instructed poor children in cities in both England and America, although they seldom cast their nets wide; they usually restricted their student bodies to their own congregations and often included children whose parents refused to pay the costs of ordinary schools even if they could afford it.[88] Thus, inasmuch as their founders celebrated their schools' civic-mindedness, they did not see themselves as capable of or responsible for universal coverage of poor children. Given the prevailing understanding that children would learn to read by memorizing their exercises and declaiming them before a critical teacher, the sheer scale of educating poor children seemed impossibly expensive. By the early nineteenth century, a large number of voluntary associations, often called "free school societies," arose to supplement charity schools by finding creative ways to instruct very large numbers of students without expending large funds for teachers.[89]

In the educational style they selected, the Lancastrian or "monitorial" system, declamation no longer enjoyed a prominent place in the classroom, and children no longer imagined they might become American Demosthenes. This system promised to educate vast numbers of students almost without teachers by organizing recitation within tiny, competitive groups of children led by older student "monitors." Joseph Lancaster assured the public that a single teacher could operate a school with as many as five hundred children, as he had demonstrated at his own London school.[90] These constantly monitored groups prompted children to learn obedience and diligence and enforced this with militaristic discipline.[91] The New York Free School Society adopted this system in 1805 and was quickly joined by other charity schools; Philadelphia schools followed suit in 1808. By the 1820s every state in the union used the Lancastrian system, even occasionally in schools for middle-class students, making it for the time the most prominent and popular educational method, and one that led to the publicly funded school movement of the 1830s and beyond.

The Lancastrian method and other attempts to provide universal education in cities were not the only reasons schoolbooks began to portray the public as more passive in the 1810s; later chapters will explore the subject in more detail. But these new conceptions of the goals of education, particularly in American cities, had long-standing repercussions on notions of the "public" as well as the state's relations with its citizens. Between approximately 1810 and 1830, American schools cultivated a nationalistic perspective among their students by celebrating political leaders as nearly mythic oratorical leaders. Such portrayals seemed to realize John Quincy Adams's prediction that, with ambition and hard work, a new generation of Americans might bring to fruition the nation's promise. But once achieved, this new collection of leaders and descriptions of the scenes of their oratorical triumphs required ordinary members of the public to play the appreciative audience rather than to become budding oratorical heroes.

In 1768 a group of Virginians commissioned a life-sized portrait of William Pitt, whom they credited with "speaking in Defence of the Claims of the American Colonies" against British tyranny—to such effect that Parliament had repealed the Stamp Act. They commissioned Charles Willson Peale, an American artist studying in London, who portrayed the prime minister not in his usual clothes of state, but in the dress of a Roman orator.[92] Pitt appears speaking on behalf of true virtue and liberty and gesturing sternly to the figure of British Liberty, who "trampl[ed] under Foot the Petition of the CONGRESS AT NEW-YORK" (fig. 5). That gesture, Peale explained in a long accompanying broadside, "makes a Figure of Rhetoric strongly and justly sarcastic on the present faint Genius of BRITISH Liberty" (fig. 6). Peale littered the portrait with contrasts between British hypocrisy and Pitt's honor; in one hand, for example, he held a copy of Magna Carta. And Americans appreciated it. Upon its arrival in Virginia, the portrait quickly gained renown; the *Virginia Gazette* noted that Pitt's "countenance appears full of fire and expression, and he looks as if he was waiting for an answer to some forcible argument he had just used." Peale took advantage of the painting's popularity to sell large facsimile engravings of it through booksellers in New York, Philadelphia, and Williamsburg, making it one of the earliest printed images in America that depicted oratorical heroism.[93]

Americans' continued celebration of Pitt long after the war reflects not only the importance of his words but the significance of oral performance and the public culture it promoted between speakers and auditors in Anglo-American culture. Good speech and conversation denoted an individual's education and social position and, more generally, how far one's larger society could be considered civilized and refined. Viewed more broadly as a cultural preoccupation, the widespread practice of oral training demon-

FIGURE 5. Charles Willson Peale's 1768 portrait of William Pitt, Earl of Chatham, in Roman "consular habit." Pitt gestures pointedly toward the figure of British Liberty, who tramples on one of the Americans' petitions to Parliament. One of the first works of Charles Willson Peale and presented to "the gentlemen of Westmoreland County, Virginia" in 1768 by Edmund Jenings. This portrait has been displayed at many historical sites in Virginia and currently is exhibited in the Westmoreland County Museum, a site specifically built for the portrait and located in Montross, Virginia.

A

DESCRIPTION

OF THE

PICTURE AND MEZZOTINTO

OF

MR. PITT,

DONE BY

CHARLES WILLSON PEALE,

OF MARYLAND.

THE Principal FIGURE is that of Mr. PITT, in a Confular Habit, fpeaking in Defence of the Claims of the AMERICAN Colonies, on the Principles of the BRITISH Conftitution.

WITH MAGNA CHARTA in one Hand, he points with the other, to the Statue of BRITISH *Liberty*, trampling under Foot the Petition of the CONGRESS at NEW-YORK.—— Some have thought it not quite proper to reprefent LIBERTY as guilty of an Action fo contrary to her genuine Spirit; for that, conducting herfelf in ftrict Propriety of Character, fhe ought not to violate, or treat with Contempt, the Rights of any one. To this it may be fufficient to fay, the Painter principally intended to allude to the Obfervation which hath been made by Hiftorians, and Writers on Government, that the *States which enjoy the higheft Degree of Liberty are apt to be oppreffive of thofe who are fubordinate, and in Subjection to them.* MONTESQUIEU, fpeaking of the Conftitution of ROME, and the Government of the ROMAN Provinces, fays, "*La Liberté croit, dans le Centre et la Tyrannie aux Extrémités:*" And again, "*La Ville ne fentoit point la Tyrannie, qui ne s' exerçoit que fur les Nations Affujettis.*" And fuppofing Mr. PITT, in his Oration, to point, as he does, at the Statue, it makes a Figure of Rhetoric ftrongly and juftly farcaftic on the prefent faint Genius of BRITISH Liberty; in which Light, Gentlemen of Reading and Tafte have been pleafed to commend it. The Fact is, that the Petition of the Congrefs at NEW-YORK, againft Acts of meer Power, adverfe to AMERICAN Rights, was rejected by the Houfe of Commons, the Guardians, the Genius, of *that* Liberty, languifhing as it *is.*

AN INDIAN is placed on the Pedeftal, in an *erect* Pofture, with an attentive Countenance, watching, as AMERICA has done for Five Years paft, the extraordinary Motions of the BRITISH Senate———He liftens to the Orator, and has a Bow in his Hand, and a Dog by his Side, to fhew the natural *Faithfulnefs and Firmnefs of* AMERICA.

IT was advifed by fome, to have had the INDIAN drawn in a dejected and melancholy Pofture: And, confidering the apparent Weaknefs of the Colonies, and the Power of the Parent Country, it might not, perhaps, have been improper to have executed it in that Manner; but in Truth the AMERICANS, being well founded in their Principles, and animated with a facred Love for their Country, have never difponded.

AN ALTAR, with a Flame is placed in the Foreground, to fhew that the Caufe of Liberty is facred, and, that therefore, they who maintain it, not only difcharge their Duty to their King and themfelves, but to GOD. It is decorated with the Heads of SIDNEY and HAMPDEN, who, with undaunted Courage, fpake, wrote, and died in Defence of the true Principles of Liberty, and of thofe Rights and Bleffings which GREAT-BRITAIN now enjoys: For, as the Banner placed between them expreffes it,

SANCTUS AMOR PATRIÆ DAT ANIMUM.

A CIVIC CROWN is laid on the Altar, as confecrated to *that* MAN who preferved his Fellow-Citizens and Subjects from Deftruction!

THE View of W——H—— is introduced in the Back Ground, not meerly as an elegant Piece of Architecture, but as it was the Place where ———— fuffered, for attempting to invade the Rights of the BRITISH Kingdoms: And it is obfervable, that the Statue and Altar of BRITISH Liberty are erected near the Spot where that great *Sacrifice* was made, through fad Neceffity, to the Honour, Happinefs, Virtue, and in one Word, to the Liberty of the BRITISH People.

THE Petition of the Congrefs at NEW-YORK, and the Reprefentation of W——H—— point out the Time, and almoft the Place, where the Speech was delivered.

THE chief Object of this Defign will be anfwered, if it manifefts, in the leaft, the Gratitude of AMERICA to his Lordfhip. It will, with Tradition, unprejudiced by the Writings of *Hirelings*, who are made to glide in with the courtly Streams of FALSHOOD, be the faithful Conveyance to Pofterity of the Knowledge of thofe GREAT THINGS which we, who are not to be impofed on by " the bufy Doings and Undoings" of the envious Great, have feen.

FIGURE 6. Charles Willson Peale's extensive "Description" of his painting of William Pitt (1768), in which he explains not only the specific allegories he employed but also the decisions he made in composing the image. Courtesy of the Library of Congress.

strated the importance of creating an engaged dynamic among the public and between the people and their leaders. When the elocution movement and school exhibitions called on children to emulate the eloquent words of civic orators like Pitt or Demosthenes, it helped Americans see themselves as bound together by a common dedication to self-improvement and civilization. In fact, the common lament that the United States lacked skilled orator-leaders helped create a sense of urgency for children to improve so they might rise to that position themselves. Long before schools became involved in fostering nationalism, elocution provided a common training and vocabulary to nonelites across the social spectrum, providing one means for them to imagine themselves as members of a public.

By the early nineteenth century, nationalist writers and artists began to find new ways to imagine the American scene that suggested the United States *had* arrived as a full-blown virtuous republic. Even George Washington, a poor public speaker, was now reimagined as an orator. Early in his tenure as president, artists still chose to portray him as a military leader, pictured on battlefields with sword in hand and horse nearby.[94] But portraits began to change at about the same time as he retired from the presidency in 1796 and offered his Farewell Address—a speech that, ironically, he never delivered orally but merely submitted for newspaper publication.[95] In the wake of these events, pictorial representations of him underwent a transformation. Gilbert Stuart was one of the first to render him as a civic orator, standing in an explicitly elocutionary pose, in the full-length "Lansdowne" portrait of 1796 that situated him in a formal room replete with books, official papers, and a chair upholstered with the stars and stripes. Copied many times in printed engravings (fig. 7), this image dramatically moved his sword from his right hand, as in earlier paintings, to his left; he now gestures gracefully and forcefully in the manner prescribed in elocution manuals (fig. 1). The oratorical pose was obvious to members of the public who studied the portrait when it made a tour of eastern cities in 1798. "G.W. is represented as delivering his last address—& is surrounded with allegories," wrote a young law clerk who was so moved by the painting that he returned a second time to appreciate it on display at New York's Tontine City Tavern.[96] Despite his well-known weaknesses in public speaking, Washington was reconceived in visual images such as these to be a civic orator who embodied—and inspired—national virtue.

Changes in imagery mirrored a nationalist shift in schoolbook content by the 1810s that conveyed the sense that the United States had finally realized its potential as a republic united by eloquence. But now that a

FIGURE 7. James Heath's *General Washington,* after Gilbert Stuart (London, 1800), was one of many engravings that circulated in England and the United States after Washington's death in 1799. Courtesy of the McAlpin Collection, New York Public Library.

pantheon of orators inspired national sentiment, they became important sources of pride in themselves—whether or not children emulated them. The altered ways of positioning schoolbook readers as passive observers rather than as would-be Washingtons indicated that conceptions of belonging to the public were also in flux, reflecting persisting debates over who counted as part of the "we."

CHAPTER 2

Vindicating Female Eloquence
GIRLS' ORATORY AND THE RISE AND FALL OF A FEMALE COUNTERPUBLIC

After reading a flattering account of a rural New Hampshire school exhibition in 1793, a resident sent an angry letter to his local newspaper. "For what purpose [are] the female pupils... taught ORATORY, or the art of public speaking?" he demanded. "As women are not admitted to speak, either in the pulpit, or at the bar, what propriety is there in teaching them that branch of education[?]" The only purpose must be to "furnish the superb THEATRE now erecting at Boston, with actors of both sexes," he speculated, playing on small-town distrust of the "Metropolis" and its vices.[1] The letter set off nearly six months of debate in Haverhill's weekly newspaper, the *Guardian of Freedom*, spearheaded by several female students who energetically defended their right to instruction in oratory. The crux of this debate, carried out within a provincial newspaper, was not whether girls should be educated, or even whether they should learn elocution. The question boiled down to whether girls' training in oratory should resemble boys'—and what it might mean for American society if it did.

A writer with the pseudonym "Aurelia" responded with utmost "indignation," claiming that "every person of a good share of common sense, who has but a small acquaintance with the first principles of Education" could perceive the value of learning public speaking—which held true as much for girls as boys. "Nothing can be a more powerful stimulous... than an expectation of appearing in public, to *perform*" before a room of critical adults, she asserted. "And when female pupils, or others are able to make a graceful appearance at a public exhibition, they certainly have it in their power to appear to advantage in every station, and in all circles—upon the stage of life."[2] Two weeks later "Almira" chimed in, asking, "Are there not other places and occasions besides the '*pulpit* and *bar*,' where, at times public speaking becomes fit and necessary, and when by the well informed, it would be esteemed an *ornament* to speak with becoming propriety?"[3] These pointed letters prompted the original correspondent to reply with considerable sarcasm: this "specimen of female delicacy, of urbanity and politeness" revealed what the public might expect "from such a female education."[4]

This debate challenges long-standing scholarly assumptions that social custom largely forbade women from public speaking during the early decades of the new United States.[5] In fact, many Americans embraced the idea that the new nation would be inhabited by well-spoken, publicly engaged women. Certainly, contemporaries took it for granted that women spoke only rarely before churches, large assemblies, or government bodies (of course, few men did so either), but they did not believe this was the sum total of "public speech" or that it was suited only to would-be formal orators or elites, as scholars have recently begun to recognize.[6] As Aurelia put it, oratorical training allowed women to "appear to advantage in every station, and in all circles"—circles that included a variety of social gatherings in everyday life. Girls as well as boys learned that polished, confident speech would make them better adults and engaged members of society, earning them the esteem of their peers and enhancing the nation as a whole. That dozens of speeches composed and delivered by schoolgirls were subsequently published in books, magazines, and newspapers from the 1780s through the early 1800s reveals not only that such orations were widespread but that they were seen as important enough to warrant publication and to earn their authors public recognition.[7]

As elocutionary education helped teach children to play their parts in public, it also showed that educated women had the potential to play important roles in American culture—roles that were not simply "private" or oriented to their place as wives and mothers, as outlined by the notion of republican womanhood.[8] By depicting skilled speech as a necessary faculty for women in a civilized society—one perfectly in keeping with a properly constituted public sphere—elocutionary practices encouraged a certain degree of female ambition and even political participation. The ubiquity of such evidence suggests that republican motherhood was by no means the only model for women seeking to define their roles in the postrevolutionary era; nor was republicanism the only language women drew on as they asserted their rights to engage in public culture. Closely following the previous chapter, this chapter continues to analyze the role of education in creating widely shared views of public engagement by demonstrating how much modes of belonging to the public differed by sex.

As the debate in the *Guardian of Freedom* illustrates, tensions surrounding women's public speech contrasted sharply with the noncontroversial nature of elocutionary exhibitions for boys. When Almira noted the importance of speaking "with becoming propriety," she acknowledged that some might still harbor doubts about women's ability to speak with reason and refinement and perhaps might even question the legitimacy of any public speech by women. Girls' orations reiterated this theme time after time by reassuring their auditors that they sought to earn approval. But female oratory could also seem potentially insurgent, for it led some to recommend an expanded position for women in public culture. Those who did so identified themselves as a female counterpublic—that is, as "members of subordinated social groups [who] invent and circulate counterdiscourses to formulate oppositional interpretations of their identities, interests, and needs" to alter the nature of the general public, as Nancy Fraser writes.[9] Some female academy students employed an assertive language of rights, citizenship, and political engagement that reflected the ideas of Mary Wollstonecraft and other female intellectuals of the era. This environment that cultivated vocal, publicly engaged women did not last long; by the 1810s the discourse about women's public roles had begun to change toward advocating exaggerated verbal modesty and decidedly away from earlier visions of female oratorical excellence. Thus, examining changing modes of education for girls throughout the early republic reveals much about conceptions of women's roles in public and political culture.

ELOCUTIONARY EDUCATION AND THE FORMATION OF FEMALE CHARACTER

"It is not unknown to you, how much wit has been scattered on the subject of the loquacity of women—and how much satire expended in ridiculing ladies who have a taste for learning," began Anna Harrington, a schoolgirl, in a 1793 speech before her Massachusetts school. "But if an eminent faculty of speech be possessed by women, for once let it be employed to a good purpose." Like many of her contemporaries, Harrington used women's "natural" facility for speech as a jumping-off point to advocate for female education. Since women were possessed of such verbal skills, they should improve their minds and their oratory to "gain the approbation of those who censure us; & to make even satirists confess, that we act with propriety," rather than succumb to supposed female propensities for prattling or scolding.[10] Harrington's ideas doubtless drew on the schoolbooks she used, which uniformly accented the ties between good speech and good character as they trained boys and girls in public speaking, and which frequently used drastic scenarios to warn their youthful readers against uncontrolled speech. Such advice had a broader significance than sheer didacticism. Authors so frequently called for the improvement of females' education in the late eighteenth century because, they argued, women represented an essential part of nexus between the progress of civilization, refinement, and increases in knowledge.

While children of both sexes often heard warnings against improperly controlled speech, both parents and schoolbook editors made it clear that girls needed to be particularly wary. "Under fourteen the foolish speeches and inconsiderate actions of a girl are in a manner overlooked & forgiven," a Connecticut father, William Edmond, wrote to his daughter in 1799. After fourteen, however, she risked marking herself as an unseemly woman:

> There are some qualities annexed to the word woman . . . which go the whole length of a character. Such as a *virtuous woman,* an *amiable woman,* a *vicious* woman, an odious woman, which have no dependence on riches or poverty & but very little on personal beauty or deformity. . . . And the English language furnishes a great variety of words, or epithets, calculated to express the degrees, by which a woman rises to the full and complete characters above mentioned.[11]

To illustrate how a woman's speech and her character became inseparable, Edmond followed this passage with a chart of twenty-nine words that he "annexed" to various feminine types. Certainly Polly did not want to be described as *tatling, noisy, gossiping,* or *scolding*; such terms made a woman *thoughtless, immodest, nasty,* and *rude.* A woman's habits of speech were not the only significant dimension of womanly conduct, but Edmond foregrounded them with his exacting attention to the epithets and compliments that defined the categories of womanhood, since a woman might gain a poor reputation no matter what her rank in society. His chart underscored his daughter's need to reform her "foolish speeches" before she was deemed a foolish woman. This father's letter conveys the intricacies of society's vocabulary for casting judgment on women.

Just as Edmond could sum up all women by categories like virtuous or vicious, so schoolbooks used fictionalized female characters to demonstrate that poor speech habits could be disastrous. Such tales could be brutally cautionary. In Arnauld Berquin's tale "The Little Prater," later anthologized as "The Little Prattler," a family undertakes to correct the incessant chitchat of their otherwise talented daughter, Leonora. "For a single fault she had unhappily contracted, was so great as to destroy the effect of all her juvenile accomplishments. The intemperance of her tongue made every one forget the graces of her understanding, and the goodness of her heart. In short, our Leonora was an intolerable prater." The story comically details Leonora's annoying tendency to leap from one topic to another, even prattling to herself when left alone in a room. Her family tries patiently to cure her of these habits, but to no avail. Finally they undertake more radical tactics, and the story takes a dark turn: when they travel from home for several days to attend a party, they leave her behind rather than risk embarrassment. "'Tis impossible for any one to bear your constant chatter," her mother explains sternly. "You would surely interrupt our pleasure, and the pleasure of the family we are now going to; and therefore for the future, when we visit, we must leave you constantly behind us." Even when they return, they only gradually allow her to join them at the dinner table. "Must I never speak, then?" she asks, and cries every day as she strains to go about her chores silently. These scenes depict her sense of isolation in chilling detail, doubtless attempting to scare their readers straight. But the author also promises a happy ending, for by these harsh measures Leonora learns self-control; now "she figures in society with credit to herself, and pleasure to her friends," the story concludes.[12] Clearly, this story advised its youthful readers, bad habits needed to be reformed early in order to avoid the severe corrective strategies of Leonora's family.

Whether or not they felt that education helped prevent their daughters from sliding into "vicious" or "prattling" talk, Americans certainly advocated it in record numbers after the Revolution. Female literacy and school attendance both rose rapidly after the mid-eighteenth century. Although an estimated 60 percent of rural adult white women were illiterate or only marginally literate by 1775 (urban whites attained far higher literacy rates), by 1825 virtually all white women over age twenty-one throughout the Northeast were literate.[13] Given that these rates apply to *adult* women, it appears that girls began to achieve almost universal literacy near the turn of the century—a remarkable generational shift. The brisk rate of change resulted partly from increased school attendance by girls after the Revolution, although they still did not attend at the same rates as boys. In fact, school attendance increased town by town even within a single state. Some towns, such as Sutton, Massachusetts, had offered free, tax-supported common-school education to girls for generations before the Revolution, while others restricted attendance to boys. Girls could not attend a town-financed school in Boston until 1789, for example, or until

1807 in Northampton—requiring parents in those areas to opt to pay for their daughters' schools.[14] Thus, although increased overall rates of school attendance may have helped boost female literacy rates, that was not the only factor.

Rising literacy and school attendance reflected the fact that, by the end of the eighteenth century, Americans had commenced a widespread reassessment of female education and women's intellectual capacities.[15] Even before Mary Wollstonecraft's *Vindication of the Rights of Woman* began to circulate in the United States, writers explored the topic of the "natural equality" of woman's intellect, decrying the earlier tendency to leave it uncultivated.[16] These sentiments accompanied the broader discussion of an educated citizenry and its relation to the nation and were voiced by conservative writers as well as progressive ones. "Since [women] have the same improveable minds as the male part of the species, why should they not be cultivated by the same method?" asked the *Young Gentleman and Lady's Monitor*.[17] Some writers went so far as to deplore women's intellectual "dependence" as singularly dangerous in a republic because it made them incapable of virtuous thought and action, just as economic dependence made a man unqualified for full citizenship in most areas. Wollstonecraft's book thus galvanized an existing discussion of female education and earned considerable popularity in the United States, appearing in four American editions as well as being excerpted in several periodicals.[18] "If [woman] be not prepared by education to become the companion of man, she will stop the progress of knowledge and virtue," Wollstonecraft wrote with a striking rhetorical vigor.[19]

Most of Wollstonecraft's American followers did not equate a woman's "station" with domesticity or motherhood—nor did they contrast the household with the public sphere—because they drew their notions of gender and social relations primarily from Scottish Enlightenment theories of civil society. Scottish theorists imagined domestic relations as organically linked to the political realm and saw the condition of women as a marker of any given society's civilized nature. They proposed, for example, that only barbaric nations kept their women ignorant or subservient. Referring to one of the most prominent of the Scottish theorists, a schoolgirl named Ann Harker explained in her 1794 commencement speech in Philadelphia that "it is observed by Lord Kaimes, that the treatment of women is always meliorated in proportion to the progress of civilization and refinement. In this age of reason, then, we are not to be surprised, if women have . . . converted their talents to the public utility."[20] These ideas contrasted with those of John Locke, whose writings provided Americans with many of their conceptions of white men's roles in society—in particular, the notion that men enjoyed the "right" to a high degree of personal autonomy in navigating the business and political worlds. In contrast, American writers applied to women Scottish theories that "treated rights as benefits, conferred by God and expressed in the performance of duties to society," as Rosemarie Zagarri has shown.[21] Drawing from two intellectual traditions to theorize differential "rights" by sex meant that Americans did not see women simply as private, domestic counterparts to men or as a part of the unfree populace against which men's freedom was measured. Rather, they viewed women as crucial to civil society—a concept that obtained in England as well as France and Germany during this era.[22]

Because they imagined educated women to be exemplars of their society's civilized nature, schoolbooks did more than simply discuss women's intellectual capacities. They viewed the education of women as important to society—and not just as wives and mothers. "The sexes are partners in the pursuit and cultivation of knowledge," one author declared; another proclaimed that "if education, in general, lies at the foundation of individual, domestic, and national happiness, this is especially the case with female education."[23] Like Wollstonecraft, some of them believed that a superficial and "trifling" education led to the "perversion" of their sex and ultimately harmed men too. Schoolbooks idealized the partnership of virtuous men and women—and demonized individuals who eschewed the rigorous education that produced such an arrangement. As one petulant coquette lamented to another in a satirical dialogue from 1797, "Well this is a pretty affair indeed that such girls as Fidelia and Lucy, who can boast of nothing but beauty, good sense education, and virtue, should gain the confidence of the finest gentlemen; and be married just when they please."[24] When books like this one set "good sense education" in such strong contrast to the coquette's "arts," they popularized female education and made it seem natural. Still other authors claimed that attaining an education actually enhanced a girl's femininity. "The domestic affections and appropriate virtues of the sex, modesty, prudence, and conjugal fidelity, far from being superseded by study and the liberal sciences, are on the contrary, both strengthened and embellished," Susannah Rowson explained in her *Present for Young Ladies*.[25]

Schools put these ideas into practice by incorporating surprising disciplinary overlap between the sexes in several subjects. In fact, boys' and girls' training in reading and elocution was virtually identical.[26] "The literary instruction of females must be conducted almost in the same way with that of boys," Rev. Samuel Magaw announced in an address before the Young Ladies' Academy of Philadelphia in 1787.[27] Schoolbooks confirmed this by specifically defining their readership as composed of both sexes with titles that referred to "young gentlemen and ladies," "young persons," "both sexes," or simply "children" or "youth." To be sure, editors often used such gender-neutral titles to sell more books. But even books with titles that specified one sex were read by both. Sally Ripley, a teenage student in rural Massachusetts, reported to her diary that she read from John Aikin's *Letters to His Son* in 1799; six-year-old William Bentley Fowle recited his lessons from the *Young Ladies Accidence* alongside the five other male students in his Boston school in 1801; and one young man wrote, "John Rafield's Never to be lent out of the Family While I live J. R. 1815," on the flyleaf of the Library of Congress copy of *The Mental Flower Garden, or An Instructive and Entertaining Companion for the Fair Sex*.[28] In this respect, schoolbooks resembled the broader genre of conduct literature, which moved away from being primarily addressed to men and, by the 1790s, displayed "an important new undercurrent of common expectations" for men and women, as Dallett Hemphill has demonstrated.[29]

Educators applied this logic to girls' elocution and public speaking because they understood that those skills were pertinent to all forms of conversation and everyday talk, not just to oratory. A girl needed proper speaking skills because she "may almost every day be obliged to speak, not only in the circle of her friends and acquaintances, but even before strangers," opined Molly Wallace in her 1792 commencement oration. A well-spoken woman "may instruct and please others," Wallace continued, but she would also expand "her own understanding."[30] Girls might commonly display their skills on semiformal occasions such as speaking in school exhibitions or before groups of adults in parlors, as when Nathan Webb reported in his diary that a "young Lady Spake a dialogue or two" at a Boston-area gathering in 1790.[31] Good speech was necessary for participation in a world that was manifestly sociable.

It was not just sociable, it was *hetero*sociable—which further confirmed the need to train boys and girls in elocution in similar ways. When schoolbook editors portrayed youths displaying their elocutionary skills in parlor settings before observant adults, they implied that this was the world they wanted children to join. Schoolbooks described this as a world in which men and women enjoyed one another's company. Both sexes might impress mixed groups of peers and social superiors by their conversation and considered opinion. Both sexes sought social respect and standing—and they sought it from each other.

In describing these refined parlor settings, schoolbooks played up understandings of sociability and conversation drawn from transatlantic sources. Just as Lord Chesterfield famously advised his son to learn the art of conversation from the tutelage of brilliant women, so some American schoolbooks advised male readers to take adult women as their models for verbal excellence. T. Knox's *Hints to Public Speakers* (1797) recommended that aspiring orators observe "the way that women express themselves when they *feel* the subject they talk upon, such as when they *pronounce* their *sorrows* for the loss of a *husband*, a *child*, or any other fond and beloved relative." Knox's recommendations fell in line with those of other writers who praised women's talent for language and expression as more "natural" and "easy" than men's, more expressive of their inner feelings; even George Washington was said to be indebted to such women for his conversational skills.[32] These depictions implied that such women were valuable aspects of the social milieus that children might inhabit.

Such portrayals also signal the difficulty of classifying parlor conversations—and the salons and levees that urban elites enjoyed—as either "public" or "private," using either Habermasian terms or contemporary late eighteenth-century usage. This difficulty distinguishes the era from the nineteenth century, when Americans increasingly perceived the home and its activities as "private" and used the rhetoric of "spheres" to demarcate them. In the eighteenth century, however, "no stable" boundary "can or could be" drawn between public and private life, as Dena Goodman has argued, nor could these qualities be correlated with the two sexes.[33] Neither can the broad range of topics discussed in parlors, which ranged from political to emotional and intimate, be simply summarized as the rational and deliberative talk of the Habermasian schema. Lawrence Klein's conclusion that "public" signaled sociability rather than isolation confirms the tendency of schoolbooks to place heavy emphasis on children's conduct in parlor gatherings.

These scholarly conclusions shed new light on the ways girls' elocutionary training reflected new views of women's place in public and in society, for in striking ways it nearly matched the same kind of training for boys. To be "agreeable," whether on the podium or in conversation, required of men and women the same clear articulation, attention to one's auditors, and "natural" correspondence between one's delivery and one's inner emotions. Moreover, specific qualities of delivery, such as modesty or boldness, were equally applicable to boys and girls.[34] Both sexes were taught to begin their speeches with modest and self-deprecating rhetorical statements. Writers grounded these rules for speaking by claiming that it was not "natural" for either sex to exhibit ambition, pride, or ostentation, since those qualities inhibited the speaker's ability to persuade. In sum, most of these rules were strikingly gender neutral.

Both sexes also learned similar techniques for gesture. Most schoolbooks included passages describing elocutionary "action," and at least four volumes devoted entirely to the art were published before 1832. Although they contained very few images to illustrate gesture and posture (and of these, the figures were male), the most extensively illustrated schoolbook of the period contained images of men *and* women. Three of the thirteen plates in Jonathan Barber's *Practical Treatise on Gesture* (1831) included images of women in a spectrum of postures that varied in dramatic effect.[35] The male figures in figure 8 display the comparatively dispassionate and controlled gestures characteristic of conventional oratory. Likewise, the modest pose of the female figure in this plate, with her crossed arms and the set of her head, exemplifies contained passions. But as figure 9 suggests, women could also gesture freely and spread their arms wide. In this respect, the dramatic and passionate poses illustrated by these female figures are comparable to those illustrated by men in figure 10. Both sexes learned to cross their arms over their chests when speaking powerfully of God; both clasped their hands in front of them when indicating hopefulness or pleading. According to the roles laid out in these images, boys and girls learned overlapping and often identical ways of making emotion visible through gesture.

Of course, that men and women employed similar poses and gestures in their declamation in no way erased distinctions between the sexes. At times in the text that accompanied his plates, Barber described a specific posture as particularly "feminine" or "masculine." For example, in describing an appropriate physical manifestation of "shame in the extreme," he suggested that to best capture this emotion, the student "sinks on the knee and covers the eyes with both hands: this is a feminine expression of it." But he used a *male* figure to illustrate this stance; obviously, a man could use a "feminine" posture to make a point with even more poignancy—and vice versa. In other words, both men and women learned how to properly express a range of sentiments, including those that carried gendered connotations.[36]

Barber's illustrations reveal *both* that the sexes learned nearly identical rules *and* that their speech was not identical: boys and girls used their bodies and voices to different effect. For example, Barber's figures disclose several key differences between "male" and "female" poses manifest in their costume and their breadth of gesture. Whereas the male figures almost uniformly wear generic, contemporary men's clothing, the women appear in costumes, as if on stage. All are dressed in classicized, draped clothing, and most also wear a crown or veil. Such representations lack self-evident meaning: the costumes may have underscored the theatricality of women's

FIGURE 8. Plate 6 from Jonathan Barber's *A Practical Treatise on Gesture* (Cambridge, 1831), illustrating some of the more dispassionate postures for public speaking. Courtesy of the American Antiquarian Society.

FIGURE 9. Plate 12 from Jonathan Barber's *A Practical Treatise on Gesture* (Cambridge, 1831), in which female figures display some of the more vivid and passionate poses. Courtesy of the American Antiquarian Society.

FIGURE 10. Plate 10 from Jonathan Barber's *A Practical Treatise on Gesture* (Cambridge, 1831), in which male figures illustrate some of the more athletic and passionate postures for public speaking. Courtesy of the American Antiquarian Society.

public speech, but they may also have suggested that public speech was best left in the hands of women with unquestioned claims to power. The images seem to evoke female monarchs or women with exceptional religious callings, but they might also have signified that women in elite social circles possessed particular rights to public speech.[37] In either case, these illustrations marked women's public speech as unusual, even if the text did not. Beyond their dress, the figures also evince distinctions in form. Unlike the male figures in Barber's book, seven of the eight female figures gaze up to the heavens, suggesting that women might be more likely to speak on topics of religion and faith. The women also keep their legs securely together, while the men exhibit more athletic "action," sometimes spreading their legs far apart as a means of dramatizing horror, recoil, or aggressive pleading.[38] Considering that this volume was intended for students rather for actors, this artistic decision was an unspoken reminder that female oratory was different and bounded by feminine "propriety," and perhaps also by class. Thus, even though most guidebooks did not distinguish between boys' and girls' speech, evidence like Barber's manual and girls' speeches reveal that contemporaries would have been aware of the differences.

The advocacy of female education in the early republic carried mixed messages about the gendered nature of speech, of course. But the larger story concerns an extraordinary reassessment of women's speech, knowledge, and intellectual capacity that had profound cultural effects during the postrevolutionary years. Considered in this light, the messages that vacillated between advocating equal access and restricting women's role in education and elocution likely reflected the uncertainty some writers felt about the implications of rapid change. Some writers and girl orators sought to recognize and uphold differences in the public presentation of the two sexes; yet even as they did so, some girls' speeches reveal that they learned to use gender differences to their rhetorical advantage.

POWER THROUGH MODESTY, OR FEMALE ORATORICAL HEROISM

One might expect that reminding girls to adhere to proper feminine behavior would implicitly discourage them from public speaking altogether. Yet girls' speeches reveal that they often learned instead to capitalize on gender differences in public speaking for greater persuasive effect. When young women delivered decorous yet eloquent speeches, they confirmed that education advanced a girl's femininity. Still, not all female oratory was consumed with asserting modesty or propriety; in fact, some girls verbalized the same desire for public success that boys expressed. These instances of female ambition were encouraged by schoolbook biographies of famous, eloquent women, stories suggesting that eloquence and knowledge could turn the educated woman into a heroine.

Both men and women struggled with the loaded terms *fame* and *ambition*, qualities that could be embraced only with moderation. Authors frequently invoked these terms when they advised would-be writers that they might seek a degree of "applause" for themselves at the same time that they forwarded the literary or intellectual reputation of the new nation.[39] In 1793 the *Lady's Magazine* urged its readers to aspire to literary greatness, assuring them that "the females of Philadelphia are by no means deficient in *those talents*, which have immortalized the names of a *Montague*, a *Craven*, a *More*, and a *Seward*, in their inimitable writings," referring to some of the most popular British female writers of the era.[40] With regard to ambition, then, men and women adhered to similar rules; but as with the elocutionary rules described above, the evidence suggests that "ambition" was a tricky subject for women. For example, when the prominent writer Judith Sargent Murray disguised her sex under the male pseudonym "the Gleaner" in the *Massachusetts Magazine*, "he" freely confessed to a "fondness for literary fame." But when Murray later revealed her sex to her readers, she felt a need to alter her tone. "I was ambitious of being considered *independent* as a *writer*," she admitted. "If I possessed any merit, I was solicitous it should remain undiminished, nor did I harbour a wish that my errors should be imputed to another." When she acceded to use an exaggeratedly feminine modesty, her tone bespoke the special importance of tempering female ambitions. Thus, even though conduct literature urged both men and women to beware of their desires for applause, it redoubled that advice when speaking solely to women.

But even if prescriptive texts emphasized caution, many schools granted girls ample chances to compete for class honors and "fame." Moreover, their founders argued that girls would benefit from the very public acknowledgment of their success. Since girls possessed a "desire for fame," John Swanwick took for granted in a speech before the Young Ladies' Academy in 1787 that they would "glow at the thought of popular applause, that will attend the successful champions in this literary race." Swanwick went on to advocate an elaborate array of prizes for the best work in each academic subject, explaining that "they ought to be delivered in the most conspicuous places, in the presence of the parents, and of all those whom the children most respect—the names of those who obtain them should be published, and every proper degree of applause and respect, at home and abroad, shown to those who have so signally distinguished themselves."[41] Thus these two sets of recommendations—to be wary of "applause" yet shower it on the deserving—were not as contradictory as they might appear. In tandem, they suggested that ambitions were appropriate female desires, provided they were carefully cloaked in modesty.

Girls' speeches clearly demonstrate their understanding of that rule—and their ability to make the most of it. Orators of both sexes in the eighteenth century were expected by long-standing convention to disavow any greed for fame in their opening statements, a self-deprecation intended to reflect the orator's gentility and training in formal oratory. When young women delivered these rhetorical gestures of humility, they did so in a specifically feminine register, and for particular effect. In most cases the young orator began her speech by modestly requesting the "approbation" of her auditors, often by directly acknowledging the comparative rarity of women's public speech. A New York schoolgirl explained in her opening lines that "awed by the presence of so respectable an audience, it is with diffidence that I appear before you," lines that would certainly have softened the critical sensibilities of her auditors.[42] But such an opening did not necessarily set the tone for the rest of the speech. In 1793 Susannah Hoar, who was probably about fourteen, opened her school's exhibition with a poem that likened her classmates to fledglings that wished to fly, "Trembling on the margin of their nest." To underscore her point, she uses "trembling" three times and "timorous souls" twice. But she uses these assertions of feminine modesty and her "fledgling" desire to please as a gambit to appeal to her audience for special consideration:

> So we this hour, with timorous souls, essay
> Our modest share of learning to display.
> Candor we ask—shall not we candor share?
> Who will deny it to the young, the fair?[43]

Girls' propensity to "tremble" thus became a means of demanding sanction, for "who will deny" friendly approbation to such proper young girls? By playfully manipulating rhetorical convention, Hoar sought to disarm her auditors with self-deprecation so she might demand their good opinion.

Others used modesty more baldly to justify increased opportunities for women's formal oratory. In a 1792 speech before the Philadelphia Young-Ladies' Academy, Molly Wallace notes that if even "veterans, in the art of public elocution" could be intimidated by a "respectable audience," "what then must my situation be, when my sex, my youth and inexperience all conspire to make me tremble at the task?" Yet rather than dwell on her "trembling" modesty as Hoar had done, Wallace makes an immediate segue—and begins to shed the veneer of feminine modesty in favor of a more rigorous logic. "With some," she states, "it has been made a question, whether [girls] ought *ever* to appear in so public a manner." She takes this as her main theme in order to dismantle it. Why, indeed, should women be taught to speak, she asks, if they are not expected to "harangue" like Cicero or Demosthenes? This question, she insists, was hypocritical if applied only to girls. Boys were taught Latin when they "will seldom have occasion, either to write or converse" in it. Likewise, "Are we taught to dance merely for the sake of being dancers? No, certainly," she answers for all present. Women should not "be deprived of what is perhaps the most effectual means of acquiring a just, natural and graceful delivery," she concludes.[44] Whereas Hoar had used gender stereotypes as a rhetorical strategy, Wallace used her modest beginning as a springboard into a more earnest and forthright criticism of restrictions on female speech, and to speaking more broadly of the benefits of women's eloquence. Defending female elocution as intrinsically valuable, she promotes women's education in more open-ended terms than the ideology of republican motherhood, which funneled a woman's "influence" into a parental or wifely role.

Molly Wallace's rapid switch from modest to diagnostic was not merely a coy manipulation of gender stereotypes and oratorical conventions but constituted a critique. Moreover, she made her impatience with gender restrictions clear without the Wollstonecraft paradigm (which her peers would use in their orations a year later), since *A Vindication* had not yet arrived in Philadelphia. But neither did she adopt the cute approach that Hoar had used. In fact, her deliberate style suited the serious question she pursued. Wallace matched the manner of her speech to its matter, displaying a developed understanding of composition and rhetorical theory.

Considering the rhetorical sophistication of such strategies, we might suspect that oratorical training was available only to the elite girls whose families who could afford to send their daughters to female academies — and, correspondingly, that the model of the erudite female speaker was available primarily to privileged, urban girls. This assumption is supported in that most extant girls' speeches derive from academies, whose elite students likely had many more opportunities to consider the implications of their speech and enact their own version of the genteel, well-spoken woman. But this model of womanhood appeared in other print formats that *were* available to nonelite and rural readers in two kinds of stories within the pages of the inexpensive schoolbooks read by virtually all schoolchildren in the greater Northeast.

The first were didactic stories designed to convince readers of the upward mobility to be achieved by education and good speech, since these allowed a child to demonstrate merit to the outside world. Schoolbooks were rife with variants of this message, often in the form of short theatrical dialogues that contrasted yokels with properly educated protagonists. In other words, rather than argue with skeptics who doubted the value of female education, these dialogues implied that uneducated girls risked being seen as ignorant and foolish. In her school exhibition in rural western Massachusetts in 1800, for example, the fourteen-year-old Sally Ripley took on the character of a crude farm girl in a dialogue, cheerfully mispronouncing terms like *mortal phlosophy* and *ratterick*. "But why do you need so much larning," she asks her better-educated friend. "No I see the trick, you mean to marry parsons, and make us poor farmers girls call you madams." She goes on to say that her family believes that "larning" makes girls "dam'd uppish" and "proud"; they see, with a good deal of prescience, that self-improvement could encourage a kind of social one-upmanship. Her friend counters these objections by arguing that far from making one a snob, education permitted a girl to "gain esteem," even, perhaps, from their town's handsome—and eligible—unmarried young parson. Faced with such appealing prospects for an estimable husband, Sally's character finally proclaims earnestly, "I'll go to school with all my heart."[45] Dialogues like this one allowed readers to imagine themselves in the role of the right-minded friend whose unstilted elocution converted her rustic neighbor.

If Sally Ripley's dialogue painted good speech as one component of self-improvement, the second group of schoolbook stories—biographical sketches of remarkable learned women—portrayed such eloquent women as potential heroines. Editors positioned these tales alongside biographies of eminent men, likely intending to inspire their readers to emulate such exemplary individuals. These stories often depicted their subjects as mobilizing virtuous speech and sentiments to effect the public good. In her 1811 schoolbook, Susannah Rowson (who directed a female academy in the Boston area) introduces a series of female biographies by stating:

> To young females, the memorials of exemplary women are peculiarly interesting. The importance of women in every civilized society is generally acknowledged, and their ascendance in forming the character of the other sex cannot be disputed; it is not alone to the nursery, or during the periods of childhood and youth, but in riper years, in the cabinet, in the camp, in almost every station in some way or other their influence is found to be unbounded.[46]

Describing the lives of such prominent figures as Lady Jane Grey, Catherine the Great, and other members of the nobility, these biographies tended to downplay the subjects' extraordinary social positions in order to detail their accomplishments. Much like contemporary portrayals of George Washington's exemplary conduct, many emphasized that even queens had to learn good manners and graceful conversation as children, and that their mastery of such skills was an important component of their prominence. The narratives' emphasis on sociability suggested these women should be remembered for their demeanor in everyday settings as much as for their social position and that, by extension, all women could aspire to the manners of queens.

Just as Rowson depicted women's influence as "unbounded," schoolbook biographies refused to portray their subjects as domestic or cloistered. Instead, they presented female readers with dramatic models to emulate.[47] Even formulaic pieces exhibited their subjects being admired in social environments such as assemblies and court circles, by men as well as by women—implying that ordinary American women could achieve the same admiration in sociable settings. Some biographies chose American women as their subjects and explicitly stressed these women's central role in galvanizing and animating polite society. The schoolbook editor Caleb Bingham delighted that "here on this western shore, we can justly boast of a Warren, a Morton, an Adams, with many others; whose talents and virtues ornament their sex, and excite emulation. Happy for the fair daughters of America, the thick mists of superstition and bigotry are vanishing away; and the sun of science begins to beam upon the land, and to irradiate the *female* mind."[48] Likewise, Benjamin Rush's frequently reprinted 1801 biography of Elizabeth Graeme Ferguson of Philadelphia celebrated her cultivated intellect and understanding as they emerged in the enlightened circle of conversationalists. It described Ferguson's Saturday evening gatherings at which she presided over a salon of intellectuals and "friends of both sexes as were considered suitable company." In this rarefied circle Ferguson, then still unmarried, claimed the highest respect for her knowledge and eloquence:

> These evenings were properly speaking, of the Attic kind. The genius of Miss Graeme evolved the heat and light that animated them. . . . She [was] instructed by the stores of knowledge contained in the historians, philosophers and poets of ancient and modern nations, which she called forth at her pleasure; and again she charmed by a profusion of original ideas, collected by her vivid and widely expanded imagination, and combined with exquisite taste and judgment into an endless variety of elegant and delightful forms. Upon these occasions her body seemed to evanish, and she appeared to be all mind.[49]

Ferguson's role in this salon bore no resemblance to that of a republican mother. Praising her brilliant intellect and imagination, this sketch notably lacked any qualifying references to stereotypical middling and modest femininity. She even appears to transcend her feminine body altogether: "Her body seemed to evanish." Here Ferguson was "all mind" yet appears neither dangerously masculine nor bold. Moreover, she energized her mind on behalf of her companions and the direction of their conversation; her ingenious pleasures benefited the group.[50] Such texts diverged from other "female" literature in that they lionized virtuous public action in real-world situations rather than focusing on family ties; "the plots encouraged girls to behave instrumentally rather than relationally," as Martha Vicinus has noted. Moreover, the narratives dramatized the need for "well-trained and controlled action" and the valuable effects of such action.[51]

Some vignettes celebrated female eloquence as a form of heroism. *The Ladies' Literary Companion* (1792) waxed lyrical about Queen Philippa's efforts to plead in court for the lives of six condemned men. Describing her speech, the author gushed, "What cogent reasoning,—what resistless eloquence, . . . *Shakespeare* himself could not have made her talk in a strain more judicious, or suitable to her request: nor the renowned Cicero, at the bar, with all his oratory, and the eyes of Rome upon him, could not have used greater weight of argument, nor powers of rhetoric, to gain the cause of his most beloved friend."[52] According to this sketch, Philippa's was an explicitly deliberative speech akin to those of male oratorical giants. Even with its hyperbole, this passage implied that all women had a right to public speech owing to historical precedent, beyond the evidence of their talent in that field. Again, such sketches idealized figures like Philippa for characteristics and action far beyond the delimited roles allotted to republican mothers, oriented primarily to their families.

It might seem impossible to trace a direct influence of biographical stories on real readers; girls may well have recognized the actions of personages such as Queen Philippa to be entertaining, full stop. But in fact, the influence of these stories is evident on at least two levels. First, female academy speeches reiterated the schoolbooks' messages about girls' oratorical heroines. The 1794 speech of Ann Harker in Philadelphia, for example, exalts "the female Iberian Cicero" who "effected a revolution, by her eloquence" against "superstition and prejudice" by opening Spanish literary and philosophical societies to women; Harker invokes this figure explicitly to inspire her fellow students.[53] References like these allowed female students to display the breadth of their knowledge, support their own public authority to speak, and even suggest that some women's public speech could be superior to men's—all of which demonstrate girls' active use of biographical sketches. Second and more abstract, broad-based archival evidence shows the direct influence of many forms of biography on ordinary readers during the early republic—readers who found these stories rousing not necessarily for their specific details but for the instrumentalist view of human action they modeled. The published lives of famous missionaries, for instance, led several early nineteenth-century American girls to dedicate themselves to mission work.[54]

Of course, that middling and rural readers would likely have read these biographical stories does not mean they would have responded in the same manner as their elite, urban counterparts who attended academies and knew *salonistes*. In addition, schoolbooks could sometimes delimit the scope of female eloquence by warning female readers that ambition and desire for "applause" were dangerously unfeminine. Still, the social world represented within schoolbooks incorporated a range of female roles that included a far more public and far less maternal position for women in American society than is generally recognized for this era. In doing so, schoolbooks reflected the cultural understanding that they were preparing children for entry into a heterosocial culture that highly valued women's conversational skills. Thus we can see that girls' conceptions of that culture ranged along a spectrum, depending on their class status and locale—and this spectrum offered a variety of opportunities for women's civic engagement.

Whether a girl took for granted that her public speech required particularly feminine declarations of modesty or criticized the limitations on girls' oratory, she participated in a cultural expansion of female public roles taking place in all schools throughout the Northeast. Girls' speeches and exhibition performances helped to familiarize their communities with women's public speech and to normalize the figure of the female orator—a shift that could have broader implications for reassessing women's participation in public. And as we shall see, some girls recognized the political potential of such roles and used their oratory to advance expansive ideas about women as public figures and as citizens.

FEMALE ACADEMIES AND THE CULTIVATION OF A FEMALE COUNTERPUBLIC

"Let me call upon all my young female friends and companions to *rouse up*, and to assist our rights!" wrote "Aurelia" during the 1793 newspaper debate over girls' oratorical education that began this chapter.[55] Her tone was strikingly different from that of most girl orators, who used a more restrained feminine register to assure audiences of their propriety. Fourteen-year-old Susanna Stearns opened her 1796 exhibition poem, for example, with the modest request, "Our stage is but the path to honest fame, / Attention then we ask."[56] Whether "asking" for attention or demanding their "rights," schoolgirls advocated for progressive opportunities for women in public and political culture. Particularly in more advanced academies, young women's self-presentation as articulate, conscientious female citizens mirrored women's increasingly bold claims to participate in the body politic in contemporary England, France, and elsewhere in the Atlantic world.[57] Aurelia's more insurgent rhetoric was far from exceptional, joining other girls' voices to help constitute a female counterpublic.

Like elementary-level common schools, academies taught virtually the same subjects to both boys and girls and employed nearly identical pedagogical methods.[58] During the 1790s and early 1800s, hundreds of academies were founded throughout the country to provide more advanced education to children—by 1855, there were 6,100 in existence, according to one source.[59] The academy was "the prevailing institution of higher schooling in eighteenth- and nineteenth-century America" for both sexes.[60] For girls, these schools provided the sole means to attain an education beyond common schools. Female academies taught subjects ranging from history and rhetoric to geography, mathematics, and the natural sciences as well as music, languages, and some fine arts such as painting or needlework; they also provided far more training in the classics and classical languages than scholars have usually recognized.[61] In addition to learning the same subjects as boys, girls attended academies in striking numbers: in fact, the percentage of girls enrolled in academies was greater than that of boys enrolled in academies and colleges between 1790 and 1830.[62]

Of course, the total number of students in academies was quite small relative to the overall population. Academies were limited primarily to elites who could afford tuition until the 1810s and 1820s, when they became increasingly affordable and attractive to the middling sorts. For example, the Young Ladies' Academy of Philadelphia, one of the most prestigious of these schools, boasted among its student body the daughters of Pennsylvania's chief justice and the treasurer of the United States and drew students from as far away as Maine and the West Indies.[63] Teachers reminded students of their privileged status by asking them to serve as exemplars for a wider public. "The greater your improved advantages have been, the more conspicuous characters you will form," John Poor told his Philadelphia graduates in 1794. "Therefore may your future demeanor be seasoned with such exemplary prudence, that the laurels you have so fairly won, may convince the rising generation of your real merit."[64] And in their speeches, girls often voiced their gratitude for the unusual advantages they enjoyed. Considered in this light, publishing girls' speeches allowed academies to substantiate their reputation and justify advanced female education; more subtly, it also confirmed the contemporary acceptance of elite women's social prominence.

Many of the young orators' speeches indicate, however, that they used the occasion of appearing on stage to do more than be "exemplary." In both content and rhetoric, they went beyond prevailing gender roles, even for elite women, and advocated expanded positions for women in the new nation. In Lexington, Massachusetts, twelve-year-old Susanna Stearns began her 1795 exhibition poem with a self-conscious reference to her appearance in public:

> What! then, I see your eyes are turned on me—
> And you may wonder well, at what you see.
> What means this little fairy—Has she to do
> A dialogue, or make a speech that's new?
> ... I come indeed to speak; but what to say,
> Aye there's the task—Suppose I talk away.

Unlike many of her peers, who began their speeches by assuring auditors of their feminine propriety, Stearns displays both charm and coyness about her goals as an orator. The playful beginning gives her some latitude to proceed in a mischievous vein: throughout she takes on the roles of a spectrum of female stereotypes, from the prude who "nip[s] up and mince[s] like th' parson's daughter," to a lady of fashion for whom no beau is good enough, to an old maid who finally marries "some cross old widower with the gout." Stearns gives each role equal time and dismisses each as quickly as the last, using humor to ridicule the emptiness of such limited female types. Her intention was not to mock women, however, but to set herself up as a strong contrast to them—a well-mannered, articulate, and educated girl who clearly had no intention of becoming a female caricature. She closed with an equally lighthearted yet open-ended suggestion: "These instances, to this conclusion bring, / That I, indeed, am fit for any thing."[65] In the context of a playful performance, this was an audacious conclusion, "indeed."

If Stearns was coy, other girl orators were explicit in expressing their desire to defy the female stereotypes that inhibited women's ambitions. In her 1791 commencement address in Philadelphia, Eliza Shrupp adopted martial metaphors and a rousing air when she turned from speaking to the exhibition audience to address her fellow students directly. "Let no obstacle retard you in your glorious progress," she commands; but she also warns them to move forward with care. "With the spirit of enterprize and emulation push forward your conquest.... Put on, then, the helmet of discretion. Accustom yourselves to some of the duties of self-denial—in this way you may hope to arrive at the Temple of Fame."[66] With her contradictory rhetoric, which counsels caution and aggression in the same breath, Shrupp reveals that she well understands that the woman who hoped to approach the "Temple of Fame" had to follow a narrow path. Even as she validates girls' ambitions, she describes the contortions required to win fame without infamy. Her sentiments seem bolder, perhaps, because she acknowledges the difficulties.

Such claims of female ambition graduated into confident assertions of female quality and oratorical ability in Priscilla Mason's 1793 address at the Young Ladies' Academy, which is easily the most assertive of all extant girls' speeches of the era. Invoking Wollstonecraft, Mason calls for "a vindication of female eloquence." Women's oratory, she argues, "is a part of the rights of woman, and must be allowed by the courtesy of Europe and America too." She acknowledges that their exercise of the right to speak might "rest like the sword in the scabbard, to be used only when the occasion requires," assuring her auditors that she seeks no large-scale reversal of sexual roles. But having reasserted gender distinctions on one level, she goes on to claim the "right" to speak at "public occasions" and thus to undermine those distinctions, at least with regard to public speech:

> Our right to instruct and to persuade cannot be disputed, if it shall appear, that we possess the talents of the orator—and have opportunities for the exercise of those talents. Is a power of speech, and volubility of expression, one of the talents of the orator? Our sex possess it in an eminent degree.
>
> Do personal attractions give charms to eloquence, and force to the orator's arguments? There is some truth mixed with the flattery we receive on this head. Do tender passions enable the orator to speak in a moving and forcible manner? This talent of the orator is confessedly ours. In all these respects the female orator stands on equal,—nay, on *superior* ground.[67]

Mason uses the universal language of elocution manuals to describe the ideal orator's attributes and claim them for her sex. Considering that women might possess a natural talent that could surpass that of men, she explains why women had not been public orators in the past: because men had historically held a monopoly on the church, the bar, and the senate. In other words, women were excluded from oratory owing to historical, not "natural," causes, calling into question the validity of that exclusion.

Mason's solution ties politics to refined sensibility and envisions a new definition of citizenship that holds a role for women. To combat women's historical exclusion from oratory and to promote national interests, she proposes that a federal senate of women be devised to oversee the "fashion and manners" of the new nation. While those topics sound trifling to modern ears, in the 1790s these terms were imbued with profound political meaning. Rosemarie Zagarri has explained that "manners" "did not simply mean proper etiquette or correct social deportment; it connoted ideas of individual morality and personal character, suggesting a strong connection between private values and public behavior."[68] Writing in 1790, an officer named James Tilton described the significance of manners: "The men possess the more ostensible powers of making and executing the laws ... [while] the women, in every free country, have an absolute control of manners: and it is confessed, that in a republic, manners are of equal importance with laws."[69] Indeed, Wollstonecraft called for a "revolution in female manners," and Mason herself distinguished these pursuits from the "servile or frivolous employments" that "degraded" women's intellects. Mason expected that this female senate would be composed of "women most noted for wisdom, learning and taste, delegated from every part of the Union" and would grant "independence" to American culture. "We cannot be independent, while we receive our fashions from other countries; nor act properly, while we imitate the manners of governments not congenial to our own," she explains. In keeping with the Scottish thinkers she studied in school, Mason imagines a world that linked independence and fashions, government and manners. The senate she proposes would harness women's unique talents, granting them a political role far beyond that of the republican mother.

Yet while fashion and manners might allow women's entry into politics, the ultimate aim of her female senate is to develop female "ambition" and improve women's deliberative skills at public discourse so they might join the men in "equal participation": "It would fire the female breast with the most generous ambition, prompting to illustrious actions. It would furnish the most noble Theatre for the display, the exercise and improvement of every faculty. It would call forth all that is human—all that is divine in the soul of woman; and having proved them equally capable with the other sex, would lead to their equal participation of honor and office."[70] Mason's senate is thus a means to a radical end: she promotes a degree of political equality rare even among those who supported the "rights of women" during the 1790s. She looks forward to the day when female senators would complete their political educations and enter a men's world of politics. As such, she advances a female counterpublic: she claims oratorical and civic power for women in order to alter the historical patterns that had inhibited them from realizing "equal participation of honor and office."

Mason's articulation of a female counterpublic also emerges in her rhetorical style. Even more than her fellow students, she employs a prose that steers clear of the feminine flourishes common to sentimental writing of the era. Instead her writing reflects a dedication to directness that Wollstonecraft associated with a radical variety of republican virtue—a clarity she approvingly termed *masculine*, as Elizabeth Wingrove has shown.[71] Delivered less than a year after the publication of *A Vindication of the Rights of Woman*, Mason's speech clearly demonstrates her debt to that writer's passion for unadorned, virtuous language, right down to borrowing the term "vindication" and other turns of phrase. Using this style grants Mason the persona of the kind of female politician who might rise to serve in the female senate. Taken as a whole, Mason's rhetoric and ideas were more heavily influenced by a strain of European radical republicanism than by American republican motherhood; her models for women's political participation drew on Wollstonecraft's bracing criticisms as well as the salons and levees where women like Elizabeth Graeme Ferguson displayed their improvisational intellects—not the virtuous household hearth.

Were Mason's argument and rhetoric far outside the mainstream of ideas about women's place in postrevolutionary society? The simple answer is yes, but such an answer fails to take into account the circulation of her ideas and similar ones, even if nonelite women were unlikely to model such public behavior. Mason's ideas were certainly not atypical among her peers. Her teachers and auditors did not just condone her oration, they published it; they clearly considered it exemplary of public speech by elite schoolgirls. Moreover, the figure of the exceptional female intellectual circulated widely, both in published girls' speeches and in biographical sketches, depicting women who considered themselves as well equipped to engage as fully in public affairs as their male counterparts.[72] Thus, even if we allow that such ideas could be enacted only by elite women, nonelites would likely have been aware of them and have viewed them as part of a spectrum of acceptable female behavior.

Within twenty years this spectrum of opinions about women's public roles would rapidly narrow. By the early 1810s the tradition of publishing girls' commencement speeches declined, and girls' expressions of ambition only rarely found a place in print culture. When Susanna Rowson published the commencement proceedings of her Boston-area academy in *A Present for Young Ladies* (1811), she included theatrical dialogues but none of her students' speeches. In 1814 a Boston schoolgirl named Amelia Russell, intent on improving herself, noted in her diary that she had "commenced a biography of Catherine 2d." Russell succinctly summarized Catherine the Great as "a woman of extraordinary talents but she sacrificed them all to ambition."[73] That she saw ambition as a quality that led Catherine to "sacrifice" her talents exemplified the shift from an earlier era when female striving tended to be viewed in more positive terms and women were allowed more room for public action.

Particularly by the 1820s, authors turned away from the open-ended notion of women's education as intrinsically valuable, advocating more gender-specific educational subjects as well as more delimited roles for women in society at large, a development Rosemarie Zagarri has called a "revolutionary backlash" to reconceptualize American politics as a sphere that decidedly excluded women's participation.[74] This shift brought new limitations on women's elocutionary education. By 1833 Almira Phelps, the well-respected principal of the Troy Female Academy in upstate New York, advocated elocution but only "confined to the fire-side, and to the domestic circle." In the same year, Lydia Sigourney similarly noted that female elocution was "particularly valuable in our sex" but described its value as strictly domestic, "because it so often gives them an opportunity of imparting pleasure and improvement to an assembled family during the winter evening, or the protracted storm."[75]

This shift toward an increasingly narrow and private conception of female eloquence reflected significant political realignments that marginalized the public contributions of elite, educated women during the early republic. The successes of the Republican Party beginning in the 1790s altered elite women's access to political authority; the new conflation of political participation with suffrage for white men was linked to the diminution of participation by women, whose access to public discourse had previously rested on their social and economic rank, as Jeanne Boydston has noted.[76] Republicans gained even more ground in this regard after William Godwin's 1798 biography of Wollstonecraft began to circulate—a book that shocked readers by its portrayal of her sexual history, views on marriage, and suicide attempts. Such revelations led to a large-scale reappraisal of the proper ends for female education, reinvigorating cultural disdain for the "learned lady," who was increasingly portrayed as a comically unattractive and unfeminine creature to warn girls of the dangers of acquiring knowledge. Increasingly, writers argued that female education should be commensurate with the cardinal feminine characteristics of modesty, selflessness, and silence. Although this transition was hardly unique to the United States, prescriptive literature tied feminine modesty to new conceptions of American identity—signaling that it played an important role in a broader reassessment and refinement of the nature of the America public.[77]

Yet this transition was accompanied by the striking democratization of female education in the early nineteenth century—at the common-school level, as we saw in the first chapter, and even more notably at the academy level. Middling families increasingly sent their daughters to academies beginning in the 1810s, a shift that accompanied—and may even have rested on—public assurances that educated girls would learn greater demureness at the schools taught by Almira Phelps, Lydia Sigourney, Catharine Beecher, and others, even when those schools actually taught their students a similar form of self-possession and confidence, as Mary Kelley has shown.[78]

Nothing more clearly signals this shift in women's public roles in early American society than the changing standards of female eloquence. All sources reveal that girls continued to learn elocution in common schools and rhetoric and oratory at academies, although they were more frequently barred from exhibition-day performances and commencement speeches. Some female academies even fostered a variety of extracurricular literary societies, debating clubs, and other groups that enhanced the girls' skills in deliberative thinking and debate.[79] But in participating in such activities, girls had to learn new forms of feminine modesty. Women increasingly jettisoned Mason's Wollstonecraftian style of plain, forthright, and ambitious rhetoric for what Granville Ganter has termed the "unexceptional" style—a humble, self-effacing voice that "pleads no trickery, and little right to declaim."[80] Women were not the only ones to use this style in the nineteenth century, but, as Ganter notes, female orators excelled in it. The modesty girls had once deployed in teasing gambits was now an end unto itself.

This tendency was exemplified in Catharine Maria Sedgwick's 1822 novel *A New-England Tale*, in which female "propriety" became the rationale for excluding girls from regular public elocution. Describing the local school's exhibition in a rural Massachusetts town, Sedgwick explains that "young men and boys were to display those powers that were developing for the pulpit, and the bar, and the political harangue. The young ladies were with obvious and singular propriety excluded from any part in the exhibition." The exception to this rule was made for the student author of the prize essay, who was asked to read his or her work before the gathered townspeople.[81] The novel uses the prize essay contest to illuminate the contrast between two adolescent female characters: the virtuous heroine, Jane, and her envious and coquettish cousin, Elvira. Though Jane wins school honors for all academic subjects, Elvira wins the composition contest and rises to deliver her essay before the assembled townspeople on the school's stage, still decorated with a royal theme for the exhibition-day play. When the curtains rise, Elvira is "seated on the throne, ambitiously arrayed in a bright scarlet Canton crape frock" and other extravagant accoutrements, while her hair flows in ringlets "in imitation of some favorite heroine." When she declaims her essay, she "spout[s] it with all the airs and graces of a sentimentalist of the beau monde," and her cheeks glow with "the pride of success and the pleasure of display." Marked by her ambition and her immodesty, Elvira earns murmurs of both praise and disapprobation from members of the audience, some of whom believe that "she look[s] too bold" to deserve compliments for her prize.[82]

Elvira's triumph is short-lived, however. An old man speaks up from the audience and proclaims with rustic good sense that, though "he was kinder-loath to spoil a young body's pleasure," he remembers reading her composition in an old Boston newspaper. Her plagiarism exposed, Elvira's prize is revoked and awarded to Jane, the second-place winner. Brought to the "throne" with her essay, Jane looks

> like the "meek usurper," reluctant to receive the honor that was forced upon her. She presented a striking contrast to the deposed sovereign. She was dressed in a plain black silk frock, and a neatly plaited muslin Vandyke.... As she unrolled the scroll she held in her hand, she ventured once to raise her eyes; she saw but one face among all the multitude—the approving, encouraging smile of her kind patron met her timid glance, and emboldened her to proceed, which she did, in a low and faltering voice, that certainly lent no grace, but the grace of modesty, to the composition.[83]

From her failure to address her auditors directly to her "faltering" air, Jane's graceless performance breaks all the rules propounded by elocutionists. Yet Jane's delivery is deemed superior to Elvira's, from the perspective of both the narrator and the fictional auditors who observe the two girls. For readers growing accustomed to prescriptive literature that increasingly emphasized the virtue of feminine modesty, Jane serves as a demure model whose public appearance, not incidentally, also draws admiration from the most eligible boy at her school. In an earlier era Jane would have been regarded as a poorly trained schoolgirl and an embarrassment to the audience, but here her modesty is romanticized and sentimentalized.

The difference between Jane's feminine reserve and Elvira's pomp is further emphasized by the politicized allusions to deposed royalty and republican virtue that pervade this vignette. Jane's sober dress contrasts with Elvira's "bright scarlet" dress and dramatizes the comparison of republicanism with monarchy. "She presented a striking contrast to the deposed sovereign," Sedgwick writes of Jane, whom she describes as "meek," "reluctant" and "embarrassed." Meanwhile, she links the royalist Elvira to the beau monde, display, novelistic excess, and even Oriental decadence (she wore a "Canton" fabric).[84] Sedgwick thus simultaneously invests Jane's poor elocutionary delivery with republican virtue and feminine propriety in ways that differed significantly from earlier views. By the 1820s the differences rather than the similarities between boys' and girls' elocutionary educations were becoming more striking. The virtuous rural American girl heroine of novels like Sedgwick's now held her tongue and cast down her eyes. Novelists not only celebrated such female behavior, they invested it with political meaning, implying that this was the proper role for women in a republic—in essence, to be the political opposite of the male citizen rather than his counterpart.

To be sure, this trend did not produce a definitive prohibition of women's public speech—even by the 1820s, as we shall see in the final chapter on Frances Wright. Nonetheless, gender ideology gradually hardened around a more retiring role for educated women and away from the open-ended depictions of female conversation and social expertise of the late eighteenth century. The new model of exaggerated modesty for women contrasted markedly with earlier visions of female oratorical and intellectual excellence that emerged in elocutionary education. Postrevolutionary ideals of women's public participation had centered on sociability and conversation that were not necessarily anchored to their influence within the family. As rarefied as such ideals might appear, they informed the ways young people from a variety of social ranks learned to conduct themselves in public. Girls learned to improve their speech and character for participation in society and alongside their male peers; performing speeches in school exhibitions became one way they learned to participate in public. And some elite young women carried these lessons further, broaching the topic of women's role within the new republic. Their oratorical performances illuminate milieus in which women were not always the political and social opposite of men and were not restricted to a sphere defined as private and domestic. "Aurelia," Priscilla Mason, Molly Wallace, and their peers used the opportunity of public address at school exhibitions to express their ambition and even to make strong, Wollstonecraft-inspired "vindications" of female eloquence.

Finally, it is worth highlighting the parallels between new ideas about women in public and changes in elocutionary education discussed in the previous chapter. Both chapters have traced the training and engagement of boys and girls in public speaking during the immediate postwar years, an encouragement that entailed new ways of thinking about the public as a whole. Spurred by a sense that America had not yet realized its potential for fine speech and refined manners, men and women cultivated their talents in speaking and made oral culture a central component of education. Inspired by Scottish Enlightenment understandings of civilization, Americans believed that only with educated men and women could their country be recognized as properly advanced to play a part on the world stage. Considering those expectations, the popular publication of girls' commencement speeches appears an unsurprising element of postwar print culture, for such examples of success could only inspire others.

Common-school and female education likewise underwent related shifts in the early nineteenth century that reconceived the way ordinary people participated in public. At the same time that schoolbooks began teaching students to venerate their national leaders' oratory and wise guidance—imagining a more passively patriotic public—popular literature began to advance a model of girlhood and womanhood that was less public and less political than before. Together, these shifts speak to the complexities and contradictions of national identification and democratization of the early nineteenth century. To take a firm hand in prescribing the manner of schoolchildren's patriotism or girls' vocal presence was to attempt to manage the public engagement of large groups within the country. And as we shall see in the final chapter of this first half of the book, print and oratory could be used to imagine an American public by constructing a cultural other. American schoolchildren and readers at large could also learn to understand their shared characteristics and national values by contrasting themselves with eloquent outsiders.

CHAPTER 3

Mourning for Logan
"INDIAN ELOQUENCE" AND THE MAKING OF AN AMERICAN PUBLIC

"I appeal to any white man to say, if ever he entered Logan's cabin hungry, and he gave him not meat; if ever he came cold and naked, and he clothed him not." With these words Logan, a Mingo Indian, began his 1774 speech, memorialized in Thomas Jefferson's *Notes on the State of Virginia* (1787). Jefferson argued that although Logan's speech came from the mouth of a "savage" in a wild land where "letters have not yet been introduced," it was equal in eloquence and sentiment to anything produced by centuries of European civilization, including the speeches of Cicero and Demosthenes. In his brief speech, Logan explains that he had been an advocate for peace throughout the bloody French and Indian War, so much so that "my countrymen pointed as they passed, and said, 'Logan is the friend of white men.'" He had even considered moving closer to white settlements, he continues, until one white man's terrible actions changed the course of his life:

> Col. Cresap, the last spring, in cold blood, and unprovoked, murdered all the relations of Logan, not sparing even my women and children. There runs not a drop of my blood in the veins of any living creatures. This called on me for revenge. I have sought it: I have killed many: I have fully glutted my vengeance. For my country, I rejoice at the beams of peace. But do not harbour a thought that mine is the joy of fear. Logan never felt fear. He will not turn on his heel to save his life. Who is there to mourn for Logan?—Not one.[1]

Yet Americans did mourn for Logan. Propelled by Jefferson's effusive praise, the speech's final melancholy plea elicited such admiration that editors reprinted it hundreds of times. Nor was it the only Indian speech to garner such attention for its eloquence. The figure of the eloquent Indian wronged by whites appeared in popular speeches, stories, and anecdotes, reprising Logan's message from the mouths of Red Jacket, Speckled Snake, Farmer's Brother, and others, each of whom, it was said, spoke with nobility and clarity when accusing the white man of treachery.[2]

Their speeches pointed out how frequently white Americans[3] had stolen land, broken treaties, murdered Indian women and children, and proselytized for a religion whose morality they seldom upheld themselves. Americans displayed a fascination with Indian eloquence nevertheless, as demonstrated by the hundreds of representations of Indian voices that appeared in a variety of print media, most notably magazines and schoolbooks. Schoolchildren throughout the Northeast memorized and recited Indian speeches in schools alongside speeches by Cicero and George Washington, as an ordinary component of learning how to read and to comport themselves. Editors of all political persuasions reproduced these speeches (and often invented them wholesale),[4] suggesting that the speeches did not cloak the agenda of a specific political faction. What made Indian eloquence and censure so prevalent in the American imagination during the early republic?

Building on earlier chapters' attention to the pedagogical practices of boys' and girls' elocution, in this chapter I analyze how those practices were used to foster national identification among schoolchildren and general readers. Print media such as schoolbooks and magazines used Indian speeches in ways that helped their readers identify as members of a white American public, unified against a shared opponent, even as these portrayals also fostered admiration of those speeches. This chapter illuminates the active involvement of nonelite editors and printers in working to construct notions of American identity and public participation. Editors advocated using Indian speeches as a means of oratorical improvement, but they also advanced powerful ideological narratives concerning the American past and whites' relation to Indians. Taken together, these educational practices and the prevalence of Indian eloquence in print culture reveal an important way that lay readers learned to think of themselves as Americans.

Americans learned this form of national and racial identification because Indian eloquence articulated a unique American history, one shaped in part by generations of white betrayal. This history made Americans appear sharply different from both their former British compatriots and the Indians with whom they shared the land.[5] By prompting their readers to feel a collective responsibility for that past, magazine and schoolbook editors also found in this story the possibility of redemption—a capacity for self-criticism that might distinguish the American character. Thus it was both the narrative put forward through Indian eloquence *and* the reiteration of American guilt in print and by schoolchildren's ventriloquy that evoked a growing identification with—and definition of—"Americanness." Together, these uses of Indian eloquence made it one of the nation's "foundational fictions," a narrative that helped to construct a coherent sense of the American past, present, and future. Like other imaginative aspects of nation building, these stories were "encouraged both by the need to fill in a history that would help to establish their legitimacy as the emerging nation and by the opportunity to direct that history toward an ideal future," as Doris Sommer has written.[6] Their widespread use in schools and popular print media cemented their importance in the postrevolutionary American imagination.

Oral and print media were deeply implicated in fostering a new national identity. Indeed, print and oratory were primary topics of discussion within these texts. In one passage, a document might explain to its readers that Indians' illiteracy made oratory essential to tribal culture and perhaps even enhanced its eloquence. In the next sentence it might identify the superiority of print and of white literacy and thus the "civilization" that derived from European antecedents. Yet again, Indian eloquence often underscored Americans' awareness that their literature and oratory still paled in comparison with Britain's. Jefferson's celebration of Logan's speech was one way of claiming that American literature was emerging on the literary scene. These multiple experiences of identity vis-à-vis the media point to the complexities and triangulations of postrevolutionary national identification.

Tales of white wrongdoing and Indian censure were not predicated on the "vanishing Indian," at least not at first, nor were they intended to provoke false sentimentality. The pedagogic uses of Indian speeches reveal this with particular clarity, since elocution taught children to internalize and harness a speech's emotion in order to deliver it with utmost persuasive power. Over time the meanings of Indian oratory changed in important ways, in part owing to regular repetition. By the early nineteenth century, print media increasingly turned readers' attention away from damning qualities of Indian censure and urged them to respond to the speeches' pathos by shedding a wistful tear for the figure of the suffering Indian.[7] In examining this shift, I draw on scholarship that has analyzed nineteenth-century "noble savage" literature, which assumed that printed representations *reflected* Indians' disappearance from power. But this chapter attributes a far more active role to print and oratory in helping to *anticipate* political possibilities than have earlier works. Of course, Indian eloquence was a literary motif, not an outright political statement; it recommended no state policy or concrete action toward the Indians. Yet as a "founding fiction," the trope of Indian eloquence provided ordinary Americans with emotional frameworks and imagined narrative outcomes for considering policies, and it thus had profound political implications. By the time political leaders began to discuss policies for removal, they used tropes appropriated from Indian oratory to do so—thereby eloquently expressing their regret for an Indian disappearance that had not yet occurred.[8]

ELOCUTION AND THE EDUCATIONAL PERFORMANCE OF INDIAN ELOQUENCE

Many of the censorious Indian speeches reprinted in American schoolbooks and magazines were delivered initially to protest specific white actions in real historical settings; and on occasion print and especially newspaper sources provided that context for their readers in detail. To name only the most famous, Logan's "lament" appeared in American newspapers shortly after a series of nearly simultaneous newspaper reports condemning Michael Cresap's bloodthirsty 1774 raid, as Robert Parkinson has shown.[9] Indeed, these stories had so frankly denounced Cresap's actions that they portrayed Logan's subsequent retaliation as a rational response. By the time the speech arrived with Lord Dunmore from the Indian front in early 1775 and "flew through all the public papers of the continent, and through the magazines and other periodical publications of Great Britain," as Thomas Jefferson remembered, the Shawnees had been roundly defeated by Dunmore's forces. As a result, Logan's speech "served as a final comment" on that vicious series of events; the early history of the speech demonstrates that popular Indian speeches could be tied to the very real stuff of Indian-white frontier conflict and tense wrangling over land, religion, and cultural integrity.[10]

But these speeches had much longer lives in print than did the histories that contextualized their initial delivery. The orations gained a new life at least partly independent of clear historical events once they were printed shorn of context-setting information. Almost from the time of its appearance, Logan's speech became a standby for memorizing and reciting in American schools. "Those who were boys at that day will now attest, that the speech of Logan used to be given them as a school exercise for repetition," Jefferson recalled.[11] The speech gained new life after Jefferson reprinted it in *Notes* in 1787, appearing on average at least three times a year in magazines and newspapers long into the 1830s and beyond—and it was cited even more frequently. Caleb Bingham included it in his wildly popular *American Preceptor* (1794), and it appeared in many other schoolbooks including McGuffey's *Readers*.[12] By 1842 a magazine editor waxed enthusiastic about the speech's pedagogical uses. He declared that "no piece of composition ever did more, if so much, as the speech of Logan . . . to form the mind and develop the latent energies of the youthful American orator. Its influence has extended even into the halls of Congress, and has been felt upon the bench and in the bar of this nation; nay more, the American pulpit has been graced by energies which that speech has, in its warmest simplicity, called forth."[13] Even allowing for hyperbole, it seems clear that the speech gained canonical status in early nineteenth-century schoolbooks. It was not the only one; nearly every example of Indian eloquence cited hereafter appeared in multiple editions and titles, almost always lacking an explanation of the speech's original delivery.

Taking on Indian voices in a pedagogical context resembled other contemporary forms of "playing Indian" across a range of activities, from treaty practices in which Anglo-American officials used Indian styles of address[14] to traditions of revelry and rebellion in which whites adopted Indian garb, such as at the Tammany Society of Philadelphia and the Boston Tea Party. As Philip Deloria has demonstrated, such "play" emerged during the revolutionary era from carnival consciousness and afforded its participants the chance to challenge authority or to engage in the playful reversal of "us" and "them."[15] But performing Indian speeches in schools was distinctive because of the complex identifications children learned early on. The basic elocutionary standards for reciting aloud from written texts demanded that one internalize a speaker's emotions and emulate the character of a virtuous orator.

"Emulation" referred to an active process by which an individual identified with an admirable model and appropriated his or her style. Emulation was not to be mistaken for passive mimicry; it was seen to be essential to developing a style of one's own. John Adams defined it as "a desire not only to equal or to resemble but to excel."[16] Benjamin Franklin explained the process most famously in his *Autobiography*: impressed with the graceful writing and refined sentiments of the influential London magazine the *Spectator*, Franklin "wished if possible to emulate it." He put the magazine aside and attempted to replicate the feeling of certain passages in his own words. Despite numerous early errors, his diligence eventually resulted in his "fancying that in certain particulars of small import I had been lucky enough to improve the method or the language."[17] For Franklin, the *Spectator* served as a model to build on and ultimately transcend. "If properly interpreted, the past was a vehicle for liberation: imitation was a form of innovation," as Jay Fliegelman has described the era's emphasis on emulation.[18] These understandings underlay schoolbook editors' choice of texts; when their titles promised the "best" or most "elegant" pieces for children to memorize, they believed that each of the examples constituted a virtuous model to emulate. Their choice of Indian speeches was hardly whimsical. It reflected a belief that these texts disseminated a form of eloquence that children could identify with and benefit from.

Moreover, most white youths would have had some form of access to these speeches owing to their frequent appearance in schoolbooks and magazines as well as in frequent schoolroom recitation. Over 30 percent of the approximately 220 American schoolbooks published between 1787 and 1830 that I analyzed contained at least one Indian speech or story. Breaking down these statistics chronologically, we find that Indian speeches and stories appeared in increasing numbers during this period, from 27.1 percent of the books published before 1810 to 33 percent after 1810. Since it was common to expect children to arrive at school with their own books and to copy pieces from one another's books to memorize, it was likely that most students either memorized an Indian speech or heard one recited by fellow classmates. In addition, students recited familiar speeches again and again until they mastered the art of effectively moving their auditors. Thomas Smith, a teenage member of a debating society in New York, for example, delivered "An Indian Warrior's Lamentation" three times before his fellows in 1792. Such repetition was standard practice: other members repeatedly took on the characters of Hamlet, Brutus, and Cato during their weekly orations, figures who likewise articulated stoic and noble virtue.[19] Clearly, the art of emulating fine oratory lay partly in repetition in order to develop one's own virtue and sensibility.

Reciting these speeches, therefore, was not just "play." Whites surely "played Indian" in other situations, but elocution saw emulation of Indian oratory as essential to larger ends. Emulation required that children adopt a strong affective identification with the speech's emotions and thus elicit their audience's sympathy for Indians. Only by doing so, these authors suggested, could they emerge as accomplished speakers themselves. In the process, they took on a doubled identity of American and Indian, eloquent both by art and by nature.

Schoolchildren and other youths regularly recited Indian speeches and transcribed them into their copybooks, but they rarely wrote more reflectively about their understanding of the text. Many examples from youths' writings imply that they thought a text's eloquence simply spoke for itself. "I am, an aged hemlock; the winds of an hundred years have blown through its branches; it is dead at the top. Those who began life with me have run away from me: Why I am suffered to remain God best knows." The schoolgirl Caroline Chester copied these words into her commonplace book in 1815 after memorizing them in school, having been touched by the pathos and simplicity of this sentiment by "Schenadoah an Indian chief who died lately aged one hundred and thirteen."[20] As in this case, schoolchildren almost never discussed their feelings about the material they memorized, Indian or otherwise—making it difficult to uncover their experience of identification and emulation. This suggests that whites' ventriloquy of Indian voices for educational self-improvement was *unremarkable*—such that the only description of Indian oratory in the schoolroom I have found is one that depicts not white children, but Cherokee children. In 1827, a Reverend Allan visited the Cherokee mission school at Creekpath, Alabama, and observed the students' "exhibition of speaking talent." "This was indeed novel and unexpected," Allan wrote, "and though the children had never witnessed any thing of the kind in their lives, yet I am confident I do not exaggerate, when I say that the performance was excellent."[21] Allan particularly praised one child's recitation of an Indian speech from Caleb Bingham's *Columbian Orator* (1797). "This piece, as you may suppose, appeared quite in keeping with the little Cherokee orator, who delivered it with great propriety," he noted. Allan's comments betrayed a degree of condescending amusement, winking at readers who could also "suppose" the incongruity of the scene. While such recitations were normative in white schools, seeing an Indian recite Indian oratory from a schoolbook was "novel." To be sure, Allan might have expressed the same wonder at untutored talent had the exhibition occurred at a white frontier school that lacked exposure to formal oratory. But it seems unlikely. His expression of surprise at the children's performance was more likely based on their "unexpected" adoption of, and skills in, *American* elocutionary practices—practices that had taught white children to appropriate Indian oratory.

White children's learning to identify with Indian orators and to express their sentiments via elocutionary education was one aspect of the larger fascination with Indian eloquence disseminated in oral and print media. Although only a small number of Indian speeches appeared in any given schoolbook, they were distinctive among the offerings. They were often some of very few pieces produced on American soil to appear in these volumes (until the 1810s, at least); they provided a pointed perspective on the history of whites in America; and they appeared so frequently as to enter an emerging canon of "American" literature, as Jefferson had predicted. These texts helped to create a more abstract set of identifications for a public of American readers. As they read Indian speeches that condemned them and their New World ancestors for wrongs, Americans engaged in rituals that signaled their unique capacity for redemption.

CULTURAL CONTRAST AND THE MAKING OF AN AMERICAN READING PUBLIC

The pedagogical uses of Indian speeches may have been new in the early republic, but Europeans had long promoted the idea that Indians had a particular capacity for eloquent oratory. This was an idea they linked to more expansive theories about social life and organization.[22] Eighteenth-century language theories identified several qualities of Indian languages as exemplary of the "primitive" stage of civilization, such as the notion that Indians had limited lexicons based almost exclusively on terms describing the material world, or that they expressed few abstract ideas compared with more "complex" European civilizations. Figuring their speech as "primitive," however, did not detract from Europeans' admiration of Indians' eloquence. Indeed, commentators suggested that the Indians' singular facility for metaphor and other vivid figures of speech developed out of necessity from their small vocabularies. For instance, the prominent British rhetorician Hugh Blair argued that the language of civilized society, having "proceeded from vivacity to accuracy; from fire to enthusiasm, to coolness and precision," had "become, in modern times, more correct . . . and accurate; but, however, less striking and animated" than those of primitive societies.[23] Such ideas about relations between language, oratory, and social organization were important features of a popular scientific discourse that emphasized comparing cultures to identify the ways complex societies might keep from becoming overcivilized.

The magazines and schoolbooks that popularized "specimens" of Indian eloquence were not primarily concerned with the scientific study of Indians and their languages, or with the accuracy of the translations and attributions. Although magazines tended to include more ethnological information than schoolbooks, both genres concentrated on presenting collections of enjoyable and informative material—which made their emphasis less newsworthy and more self-consciously literary than newspapers' selections. Editors used the figure of the eloquent Indian to raise topics that tied together the nature of American political society, the nation's relation to Indians, and the cultivation of a humanitarian sensibility among readers. The more they stressed American culpability for Indian suffering, the more they urged readers to see themselves as belonging to a collective reading public.

Magazine portrayals of native eloquence invariably stressed its centrality to good order in Indian society—making clear comparisons with American public culture. Introducing Logan's speech to his readers, the editor of the *South Carolina Weekly Museum*, a literary miscellany, explained in 1797 that "the principles of their society forbidding all compulsion, they are to be led to duty and to enterprise by personal influence and persuasion. Hence, eloquence in council, bravery and address in war, become the foundations of all consequence with them."[24] Likewise, an issue of the *Monthly Miscellany* reprinted Benjamin Franklin's statement that "all their government is by the counsel or advice of the sages; there is no force, there are no prisons, no officers to compel obedience, or inflict punishment. Hence they generally study oratory; the best speaker having the most influence."[25] Such accounts suggested that Indians may have achieved a degree of republican virtue and sensibility unknown in world history since classical days. If eloquence was the foundation of political harmony in simple societies, this implied, oratory might invigorate American society as well.

Observers' connections between oratory and good government also appeared in their descriptions of the Indian rank and file. In these renderings, Indian audiences were orderly and prepared by long experience to weigh thoughtfully the ideas of their eloquent leaders—descriptions that suggested to magazine readers that unruly Americans had much to learn. The contrast between American rudeness and Indian decorum was underscored in numerous accounts. "Nothing is more edifying than their behaviour in their publick councils and assemblies," stated a 1794 issue of the *Massachusetts Magazine*, one of the most respected and long-lived eighteenth-century American periodicals. "Every man is heard in his turn, according to the rank he holds by his years, his wisdom, or his services to his country. Not so much as a whisper is heard to interrupt the speaker: No indecent reflections, no ill timed applause."[26] This was a portrait not just of well-behaved Indian audiences, but of discerning, rational auditors—and as such it indirectly criticized the rambunctious, partisan United States of the 1790s and early 1800s. The thinly cloaked complaint about American audiences revealed the Federalist leanings of the *Magazine*'s editor. But Republican and Jeffersonian editors used similar portrayals, suggesting that representations of Indian eloquence were plastic enough to be useful to all manner of partisans of the period. A 1791 essay in the *Universal Asylum*, for example, went so far as to compare the discriminating Indian audience to the "fine ear [of] the people of Athens"—the ur-model of a virtuous political culture galvanized by oratory.²⁷ To link savage Indian auditors and the citizens of classical Greece was to suggest that eloquence provided the glue between leaders and citizens, rendering more virtuous all who listened with close attention to a thoughtful speech. By reproducing that relationship, Americans could benefit their nation.

Some writers drew explicit comparisons between Indians and European culture by placing critical statements directly into the mouths of the Indians they described. Indians "are never in a hurry to speak before they have thought well upon the matter, and are sure that the person who spoke before them had finished all he had to say: They have therefore the greatest contempt for the vivacity of the Europeans, who generally interrupt each other, or speak all together," the *Massachusetts Magazine* article continued.²⁸ The ethnographer James Adair, who wrote of the Indians of the greater Southeast with unusual admiration, also used Indian voices to criticize white culture. "They say, if our laws were honest, or wisely framed, they would be plain and few, that the poor people would understand them and remember them, as well as the rich . . . that simple nature enables every person to be a proper judge of promoting good, and preventing evil."²⁹ This critique hit several targets at once—the social inequalities, the deceptive legalisms, and the "unnatural" social order of an overrefined and corrupt European culture. By confronting their readers with these judgments, magazine editors proposed that even illiterate Indian observers had gained sufficient information about their white counterparts to deem them unmannered—a devastating assessment from "uncivilized" Indian critics. These representations criticized the failings of an overcivilized European culture and presented American readers with a clear vision of their republic's faults. They might be rude, but Americans could change their ways by virtue of their access to print.

By the late eighteenth century, readers had grown accustomed to a literary form of cultural comparison, frequently conveyed through orientalist texts such as Montesquieu's *Persian Letters* (1742) that figured a racial and cultural other as perfectly positioned to perceive the faults of white society. Again, the real focus of this literature remained squarely on Europe and was not intended to offer insights about the racial other. By emphasizing the vast cultural differences between publics, this comparative discourse encouraged readers to identify as members of a racial or national community in part by underscoring its flaws and contradictions. To uphold the virtues and consistency of cultural outsiders was to provide a model for the improvement of American political culture. Eloquent Indians were the perfect figures to articulate republican virtue. Unconcerned with accepted hierarchies and positioned outside American culture, they were uniquely situated to speak truth and censure wrongs. As depicted in one schoolbook piece, whites were warned that Indians "will tell you some truths which you must necessarily hear."[30] Virtuous readers "must necessarily" listen.

Indian speeches cried deceit and betrayal in urgent terms and used the first person to create an immediacy that heightened both the indictment and the need for reform. They especially spoke of white dishonesty and its consequences. Caleb Bingham, a prominent Boston school reformer and Republican, included a dialogue in his *Columbian Orator* that lambasted insincerity. It depicted an Indian telling his white counterpart, "This is the way you talk; you act differently. You have good on your tongue, but bad in your heart."[31] Federalist editors made similar choices to include censorious Indians. J. Bemis, a Federalist editor in upstate New York, published a speech in which Farmer's Brother similarly denounced white untrustworthiness:

> The white men with sweet voices and smiling faces told us they loved us, and that they would not cheat us, but that the king's children on the other side [of] the lake would cheat us. When we go on the other side [of] the lake[,] the king's children tell us your people will cheat us, but with sweet voices and smiling faces assure us of their love and that they will not cheat us. These things puzzle our heads, and we believe that the Indians must take care of themselves, and not trust either in your people or in the king's children.[32]

The divide between whites' words and actions clearly went beyond hypocrisy and became treachery when Indians were so frequently swindled. And these sometimes fictional Indian speakers did not hesitate to object in forthright terms. The dialogue from the *Columbian Orator* continued, "You call us brothers, but you treat us like beasts; you wish to trade with us, that you may cheat us; you would give us peace, but you would take our lands, and leave us nothing worth fighting for."[33] The blunt insistence of such passages portrays Indians as plainspoken and clearheaded, deserving of consideration.

Editors of magazines and schoolbooks helped their readers make distinctions between Americans and their Indian censors by inserting editorial comments on Indian eloquence into many of their articles to guide their readers' interpretations. One example is the intervention in 1787 by Noah Webster, the patriotic Federalist editor of the *American Magazine*, in Pocahontas's much-reprinted seventeenth-century speech in which she reproaches Captain John Smith for failing to adhere to the Indian rules of reciprocity and the bonds of kinship. Her speech ends with the damning statement that the Indians must always be skeptical because whites "will lie much."[34] Webster responded to this with a footnote gloss observing, "This charge is just; civilized men lie more than savages." Such a matter-of-fact statement might have implied that a marker of "civilization" ought to be to acknowledge one's own hypocrisy. Webster went on to note: "How ought Christians to blush—to be charged with lying and ingratitude by savages!"[35] In like manner, an 1829 issue of the *Christian Register* (a Unitarian periodical that devoted most of its pages to religious texts) reprinted a speech by Speckled Snake that struck a sarcastic tone to describe a harrowing history of Indian removal and cruelty by white Americans. The "white man ... speaks with a straight tongue, and will not lie," he states. "Our great father says we must go beyond the Mississippi. We shall there be under his care, and experience his kindness. He is very good! We have felt it all before!" To eliminate the possibility of misreading this statement, the *Register*'s editor instructed his readers, "A vein of cutting irony runs through it which indicates great sensibility to the wrongs which the native tribes have sustained."[36] Positioning themselves as cultural mediators in the new republic, editors made comments that reiterated the texts' moral meaning for any who might be inclined to evade it.

Such editorial interventions may have been ham-fisted, but they had the potential to evoke a very specific form of identification in readers as members of a shared reading public. The potent combination of appreciation of Indian eloquence with pointed reminders of white culpability allowed editors to demonstrate what acquiescence and regret might look like. As a result, we can see that these interventions had a broader effect: to help a potentially disparate readership identify the moral or sentimental characteristics that tied white Americans together. And because editors took pains to remind readers that Indians lacked access to print, these (printed) comments served as an extra distinguishing layer to mark the difference between guilty American readers and eloquent Indian victims. Print identified white guilt, underscored it, and illustrated a solution—at least insofar as it proposed regret as the proper emotional response. The use of Indian censure as a form of cultural critique asserted and exemplified a capacity for self-criticism that, in the end, distinguished an American reading public from the Indians they emulated, much as antislavery humanitarianism had helped to define a certain version of Britishness in the 1770s.[37] They may have been guilty, but they were capable of self-reflection.

The very admiration and emulation of Indian eloquence that editors encouraged constructed a divide between Indian and white identities. Editors could call a speech sublime in one sentence and, in the next, identify an appropriately genteel or civilized response on behalf of their white readers. "We cannot read this address of Logan, without feeling the most generous emotions," Noah Webster wrote in the *American Magazine* in 1788. "We love him for his hospitality, peaceable disposition, and unshaken attachment to the whites—We detest the murder of his family, and can hardly withhold a sympathetic tear for his loss."[38] Editors articulated both the readers' collective identity ("we") and their response ("a sympathetic tear"). In a similar vein, an editor of the *Monthly Anthology* remarked that Indian eloquence exhibited brilliance "far, far beyond what we should have expected to find in the wandering tribes of Indians."[39] By invoking these references to "we" and "us," editors worked to unify their readers through the act of exclusion. They placed Indians on display as objects of "love" and sympathy at the same time as they constructed an imagined reading public that by definition contained no Indian readers, no members of "wandering tribes." White readers, these editors suggested, were uniquely qualified to summon up the appropriate moral sentiments in response to the Indians' pathos.

These invocations of a white "we" vividly displayed one of the forms of constructing a national identity by means of triangulation: America was "both aboriginal and European and yet was also neither," as Philip Deloria has explained. This manner of constructing a national identity had a seesaw quality: at times, representations of Indian eloquence demanded a strong identification with the Indians to help Americans reject their British past, while at other times they tilted in the opposite direction. This "prevented its creators from ever effectively developing a positive, stand-alone identity that did not rely heavily on either a British or American foil."[40] The frequent mentions in American print media of English and Indian oratory thus provided readers with two very different sources of emulation and counteridentification, during an era when these media sought to contribute to national identity. As they read about cultural others, readers learned to imagine Americanness as a quality that borrowed from yet "perfected" those other identities.

If earlier depictions of Indian eloquence referred mainly to "whites" and "Indians," editors increasingly made that "we" even more specific and depicted their readers as exclusively American. Following one particularly pointed anecdote about attempts to steal Indian lands, the moderate

Federalist editor Mathew Carey asked his readers, "Americans! Is this the people whom you accuse of *perfidy*? When you have removed them from their native feasts, will you place in their stead a people of *better* principles and manners?"[41] The message was clear: the very "Americans!" who perused magazines like the *American Museum* were implicated in removing and replacing the highly principled Indians. This passage carried a particularly fraught combination of direct address to Americans and indictment of American crimes and was all the more powerful because it was based on a prediction of crime ("*when* you have removed them") resulting from American expansion into the interior.

Carey's anticipatory "when you have removed them" comment was related to an emerging narrative of American triumph and Indian decline in representations of Indian eloquence. This narrative, in which Indian orators remembered the time "when we were great and you were small," presented a new version of national history, a version that centered on American-Indian relations (rather than American-European) and traced a reversal of fortunes that began long before the Revolution. Long ago, this story explained, "The white people were small, but we were very numerous and strong; we defended you in that low state," a Stockbridge Indian was quoted in a 1798 issue of the *Weekly Magazine*, a New York–based literary miscellany. "But now the case is altered; you are numerous and strong, but we are few and weak: therefore we expect that you will act by these circumstances, as we did by you."[42] In 1809, Red Jacket told this story most famously as a trajectory from a prelapsarian peace to conflict triggered by white dishonesty and greed for land. "There was a time when our forefathers owned this great island. Their seats extended from the rising to the setting sun. The Great Spirit made it for the use of . . . his red children, because HE loved them." This land was rich and plentiful, edenic:

> But an evil day came upon us. Your forefathers crossed the great water, and landed on this island. Their numbers were small. . . . We took them to be friends. They called us brothers. We believed them, and gave them a larger seat.
> . . . *Brother*; Our seats were once large and yours were small. You have now become a great people, and we have scarcely a place left to spread our blankets. You have got our country, but are not satisfied; you want to force your religion upon us.[43]

This narrative constructed a new foundation for an American historical genesis that lay not in England but rather in shifting power relations between whites and Indians on American soil. It gave Americans a history that marked their uniqueness from Europeans and antedated—even ignored—the Revolution as the moment that birthed the nation. As such, it represented an important means by which postrevolutionary Americans articulated their nationality: they obfuscated how far it was a contemporary construct by claiming to have inherited their place by means of a long history.⁴⁴

The story of "when we were great and you were small" also pointed out the moral responsibilities of the powerful toward the weak and linked Indian eloquence to the tradition of the jeremiad in American culture, a tradition alive and well during the early republic, as Sacvan Bercovitch has shown.⁴⁵ Indian speeches functioned much as the jeremiad had: they chastised a prosperous but ungrateful people for betraying their own ideals and not living up to their moral obligations. In the process, it rhetorically bound together its reading audiences as a body that shared these responsibilities. The jeremiad acted as a "ritual of consensus" that reminded its audience of the importance of piety or morality as well as prosperity. After the Revolution, as Bercovitch has demonstrated, political leaders used the jeremiad style not only to enact unity, but also to guarantee their authority in the new nation. By that time it had so long been used, especially in New England, that the jeremiad itself had become part and parcel of the ideology of an American past. Whereas early jeremiads had warned colonists against falling away from their faith, after the Revolution they engaged a national audience in a ritual that imagined an accountable future based on a shared culture and history.

We cannot dismiss the censure of the period before 1810 as producing only crocodile tears or as masking brutal reality. But neither did it produce altered political relations or a lay movement to remedy policies in the Indians' favor. In this regard it constituted one aspect of eighteenth-century humanitarianism and most specifically represents a parallel discourse to the antislavery sentiment that emerged in midcentury Britain—a prevalent and even fashionable sentiment that long lacked an abolitionist movement behind it and that used many of the same rhetorical techniques of censure and direct address. Like early antislavery writing, sensitive portrayals of Indians remained largely unspecific about regional or tribal distinctions and avoided identifying villains by name. In the new United States, Indian censure likewise sought to convert readers into feeling humanitarians and to grant that sensibility a nationalistic cast. It helped to articulate a triangulated American identity—one that emulated the Indians' natural virtue and eloquence even as it aspired to a literary excellence like that of Europeans.

It used a blameworthy narrative of American history to heighten the need for national and humanitarian engagement. But if these speeches created a sense of shared responsibility for wrongs against the Indians, they offered no plan to redress those wrongs. Whereas sympathy for the enslaved African led eventually to abolitionism, the case of the Indians reflects more clearly what Christopher Leslie Brown calls "the wide gulf that divides the mere perception of a moral wrong from decisions to seek a remedy."[46]

Most telling were the moments when ordinary men—missionaries, government agents, soldiers—recorded the Indian speeches they heard while working in the backcountry. The letters and diaries of these individuals often contained copies of Indian orations, and while these travelers provided little information about the context of a speech's delivery (or who translated it), they clearly felt that such eloquence required full transcription. Such acts placed these diarists and correspondents in an awkward position: appreciators of Indian eloquence, yet also the agents of change in the Indians' lives. A young missionary working among the Oneidas in 1791 recorded a speech by "a young man of considerable understanding" that queried God's treatment of the Indians. "How can God be just in making such a differance between Indians and white people? did it not appear manifest that God never intended Indians should rise like white people?" The earnest Christian attempted to answer these questions: "In general I observed . . . that Indians did not obay that first commandment of God in tilling and cultivating the earth for their living. &c. &c.," a response that likely held as little purchase as this tepid account implies.[47] Other Americans recorded speeches that more forcefully recited familiar themes of betrayal, as when Henry Knox sent back speeches by Cornplanter and other Senecas detailing a long history of broken treaties. "Father, Your commissioners . . . did most solemnly promise, that we should be secured in the peaceable possession of the lands which we inhabited East and north of that line; Does this promise bind you?"[48] Of course, such speeches might be put to a variety of uses by their recipients—to record tribal understandings of earlier treaties, for example. But their purporting to be transcriptions of Indians' speeches that probed important questions of their relationship with whites made them resemble the presentation of published speeches in magazines and schoolbooks. These manuscripts suggest that, given the opportunity, lay Americans became active recorders of original Indian speeches in terms similar to those that appeared in print.

Indian eloquence was put to numerous uses in postrevolutionary America: to offer a model of good government oriented around an oratorical bond between leaders and the public; to humble a reading public by displaying the model audience behavior of "savages"; and to use print culture as a means of fostering affective ties among white readers. In each of these respects, Indian oratory was used to call forth an American public and to help the people imagine a bright national future. And soon these representations also began to resolve the problem of censure by envisioning the disappearance of the Indian as regrettable but inevitable.

TURNING CENSURE INTO "SYMPATHETIC TEARS" FOR THE DYING INDIAN

One of the most powerful representations of "inevitable" Indian demise was Logan's speech. With his family murdered by a white soldier, he asks in conclusion, "Who is there to mourn for Logan?—Not one," positioning himself as the last Indian and inviting his white audience to envision his death. Although as early as the 1770s Indian speeches like this foreshadowed the speaker's disappearance, the ones that appeared in magazines and schoolbooks usually did not stress the Indian's death until the 1810s and later, at which point the shift in emphasis is striking. Gradually, sentimental images predominated. By underscoring the Indian's lament, melancholy deathbed speeches portrayed Indians as a vanishing people and gradually overshadowed representations of forthright Indian censors. The print media of the early national period helped American readers view Indian eloquence as pathetic in a manner that gradually silenced real Indians.

Why did caring portrayals of eloquent Indians fail to produce changes in Americans' policies and actions, the way antislavery sentiment evolved into a political movement in Britain and the United States? Clearly the plight of "the poor Indian" never achieved the same moral urgency as that of enslaved peoples, perhaps especially because of the ways notions of slavery and freedom were deployed during the war. The ethical issues relevant to the Indian case were less serviceable in part because they were less clear-cut: after all, the British were guilty of offenses against Indians too. In fact, the flowering of an antislavery movement may have monopolized humanitarian sentiment at the time. Most of all, as Christopher Brown as shown, it is less surprising that a movement on behalf of Indians did not materialize than that an abolitionist movement *did*.[49] That discussions of Indians remained limited to sentimental effusions is far more typical of humanitarian thought of the era and reveals how seldom political action followed in its wake. As a result, it is important to see how literary representations of eloquent Indians helped to contain the emotional effects of censure and to offer means of resolution.

Even before the full-blown literary arrival of the "vanishing Indian" in the nineteenth century, magazines and schoolbooks often framed Indian speeches in ways that contradicted the message of censure. Some schoolbook editors lumped all Indian documents together, a habit that emphasized the speeches' generic, timeless qualities and finessed the distinctions between authentic speeches and those invented by editors. Only in rare cases did editors attempt to authenticate a speech by mentioning its translator or its provenance; several very different versions of Logan's speech circulated during the early republic. At times they displayed no interest in whether a speech was authentic. One magazine writer, for example, described being entranced by a passage in one of Lord Erskine's volumes "in which he either invents or relates the speech of an American chieftain." Whether the speech was genuine or invented, the author explained, "I have no means of ascertaining; but be it what it may, there is a soul-stirring energy about it which few can peruse without excitement—it is a short and splendid specimen of nature's eloquence."[50] At times schoolbooks even grouped Indian speeches in a category called "pathetic eloquence," whereas Anglo-American speeches were placed into such categories as "eloquence of the bar" and "legislative eloquence." Under headings such as "Specimen of Indian Eloquence" or "Indian Speech," magazines frequently stripped the speeches of the orator's name, tribal affiliation, date, and place of delivery. The articles that did identify the speech's date or speaker's name reveal that most of these reprinted speeches originated during the colonial era, sometimes as early as the seventeenth century, doubtless making their emotional impact somewhat abstract.[51]

In addition, anthologized Indian speeches referred to broad shifts in power over long expanses of time, which tended to distract from the theme of responsibility. Others traced such a long trajectory of Anglo-American progress and Indian decline that they denounced moral wrongs only in the most general terms. By the same token, other speeches decried offenses so specific in nature—for example, Logan's accusation that Colonel Cresap had murdered his family—that readers may have condemned the crime as a local one without feeling implicated in the ongoing suffering of Indian tribes. In short, representations of Indian eloquence offered no coherent agenda for altered political relations, nor did they inadvertently bring about policy changes in the Indians' favor.

When literary representations of the vanishing Indian began to recur frequently in print, they were by no means accurate portrayals of demographic trends or the failure of United States–Indian diplomacy. In fact, Indian-white relations varied widely by region and by tribe, making it impossible for historians to advance comprehensive generalizations about them. For example, at the same time that some tribes may have fought losing battles as they tenaciously contested white encroachment onto their land, others succeeded in regaining land and restoring their homes and cultural practices. Neither did other punitive methods of control, such as the determined pursuit of Indian conversion and "civilization," lead directly to Indian decline or removal. When the federal government controversially advocated Indian removal among tribes of the Southeast in 1830 and afterward, many tribes retained some semblance of sovereignty and found some success in maintaining their distinct cultures, as James Merrell has shown.[52] In addition to persisting on the frontier, Native Americans increasingly gained a place in print as writers. Adding to the variability of portrayals of current Indian affairs, reports on Indian-white tensions varied wildly in their assessments, which meant that contemporaries could not make blanket assessments either. Both whites and tribal leaders might exaggerate or downplay Indian power in a region. In sum, none of these shifts absolutely circumscribed the Indians' future, nor did contemporaries share a clear (much less accurate) picture of Indian affairs. Considering this situation, the reproduction of eloquent Indian speeches that emphasized the orator's imminent death represented a far more consistent narrative than was otherwise available. That these became common long before the political or demographic facts corresponded shows that the discourse of Indian eloquence became a way Americans could justify policies of removal.

If "vanishing Indian" imagery did not clearly reflect political or demographic reality, it is worth looking to the printing industry and literary production, where this narrative of decline arose, to find its origins. One of the ways publications like schoolbooks and magazines helped to imagine national unity was by popularizing a centrist, urban (and urbane) tone that displayed little concern about Indians as a threat. In part this tone reflected the fact that, after 1790, most new published texts *were* urban, insofar as they mostly first emerged from presses in Boston, New York, and Philadelphia before they were reprinted in small towns or rural areas. Rural or small-town presses still outnumbered those in cities, but those printers tended to take fewer publishing risks than their urban counterparts because of the costs involved in printing—for labor, type, paper, and binding. Publishing a new book or an untested author represented a significant outlay of capital that had a small chance of paying off.[53] As a result, rural printers chose instead to reprint established material, especially titles that earned a printer's bread-and-butter income: almanacs, devotional works, and schoolbooks, as well as books and newspaper stories that originated in cities.[54] This was true even for anthologized texts like schoolbooks; rural printers often elected to reprint a popular volume rather than spend money on an untried book. As a result of the 1790 federal copyright law, these printers were required to pay publishers for the right to reprint texts. Eventually, publishers like Mathew Carey also sent book peddlers into the countryside and opened branch stores in the backcountry. The shift toward urban publication resulted from urban publishers' economic wherewithal and their desire for expansion as well as the support of the copyright system; but its cultural effects were much broader. Publishers sought ways of tailoring their offerings to appeal to rural readers, but they did not publish books specifically for that market. American readers in both urban and rural areas came across similar fare in the books and magazines they purchased. In the process, they implicitly acknowledged that urban printed materials now possessed a certain authority, if only because they seemed to be salable. When such books presented information on Indians, they reflected a perspective that usually originated in the city, far from the rural or frontier locations closer to actual Indian populations. As a result, urban publications often portrayed Indians as more abstract than threatening.

One example of this shift is the 1809 publication of two Indian speeches in the *Monthly Anthology*, a Boston magazine known for its original, high-quality material. These speeches were submitted by a subscriber in rural Canandaigua, New York, whose comments were published in full by the magazine. Using a refined voice, he apologized for his delay in dispatching the speeches (they were dated 1798 and 1805), explaining that he had waited for a reliable source to carry them to Albany, where dependable conveyance to Boston could be secured.[55] These comments gave the article an air of authenticity and helped to support the magazine's reputation as a central clearinghouse of new information. At the same time, publication in the magazine certified the literary importance of the speeches and, to some extent, the value of its rural correspondents; the magazine made a point of noting, in a prominent subtitle, that the speeches had been submitted "FOR THE ANTHOLOGY" alone. That latter claim was not exactly true: the subscriber had also sent the speeches to his local newspaper, the *Ontario Repository*, but not until he heard that the speeches had arrived in Boston; as a result, their publication in the two venues was almost simultaneous. Two years later, a Canandaigua editor included them, along with most of the correspondent's remarks from the *Anthology*, in a pamphlet titled *Native Eloquence*.[56] In this not atypical case, information dissemination proceeded from rural locale to urban press and back to rural press, making the speeches seem worthy of attention from an American public for being vetted by a prominent urban periodical.

The prefatory comments by the "subscriber" accentuated the speeches' literary qualities, making clear his affiliation with the *Anthology*'s urbane readers (despite his home far to the west) rather than a frontier populace wary of Indian threat. In them he identifies himself as one of those right-minded whites who appreciate specimens of native eloquence: "I confess that, in perusing his speech, I felt humbled in the view of myself, considering the superiour advantages I had enjoyed from childhood, to those granted to this man of the woods," he explains, likely anticipating some of his readers' responses as well.[57] His emphasis is particularly noteworthy because one of the speeches, by the prominent Iroquois leader Red Jacket, condemned the hypocrisy of Christian missionaries and forecast a dark future for Indian-white relations on the frontier. But rather than draw attention to the speech's references to aggressive white frontier settlers and zealous Christian hypocrites, the correspondent refers to Red Jacket's "beauties of imagery, united with a shrewdness of remark and an extent of information," focusing squarely on the aesthetic pleasure granted by the speech. In this way publications like the *Anthology* presented the Indians as the objects of literary appreciation rather than as a political presence in their own right.

The article also shows that urban editors mediated Indian speeches in ways that rid them of a sense of immediacy and realism. Editors in the early nineteenth century embraced a belletristic writing style that stressed the aesthetic experience of elegant language and endorsed a perspective on Indians that drew attention away from the theme of Indian censure. This style, borrowed from British literature of the day and often referred to as "polite literature" or "belles lettres," did more rhetorically than imagine right-thinking, like-minded reading audiences, as discussed above: belletristic writing also helped all publications seem less provincial and more uniformly "elegant."[58] Thus, publication by urban presses increasingly granted a text literary value at the same time that publication became invested with urbanity, which had important effects on portrayals of Indian eloquence.

The effects of this belletristic style on Indian eloquence are illustrated by the significant alterations some stories underwent during the early nineteenth century, alterations that downplayed readers' sense of responsibility in favor of easy sentimentalism. One prominent example is the changing representation of Pocahontas. Until the 1790s, editors reprinted John

Smith's original account, which ended with Pocahontas's sharply worded rebuke to Smith about whites who "lie much." Beginning in the 1790s, many editors began to substitute a new version by the Marquis de Chastellux that altered the meaning and power of Pocahontas's speech, largely by finessing the question of white dishonesty. In this account Smith greets Pocahontas in London with a politeness appropriate for the etiquette of English society. She misinterprets his formality as an absence of affection and, as a result, weeps "bitterly." "Didst thou not assure me, that if I went into thy country, thou wouldst be my father, and that I should be thy daughter? Thou hast deceived me, and behold me, now here, a stranger and an orphan," says the new incarnation of Pocahontas, now no longer angry at the lack of reciprocity among kin. Seemingly eager to resolve what is now portrayed as a personal misunderstanding, Chastellux invented a quick resolution to the story. "It was not hard for the Captain to make his peace with this charming creature, whom he tenderly loved. He presented her to several people of the first quality."[59] Problem solved, this version implies. She still insists that Smith "hast deceived" her for abandoning his fatherly responsibility to serve as her guide, but the accusation loses the political effect of the original, which had emphasized Smith's political betrayal of his ally. In this version, Pocahontas is entitled to Smith's affection not as her father's diplomatic emissary, but because she is a "charming creature" deserving of his "tender love."

A successive, anonymously written version of Pocahontas's story rapidly gained in popularity beginning about 1801. Even more than Chastellux's, this version shifts the story's earlier emphasis and eliminates Pocahontas's voice altogether. Frequently titled "A Sketch of the Life of Pocahontas," it obscures the source of the conflict between Smith and Pocahontas so profoundly that the narrative becomes rather confusing. "Smith called on Pocahontas soon after her arrival. Her astonishment was at first succeeded by contempt. But the resentment of wounded pride soon yielded to tender sentiments. In a private interview she heard his explanation, and ever after caressed him with the fondness of a sister."[60] This pared-down version maintains the sense of conflict between Smith and Pocahontas but eschews even Chastellux's simplistic explanations. In fact, its vague allusions to "wounded pride" and "tender sentiments" almost allow one to forget that Pocahontas was an Indian. It also underscores Chastellux's message that Smith's affection for her might overcome all quarrels between them. These successive retellings of the story reveal the gradual dissolution of her original censure into sentimental affect: it would not be long before writers would transform their relationship into star-crossed love.[61]

When Logan's speech appeared alongside sentimental poetry or the new story of Pocahontas, it resided in a literary world where affective quality was privileged above social context—a world that evoked urban gentility and refined pathos rather than the gritty stuff of racial strife and frontier skirmishes and was notably different from pre-1810 popular representations of Indians. Taken together, the feeble links to the politics of Indian affairs, the assertion of an urban perspective, and the focus on the literary enjoyment of Indian eloquence constitute some of the ways print media increasingly turned readers' attention away from censure.

As Indian eloquence came to serve sentimental ends, it increasingly lost its place as a didactic tool designed to teach political virtue. Instead, beginning in the 1810s, schoolbooks included progressively more speeches by white American politicians, who now appeared to have overcome their earlier oratorical inadequacies. Speeches by legislators like Fisher Ames, Daniel Webster, and William Wirt appeared in growing numbers to supplant those by English orators. Indian eloquence was still common in schoolbooks (and, as mentioned above, appeared even more frequently), but it was used for different purposes now that American oratory could provide the civic glue between public and nation and confirm the fruition of eloquence in the United States. The muscular nationalistic inclinations of American schoolbooks and magazines replaced the censuring Indian as a model of eloquence and political virtue and transformed him into a sentimental figure.

The narrative power of Indian eloquence remained, but it was appropriated by whites. Indeed, perhaps because they had learned the plainspoken tones and clearheaded directness of schoolbook versions of Indian speeches as children, political leaders increasingly used familiar motifs from Indian eloquence to comment on conflicts between whites and Indians during the 1810s and 1820s, particularly in oratorical settings where their narrative drive might have the most impact. Speeches before Congress, for example, now recycled literary narratives borrowed from Indian oratory for use in discussions of Indian policy—following the pattern of emulation that had been recommended by elocution manuals, except that now these speeches exercised a burly nationalism. In 1819 the political orator Henry Clay told a familiar narrative of American history. Back in colonial times, he told Congress, "we were weak, and . . . [the Indians] were comparatively strong." Now "we are powerful and they are weak: . . . to use a figure drawn from their own sublime eloquence, the poor children of the forest have been driven by the great wave which has flowed in from the Atlantic ocean almost to the base of the Rocky Mountains."[62] Clay borrowed the "when we were great and you were small" motif to confirm the decline of Indian might as it puffed American power; Lewis Cass and Andrew Jackson would do the same as they discussed Cherokee removal in 1830, perhaps as one means of expressing regret as they pushed Indians off their land.[63]

Nor were such uses limited to political oratory. Perhaps the most powerful venues for appropriating Indian eloquence and disseminating the fiction of the vanishing eloquent Indian were novels and the Indian dramas of the stage. Novelists like James Fenimore Cooper and the playwrights who wrote *Metamora* and similar plays mythologized the "vanishing Indian." As John Frederick has shown, three-quarters of all the figurative expressions used by Indians in Cooper's novels were lifted directly from the Indian speeches and ethnological accounts of Indian eloquence circulating widely in the early republic.[64] The use of purportedly authentic Indian eloquence for such maudlin, romanticized ends could even be undertaken by writers who themselves had encountered Indian violence on the frontier. When he was a child, Joseph Doddridge and his family abandoned their home in western Pennsylvania to escape Logan, who sought to "glut" his "vengeance" on white communities for the murder of his family. Yet by the 1820s Doddridge—now an Episcopal minister and missionary—had composed numerous sympathetic paeans to the Indians and to Logan in particular, fully participating in the cult of Indian eloquence.[65] The very foundational fiction that had earlier encouraged white readers to imagine themselves as American now seemed to explain, in the most dispassionate terms, Indian removal and disappearance.

If the patterns and phrasings of Indian eloquence appeared with increasing frequency in white writing, such rhetoric fell out of use in Native Americans' political oratory, for it now gave them little political purchase. Most Indian orators eschewed such old chestnuts when they discussed matters of political import. Cherokees in particular adopted far different rhetorical strategies in defending their lands and only rarely issued their memorials by deploying eloquent narratives of white betrayal and hypocrisy. The vast outpouring of public support for the Cherokees' cause, particularly from readers of evangelical magazines, was based on their adoption of "civilized" practices and Christianity (which, supporters argued, made them indistinguishable from other Georgia farmers), not their maintenance of quaint oratorical traditions.[66] In general, Indians reserved those narratives and metaphorical cadences for ceremonial occasions, as when William Apess delivered his "Eulogy on King Philip" in 1836, and for missionary pleas or commercial performances, as when Red Jacket delivered a series of speeches in theaters during 1828 and 1829 accompanied by a troupe of Indian dancers, which allowed him to fund his trips to Washington to formally protest white intrusion onto Indian lands.⁶⁷

Descriptions of Indian eloquence now possessed an assured tone that easily acknowledged crimes against the Indians as an accepted fact but no longer paused to consider how this reflected on the American republic. "It is because our American Indians have endured so many unredressed wrongs ... that they can never see the face of a white man, or think of their former privileges, without being aroused to the highest indignation," *The Manuscript* explained in matter-of-fact terms in 1828. "Who can wonder, then, if the most highly gifted of their nation give vent ... and melt the hearts of those to whom they communicate their wrongs?"⁶⁸ Schoolbooks could go even further in appropriating Indian eloquence to relegate Indians to a place in American memory, a tendency that flowered during the late 1820s. Adopting an authoritative tone, Samuel Willard's *Secondary Lessons, or The Improved Reader* (1827) informed its readers that "the character of the Indians is not so noble now, as it once was. Though in some respects dreadful, it has been very interesting.... Their diminution is indeed our wealth and peace; but still we would drop a tear over the decline of those, who had the first right to this pleasant land, and who, before they were corrupted by us, were in many things worthy of admiration."⁶⁹ Here, as in numerous other schoolbook vignettes during the 1820s, the aestheticizing move matured into full-fledged dismissal. Willard acknowledges whites' responsibility for Indian "corruption" (this was doubtless a reference to alcohol), but he proposes merely that his readers "drop a tear" for the "not so noble" Indians. As in the final sentimentalized version of the Pocahontas story, Willard jettisoned Indian voices altogether, replacing them with faint-hearted tributes that recalled Indian power only long enough to evoke sentiment.

The implications of eliminating Indian voices—even fictionalized ones— were sweeping and helped configure a new perspective on American history and identity in schoolbooks. Rather than invoke guilt over broken promises or remember the days when Indians were "great" and whites were "small," stories defined their white readers as the heirs to the Indians' original status as the first "Americans." A dialogue from *Boston Reading Lessons* (1828) demonstrates this tendency:

EDWARD. Mamma, will you decide which of us two is right? Charles says we are Americans, and I think that we are English.
MOTHER. What makes you think so, child?
EDWARD. Because we speak English, and I know that we are not Americans, because I saw in my new picture-book that Americans

look like Indians, and that they wear nothing but skins and blankets, and live in wigwams.

CHARLES. And I know we are not Englishmen, because we do not live in England. I know by the map that England is a great way off, and that we live in America.

MOTHER. You are both partly right and partly wrong. We are Americans because we were born in America. We speak English because our great grandfathers, two hundred years ago, were English people. They came across the sea to this country, when it was covered with woods, and built houses, and made it their home. They taught their children and their children's children to speak English as well as they, and it is for this reason that we speak the English language, although we live in America.

But there were other Americans, a long time before our forefathers came here, who lived in the woods, and got their living by hunting and fishing. These Americans we call Indians. There are but few of them now left among us, but in some parts of America, they are the only inhabitants.[70]

In this vignette, "Mother" teaches her children to know their American identity by displacing the Indians' claim to Americanness both in time and in language. She acknowledges that, by their presence in the American "woods," the Indians were once (and in some distant places still are) the "other Americans," but whites have superseded them. This passage also implies that it may simply be a matter of time before the remaining Indian habitations become a thing of the past. Intended for schoolrooms, this dialogue replaced direct Indian voices with bookish white children who represented Indians as wearing "nothing but skins and blankets" and living in wigwams— that is, as so distinct from white children as to lead Edward to determine they cannot both be "American." When Mother resolves these questions of identity, she also juxtaposes the historical trajectory of Indian demise with a Whiggish tale of the Americanization of English descendants—a tale that noticeably lacks even the gesture of a "sympathetic tear."

Looking back to the 1827 case of Reverend Allan, who watched a Cherokee child recite an Indian speech from the *Columbian Orator*, we can see an additional source of Allan's surprise. By that date, whites like Allan would not just be struck by the incongruity of an Indian child's appropriating white educational practices; they would also have viewed it as an example of Indians' *reappropriating* their own oratory for this purpose—which would indeed have seemed amusing. Such an act ran contrary to the narratives of Indian decline and white ascendance, presented in popular stories that increasingly eliminated Indian voices, that packaged American history and identity and, by the late 1820s, made the consideration of Indian removal seem natural. Whites had learned to feel rueful about Indian disappearance; with the exception of a few abolitionists, Americans saw no other end to the story. They had also learned resignation, having now largely resolved the ambivalence over Indian suffering. The invocation of this oratorical style now told reading audiences that America could move ahead without the Indians. The evolution of Indian eloquence in print and pedagogy had played an important role in forming a coherent sense of the American public, its foundational history and its future.

But as much as print had sentimentalized Indian eloquence by the 1830s, it should not overshadow the more hard-hitting tone of earlier literature during the several decades immediately after the Revolution. When censorious Indian speeches spoke in stoic terms of Indian suffering, they called forth audiences of American readers as sensitive humanitarians unified by guilt and by history—much as the jeremiad had long reminded its audience of their sins and called for redemption. The genre of Indian eloquence served as a model of fine oratory that Americans might emulate to cultivate a more active and dynamic relationship between political leaders and the public—a model more in keeping with American virtue than European oratory, which evoked less republican sentiments. And finally, it helped anchor literature, reading, and print to the very nature of republican society by striking a sharp contrast to the Indians' illiteracy. Taken together, representations of Indian eloquence worked on multiple levels to permit white Americans to think about themselves, their political culture, and their relation to the Indians in a way that seemed to promise a bright future. And citizens of the United States would be poised to realize that future in later decades, when they folded that early rhetoric of guilt and responsibility into a confident narrative of Indian decline and white ascendancy.

What do analyses of boys' and girls' elocution and representations of orators—Indian and otherwise—tell us about the making of an American public after the Revolution? Three important phenomena emerge from the previous chapters in part 1 of *A Nation of Speechifiers*, each of which has taken a broad view of the fifty-year period after the Revolution.

The first phenomenon uses schoolbooks and elocution to shed new light on the cultural dissemination of ideas. As Trish Loughran has demonstrated, the circulation of print took place locally and often unpredictably;

the new nation lacked the material infrastructure to ensure the widespread diffusion of even the most popular texts such as *Common Sense*. Thus she calls the notion of a cross-regional system of print diffusion a "postindustrial fantasy," a position that is thoroughly convincing.[71] Certainly no single schoolbook title could claim universal diffusion. Yet as these chapters have shown, we can still trace the diffusion of ideas as they appeared in hundreds of locally printed and locally disseminated titles that anthologized from one another, genres such as schoolbooks, newspapers, and magazines. Moreover, these texts' uses in fostering the practices of elocution and the circulation of admirable orations helped to spread ideas about public speech, idealized behavior, and good leadership. The nearly uniform practices of school recitations and exhibitions across regions of the American Northeast indicate that we can find a middle position between older scholarship that fantasized about print's quickly diffusing nationalistic views and Loughran's portrayal of a radically local and discrete print culture.

That national sentiment appeared so slowly and intermittently in these texts and in elocutionary practices further clarifies that print culture cannot be fantasized to have been the tool of would-be nation builders immediately after the Revolution. But as I have shown, these books and practices *did* foster shared understandings of public participation and ideal public behavior before the 1810s, even if they did not yet grant it a nationalistic cast. In teaching boys and girls to speak and gesture in particular ways, they developed a normative view of appropriate public behavior that nonelites applied to themselves as well as to the public speakers they observed. These texts and practices called forth from their readers shared views of sensibility, civilization, and—in the case of Indian eloquence—history. The concern that the new United States lacked visible leader-orators led schoolbook and magazine editors to elicit from their readers a sense of responsibility for self-improvement. Elocutionary forms of speechifying declared one's engagement in a wider public by displaying one's adoption of the elegant sentences, graceful gestures, and right-thinking emotions that seemed to signal Americans' civilized nature. Together these chapters illustrate some of the uneven and open-ended processes by which ordinary people identified as members of a public. In this regard, we can see that a sense of public participation preceded national identification and provided the basis for its articulation.

Finally, representations of the public at large underwent important shifts after 1810, the most striking being the concomitant rise of a coherent nationalism in print culture and elocutionary education, on the one hand, and on the other, increasingly contained views of public participation, especially by poorer whites, girls, and literary Indians. During the second half of the early republic, oratory and print media reimagined the public order—evoking schoolchildren who uncritically admired their leaders, girls who embraced their domestic and nonpolitical roles, and Indians worthy primarily of pity. Although such prescriptive views of the public may not have been embraced wholesale by nonelite readers and auditors—or disseminated uniformly—these perspectives exemplified a gradual reorganization of the American public by powerful cultural mediators who exerted a strong voice in print and oratory. Books and orations now called for different forms of public participation by ordinary men and women. These demonstrate yet again that early nineteenth-century "democratization" was deeply differentiated by class, sex, and race.

These social dynamics are illustrated more specifically in part 2, which uses three sites to examine forms of public participation and debates over the definition of the American public throughout the early republic. These chapters each take place outside classrooms, yet all show the influence of elocution in fostering public engagement and identification; they especially focus on groups who sought to play active roles in shaping public opinion during the early republic. As we shall see, men and women fought bitterly over the definition of an American public and a properly constituted public sphere, imagining political cultures more hospitable to individuals like them and more reflective of the United States they sought to realize.

PART 2

Contesting Public Participation: Debates over "the Public"

CHAPTER 4

"A Club Is a Nation in Miniature"

YOUNG MEN ON THE MAKE AND THEIR DEBATING SOCIETIES

> Do you know my good friend of a belles-lettres club,
> That meet in this city, their talents to rub,
> With writings and spouting, with essays and speeches
> On Caesar's old jacket, or Hannibal's breeches?

So began a manuscript poem titled "The Tullian Society: A City Eclogue" by a young Philadelphian, Joseph Hornor.[1] To twenty-first-century ears the poem sounds hopelessly pretentious: it celebrates the members' freewheeling, educated club conversation and their talents in "writing and spouting" in the vein of the classical greats. Even when Hornor mocked the personal quirks of each of the Society's eight members, including himself, he made clear that it was all in good fun—intended to add to the group's pleasure in gathering together. Clearly the Tullians' humor played an important role in their cultivation of male friendship, in the same way as better-known late nineteenth-century urban fraternal clubs, which came to symbolize exclusivity, elitism, and humor, often at women's expense.[2] Men's clubs like Hornor's appear, at least at first, to have been concerned with cultivating rich private lives for men eager for a break from business, politics, and the public sphere.

During the early republic, however, belonging to a debating society announced one's *lack* of position more often than the reverse, since these groups promised to further a young man's entry into public life by cultivating his speech, conduct, and relationships. Men like Hornor did not join literary and debating societies because they were socially established and bored, nor were clubs the bastions of the privileged. The vast majority of these groups consisted of strikingly young, unmarried men (typically in their teens and early twenties) who, with few exceptions, held no social position and did not come from prominent families.[3] They worked as clerks, journeyman artisans, and teachers; sometimes they were still in school or were training to be lawyers or doctors but had not yet assumed practices of their own. In fact, it was their youth and relative social insecurity that led them to join these clubs, for membership provided practice in self-presentation as well as friendships with men who similarly sought to establish themselves in a competitive market environment.[4] Joining a club could teach young men new ways of imagining themselves as members of a broader public, for—as one member of New York's Calliopean Society put it—"a Club is a nation in miniature."[5]

Part 2 of *A Nation of Speechifiers* examines moments of contestation over the definition of the public. Each chapter focuses on a specific site—a group or an event—in which a variety of individuals debated or challenged prevailing views of the American public and its role in political culture. My close attention to the Calliopean Society in this chapter illustrates how one group of men underwent transformation in their collective understanding of themselves as members of the public. Moreover, because the Calliopeans wrote for and edited the *New-York Magazine, or Literary Repository* (1790–97), their minute books and published writings provide especially rich detail of how they imagined themselves to be the *makers* of public opinion as well. Indeed, they liked to remind their readers that they were members of a men's club through a monthly column titled "The Club" (subsequently renamed "The Drone") that depicted an idealized version of their conversations and opinions.[6] The young men who joined this association were, of course, a highly specific group, so rather than attempt to claim they were "representative" of other men, I seek to show how the particular events of the 1790s transformed their understanding of themselves and their self-portrayals in print.

In addition, this chapter and those that follow demonstrate the long reach of elocutionary ideas about speech, writing, and public engagement, which extended beyond one's school years. The very nature of a debating society in this era took for granted that facility in public speech was essential for a man's professional advancement. When the Calliopeans engaged in debate or oratory and criticized one another's writings, they employed elocutionary theories and sometimes even drew their speeches or themes from the schoolbooks discussed in earlier chapters. In doing so, these middling men expressed their belief that debating and writing about a wide range of topics helped to create individuals well suited to face the requirements of public engagement and citizenry—ideas themselves drawn from the broader elocutionary culture of the time.

The Calliopeans were engaged in projects of self-making at the same time that they felt themselves to be participants in the political and literary advancement of the nation. Whereas most scholars who have studied young men's associations have marked a divide between partisan groups and literary or self-improvement groups, this chapter demonstrates that during the early republic political and literary topics were not distinct but were interrelated, mutually constitutive categories. My focus on the important interactions between the club members' "private" discussions and their "public" face in the magazine shows that they believed their society could be a model for public discussion and debate at large. This belief emerges with particular clarity in the evolution of their views of democratic politics. Increasingly inspired by the heady ideas of the French Revolution and works by Thomas Paine and other figures, in their club meetings the Calliopeans advocated a radically engaged and participatory public. Slightly more circumspect in the magazine, they still clearly elicited a pro-French, democratic perspective from their readers. But when a conservative political backlash stigmatized societies as divisive forces in American society, the Calliopeans turned away from political commentary and instead directed their attention to commenting on women, gender roles, and courtship. In doing so, they used the magazine to declare themselves as public arbiters who guided and governed civil dependents, especially women. Such literary moves permitted them to imagine themselves at the center of an American public, and their celebration of male association and mutual improvement strongly asserted the place of young men on the make in both the market and civic culture—to some extent at the expense of others.

YOUNG MEN ON THE MAKE IN SPEECH AND PRINT

In September 1794, twenty-four-year-old John Barent Johnson held memberships in the Uranian Society, Tammany Society, Democratic Society, Cliosophic Society, Calliopean Society, Black Friars, Freemasons, and a group he abbreviated in diary entries as the "Cons. Soc." Until recently he had also belonged to a society at Columbia College and to the Theological Society, since he was studying for the ministry. This array of memberships was striking because, on top of the costs of dues and other club fees, Johnson had moved home to Brooklyn in 1792 after graduating, which increased exponentially the time and money he spent taking the ferry across the river to attend meetings.[7] Still, it was not Johnson's ability to afford these expenses that made his associations exceptional but that he had time for all of them: many groups demanded that their members dedicate one evening each week to club debate and discussion, entertainments that usually required them to memorize material or prepare debate topics ahead of time. As a member of eight societies, Johnson clearly spent most of his time in association with other men.

Contemporaries celebrated the notion of homosocial *association*—and even more so *friendship*—because they believed these bonds enhanced all other relationships. Association smoothed the way for business transactions and political discussions, to be sure, but it also allowed men to emulate one another's manners, demeanor, wit, and knowledge in ways that they thought made all of society more civilized.[8] Provided, that is, that one chose to associate with upstanding fellows. In the most idealized portrayals, friendship with the right individuals helped young people polish their rough edges. A formal society could take those benefits to a new level: "The objects of this Society are, to investigate the means of promoting the happyness of Mankind, to discuss all useful and interesting Subjects, except those which tend to Religious Controversy, to strengthen those benevolent ties which bond us together, and to assist each other in all our honorable designs Relative to this association," stated Baltimore's Society for the Attainment of Useful Knowledge in 1797.[9] The Calliopean Society of New York boiled it down to a more straightforward club motto: "Friendship and Improvement," which they had engraved on medals for each member to wear at all times—or risk being fined (fig. 11).

On the surface it might appear that mutual improvement and literary societies like the Calliopeans had far different aims and practices than secret societies like the Black Friars and Masons, based on a shared morality and mystical knowledge; than ethnic groups like the German Society; and than partisan political groups like the Democratic-Republicans. In their practices and aims, however, such groups shared important commonalities, beginning with a strict organizational framework. Each had an elaborate written constitution, rules, and bylaws and a restrictive system for admitting new members—documents that members painstakingly debated and revised in the earliest days of club formation, then copied into a minute book in a formal hand. They also arranged similar activities for club meetings. Many held debates or featured weekly orators, whether or not they were "literary" or debating societies, and many used classically inspired club names to signal their connection to ancient knowledge (the Calliopeans

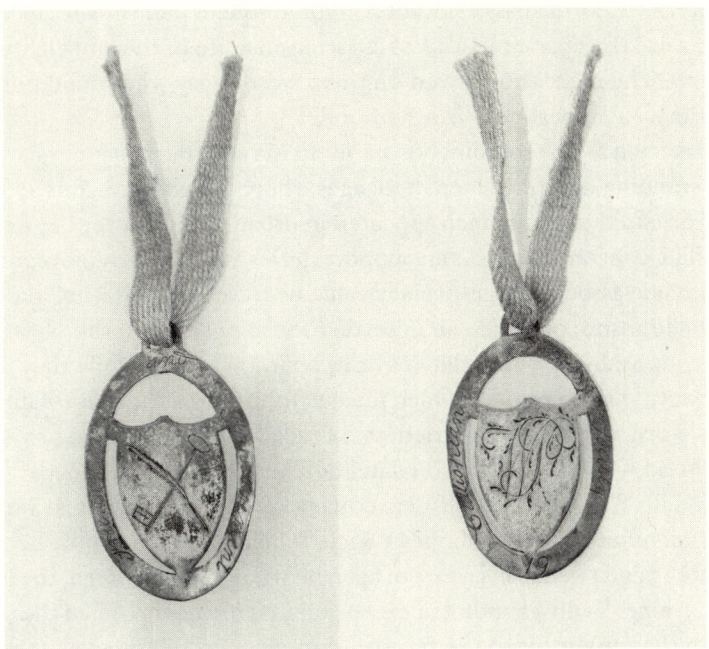

FIGURE 11. A Calliopean Society member's medal, 1789. Engraved around the sides is the club's motto, "Friendship and Improvement," and in the center are a crossed pen and key, symbolizing learning and the key to knowledge. On the reverse is written "Calliopean Society" and the member's number. Courtesy of the New-York Historical Society.

drew their name from Calliope, the Greek muse of eloquence and epic poetry). New York's Tammany Society, for example, slowly evolved during the 1790s from a fraternal group that affected an "ancient" mystical connection to Indians to a partisan democratic organization.[10] Most established small libraries for their members, thus taking on some of the trappings of a library society, and all featured periodic ceremonial speeches that might be printed in magazines or pamphlets.[11] Once admitted, the members of each group adhered to exacting and rigidly enforced rules of discipline and secrecy. The Calliopeans regularly fined members for "neglecting duty," skipping meetings, using indecent language, failing to return library books, interrupting the orderly nature of club debate, and misspellings (a penny a word); if a member persistently failed to follow these standards, he was expelled with a flourish. On anniversaries and other occasions, each club pulled out the stops with dinners, drinking, toasts, songs, poetry, and revelry, events that gave members ample opportunity to herald the delights of fraternity. Formality, celebration, rigor, frequent punishment, idealism: these were the characteristics of associational life in the late eighteenth century. The men who thrived on them were those who found punitive orderliness as appealing as brotherhood.[12]

Inasmuch as this combination of discipline and fraternity may have had long-standing appeal to men of all ages, there are good reasons so many clubs oriented to young men appeared in urban settings after the Revolution. The concomitant risks and opportunities available in rapidly growing cities made associations especially valuable to young men who, like John Barent Johnson, occupied an unsettled social position in the New York of the 1790s, living with relatives or in boardinghouses while they found their way.[13] Like most urban men his age, Johnson was not yet established in his work, nor was he married, two crucial steps in a man's rise to full adulthood—in fact, in Johnson datelined his letters to his friends "Bachelors Hall, Brooklyn," a self-deprecating reference to living at home.[14] Most members of the Calliopean Society belonged to a cohort between seventeen and twenty-five years of age; the youngest was fifteen, the oldest twenty-nine. With a handful of exceptions, its members lacked the family wealth that might speed the transition to manhood. Moreover, owing to the rapidly changing nature of postwar urban labor, professionalization, and mastery, they often launched their careers without the assistance and protection of older men. Their fathers' generation had benefited from comparatively stable vocational patterns: they could generally expect to inherit farmland, advance from apprentice to journeyman under the guidance of a master artisan, or gain assistance in business from fathers or relatives. But after the war, occupational paths became less predictable, particularly in cities. Young men "groped their way toward autonomy" by trying out different jobs and by moving between rural and urban settings, as Daniel Cohen has explained. This uncertainty could delay a man's ability to marry, contributing to a sense of generational cohesion in postwar culture, since men "may have naturally resented a perceived absence of adequate support from their elders."[15] Clubs helped compensate by substituting the friendship and strictness of one's peers.

They also provided a sense of regularity, which may have been welcome in an environment where the economy fluctuated as wildly as it did during these years. Tales of men's failures in business ventures were legion; at several points during the 1780s and 1790s speculation in risky markets led to waves of bankruptcies and massive personal losses. In contrast, attending weekly club meetings was predictable. More important, meetings offered men the chance to cultivate the kind of refined public persona they had learned about in schoolbooks: the well-spoken, graceful man who impressed his superiors and drew the admiration and emulation of his friends.

Founded in 1788, the Calliopean Society met on Tuesdays in a small rented room for an evening of oratory, debate, and conversation that lasted as long as four hours.[16] Each evening's formal events were arranged the week before. As many as four "orators" declaimed memorized speeches or pieces, often lifted directly from school anthologies and utilizing the same elocutionary skills they described. In December 1788, for example, Gerard Depeyster recited "The Dying Christian's Soliloquy" and B. Payne performed "Mr. Barlow's Oration before the Cincinnati." They particularly favored selections from *Hamlet* and Joseph Addison's play *Cato* (in 1791 alone, members spoke from *Cato* thirteen times).[17] In addition, each evening featured up to five "composers" who read aloud poetry or essays of their own composition on topics from "On Society" to the philosophical "A Letter on Pardon," or subjects that touched on contemporary political culture, as in the essay "On the Flourishing State of Manufactures in America." Each composition was then handed to a fellow member who dedicated a week to editing and criticizing it, paying rigorous attention to originality and elegance. Sometimes a composition required so much work that a member chose to resubmit it several weeks later for further advice.

Such mutual criticism came with tensions, especially when the society created a Committee of Examination to review each composition formally. This committee proved nearly impossible to please. In addition to dismissive comments about authors' poor "stile" or lack of originality, examiners expressed huffy frustration with poor grammar and spelling as well as "indecent" subject matter. "The defects in these pages are so striking to the ear, that they do not require to be particularly pointed out," they complained of one poem, though they ultimately conceded that its occasional "beauties" of sentiment were "sufficient to atone for their trifling imperfections."[18] By July 1792 the committee issued a stern rebuke to fellow members for submitting few worthwhile compositions. "The observations are sometimes trite, improperly applied or arranged, or incompatible," the committee explained. Within a year the suggestions had become so harsh that an impasse developed between the committee and the broader membership: some refused to offer their writing for such abuse, while others submitted anonymous essays denouncing or ridiculing fellow members. With the prim tone of a schoolmaster, the committee reminded fellow members that they should view composition as a "pleasing employment of their leisure" rather than "a subject of complaint."[19]

The task that engaged every member equally was each evening's "dispute." Each man was arbitrarily assigned to one of two sides and instructed to follow strict rules. According to club bylaws all speech had to be extemporaneous. No one could speak a second time until each of his fellows had spoken once, and members whose comments were too long or who interrupted were reproved by the president (or by the censor, a position created after debates in 1793 became overly heated). After a considerable period of debate, the members stopped speaking and voted on which side had made the more convincing case. The club secretary dutifully recorded the topic of each night's debate and its conclusion. When they debated such topics as "whether Polygamy is usefull to Society," "whether the Theatre ought to be tolerated in this place," and "weather Brutus was justifiable in killing Cesar," they voted no in each case.[20] The outcomes of these debates may appear somewhat predictable, but the nature of the questions reveals why societies like the Calliopeans felt so strongly about secrecy: any member asked to defend polygamy for the sake of debate might not want his arguments publicized. The art of staging a good debate was not necessarily to come up with a probing or important political question but to field one that would test the elocutionary and argumentative talents of men on both sides for the evening. The club's secrecy let its members speak freely—in debate as well as in conversation.[21]

Secrecy did not wholly make club debates "private," however. Members tried out forms of address, personae, and arguments that would enhance their lives as businessmen and citizens. Moreover, the rules and format of their debates signaled important understandings of public discourse overall. Unlike the style of debate within the earliest college debating clubs in the 1720s, which were more scripted and claimed to be oriented toward the pursuit of truth, postrevolutionary societies emphasized that debate was intended to develop the skills of logical argument and extemporaneous presentation; there was no "true" answer.[22] Such shifts marked a new acceptance of disagreement and even contention that was, in principle, free of narrow personal interest. Such rules sought to ensure that personal beliefs or business connections did not inflame members' passions during debate.[23] One Baltimore society went so far as to stipulate in its bylaws that "no member shall be accountable . . . for any expression in debate."[24] In this regard groups like the Calliopeans differed significantly from the London debating societies and "mooting clubs," which were highly visible and commercial institutions that attracted hundreds of audience members each week—so popular, indeed, that notices of their events appeared in American newspapers.[25] Instead, the Calliopeans and dozens of nearly identical

American groups sought to meet the needs of young men wanting to establish themselves in a climate that privileged the "pursuit of knowledge under difficulties," as one contemporary put it.[26] Debating societies constituted a place for youths to hone public selves via speech and composition outside school or college.[27] This environment might be invaluable, especially if one sought to assume a vocation far removed than that of one's father.

And in fact, evidence on the Calliopeans' backgrounds and their subsequent courses shows that these men did pursue different careers than their fathers had. Over three-quarters of the fathers whose professions have been identified were farmers, artisans, and small shopkeepers, while at the high end of the spectrum approximately one-sixth were professionals, merchants, high-ranking officers, or members of the legislature (and at the other end, 5 percent were unskilled workers). Thomas Stagg Jr. and his family are representative of most members. Stagg joined the Calliopeans in 1788, when his father worked as a baker on Greenwich Street. By 1794 the city directory listed Thomas Jr. with an imposing-sounding merchant office on Ann Street. Likewise, Joseph Rose's father worked as a distiller, but his son had grander designs. By the end of Joseph's tenure in the Calliopean Society he had formed a partnership with fellow member Thomas Stoutinburgh as merchants and insurance brokers; by 1800 he had established his own independent merchant office.[28] In all, a full 60 percent of the members whose own occupations can be ascertained entered professional, mercantile, or otherwise "high white-collar" careers.[29] An additional 13 percent attained "low white-collar" positions such as accountants, teachers, and clerks, while 25 percent had careers as artisans and shopkeepers or in small manufactures.[30]

To be sure, this generational shift toward the professions and mercantile trade does not necessarily signal dramatic upward financial mobility. A jeweler, coach manufacturer, or ironmonger may well have prospered while a small merchant or physician might not.[31] Moreover, a close look at the early careers of these young men shows that in at least seven cases they shifted from one kind of work to another. Henry Hunt, for example, appeared in the 1793 directory as a merchant and glovemaker but by 1800 was listed as a grocer. Likewise, Jeremiah Hallet was listed as a merchant in 1792, an ironmonger in 1793, and a hardware store owner by 1795. Whether they reaped more status and financial rewards than their fathers, however, is less important than that so many of them sought out white-collar positions rather than artisanal paths like their fathers. Indeed, the apparently mutually encouraged shift of this group toward new lines of work demonstrates that young men's societies constituted an important site for middle-class formation in this era, beyond those detailed by Stuart Blumin, Richard Bushman, Mary Ryan, and others.[32] Likely influenced by their connections within the club, the Calliopeans apparently drew members based not on their current class position but on their imagined future as respected and possibly influential public figures; the club helped socialize one another into a world in which the old rules no longer carried so much weight.[33]

In all these respects, the Calliopean Society likely was nearly identical to similar societies of the era, though it differed in that the members started writing and editing the *New-York Magazine* in early 1790, after the club had existed for little more than a year. Their "The Club" columns became the place where they took turns presenting an idealized version of themselves and their club conversations. These columns nearly always opened each issue of the magazine, helping to frame the entire publication as one vetted and approved by a group of "gentlemen," as they announced in their June 1790 issue. As I have shown elsewhere, a significant percentage of American magazines claimed to be edited by "societies of gentlemen," but most readers probably did not expect such a group to be made up of men as young and inexperienced as those of the Calliopean Society.[34] Doubtless aware of this, the members worked hard to conceal their collective age and status in the magazine's pages by implying that they were significantly older, more established, and less politically partisan than they were.

The Calliopeans undertook the task of editing within the social, spoken, and local environment of club meetings. The club seems to have determined whether to publish a piece by how it sounded when read aloud—revealing how far oral delivery, even the reader's skill, and perhaps also the food and drink on a particular night affected publication decisions. Building on their existing practice of reading aloud and criticizing one another's compositions as one aspect of ordinary club practice, the Calliopeans used a similar approach when they considered submissions to the magazine by members of the public. After reading a piece aloud at a meeting, they assigned one member to submit an extensive analysis to the Committee of Examination, which determined whether to publish it.

Although their records provide few details about the conversations during these meetings, comparable proceedings can be found in the records of Boston's Anthology Society, which published the *Monthly Anthology* between 1803 and 1811. These men readily acknowledged that the oral performance of written work affected their publication decisions. "Lines from Baltimore signed 'Sedley' were rejected, owing either to the bad reading of the Secretary, or their intrinsick worthlessness," recorded the self-same secretary in 1807, even as his humor suggests that the bad reading was not really the problem. Sometimes they were more lenient toward items read by the author. "Mr. Stickney read his Remarker piece on political bigotry, which was accepted, though we were almost out of breath in hearing some of his long sentences." Even rejected pieces might provoke considerable club conversation. "The review was so strangely written, with such a mixture of good & unimportant matter, with such curious compliments & remarks in so singular a phraseology, that it afforded much pleasant talk to the Society," the secretary wrote after a particularly enjoyable night.[35] Published items had to survive both oral and written criticism—and perhaps the "bad reading of the Secretary" as well. These meeting minutes display the social context within which publication took place: reading a submission aloud could expose labyrinthine sentences and awkward transitions or open it to ridicule by a clubby roomful of highly critical men, some of whom may well have seen these essays primarily as entertaining fodder for an evening of drinking and dining.

Believing that successful men were made rather than born, these young men created a club to establish the discipline and friendships that would help them advance in business. Their debate, oratory, and editing of the magazine presumed that they required those skills to proceed into their adult lives. They learned to portray themselves as if they had already arrived, with the confident, masterful voices that glided over their true age and status. In this regard the Calliopeans represent a sharp contrast with the young women orators analyzed above: they eschewed the special pleas and coy rhetorical gambits used by their female peers to advance women's oratory and civic engagement. These men felt no need to articulate a counterpublic position asking society to welcome their literary and political contributions. Instead, the Calliopeans and similar middling young men used their club writings, debates, and oratory as opportunities to rehearse the roles of the successful men they expected to become—thereby endorsing prevailing notions that business and public discourse should be dominated by well-spoken, well-connected men. No matter how similar the elocutionary training for the sexes during the 1790s, ambitious boys learned simply to inhabit the confident public voices and personae of gentlemen rather than to vindicate themselves.

Seen in this light, it appears unsurprising that young men would go further and seek to be *makers* of public opinion in the magazine. The Calliopeans viewed the combination of impromptu conversation and formally choreographed debate, as well as its mix of literary and political subject matter, as a model of harmonious and sociable discourse that all members of the public might emulate. Thus, when they inserted a fictionalized version of themselves in their column "The Club," they sought to shape not only their readers' opinions but also the style and practice of public conversation.

THE CLUB AND PUBLIC DISCOURSE IN AN AGE OF DEMOCRACY AND COUNTERREVOLUTION

The members who wrote for their collaborative column addressed both serious and humorous topics, but they perennially returned to one subject: the ways club conversation and sociability constituted a model for broader public discourse. In the first "The Club" column in June 1790, one writer-member explained that he and his fellows had determined to write and edit the *New-York Magazine* because they felt they could be most "serviceable to the community" if they presented "the subjects of our conversation . . . to the public," since their conversations were exemplary of free public discourse:

> As each individual naturally expresses his mind with freedom, and according to his own opinion of things, various lights are thrown on the same subject; and the discussion of the question, while it tends to amuse, always serves to inform. It may be readily concluded, that there can be no want of matter for conversation, whilst this city is the seat of the general government; and the politics of the week are sure to be discussed, with all the earnestness natural to a people, alive to every action of their rulers.[36]

This was the very picture of idealized public discussion: the diverse conversation of "a people, alive" and as ready to be engaged in political debate as in amusing diversions. His recurring use of "natural" undergirded his admiring portrayal of clubs, since it suggested to readers that societies enhanced an individual's "natural" capacity for intelligent, earnest public discussion. According to this view, the crucial component of an ideal public forum was not unanimity but diversity of opinion, spoken in an environment of "freedom" and "earnestness." Describing the club to the magazine's readers in this fashion allowed the writer to draw a connection between the discussions in his club and the experience of reading the magazine—readers could catch glimpses of the men's conversations and join in through the medium of print.

Shaping public discussion and even political culture proved to be an important element of the Calliopeans' work with the magazine. They imagined an integral relation between their club conversations and the improvement of the public overall. As a result, they advertised in their published columns the notion that the club was metonymically related to the nation as a whole: the heterogeneity of their discussion might be a model for reasoned public exchange in general. The magazine's combination of literary and political subject matter enhanced the men's claim to be expansive thinkers fully engaged in public life. As we shall see, this public self-presentation gained in appeal and political significance as a result of debates in the mid-1790s about the nature of the public vis-à-vis its political leaders.

Especially in the magazine's early days, "The Club" insisted that a truly ideal form of public discussion took place in clubs and societies.[37] To some degree, this was a defensive claim. American clubs had acquired a bad name during the Revolution, when political leaders had accused such minority partisan societies as the Republicans and the Whigs of falsely claiming to speak for all the people.[38] Questions still lingered by the early 1790s, so that the Calliopeans felt it necessary to address them directly in their earliest columns by depicting a "debate" among the fictional members of "The Club." One member, the author explained, had asserted "that great advantage as well as pleasure result from small clubs and societies, composed of characters who have a similarity of taste and opinions." But his fellows would not permit such a platitude to go unchallenged. One of them "warmly contended" that dividing the population into groups by "peculiarity of character, or difference of political or religious tenets [would allow those individuals to overlook] the great and important interests of humanity" so that "a spirit of diffusive liberality would be swallowed up by those subordinate institutions." He even warned that such behavior might "beget a party spirit." Finally, a third intervened to reconcile their differences. This man granted that some groups had the potential to "diminish our regard to the general welfare of society," as the second member had suggested. Still, he pointed out that American society was rife with "local attachments" and "small districts and associations" that posed no threat, such as the relationship between the state of New York and the United States or the city of Boston and the state of Massachusetts. Surely, he insisted, it was possible to maintain affection for clubs and societies without leading to hopeless social division. Membership in a club was wholly compatible with being American, he argued: one affiliation enhanced the other, reinforcing one's attachment to the larger, more abstract entity—thus incorporating a version of the arguments made in *The Federalist #2*. His own participation had convinced him that "we should now consider ourselves as Americans, and should deem every regulation wrong, that holds us up to view in any other character."³⁹ Mediating between the first two positions allowed the column's author to assert that the very nature of considered, dialectical conversation in clubs was patriotic.⁴⁰

Such idealized portrayals of public involvement also signaled the men's political (and eventually partisan) inclinations. Although most Americans agreed that public opinion rendered a republican government legitimate and stable, political leaders disagreed about whether it ought to influence policy or simply reflect the people's consent for their leaders to govern on behalf of the general public good. Jefferson worried that the people had become so distracted by making money that they had failed to maintain "a due respect for their rights"—and government had followed suit, forgetting its obligations to the people. "The shackles . . . will remain on us long, and will be made heavier, till our rights shall revive, or expire in a convulsion," he warned in *Notes on the State of Virginia*.⁴¹ James Madison, on the other hand, believed that allowing public opinion too active a role would constrain government in its important business, while Alexander Hamilton advocated that government maintain a healthy distance between leaders and the public. Meanwhile, a growing group of politicized nonelites increasingly argued that the people could play an active and even radically participatory role in decision making and policy formation by state and federal governments—a position increasingly embraced by the Calliopeans.⁴²

Their club records reveal that during their earliest years they shifted from a general attention to politics to explicit partisanship. At first they permitted the discussion of political matters in debates solely in the most general, and often idealized, terms: they queried the philosophical value of certain policies rather than addressing specific events of the political moment. For example, during 1789 and early 1790 they debated "Whether or no the Importation of Tea is Necessary" (and determined no at the end of the debate), "whether a Republican form of Government is preferable to a Monarchal one" (yes), and "Whither it is politic in government to give way to the Desires of the people" (no).⁴³ Most of these questions struck the same tone as other debate topics on less obviously political matters, such as "Whether Avarice or Ambition is the most advantage to Society" (ambition) and "Whether public brothels ought to be tolerated" (no)—that is, their questions asked members to take positions that ranged from practical to philosophical while steering clear of anything that reeked of partisanship or risked real political conflict, since the club included members with a range of political inclinations.⁴⁴ They never discussed the value of the new federal Constitution, controversially ratified in New York only a few months before the club's founding, or the Bill of Rights.⁴⁵

But during the 1790s their meetings and publications reveal that the group increasingly addressed political issues directly and began to lean collectively toward republican and eventually more radical pro-French politics. In this regard the group resembled similar groups of white men who formed Democratic-Republican societies in many locales between approximately 1792 and 1796.[46] At first, in mid-1790, the Calliopeans began debating some of the politics of the day, such as "Whether it is politic to manumit the Slaves" (yes), "Whether it would be politic for the United States to Raise and Maintain a Standing Army" (no), and "Wether the governor was Justifiable in releasing Morehouse" (yes)—a man initially sentenced to death for fraud.[47] By using terms such as "justifiable" and "politic," they maintained the philosophical tone of earlier questions, even as they now focused on topical issues. During 1791 and 1792 the subjects of their weekly orations and compositions also turned more toward contemporary politics. Garret Abeel rehearsed an oration "On the American and French Revolutions" at several meetings; Joseph Rose and others composed pieces that celebrated the Tammany Society; and John Duryee delivered an oration "for the benefit of the weavers in Ireland" (in 1792 the weavers, inspired by the democratic writings of Thomas Paine and tied to the radical United Irishmen, were striking for the right to vote, better representation for ordinary people, and parliamentary reform).[48] Of course, a political topic debated one week might well be followed by a more traditional topic the next; the Calliopeans' weekly meetings never focused solely on contemporary politics or radical subjects. Still, their increasing appearance clearly shows that the members gradually added a political component to the club's purpose. In doing so they spurred one another to advance democratic visions of an active and critical citizenry.

Their embrace of republican politics also revealed a vision of intellectual men engaging fully in political and social transformation. These were not individuals who remained disengaged from democratic movements. Political and literary discussion had the potential to achieve two goals: to perfect one's dedication to the nation and to forward one's personal ambitions, aims that were viewed as perfectly consonant with one another. For example, when they urged readers to submit their work for publication in the magazine, they explained that "Patriotism may here find its dearest object—Ambition may receive its richest meed—Patriotism may exert itself in perfecting and supporting a government founded on equal liberty, and whose object is the happiness of all its citizens—Ambition may be rewarded by the love of a grateful and an enlightened people."[49] By tying their literary and aesthetic concerns to broader movements for independence, these men sought to position intellectuals at the center of their vision of a new public culture in America and perhaps even in the world at large, as Bryan Waterman has shown for a contemporaneous New York club.[50]

Their political concerns grew more pronounced in 1793 and 1794, when fully two-thirds of their debates covered political topics, approximately 20 percent relating to the French Revolution. They debated such questions as "Would a revolution in the English Government be of advantage to the present Generation?" (yes), "Would the French Nation be justifiable in beheading Louis XVI?" (yes), "Is Paines book called the age of reason likely to produce more good or evil in the world?" (good), and "Is not America bound in justice to assist France in her struggle for liberty?" (no). During one particularly active month of debates in early 1794 they voted to install strict term limits for political representatives, to support France in its war (rather than "the despots leagued against her"), to maintain an individual citizen's right to bring suit against a state, and to condemn the United States' treatment of Citizen Genet—a full catalog of Democratic-Republican concerns.[51] In fact, for seven months during 1794 they even took to calling one another by the French designation "citizen," a term that other democratic radicals heralded: "*Citizen* implies the right to think, and the right to think implies an analysis of governmental doctrines and measures," explained an essay in Philadelphia's *General Advertiser* in 1794—a sentiment the Calliopeans appear to have embraced.[52]

Their views of public engagement and a properly constituted public sphere appeared as primary themes in the magazine, although there the men were more circumspect in advancing these as partisan views than in club meetings.[53] The *New-York Magazine*'s content displayed a strong pro-French bias, and its political and social commentaries tied it to "the new republicanism" to an extent unique among American magazines of the period.[54] It resembled the republican and radical newspapers of the era, edited by similarly young men inspired by the democratic possibilities of the French Revolution and the writings of Thomas Paine. The magazine's selections long had included excerpts of French literature and poetry, but now they comprised such items as the "Petition of Madame Guillon" delivered to the French National Assembly and an "Address" describing conflicts within Paris between "true republicans" and "federalists" during the beginning of the Reign of Terror.[55] The magazine's attention to these themes reflected the enthusiastic support for the Revolution by many urban Americans, whose festive celebrations of the Revolution became so popular and widespread that they temporarily surpassed Fourth of July rites, as Simon Newman has demonstrated.[56]

But that enthusiasm did not survive the news of the Terror—either among pro-French Americans in general or in the pages of the *New-York Magazine*. The magazine's French bias became so controversial by the beginning of the Terror that the editors felt obliged to deny it in their January 1794 issue, asserting somewhat implausibly that they had always remained strictly impartial. Despite this disclaimer, the editors pulled back sharply from publishing supportive essays on France.[57] The club's meeting minutes likewise reflect a quiet retreat from the group's earlier sentiments.

Changes in public opinion on the French Revolution strongly affected perceptions of clubs in the United States during 1794. Owing to Americans' growing understanding of the Jacobin Clubs' involvement in radicalizing French politics and in the ten-month-long Terror, in late spring fears of American clubs began to spread. Those fears accelerated in September, when George Washington himself condemned "certain self-created societies"—specifically, the Democratic-Republican societies—for allegedly playing a role in the Whiskey Rebellion. These "combinations of men, careless of consequence" had "disseminated, from an ignorance or perversion of facts, suspicions, jealousies, and accusations of the whole government," Washington declared.[58] Federalists and the Washington administration used the backlash against political clubs as an opportunity to denounce those who, like the Democratic-Republicans, criticized specific government actions and advocated a stronger public voice in politics. Together the confluence of fears about American political clubs and the devolving situation in France led the Calliopeans to adopt a defensive public stance regarding their own club. By June 1794 they suspended writing "The Drone" altogether (they would resume eighteen months later), perhaps in response to mounting antagonism to clubs, and considerably shortened the magazine's overall length, perhaps owing to disappointing subscription sales.

But even before "The Drone" was suspended, the columns had switched their tone from earnest to comical. This shift had a crucial effect on the men's self-portrayal and the public they called forth from their readers. They now altered the way they positioned themselves as the writer-editors of the magazine, affecting to be less the moderators of a right-minded, earnest public conversation than men with primarily impertinent and trivial pursuits, whose sense of humor tended toward the ridiculous.[59] However intelligent and learned they ultimately appeared, they cultivated ineffectual, apolitical personae. They now downplayed their significance in moderating and modeling an idealized form of conversation that might have political import.

They achieved this self-portrayal especially through satire. Their humorous columns of the mid-1790s often focused on language itself, probing the boundary between proper and deceptive speech as they pretended to appreciate the latter. This fixation on language and usage may have meant that the controversies surrounding clubs had led the Calliopeans to transform their earlier advocacy of democratic public conversation into a more one-sided banter. One 1794 column, for example, advanced a mock celebration of *"Lying"* as a useful and "universally applicable," if sorely overlooked, figure of rhetoric. "It must be evident to every one who is acquainted with the beauties of language, that the plain, simple, relation of *matter of fact*, without *embellishment* of some kind, is a very dry, uninteresting task, both to the speaker and hearers," explained the author. Convinced of the "utility" of lies to invigorate rhetoric, he now proposed to open an academy to teach "the *science of lying*"—and to give readers a taste of its wonders, he briefly dissected the genera, species, and varieties of such lies as "the stretch," "the bounce," and "the humbug." "I mean to make my pupils acquainted with the theory of these principles . . . [and] to instruct them in the application of these principles to practice," he explained.[60]

Mock paeans such as this allowed the men to satirize the self-important classification schemas of elocution manuals and magazine literature that purported to categorize various forms of useful knowledge. They also mocked the Calliopeans' own earlier claims to be a model of public discourse: in fact, the columns offered instead an antimodel. More broadly, it allowed them to skew the magazine in the direction of high literary wit for like-minded readers and away from a dangerous—and unprofitable—preoccupation with politics.[61]

In 1796 "The Drone" revealed to its readers another seldom-recognized source of oral brilliance: the "eloquence of the counter." Alongside ministers, lawyers, and senators, the author explained, the shop clerk should be celebrated as a special font of eloquence in American society. Indeed, the writer insisted, the salesclerk required "a greater proportion of genius, ability, presence of mind, and skilfulness of address" than the others, for he had to adapt his pitch extemporaneously when faced with myriad unexpected circumstances and different customers. Although he was limited in inventiveness as a result of his merchandise—"gauze could not be with propriety praised for its strength"—the author celebrated the clerk's virtuoso ability to think on his feet while negotiating customer psychology and the vagaries of consumer taste. "One person would despise an article for the same reason that would most strongly recommend it to another," which required the clerk "to persuade a young lady that any thing you would sell is strong, and will wear well" and then to turn around and "tell a Dutchman from Kinderhook, that it is the tip of the mode, fine, and of the most fashionable colours."[62] To trumpet the sales pitch was to temporarily erase the distinction between straightforward, upright speech and verbal pandering, even as the essay ultimately lampooned the clerk's patter as hucksterism.

Such satirical attention to proper and improper uses of language implied that the Calliopeans now imagined their relation to their reading public in different terms. While their mock analyses of the beauties of lying and swearing may still have called forth an image of a reading public well aware of the differences between virtue and deception, the Calliopeans' columns and their work in the magazine overall had lost their early idealism to represent the "nation in miniature." And indeed, clubs became a subject debated in magazines and viewed skeptically even by members. An 1800 essay in the *Philadelphia Repository*, for example, lodged two primary complaints about debating societies. First, "they prevent that care and attention to business, which is requisite to the satisfaction of the employer, and the peace of the employed" by encouraging men to prepare for debates about which they knew nothing. In other words, the clubs' pursuits were a frivolous diversion from the practical knowledge needed to fulfill their members' job obligations. Second, the author argued, societies "tend to associate characters of moral and immoral import," linking young men "in *private*, [with those] with whom in *public*, they would be ashamed to be seen."[63] This implication of moral contamination suggests alarm about youths' abilities to regulate themselves and a fear of their autonomous peer culture. By the time the twenty-two-year-old John Gallison joined the Columbian Society in 1810, he felt it necessary to tell his diary that "it is not my intention to have my individual sentiments at all controlled by those of any part or body of men with whom I may be joined. I shall agree with them in some things & in other differ.—Considering this to be a society for the purposes of free inquiry & discussion, I shall employ its advantages to that purpose."[64]

As the optimistic narrative of the pro-French radicals came to an end, the Calliopeans released themselves from the position of public intellectuals interested in both social and political concerns. The writerly voice they settled on by 1796—sardonic, self-mocking—may have been more assured than the earnest one they began with, but it also separated their literary magazine from the heady political environment of the time. In fact, as Albrecht Koschnik has shown, the young men's groups that did retain clear partisan inclinations during the early nineteenth century tended to be Federalists.[65] Like Joseph Dennie and other quasi-aristocratic Federalists of the era, they escaped into the world of literature as a space of pure aesthetics unsullied by partisanship—a move that framed their intellectualism as legitimate and worthy of respect.⁶⁶ Their eagerness to protect the magazine from the taint of "self-created societies" meant they no longer saw democratic politics as an appropriate subject for their writings. They turned toward easier targets: women, gender behavior, and the field of courtship.

MODELING MANLINESS IN PRINT AND PUBLIC

Simply because they ceased publishing articles explicitly about politics did not mean the *New-York Magazine* went apolitical after 1794. This is particularly true for the numerous writings on gender relations and courtship, subjects that had long occupied them but that received renewed attention in the wake of the backlash against political clubs. These concerns reflected, of course, the circumstance that most of the Calliopeans were themselves far from assured of success in courtship. In fact, the magazine's preoccupation with gender displayed a primary interest in the topics of manliness, proper male behavior in courtship, and men's self-presentation in professional life. Writing on manliness and courtship did not just reflect their uncertain status in life; it provided a safe haven for a self-described club of "drones" or "old bachelors" to steer clear of accusations of political machinations while still commenting extensively on American life.

The Calliopeans' columns on gender relations and courtship manifested a striking ambivalence about women and an uncertainty about their roles as marriageable men. To take one example, the Calliopeans published an essay in a 1793 "Drone" column that purported to rank spinsters "in two different classes": "those who are such *by imprudence*, or *by misfortune*." Both types, the essay charged, were sorry characters indeed—and the author used a series of comic caricatures to account for their single condition. Whereas Clarissa proudly refused to display interest in any suitor "until her season for conquest was past," the flirtatious Harlotta "was under engagements to four different gentlemen at one time. She disappointed them all!" Meanwhile, the fortune-seeking Harriot "pretended to despise every body; she could find no person rich enough; her ideas were exalted and she longed to be married, if she *must* be married at all, to a man of *fortune* and *distinction*." She got what she deserved when she was humiliated to discover that the German baron she favored was only a French periwig maker in disguise. In lampooning old maids for their readers' amusement, the youthful author and his fellow editors sermonized at women's expense. The moral lesson was that "to deserve well of society, it is necessary we should be beneficial to it": since spinsters were useless to society, young women should be warned to avoid the behavior that led to this condition. "On persons such as these, the world delights to crack its jokes," the author concluded.[67]

But just as this essay veered dangerously close to unabashed misogyny, the author pulled back and assumed a more sober tone by quoting an "old woman" correspondent whose sad life story was intended to humble male readers who took too much pleasure in mocking old maids. Whereas men find happiness and social esteem "in serving your country; your wounds have attached honour to your names," she wrote, women who lost out in the courtship game were truly pitiable. "I, on the other hand, have grown old in a single life, without having enjoyed the satisfaction of hearing a man of any description whatever ... ever make a declaration that he loved me. I have of course run through life ... without answering one valuable purpose: I have injured nobody it is true, but I have also done nobody any good." After transcribing her sorry tale, the Drones "hesitated not a moment to declare" that single women were far more "unfortunate" than bachelors.

The ambivalence of this single column reflects the Calliopeans' overall take on women in the *New-York Magazine*. Even as they occasionally mocked or ridiculed women, the magazine also featured them prominently in its pages—both as authors and as admirable subjects. They published works by prominent American writers Hannah Foster, Judith Sargent Murray, and Susannah Rowson and featured excerpts of Mary Wollstonecraft's *Vindication of the Rights of Woman* shortly after its publication. "While thousands are shedding their blood in asserting the *Rights of Man*, a Female has lately wielded her Pen, and we think with great success, in vindicating the *Rights of Woman*," they wrote by means of introduction.[68] To encourage a larger female readership and submissions from women writers, the magazine's first issue featured a letter from "Maria Morelove" that promised she would support the new magazine by urging her female friends to purchase subscriptions and to think of the journal as "a place in which to deposit our sentiments." Although the editors probably wrote Morelove's letter themselves, it likely served the purpose of welcoming women to submit their work to the magazine.[69] The editors' overall ambivalence toward women infused a large number of the magazine's many essays on gender, particularly in the Calliopeans' "Club" and "Drone" columns, during an era when marriage and courtship were almost as much in flux as work and politics.

The men's preoccupation with gender surfaced in the club's private meetings. "Which is the most happy state, matrimony or celibacy?" the Calliopeans asked in an early club debate in May 1789. Other debates centered on such topics as whether children ought to marry without their parents' consent, whether beauty or wit was more beneficial to women, and whether bachelors over age twenty-eight should be taxed by the state.[70] Striking an exceptionally legalistic mood, one 1792 debate queried, "Would it not be for the advantage of Society, if the term of Marriage between persons of less than 35 Years of age, were restricted to 7 years, allowing them at the expiration of that term, if agreeable to both parties to renew their contract; the man in all cases to support his children?" (no). Approximately one-third of the Calliopeans' debates revolved around topics of gender and relations between the sexes, a preoccupation also exhibited by other Anglo-American debating clubs of the era.[71] This fixation was even more prominent when the men represented themselves in the "Club" and "Drone" columns, of which nearly half probed such matters in detail.

In this regard, "Drone Club" was a felicitous name for the Calliopean Society's alter ego within the magazine. It allowed them to make a great show of mocking themselves as droning on about useless topics and contributing little to society, yet it also sent potent messages about the members' unmarried status and sexual anxieties. In disguise as Drones, the Calliopeans shed the youthful idealism they displayed in private club meetings (as when they voted that dissimulation was not integral to the female character in a July 1789 debate) and put on the writerly personae of wise "old bachelors." They had no real reason to portray themselves thus: men married on average at twenty-five, leaving the Calliopeans too young to warrant the characterization.[72] But in print this persona allowed them to appear canny in the mysteries of courtship and skeptical about gender ideals. Whether their unmarried and childless status was "*by imprudence* or *by misfortune*," they did not tell; but affecting this world-weary, sardonic, and even mock-tragic perspective made them sound all the more proficient in diagnosing the foibles of relations between the sexes—since after all they had forsaken romance and resigned themselves to bachelorhood. More than the other topics they plumbed in their columns, gender themes allowed them to sound assured as they navigated between the strictures of societal expectations and the dangers of abandoning those mores.

A letter from "Miss Henrietta Misslove," almost certainly composed by one of the Calliopeans, helped to confirm this collective persona. It opened with a bit of raillery that referred to the Drones as "a set of old bachelors; for you must know I term an old bachelor a very *drone* in society, and as much deserving to be excluded from the enjoyment of it as a drone from the benefits of the hive." In the same vein, she opined that "a worn-out rake and an old bachelor are with me synonymous terms."[73] Her jibes captured the image of men redundant in society, past their prime, and withdrawn after leading lives of pleasure; she affected to disdain them for their past behavior toward women and implied that they deserved their social ostracism.

The rest of Misslove's letter took a different tone, however: she solicited their help as sage experts in the ways of love, calling on them to serve as public mediators with the capacity to affect readers' behavior. In making this transition, she revealed the true reasons for her cynicism about men. Years before, she said, she had fallen in love with a rake who had duped her into believing he loved her. His abandonment caused her to suffer "miseries," even more so when she heard that he had gone on to use "the same deceit with several others." Her tale exposed the devastating effects of such cavalier behavior toward women: even though she had since been visited by a number of honest suitors, she knew she could never love another. Her deception by this man had rendered her an unwilling spinster, hardened by experience. In fact, Misslove confessed bitterly, she could have "been settled with *as good a man* as perhaps can be found; but as I know them all to be a set of *deceivers*, and have for some time entertained a hearty contempt for the *whole sex*." She urged the Drones to use the magazine to advise rakish men to repent of behavior that inflicted enduring harm on women like her. Rakes eventually "see the errors of their conduct, and bewail their situation," she believed; "but the worst part of their character then is, that they are sorry only for themselves, and seldom or never reflect on the sorrows their conduct may have entailed upon others." A public discussion of her plight, she hoped, would prompt these men's consciences. In appealing to the club, Misslove asked them to advise other men for women's benefit. Thus, even after she initially charged the Drones with being "worn-out rakes," in the end she rehabilitated them because of their capacity to reach a public audience and serve as sympathetic supporters of wronged womanhood.

Why such disproportionate attention to the "problem" of bachelors and spinsters? The recurring themes in these tales—deception, misplaced affection, and being rendered socially "useless"—confirm that the dilemmas of courtship proved directly analogous to troubling aspects of postrevolutionary political culture.[74] Just as the people's trust in their elected representatives might be abused, so the norms of courtship permitted great dishonesty by disreputable rakes and coquettes. And as government corruption by the few effectively disfranchised the many and rendered them politically "useless," becoming a spinster or bachelor by the "misfortune" of duplicity left one *socially* useless in the Calliopeans' numerous stories. Conniving characters such as "Clarissa" and "Harlotta" may have gotten what they deserved when they failed to marry, but their deception had serious social costs. Tales about bachelors and old maids were not merely metaphors for public participation and political engagement; in postrevolutionary America, marriage fell just short of a requirement for most men to attain full cultural and economic independence, and thereby political standing. The Calliopeans' fixation with these topics thereby reflected not only their own unease about being young, unmarried, and unsettled in business but their awareness of the intimate connections between courtship and civic life. While such stories afforded high entertainment value, they also allowed young men to write obliquely about the political culture that continued to engage them privately—and perhaps to manage their anxieties as well.

These themes intertwined in a piece they published in 1793, "An Oration on the Question, 'Which is the More Eligible for a Wife, a *Widow* or an *Old Maid?*'" written in the style of a position statement for a debate, advancing with oratorical flourish and manifest silliness the argument that one should marry spinsters rather than widows.[75] As self-consciously absurd as it was, the essay largely revolved around the problem of which type of woman would love her husband wholeheartedly and without guile. In this regard, the author explained, widows ought to be viewed with a high degree of skepticism. "The wife, who has buried one or two husbands, on a slight disagreement with her second or third, will soon wish him to sleep in peace with her departed predecessor, from her hope of being more lucky in her next adventure," he wrote with evident enjoyment. In contrast, "He who marries an Old Maid, has a much greater chance of being invariably beloved by his wife, or in other words, of being happy in wedlock," since a woman loved most whom she loved first. Clearly, happiness in wedlock transcended the needs of two individuals: society in general would be better off if wives adored their husbands completely. Added to this was the second rationale for marrying a spinster: it allowed her to be "useful" to society. It was a crime to keep her "an utter stranger to the cares or to the delights of an important office, which she is equally ready to assume, and equally able to support," the author advanced in grand style.[76] This vision of an ordered society, in which each woman could dream of holding her own "office" of marriage and unconditional love for her husband, was—not coincidentally—sharply focused on its benefits to husbands.

On a broader level, this putting on and taking off multiple male perspectives reveals that the forums of the magazine and club compositions were perfect sites for contributing to a masculinist discourse on public inclusion and exclusion.[77] They no longer had radically democratic politics by which to stake claims to participation, but they could use gender politics to do so. Playing a wide range of men's roles (and female personae as well) allowed them to hold themselves up as virtuoso male writers, capable of directing the conversation about gender. This position was akin to Homi Bhabha's concept of masculinity as "an enunciative position"—in this case, the particularly masterful position of articulating a series of male types and antitypes (bachelors, rakes, and so on).[78] Carroll Smith-Rosenberg argues that "we cannot fully understand the construction of a new sexual and domestic female . . . unless we view it against the constantly changing construction of the male citizen," constructions the Calliopeans themselves helped to articulate.[79] Whether they portrayed women and men as virtuous or vicious was beside the point: in the *New-York Magazine* the Calliopeans toyed with all of them. It was less significant to identify a single appropriate mode of manliness than to be the puppeteers of them all.

This is not to say they necessarily knew where they were going in their depictions of men and women. In fact, their play with gender conventions sometimes appeared as thinly disguised sexual descriptions. Although sexual themes only seldom found overt expression in self-consciously "elegant" publications like the *New-York Magazine*, portrayals of bachelors and spinsters particularly lent themselves to unsubtle sexual references. Take, for example, an extensive depiction of the old maid from the "Oration" that describes her growing love for her husband: "Like an inexperienced but a passionate naturalist, she continues to survey the new and sole object of her contemplation, not only with unremitting assiduity, but with increasing amazement and delight. He fills her eye; he occupies her mind; he engrosses her heart." In contrast, the writer compared the purported appeal of the widow—her alluring feminine sorrow—to "the moan of the hyaena, that artful, destructive, and insatiable creature, who is said by the ancient naturalists to lure into her den, by a treacherous cry of distress, the unwary traveller whom she intends to devour."[80] Passages like these added a degree of prurient titillation to a discussion of a properly constituted public and hinted at the urban "pleasure culture" that urban young men had accepted as an aspect of their social landscape since midcentury.[81] Thus, even as this writer seemed to condone a tidy vision of society in which all spinsters might find husbands, he also used the piece to sneak in some of the masculine humor of broadsides, bawdy houses, and street culture. Writings like this reveal that the *New-York Magazine* ultimately upheld not just a masculine perspective on gender relations, but masculine prerogative.

This portrayal of the untrustworthy and sexually voracious widow was relatively unusual in the magazine, however. In general, it was men whom the Calliopeans tended to portray in suspect terms; in many of their accounts men tended toward the bad choices, misplaced priorities, or outright selfishness that had dire social consequences.[82] In this regard the case of the Calliopeans casts new light on the construction of manliness in postrevolutionary America. Whereas Smith-Rosenberg has concluded that much postrevolutionary magazine writing defined the new bourgeois man in contradistinction to women, the Calliopeans' many writings displayed much more transparently men's struggle to define and adhere to the codes of appropriate manhood.[83] Rather than denounce women as lacking virtue, these writers created a cast of middling male characters who erred in judgment with regard to personal behavior, priorities, and the treatment of women. And when they did, they served themselves up to the watchful eyes of the wise "old bachelors" whose unmarried status made them—like the outsider-censor, the eloquent Indian—incapable of ideal manhood, yet in the perfect position to correct behavior in others.

The Calliopeans especially liked to contrast their own right-minded views with the letters they received from characters such as "Anthony Anxious," who begged for advice. This character appeared shortly after the "Henrietta Misslove" column and functioned as her counterpart: a male suitor distressed by the conflict between his heart and his determination to remain honorable. Anxious explained that although he was engaged to another, he had since fallen hopelessly in love with Julia, a daughter of family friends who had returned to the city for the first time since childhood, now "transformed" into Anxious's ideal of womanhood. Even though Julia was also engaged, his feelings for her were so powerful that he now doubted the propriety of following through with his upcoming wedding. "Shall I go and deliver myself up" to his fiancée in marriage, he asked, but "withhold from her my heart?" After detailing his conflict for nearly three pages, Anxious concluded his letter by begging for assistance and promising to follow their recommendations exactly, placing his future in the hands of these knowing "gentlemen."

The Drones were unswayed by the correspondent's romantic feelings and unequivocal in their reply. "It is clearly his duty, and will be essential to his happiness, to comply with the engagements of honour and affection" rather than abandon them for the "romantic work of the imagination" that drew him to Julia. Indeed, assured of his fiancée's "unalienable love" as well as "long acquaintance" with her virtues, they sternly explained that "he should think himself happy" to comply with the marriage, for "few are favoured with all these advantages."[84] A man's "happiness," they asserted, derived not from succumbing to his desire but from upholding his honor and fulfilling his responsibilities to others. The conservatism of this advice may have gained a particular poignancy because it came from the pens of old bachelors who claimed they knew too well what it meant for men to lack honor and responsibility. But the real fun of the "letter" and its response was that the Calliopeans got to play both roles—hapless suitor and stern advisers—in the vein of literature written in epistolary form.[85] Hewing to the line of conservative male values may have been the final moral of this story, but as with so much of the era's sentimental literature on courtship and seduction, the "Drones" made sure to give full voice to Anxious's romantic yet hopeless perspective as well.

After the column's eighteen-month hiatus during the anticlub panic, the Drones added a new facet to their depictions of proper manhood: a thoroughgoing skepticism of political partisanship. They published a portrait of George Washington in February 1797 that stressed his political evenhandedness and the "unanimity" of the people's love of him; they followed it in March with John Adams's inauguration speech decrying faction.[86] Literary sketches that depicted masculinity likewise emphasized that right-minded men disdained party, as the editors portrayed themselves as fully on board with the new political regime.

The Calliopeans' turn to gendered themes in their *New-York Magazine* writings granted them a new purchase for commenting on public culture. Such topics helped resolve the problems they faced during the political backlash against "self-created societies" in the mid-1790s, since they could continue to write about a properly constituted public sphere in ways that steered clear of accusations of partisanship. Holding forth on matters of courtship and gendered behavior articulated a particular vision of social relations, one that decried duplicity and called forth honorable manliness and dutiful femininity from their readers. This was, overall, a deeply masculinist view of society. To be sure, they featured female writers and subjects throughout the magazine—yet as these passages have shown, they ultimately used women as foils for the complex elaboration of male subjectivity.

When member Richard Bingham Davis died unexpectedly in 1799 at age twenty-eight, his fellows compiled a biography and collected his poems in a small publication.[87] Davis had written several of their favorite pieces but was most fondly remembered for his "Mr. Martlet," a peculiar and philosophical character that he painted in loving detail beginning in 1792, when he was twenty-one.[88] Martlet was a "member of the republic of letters" and an "old bachelor" who had proved hopeless with women. Quiet and something of a misanthrope, he had found his métier in the club, where he earned his fellow members' gratitude for proposing that they compile their conversations for publication in the *New-York Magazine*. In a dramatic moment, Martlet nominates "The Drone" as the moniker for the club's combined literary efforts. When his fellows appear mystified by this suggestion, he explains that society unjustly presumes "drones to be the most useless and unprofitable members of the community of bees, because they do not work with the rest, nor apply their whole attention to laborious occupations."[89] Delighted with the notion that they might appropriate such a characterization and turn it to their advantage, the Calliopeans thereafter celebrated it and continued to write Martlet into subsequent columns. When Davis died, his friends insisted the character had been autobiographical, and they set out to portray Davis in nearly identical terms—except that they stressed his Martlet-style derision not just of the marketplace, but of party politics as well.

Misanthrope, bachelor, unsuccessful in business: Richard Davis was hardly representative of an ideal man according to the Calliopeans' earlier reckoning, yet he easily received the most effusive eulogy of the dozen members who died during the yellow fever outbreaks of the 1790s.[90] Considering the timing of his death, it appears to have afforded his fellow members the chance to reimagine their club according to newly acceptable standards. Davis was, according to his biographers, happiest in the company of his friends and miserable when forced to face the hypocrisies of a mercantile economy and partisan politics. Possessed of prodigious "literary acquirements," he temporarily abandoned his craft as a carver and gilder in 1796 to edit the *Diary*, a weekly literary newspaper. But this turned out to be an unfortunate choice, for he was daily affronted by the incompatibility of literature and the market—an early expression of a tension that would become a central feature of the complaints of self-described "serious" writers.[91] He especially felt insulted by his readers' lack of interest in his writings. "The richest effusions of his muse were lost amid the rubbish of advertisements; and his essays, whether of an instructive or amusing nature, were supplanted in interest by mercantile details, which were considered of far superior importance by his commercial readers." Even worse was the partisan nature of the press. As a "lover of truth," they wrote, he "could not endure the tale of slander" or the political self-promotion of other editors. After "a year's irksome experience . . . he abandoned it with disgust."[92] All told, his biographers created a tale of a right-minded man, a true intellectual, betrayed by a public more concerned with superficial matters than with the "truth" revealed in fine writing and poetry. Davis and Martlet became equivalent, exemplary of a high-minded literary stance that retreated from a market-driven, fractious urban culture. Davis's eulogizers romanticized his social isolation and commended his distaste for ordinary readers who failed to appreciate his published offerings.

If this semitragic version of Davis's life was appealing to his friends by the late 1790s, it represented a new view of the Calliopeans and their relation to the public, specifically resulting from the Jacobin and Illuminati anxieties of the 1790s. In depicting themselves all along as a "society of gentlemen," they likely always hoped to be seen as intellectuals. But whereas their earlier intellectual pursuits had been infused with enthusiasm for social engagement and advocacy of radical democratic politics, by the mid-1790s they reconfigured their magazine personae and now appeared as misanthropic old bachelors—skeptical of women, withdrawn from popular politics, and mocking of the striving of ordinary people. Such self-portrayals would have relieved the club of the taint of radicalism, but they also misrepresented most of the real-life Calliopeans, who collectively thrived as businessmen, professionals, and artisans in the city. These men embraced the emergent features of the new republic—an orientation to the marketplace, partisan politics, and a desire for normative marriage. In print they now seemed aloof from, and disdainful of, the hustle and bustle of urban life. Initially this defensive posture protected intellectuals; but it did not change as time passed and the perceived danger of political radicalism faded. Throughout the early nineteenth century, self-described intellectuals of all political stripes adopted self-characterizations suspicious of the general public and of mainstream taste.

The evolution of the Calliopeans' views of the public and of public participation demonstrates both the importance of oral and written performance and the ways such performances could be revised in profound ways over short periods, evoking quite new understandings of the public. The Calliopeans may have been long out of common school, but the elocution movement continued to shape how they made themselves into successful men. The activities of performing speech and writing for one another mirrored contemporary schoolbooks' emphasis on polishing one's rough edges by means of friendly yet critical mutual assistance. Emphasizing that the *New-York Magazine* had been edited by a "society of gentlemen" further underscored the significance of sociability, orality, and sensibility as the ties that bound the public together in shared feeling. When they shifted from seeing their club as "a nation in miniature" to believing it capable of fostering revolutionary democratic spirit, they indicated a new faith in the ties between sociable clubs, print, and the reading public in effecting a better public and political culture—and not incidentally displayed strong overlap between the club's actual proceedings and their representation in print. But faced with counterrevolutionary political conditions, the Calliopeans reframed their relation to the public. The "Drone" columns indicated that clubs were no longer vital to a properly constituted public sphere but were best suited to elaborating the complexities of a middling male subjectivity. Only in the guise of "old bachelors" and on the subjects of courtship and gender relations did they now pretend to serve as arbiters of public opinion; they protected the club's private affairs behind idiosyncratic print personae such as Mr. Martlet.

The anticlub bias faced by the Calliopeans did not last long; indeed, as Alexis de Tocqueville famously remarked, the early nineteenth century was singular for the outpouring of organizations and societies, few of which faced political criticism. "The Americans make associations to give entertainments, to found seminaries, to build inns, to construct churches, to diffuse books, to send missionaries to the antipodes; in this manner they found hospitals, prisons, and schools. If it is proposed to inculcate some truth or to foster some feeling by the encouragement of a great example, they form a society," he wrote wryly in *Democracy in America*. But as much as such interest-based groups believed they might improve society, they did not see themselves as so heterogeneous that they were "nations in miniature," nor did they pretend to represent Americans as a whole, even if they sought wide support. When they addressed the public in speech or print, representatives of nineteenth-century associations acknowledged that their members had come together owing to common backgrounds or single-minded reform aims, and they sought to persuade audiences of the importance of their concerns. As societies in the early nineteenth century became more prevalent, they began to reflect pervasive social divisions. As a result, we see with increasing frequency a growing tension in American public discourse during this era between the fantasy of social harmony and unity among the public, on the one hand, and on the other growing divides between divergent interests and social groups.

CHAPTER 5

Saint Franklin

JOURNEYMEN PRINTERS AND THE
MEDIUM OF DEMOCRATIC VIRTUE

Many men and women expressed their admiration of Benjamin Franklin after his death in 1790, but none were more vocally ardent than American journeymen printers. These men adopted Franklin as "the patron of our art" and sang out their appreciation in odes, addresses, and toasts. In a typical paean, Adoniram Chandler, a member of the New-York Typographical Society of journeymen printers, stated that Franklin was "sacred to the sons of freedom; a name unrivalled in the annals of our nation's glory: and while the land which gave its bearer birth, holds on its surface the faintest glimmerings of civilization, among the most conspicuous of its traits, let there be seen the name of Franklin."[1] Jefferson Clark, another journeyman, called him "the most rational of *all* philosophers. No individual ever possessed a more just understanding, or was so seldom obstructed in the use of it by indolence or authority."[2] These were by no means the most hyperbolic of these documents.

Closely following the analysis of the Calliopean Society, this chapter examines associations made up of men like Chandler and Clark: journeymen printers' societies ("typographical societies," as they called themselves) designed to help one another and assert their right to public respect. Claiming a close connection to Franklin helped them do so, for at the turn of the nineteenth century journeymen occupied a tenuous social position. Franklin's remarkable tale of upward mobility—hard work and self-education leading to mastery and social prominence—seemed to promise similar possibilities for men who now worked for wages under master artisans. It certainly helped the men claim the right to public respect. Yet by that time, even the most self-denying efforts only seldom allowed a journeyman to open his own shop; the percentage of those lucky enough to do so had been plummeting since the mid-eighteenth century.[3] This made it all the more important that journeymen publicly pronounce their intelligence and social value. Invoking Franklin's name became a cornerstone of journeymen's self-identification with print and the democratic connotations that accrued to it in the early nineteenth century.

Unlike the Calliopeans, who assumed the voices of the powerful men they hoped to become, journeymen struggled to distinguish themselves publicly as independent agents or as spokesmen for the public at large. They ultimately situated themselves in an ambiguous position between independence and deference to their masters, a characterization that appeared in both their celebratory orations and their battles over fair pay. On one hand, their societies mimicked Franklin in strongly tying the democratic nature of print to the person of the journeyman printer. In this iteration, the printer's daily work with the enlightening medium of print liberated and educated him as a free thinker, just as it had done for Franklin. Yet on the other hand, journeymen celebrated the harmonious craft workshop as a synecdoche for the public at large—a characterization fraught with difficulties. This resembled the Calliopeans' view of their club as a circle of rational debate and conversation, but it could not escape the hierarchy of the craft workshop, in which journeymen depended on the benevolence and goodwill of their masters. Even when journeymen acted as boosters for the domestic print trade—strongly mobilizing nationalistic rhetoric to tout American imprints—they found it necessary to identify so closely with their masters as united printers that it became difficult to launch campaigns *against* them for better wages. Such ambiguities imply that journeymen felt the need to articulate why they deserved full public participation and how much they desired it. Here we see more vividly than in previous chapters the potential fragility of such self-fashioning, particularly when a master was willing to dismiss them as mere laborers, as we shall see occurring during a prolonged labor dispute in Washington, DC, in the early 1830s.

Thus this chapter examines the typographical societies' public representations of themselves and their vision of an idealized American public that emerged in their various endeavors—from celebrating their "art" and promoting domestic print to protecting their wages, all of which required speechifying and publishing their ideas.[4] In some respects these articulations exemplify the artisan republicanism described by Sean Wilentz and others.[5] But journeymen printers also had a savvy and highly self-interested side. As they celebrated the medium of print, they identified themselves as its central agents; as they heralded the role of print in forwarding democracy, they characterized themselves as the most immediate beneficiaries of its enlightening power. Yet when faced with declining wages and poor jobs, they had trouble finding a successful mode of redress—since such conditions inhibited their chances of improving themselves and destroyed the idealized image of the harmonious workshop. Journeymen were not the only wage laborers who struggled to portray themselves as full members of the public—but their story illuminates the difficulties of others in that position.[6] Whereas the middling Calliopeans saw ample opportunities for personal advancement, workingmen more often found themselves defending an increasingly constricted way of life.

WAGE SETTING, MUTUAL REGULATION, AND THE RHETORIC OF MANLINESS

When a journeyman finally graduated from wage labor and established his own shop, he frequently sought to gain clients by announcing that he had come up via "regular" training—that is, up the ladder from apprentice to journeyman to master. In 1802, when Sydney Andrews publicized in the New York newspapers that he had "commenced the PRINTING BUSINESS," he appealed to potential customers by explaining that "having been regularly bred to the business in one of the first houses in this country, he trusts that he shall be able to give ample satisfaction."[7] To assert one's identity as a "regular" printer was to proclaim that one had gained the proper education necessary to produce fine work. But it also affirmed the custom inherent in the system and promised that the new master would uphold those rules with his own apprentices and journeymen.[8] These ideas about the relations between masters and employees became increasingly contested during the early nineteenth century. The societies' mutual regulation efforts—which constituted one important part of their overall goal—reflected the men's desire to depict themselves as the worthy partners of their masters, even at the expense of maintaining loyalty among journeymen.[9]

Journeymen printers' societies emerged for the first time in America as a result of wage disputes shortly after the Revolution, an era when the fluctuating economic conditions the industry faced were gradually changing the nature of the craft. For decades during the colonial era, master printers in larger cities had joined together to set uniform scales of wages—scales that ensured less competition over labor.[10] But the postwar depression was so profound that masters faced impossible economic dilemmas. "It is afflicting to think of selling my office, which at times, is productive, but the times are so solitary," wrote Philadelphia printer Robert Aitken to a New York colleague. "We have not 2 [pounds] of printing at present to do, it never was so since I knew any thing of the business. . . . Money is so scarce, we cannot even pay wages."[11] Other printers wrote to their peers in other cities offering to take on "the printing of a work or two" at rock-bottom rates.[12] At the height of the depression in 1786, Philadelphia masters proposed dropping wages from 45 to 35 shillings a week—a 22 percent pay decrease for laborers.

In response, journeymen printers initiated the first-known American labor walkout by forming a "combination" that successfully prevented the pay cut, guaranteeing that their pay would remain at the same level.[13] Flushed with success, they formed a journeymen printers' organization that lasted at least ten years; after it failed during the late 1790s, the even more vigilant Philadelphia Typographical Society arose in 1802, a group of approximately sixty members who had enough funds to hold monthly meetings in a rented room. Likewise, when New York's Franklin Typographical Society dissolved in 1804, it was replaced by the New-York Typographical Society, a group of about fifty men with an invigorated sense of purpose who met weekly at the home of David Reins, one of its directors.[14] Like the Calliopeans and so many other young men's groups, each typographical society took care to uphold strict rules for decorum and encouraged members to speak with propriety.[15]

Journeymen printers in Baltimore, Philadelphia, New York, Boston, and Albany developed their societies in close coordination, trying to uphold the "regular" apprentice-to-master route.[16] It was not an easy job, particularly since journeymen printers were highly itinerant, moving frequently in search of better pay, more secure positions, and ultimately opportunities to establish their own shops. The Philadelphia Typographical Society's records of new members, for example, show that just as many men were outsiders as had been born in the city; a significant minority of these had arrived from Europe or such remote American locales as North Carolina and Utica, New York.[17] Such "birds of passage," as the New-York Typographical Society termed them, included men who had run away from their apprenticeships to seek a fresh start in the city, as Franklin had done long before.[18] Certainly the itinerancy of journeymen could allow a man to find a new job with few questions about his past. Others did not bother to hide their lack of training but agreed to work as "half-way journeymen" or "two-thirders," that is, for only half or two-thirds the rate of a properly trained man.[19] Joining a typographical society signaled one's adherence—by pledge at least—to the orderly progression from apprentice to journeyman, thus granting the society a rare sense of control over the workforce.

Of course, monitoring men's status as regularly trained was only part of moderating labor conditions; typographical societies also fretted about an oversaturated market when large numbers of journeymen arrived looking for work. Societies frequently undertook a two-sided defense—discouraging new arrivals and the unscrupulous employment practices of masters alike. When a group of masters posted a notice in Philadelphia-area newspapers urging "SOBER young men" from the countryside to apply for work at "the highest prices," the Typographical Society paid for a counternotice immediately below it, disputing these claims (fig. 12). The society's headline, "TO PRINTERS," captured the two aspects of the advertisement. On the one hand, it advised young men to ignore the "*delusive*" promises made in the masters' advertisement, urging them not to "stray from their masters."[20] But the more aggressive—and barely cloaked—criticism focused on the masters who deluded those tempted by better wages. The society clearly felt these masters had abused the trust of their journeymen and deserved to be exposed.

In most circumstances, however, typographical societies combined firm insistence on fair wages with pronounced deference to masters in order to uphold a specific vision of their "mutual friendship." That is, they sustained the view that a moral economy dictated their relationship. In 1802 and 1803 the newly formed Philadelphia Typographical Society dedicated nearly one in every four meetings to wages or the treatment of its members. They "summoned" Robert Maxwell to appear "before the Directors to answer certain questions" about his employer, who had hired another journeyman to work below rate.[21] Likewise, in 1809 the newly formed New-York Typographical Society sent a letter directly to each of the city's master printers that broached the topic of setting a fair scale:

> Between employers and the employed there are mutual interests depending; mutual duties to be performed. To the end that these may result in harmony . . . we the journeymen printers of the City of New York, having duly and deliberately taken into consideration the present irregular state of the prices in many of the printing offices, and conceiving that they are inadequate to a comfortable subsistence, have united ourselves into an association for the purpose of regulating and establishing the same. The annexed List, framed with a due deference to justice and equability, is presented with a view that it may meet your approbation.[22]

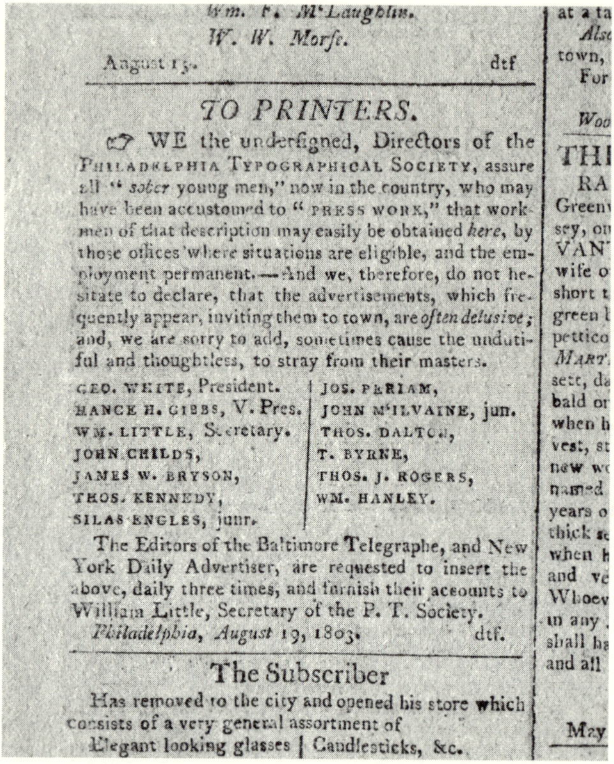

Wm. F. M'Laughlin.
W. W. Morse.
August 13. dtf

TO PRINTERS.

☞ WE the undersigned, Directors of the PHILADELPHIA TYPOGRAPHICAL SOCIETY, assure all "*sober* young men," now in the country, who may have been accustomed to "PRESS WORK," that workmen of that description may easily be obtained *here*, by those offices where situations are eligible, and the employment permanent.—And we, therefore, do not hesitate to declare, that the advertisements, which frequently appear, inviting them to town, are *often delusive*; and, we are sorry to add, sometimes cause the undutiful and thoughtless, to stray from their masters.

GEO. WHITE, President.
HANCE H. GIBBS, V. Pres.
WM. LITTLE, Secretary.
JOHN CHILDS,
JAMES W. BRYSON,
THOS. KENNEDY,
SILAS ENGLES, junr.
JOS. PERIAM,
JOHN M'ILVAINE, jun.
THOS. DALTON,
T. BYRNE,
THOS. J. ROGERS,
WM. HANLEY.

The Editors of the Baltimore Telegraphe, and New York Daily Advertiser, are requested to insert the above, daily three times, and furnish their accounts to William Little, Secretary of the P. T. Society.
Philadelphia, August 19, 1803. dtf.

The Subscriber
Has removed to the city and opened his store which consists of a very general assortment of
Elegant looking glasses | Candlesticks, &c.

FIGURE 12. A notice in the *Gazette of the United States* of August 1803 posted by the Philadelphia Typographical Society, complaining about an earlier advertisement by master printers advertising ready work in their offices. Courtesy of the American Antiquarian Society.

This carefully worded letter conveyed the journeymen's ideal relationship with their masters: collegial and moderate. It firmly laid out the journeymen's needs, but within the context of "mutual interests" and "mutual duties" between masters and workers. Its muscularity in claiming that low prices were "inadequate" was self-consciously paired with its courteous references to "a due deference to justice and equability" and the writers' desire for "approbation." In other words, even when journeymen were most exercised by a wage campaign, they preferred to represent their concerns as fundamentally the same as their masters.' As the Philadelphia Typographical Society put it in a letter to the city's employing printers, only with fair wages could they "act as men towards men. Indeed, we cherish a hope, that the time is not far distant, when the *employer* and the *employed* will vie with each other, the one, in *allowing* a competent salary, the other, in *deserving* it."[23] They did not constitute a "class" at odds with their "bosses," as later labor organizations would situate themselves; rather, they portrayed their interests as primarily harmonious and cordial.

The typographical societies' views of regular training and their handling of wage setting and other labor matters demonstrate contradictory views of themselves as members of the American public that contrasts with the figures examined in earlier chapters. Whereas schoolchildren or young men and women learned to portray themselves as independent civic actors, journeymen remained bound to the model of the harmonious craft workshop—an almost familial model they held up as an exemplar for the public as a whole, yet one that severely limited their potential independence. The long guild tradition that inspired adherence to the workshop model took hierarchy for granted: now that few journeymen advanced to the position of master, their idealized workplace restricted how far journeymen could reinterpret the relationship between masters and laborers, no matter how hard they tried. Thus they found themselves working at cross purposes in their wage-setting and celebratory activities. Heralding the democratic nature of print helped journeymen portray themselves as full participants in public culture—active, virtuous, and self-educated along the lines of Franklin. At the same time, however, they would not divorce themselves and their products from the hierarchy of "regular" training that signaled that a man had advanced up the ladder by improving his skills and meeting his obligations to superiors. Typographical societies thus set prerequisites for civic participation: using regular training as a metaphor for participation in a properly constituted public had clear limitations.

Journeymen may have had contradictory claims about their right to public participation in general, but in negotiations over the wage list they became prickly about the masters' language and rhetorical tone, for it signaled respect. More important, it illustrated the satisfaction journeymen might experience by impressing their masters with reasoned arguments and well-formed sentences. After receiving an initial written response from the masters regarding a wage list in 1809, the New York journeymen reported that they "disliked the stile of the note, which savoured much of despotism." But their subsequent meeting with the masters was far more gratifying: the masters had "met them with a frankness which was highly honorable to themselves, and pleasing to the committee." When the masters acceded to nearly all the specifics of the Typographical Society's wage requests, the journeymen determined to debate the remaining "small" matters among themselves in a long society meeting—which again the secretary described in terms of the journeymen's skills in reasoned discussion. "It would be impossible to follow the members in their arguments through the course of the debate that ensued, in which was displayed a spirit worthy [of] the cause in which we are engaged, and an eloquence that would have graced a senate house," he recorded.[24] Concluding these negotiations thus proved rewarding for the journeymen on two levels: they had arrived at a fitting set of wages after formally debating with their masters; and they had done so in a "stile" and with an "eloquence" that distinguished them as worthy—as men, workers, equals. In this regard, the societies' wage-setting negotiations let them portray themselves as worthy peers alongside their masters and articulate their vision of the journeymen's place in society.

By the 1810s, most of the East Coast–based typographical societies had settled into a long period of little conflict with employers. In fact, most of them now downplayed the wage-protection approach and emphasized instead a strong mutual affinity with their masters.[25] When they did engage in wage-setting work, they primarily sought to regulate the labor of fellow journeymen rather than complain that masters had broken from the scale of wages. In several cases typographical societies claimed they would join with the masters to promote the art of printing by purging the craft of the corruption of improperly trained employees. "To render an art respectable, it is indispensably necessary that its professors should be perfect masters of their calling; which can only be acquired by serving a proper apprenticeship," the New York group wrote in an appeal to local masters. In doing so, they pointed out that journeymen and masters shared the same goals—to prevent "the professors of this noble art" from "sinking in the estimation of the community."[26] When they claimed they shared their masters' vision of society, they represented themselves as aspiring to be on the same civic terms.

For a variety of reasons—desperation for paying work, ignorance of the scales, lack of interest in worker solidarity—hundreds of regularly trained journeymen simply opted to work below rate, infuriating those who faithfully adhered to society rules. In 1803 the Philadelphia Typographical Society noted with alarm that as many as seventy journeymen printers in city shops had disdained membership in the organization, undermining the group's ability to uphold their new scale. To resolve this problem, the organization met with representatives of nonmember journeymen and successfully earned their promise to "adopt such measures as they may deem proper for the general good and protection of the business."[27] Likewise, during its first two years, the newly formed New-York Typographical Society regularly chastised journeymen who worked for cut rates ("rats," as they would call them by 1816) in order to protect the fortunes of all members. When angry words failed, they tried guilt. In a circular letter to other East Coast typographical societies, they waxed eloquent: "There is nothing which acts more powerfully on the human mind than shame: It makes the coward bold; the miser generous; and it is to be hoped that it will ever deter a journeyman printer from conducting unworthily towards his brethren, where inate principle is wanting."[28] By 1811 the societies manifested so much concern about "rats" and "half-way journeymen" that those men became their primary object of scrutiny rather than the masters who defied the scale in hiring them. Such behavior, it seemed, flew in the face of the societies' desire to appear as men worthy of wholehearted public regard.

When they claimed that "rats" were to blame for degrading the collective value of their labor, they granted primary control over their fates to journeymen rather than to masters. The typographical societies' vigilance in policing one another largely reflected their belief that, to realize a harmonious work culture, it was journeymen rather than masters who required a firm hand. The Albany Typographical Society went so far as to blackball offenders and mail their names to each of the typographical societies throughout the country, arguing that "from self-interest or perverseness [they] endeavor to defeat the object" of the typographical societies.[29] Likewise, the Columbia Typographical Society in Washington, DC, grew more vigilant about regular training by requiring each new member to prove or pledge that he had completed a full apprenticeship. This society also required that each member carry his certificate of membership while at work or if he traveled out of town to work.[30] In short, the overwhelming tendency by typographical societies was not to do battle with masters over fair pay, but to browbeat fellow journeymen into adhering to the wage scales they had established. They thus created a culture that placed the onus on journeymen themselves for upholding wage scales—seldom consigning blame more broadly to changes in the industry that had progressively devalued their labor. Punitive to be sure, this vision of American society nevertheless put journeymen themselves in control of their futures.

Only on occasion did they make exceptions. After blackballing Stephen Dorion, the Albany Typographical Society sent a second circular letter withdrawing that charge, since on reviewing his case they recognized that

> he was among the first of those who refused to comply with the views of the employers and consequently lost his situation. He went to New York in pursuit of work but could not procure any. He returned again to this city and after sacrificing all his property, amounting to about $100, besides contracting a heavy debt for the support of his

family, with starvation staring him in the face, without the least hope or possibility of procuring any assistance from our society, and, from the conviction that "rats" in abundance could be procured to carry on the work of destruction, he chose rather to work at reduced wages than to become an inhabitant of a gaol or a poorhouse. Therefore we hope he may be exonerated from the odious appellation of "rat."[31]

Shut out from work after adhering to the Typographical Society's rules, Dorion had few options. Yet the society treated cases like his as instances of individual hardship rather than as representative of larger trends within the industry. During the 1810s and 1820s the typographical societies engaged in no broader discussion of labor questions in the printing industry, electing to continue demonizing "rats" and to forge stronger alliances with masters by asking them to abstain from hiring "irregular" men.

At the same time, the industry manifested changes that would eventually have profound effects on the labor within print shops. During the 1810s several masters began to experiment with stereotyping—casting creating permanent metal printing plates of a book's text from molds of set type. With these permanent plates, a book could be reprinted multiple times over decades without keeping the original type standing or resetting it. Moreover, unlike standing type, stereotype plates were easily stored. Although at first stereotyping was cost-effective only for the most popular, frequently reprinted books (Bibles and schoolbooks), this method saved time and the enormous cost of composing so that printers could produce frequent small editions of popular books. By the 1820s stereotypers even offered classical texts for sale to colleges and Latin grammar schools, texts that were far less popular than Bibles but that required care and expertise to set properly.[32] Technological changes such as these meant that some shops kept fewer men working in composition (typesetting), one of the skilled duties on the shop floor that offered better pay. The replacement of compositors with unskilled labor in some shops dealt a serious blow to journeymen's self-portrayal as worthy craftsmen with valued skills.

Their responses to new labor pressures was to use even stronger rhetoric distinguishing regular men from "rats" and to ascribe new masculine significance to the "education" apprentices received by serving their full term. Typographical societies wrote with mounting anxiety of the harm done to boys who abandoned their apprenticeships too early. In 1811 the New York society warned local masters in an alarmist vein: "Becoming the masters of their own conduct at a period of life, when they are incapable of governing their passions and propensities, they plunge headlong into every species of dissipation, and are often debilitated by debauchery and disease before they arrive to the state of manhood."[33] By stating that boys were "incapable" of manly self-control because of their youth, the society implied that fully trained journeymen were "men" by virtue of the double responsibilities to the craft and to their families. This statement also implicitly likened the journeymen's manly behavior to that of their masters, reflecting long-standing views of the value of regular training. "It was actually engaging in manly work that conferred masculinity on the apprentice," Ava Baron explains in a pathbreaking essay on gender and labor. "A boy's completion of an apprenticeship simultaneously symbolized passage into manhood and into skilled 'competent' worker status." Indeed, when journeymen made increasing use of such gendered language to demonize the "boys" and (later) women workers whose cheap labor posed a threat, they even more strongly asked their masters to consider them manly equals whose need for a "man's" wage made them peers. In later years journeymen went so far as to call rats "prostitutes."[34]

The connections journeymen forged with their masters extended even to society meetings, so much so that some journeymen worried about their organizations' integrity. By the 1810s and 1820s, most journeyman printers' societies included masters as voting members. Some were men who had managed to open their own shops and never suspended their memberships, who may have sought to sustain the ties of friendship and conviviality established during their formative years. Some, perhaps, also wanted to maintain access to the societies' mutual assistance programs, which pooled membership fees to aid sick members or widows and children. Other masters received honorary memberships as evidence of the goodwill between the two groups; some who were not members were invited to annual typographical society celebrations. For example, the Columbia Typographical Society invited fifteen prominent masters from the Washington, DC, area to their 1825 annual meeting. They also took care to list those names when they published accounts of the night's proceedings. In such circumstances, journeymen made a great show of speaking to their masters in highly deferential terms. When the Philadelphia Typographical Society offered an honorary membership to the prominent printer Mathew Carey, for example, they did so in an eloquent letter that left him in no doubt of their humble admiration as they expressed their "sense of gratitude for your unwearied exertions in promoting the interests of the professors of the *ars artium*." "Though [the honorary membership] should be of but little consequence to you," they added, "it is the only mode left us to pay respect where we think it due."[35]

But lasting harmony with masters proved elusive. The New York society eventually begrudged the influence of masters within the organization, and in 1815 they considered whether to prohibit those men from voting. That conflict, in combination with a proposal to cancel the memberships of all who had fallen behind in their dues, would have decimated the society's ranks, from 120 active members to only 19.[36] Two years later, when the society sought incorporation from the state of New York, the legislature granted it only on condition that they cease to act as a protective wage-setting organization and focus entirely on celebrations and mutual assistance. Bereft of a healthy membership and eager to protect funds dedicated to helping the sick, they agreed. "Truly, this is a mutual benefit society," they reasoned during the 1818 meeting announcing the change. "In supporting the true character of this institution we advance the cause of mankind, by raising up the light of improvement in its front, and chasing away the glittering appearances that dazling dance upon the surface of corruption."[37] If they retained their appreciation for eloquence, they had lost the potential to bare their teeth.

As we have seen, journeymen printers' relationship to masters reflected their hopes that they might become masters themselves, even in a grim labor market. Determining whether to portray themselves as dutiful subordinates or civic equals was a fraught question, as George Churchill indicated at the conclusion of his 1813 oration before the Albany Typographical Society. "Some of us will, doubtless, one day be called to the honorable, the important, the responsible task of conducting the Press," he said with evident reverence for his craft. But until that time, "my friends, however humble our situation in life—however unknown to fame—each of us possesses some degree of power to aid in the great work of ameliorating the condition of mankind."[38] Churchill's notion that journeymen had "some degree of power" nicely encapsulated their sense of ambivalence when they contrasted themselves with "honorable, the important" work of running one's own shop. Such statements are all the more poignant when we consider that printers were some of the most literate and, of course, frequently published workingmen; journeymen in other crafts experienced similar conflicts, even if they left behind few written memorials. In sum, journeymen printers' struggles to view themselves as integral to the public good were likely representative of journeymen at large—and demonstrate their constricting possibilities as the apprenticeship system deteriorated in the early republic.

Typographical societies did not dwell on such reminders, however, electing instead to allow journeymen to demonstrate mastery in other ways. In numerous speeches and publications that emerged from mutual-improvement activities and ceremonial events, journeymen demonstrated that they had mastered the educated voice and reasoned tones of full citizens—and were even more worthy of public participation because of their daily work with print.

SELF-IMPROVEMENT AND THE DEMOCRATIC MEDIUM OF PRINT

Journeymen in all the mechanical arts were given to making hyperbolic statements about the significance of their professions in toasts, celebratory orations, and parades. But unlike carpenters, tailors, or bakers, journeymen printers had the unprecedented advantage of ready access to print to proclaim the superiority of their product. In fact, they frequently called printing "the art preservative of all arts" or claimed that printing was "the source of knowledge," as did the New-York Typographical Society's membership certificate (fig. 13). Such boosterism for the print medium allowed printers to position themselves as parallel to their masters, who likewise undertook campaigns to puff and protect American publications in the early years of the nineteenth century. In devoting so many of their public writings to such declarations, typographical societies clearly sought to convey organizational goals far beyond mutual economic assistance and wage setting. As typographical societies dedicated themselves to self-improvement and to promoting American printing, they strongly resembled literary and debating societies like the Calliopeans.

The notion that printing was "the art preservative of all arts" emerged from a narrative that printers had embellished for generations in Europe and that had taken on a particularly patriotic tenor in the early United States. This story hit the same notes in virtually every retelling. In medieval times, they said, knowledge was controlled by only a few, leaving the vast population in "ignorance, barbarism, superstition, and bigotry," as George Churchill put it in an oration before the Albany Typographical Society.[39] With the invention of printing and the refinement of its technology by Faust, Gutenberg, and other key innovators, information began to spread in waves to larger and larger portions of the public, slowly "banish[ing] baleful superstition from the world" and replacing it with reason.[40] Print disseminated information about science, letters, and politics; and in describing this rising spread of knowledge, journeymen's speeches invariably waxed dramatic as they implied the largest effects of printing and knowledge. "By degrees, it inspired the human mind with new faculties—bid it penetrate

FIGURE 13. Membership certificate for the New-York Typographical Society, 1829. Note the forward movement depicted in the image: from the darkness and ignorance of the figures on the left to the triumphant arrival of Liberty on the right—via the light that literally emerges from the bed of the press. Courtesy of the New York Public Library.

through the thick veil of error and prejudice, and dare to think for itself," William Burdick told a group of Boston printers in 1802. "The rights and the happiness of our species began to be justly appreciated, and properly asserted."[41] With such a lead-in, listeners could anticipate the next chapter: the effect of print in America and the resulting rejection of monarchy and tyrannical authority as ordinary people gleaned new enlightenment and developed confidence in their own judgment. Journeymen orators traced the critical role of print and the work of brave, patriotic printers during the Revolution, then concluded with a crescendo of optimism and faith in future progress—liberally punctuated with exclamation points. On "this side of the Atlantic," Adoniram Chandler told the New-York Typographical Society, "people of all ranks enjoy the free privilege of discussion; where the reasoning faculties of every citizen are called into action; and the Press, unrestrained, forms the grand bulwark of our National Independence!"[42] Such speeches implied that democracy was so dependent on print that the creation of the United States was unthinkable without it. Ebenezer Mack's oration drew a direct connection between the triumph of print and the spread of common schools in America: "In every village—in every country town—and often amidst the dark wilderness, where culture has scarce lopped the branches of the pine to admit the light of heaven—we behold temples arising, dedicated to KNOWLEDGE."[43] The societies' illustrated membership certificates invariably placed the image of the press at the center, backlit to suggest its almost supernatural power in compelling the attention of the ignorant and enslaved, to reinforce the influence and authority of this technology (fig. 14).

By advancing the claim that print was integral to democracy, journeymen characterized themselves as the first beneficiaries of print's enlightening power. Print was, they argued, *the* democratic medium. By adopting this line as their own, journeymen printers allied themselves with their masters in a unified effort to promote print generally and, more specifically, to urge Americans to buy domestic publications. The strategy highlighted the stark differences between early nineteenth-century typographical societies and later labor organizations. Characterizing themselves as the future peers of their employers in this cause at least, in their writings and speeches journeymen printers upheld the same deferential relationship with their masters that they had cultivated during wage discussions. Their agency in promoting the "art of printing" helped to unify wage laborers and masters in the shared goal of forwarding their products.[44] Together, they sought to convince the public that print was the quintessential medium for fostering democracy.

Their printed speeches display journeymen's eagerness to be viewed as fully deserving of a public voice. Demonstrating their facility in mainstream styles of oratory indicated that the men possessed advanced forms of elocutionary knowledge required to compose and deliver such speeches. Indeed, in "Hymn: The Art of Printing," a member of Boston's Franklin Typographical Society referred to printing as *"the art of speaking to the eyes."*[45] Like the Fourth of July speeches they set in type, journeymen's orations touched on patriotic themes, most frequently by tying the art of printing to a tale of American progress. In this way printers sought to distinguish themselves from other "meer mechanics" by virtue of print's postrevolutionary

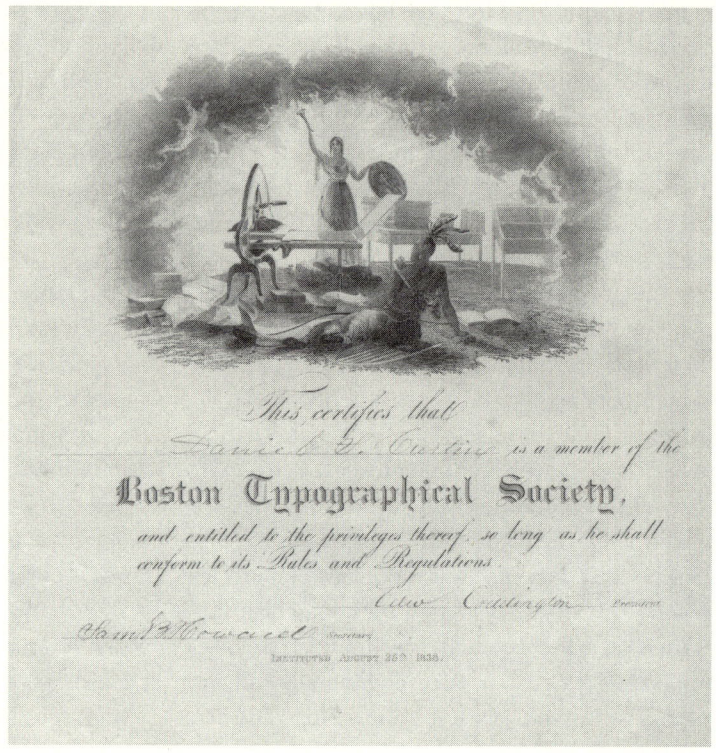

FIGURE 14. Membership certificate for the Boston Typographical Society. The majesty of the press is emphasized by backlighting it with glowing rays of light and a celebratory figure of Liberty, while the prostrate Indian can only look on with admiration from the darkness in front. Courtesy of Special Collections, Butler Library, Columbia University.

importance, as Stephen Botein has shown.[46] In addition, they referenced some of the most prominent political themes of the day. For example, when John Clough spoke before the Franklin Typographical Association in 1801, he dedicated much of the early part of his speech to commemorating Washington, who had died a year before.[47] George Asbridge's 1811 speech took a moment to decry the African slave trade, from which the United States had withdrawn three years earlier, even though his larger point was to lament Africans' "ignorance" owing to their lack of access to democratizing print materials.[48]

Adhering to widely shared styles of oratorical address and touching on familiar political themes granted the journeymen's speeches an air of self-conscious elegance and even authority in the public sphere. Nothing in the speeches suggested they did not already have the right to speak. Each speaker opened with modest disclaimers, purporting to be embarrassed about his lack of oratorical skills and hesitant to appear before a worthy audience, but they did so as conventional rhetorical maneuvering, not because as workingmen they felt inadequate to a public appearance. These rhetorical moves made journeymen's speeches appear more solidly mainstream, not less so.

Moreover, by arranging for their society's speeches to be printed—either in local periodicals or, more grandly and expensively, as stand-alone pamphlets—the men demonstrated skills in speechifying to a wide public audience. They found other ways of exhibiting their writerly polish as well. When the Philadelphia Typographical Society donated the hefty sum of $83.60 to help ailing fellows in New York after a yellow fever outbreak in 1803, the two societies exchanged self-consciously elegant letters acknowledging the gift and confirming the friendship between the groups.[49] "Those shall not fail of tasting the sweet cup of friendship, so amply filled by their brethren," the Franklin Society wrote with flourish to its Philadelphia fellows, who promptly copied entire correspondence into their records and published a notice of their generosity in *Poulson's American Daily Advertiser*.[50] In the careful wording of both their speeches and their published correspondence, journeymen demonstrated their mastery of public discursive conventions.

Such self-portrayals in print coexisted with the published proceedings of their societies' annual celebrations, which prominently featured the toasts and comic puns delivered. No matter how reverent and patriotic those toasts might be (or how lavishly they described the "elegant repast" they had eaten),[51] these depictions also proclaimed the men's status as workingmen and their alternately raucous and earnest enjoyment of one another's company. When they published John Clough's speech, for example, the Franklin Society appended to the pamphlet its list of toasts, about half of which were solemn, such as their "silent applause" for the fallen heroes of "Independence" or their toast to "The Press—May it be free as air, beneficial as light, and as congenial to Liberty, as sun-beams to vegetation." The other half played so liberally on the double meanings of printers' lingo as to evoke the smell of the taverns where the toasts were delivered, such as their toast to Franklin:

> To BENJAMIN FRANKLIN, the pride of our profession—
> His *heap* is *off*—his *balls* are *dry*,
> His *press* is *stript*—his *form* in *pye;*

His *case* within the *rack* is plac'd,
His *galley's warp'd*—his *frame unbrac'd;*
Yet shall the WORK he left behind,
Impress his worth on every mind;
While each his honor'd Image bears,
Grav'd on the Badge his bosom wears,
Shall cry, and press it to his heart,
Behold, "The Patron of our Art!"[52]

No matter how bizarre it might appear to celebrate Franklin by drawing out an elaborate description of his dead, decaying body ("his *press* is *stript*—his *form* in *pye*"), those puns only lent more boisterous pleasure to their half-serious intention of celebrating their "Art" as well as their fraternity. When they published accounts of the "hilarity and social glee [that] prevailed throughout the evening" on anniversary celebrations, they wanted newspaper readers to recognize that part of their hilarity was their enjoyment of wordplay—a pleasure derived from the nature of their everyday work with words and expression.[53] The New-York Typographical Society publicized that combination of puns and patriotism in an 1811 broadside after its anniversary events (fig. 15).

Together, their wordplay and celebratory tributes to print helped personify the American print industry as journeymen implicated themselves in the powerful patriotic narrative of the double ascendancy of print and democracy in America. The deep identification with their product that journeymen printers expressed in toast after toast was unusual among journeymen at large. By promising to emulate Franklin as the model printer-citizen, and by celebrating and encouraging one another's literary endeavors and skill with puns, journeymen printers aggressively represented themselves not just as fine workmen and artisans but as uniquely literate Americans who performed a labor vital to the sustenance of the republic.

Journeymen printers' careful self-representations in print reflected a deep consciousness that they needed skill in writing and speaking to appeal to the public as well as to their masters. The records of the New-York Typographical Society reveal this consciousness in detail. Throughout the 1810s the society fostered educational programs and offered rewards to members for improving their self-presentation. In 1811 they offered a medal (worth $10, they took pains to note) "to the person who will compose the best ode, on the art of printing, to be sung at the anniversary celebration," to be chosen by the members as a whole.[54] By 1813 the group determined that in addition to the annual oration delivered on the Fourth of July, each monthly meeting would feature an orator selected from the ranks, to improve members' skill

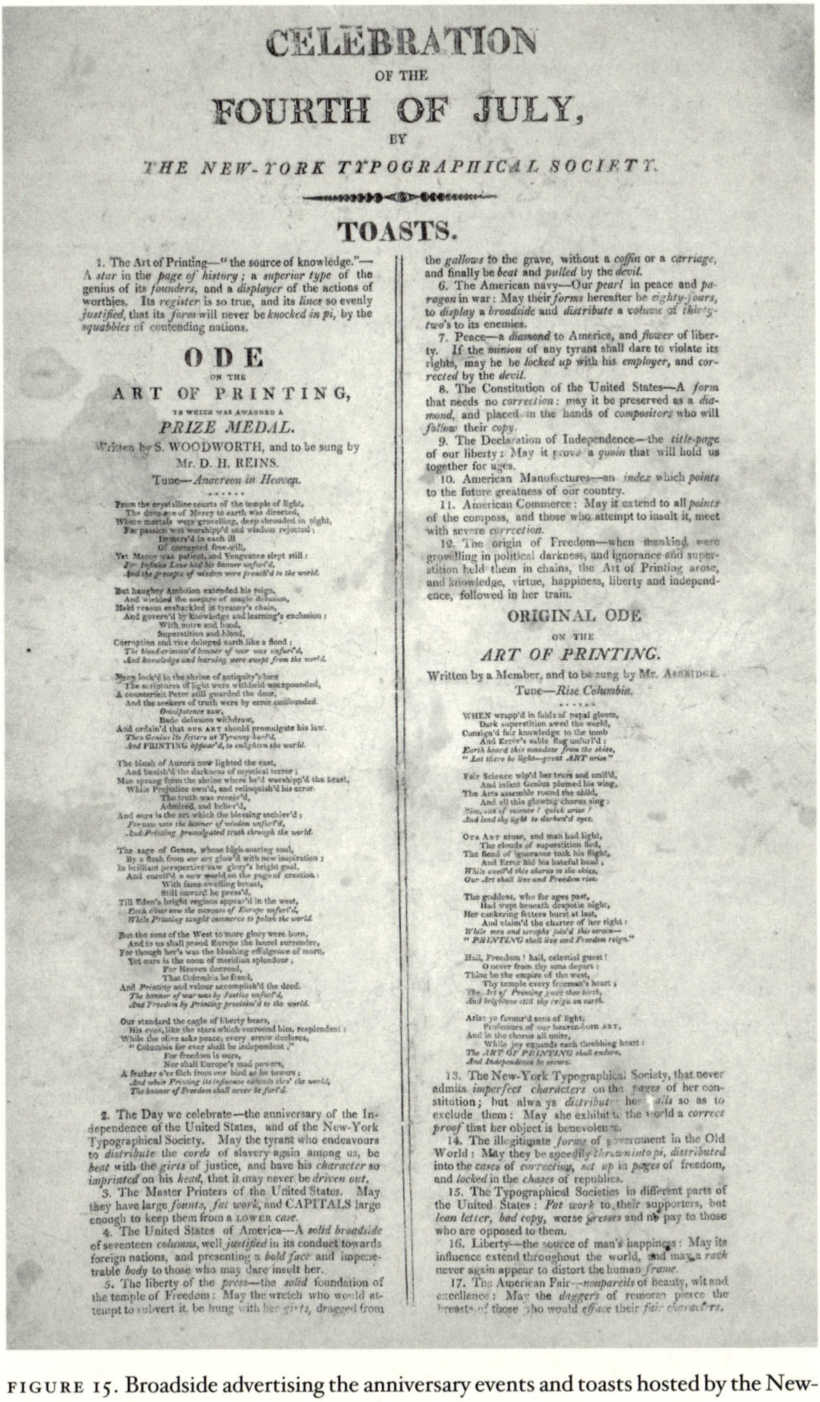

FIGURE 15. Broadside advertising the anniversary events and toasts hosted by the New-York Typographical Society, 1811, including two original odes on the "Art of Printing," one of which received the society's prize medal. Courtesy of the Library of Congress.

in public speaking. Moreover, "it would have a tendency both to edify and improve, and give a greater degree of interest and importance to this Society," the secretary explained in the meeting minutes.⁵⁵ Three years later its members formed a "Literary Club . . . for the encouragement of literature, and to promote an enquiry into the origin and progress of the Art of Printing, and to endeavor to make ourselves by mutual exertion more generally acquainted with the theoretical parts of that Science."⁵⁶ Efforts like these, which remained largely out of the public eye, show how the society's public assertions that its members were literate, knowledgeable men were backed up by systematic attempts at mutual improvement and education. Such efforts resembled those of master printers' groups such as Boston's Faustus Association, which formed a membership library and encouraged its members to present addresses at each meeting and speak on "any improvements which they may have discovered" that might "add to the neatness, facility, or profit of the trade"—most of which consisted of comparative reports on paper and ink quality.⁵⁷ For the most part these mutual education efforts anticipated similar programs during the 1810s and 1820s by mechanics' and apprentices' societies and resembled the ad hoc literary and debating societies that now dotted small towns and cities in the Northeast.⁵⁸

The purpose of these programs went beyond their benefit to individual journeymen; having well-spoken, knowledgeable members made typographical societies look good. Savvy in the twin importance of what Franklin identified as the *"reality"* of hard work and the "appearance" of it, printers took care to publish notices of society events because they displayed the right image to the public. Nothing could better illustrate the typographical societies' anxiety about public image than an 1810 case of plagiarism. A week after Joseph Gleason delivered the New-York Typographical Society's annual oration, the company announced that it was so pleased with the speech that it wanted to publish it, and it sent him a highly complimentary letter requesting the text. Like speakers in previous years, Gleason demurred in a finely worded letter that "begged to assure" the society that "their approval of the Address is sufficient to compensate me for the ardor of the undertaking, and the reluctancy with which I undertook the discharge of so important a duty."⁵⁹ Even though he claimed to have sent the manuscript to a brother out of state, the society proved so persistent that Gleason eventually submitted the text for publication. But within a week, owing to "a fortuitous circumstance, that may be ranked among the *marvelous*," the society discovered that it had been lifted directly from a published Harvard commencement speech and presented as Gleason's *"own* production." The society's outrage was palpable. With flourish, the officers announced that they would keep Gleason's manuscript with the society's official papers and record the full account of the plagiarism on the verso of the title page; in addition, they composed a letter to him expressing their "indignation . . . at the insult put upon the Society" and officially rescinded their earlier gratitude.[60]

Why was a plagiarized anniversary address so offensive to the membership? Because it eroded the men's ability to be recognized as writers and wordsmiths in their own right, quite apart from the labor they performed in bringing other people's words into print. In numerous published pieces throughout the early nineteenth century, they sought to end the comic and denigrating representations of journeymen as inveterate drunks, ignorant and otherwise in need of the master's firm hand—perhaps even drinking away their ambition, as in Franklin's characterization of British pressmen. The negative representations that appeared in print throughout the early republic picked up on long-standing views of the journeyman as not yet prepared for mastery. They also added new political valences. The *Boston Recorder* fretted in 1828 that an immoral, unprincipled, and intemperate journeyman printer "will be corrupting the sentiments of thousands around him, and undermining the foundations of our Republican institutions" by failing to bring important information to the public.[61] Such digs at journeymen may have fueled stereotypes, but the essay actually confirmed what typographical societies had emphasized for years: that the journeyman printer had more responsibility than journeymen in other lines of work owing to the special place print held in a republic. Societies understood that the depiction of journeymen as hard drinking and ill informed hurt the opportunities of all of them advance to the position of master.

Journeymen countered stereotypes by attempting to show the public how crucial was their role in polishing manuscripts for publication—and how talented they were with ideas and exposition. They particularly insisted that they had gained this knowledge on the job. They frequently inserted short pieces in magazines and newspapers reminding readers how often they corrected writers' spelling, grammar, lapses in logic, and even references in other languages. "By far the greater part of the errors which disgrace the productions of the modern press are *autorial* oversights," one journeyman wrote in 1807. "We journeymen printers (and few of us are *professed conjurers*) frequently need all the sagacity of an Oedipus, with the keen eyes of a Lynceus to decipher a writer's meaning."[62] With such highbrow classical references, the writer implied (and perhaps exaggerated) the kinds of literary knowledge an ordinary journeyman printer might draw on in his work. Nor was this passage unusual. Complaining of having to set type for a poorly written "Essay on the Influence of Kant's Philosophy," one journeyman-essayist described the author's unintelligible prose and ill-conceived logic. "The shade of Dido was not more unwelcome to Aeneas, or the apparition of Banquo to Macbeth," he wrote, thereby assuring his readers that few ideas went over his head. Even faced with such a task, within an hour he "had succeeded in reducing the metaphysical chaos to something like *'pure reason,' ex fumo dare lucem*" and had rewritten the piece so it made sense to an educated audience.[63] His point was clear: authors with fancy educational pedigrees had nothing on journeyman printers, educated on the job with an eye toward practical reason. He also slipped in a gratuitous reference to his knowledge of Latin, implying that many journeymen held such knowledge precisely for the purpose of editing and proofreading academic texts.[64]

The larger point of such published essays was not just to parade journeymen's knowledge but to display to the public how much a printer served as an intellectual medium for an author's ideas—a vital channel between author and the reading public. In fact, by insisting with such vehemence that most texts required significant editorial intervention, journeyman writers sometimes portrayed themselves in highly gendered and even sexual terms. "The printer it is who *consummates* the author's conceptions. The mechanic puts the finishing strokes to the finest dreams of the imagination," continued the journeyman who had polished the essay on Kant. Without the printer, "What a poor dreaming, fruitless, futile thing, is a wit. He is a soul without a body—a soldier, with 'lots of courage,' and no sword."[65] In no uncertain terms, this writer made a big claim on behalf of his fellow printers: not only were they possessed of high levels of knowledge and positioned as important mediators to the public, but these qualities made them manly, virile, potent figures.

Such overt assertions about the powerful role of journeymen printers were unusual; on the whole they preferred to serve as cheerleaders for the magic powers of print. But make no mistake: these public pronouncements were far from self-effacing. Each proclaimed in the same breath the value of the print medium and the self-taught knowledge and even eloquence of the journeyman printer. Consider the toasts that the Philadelphia Typographical Society decided to print after its 1824 anniversary dinner:

> By Mr. Adam Ramage—May we always *Press* on, but never feel oppression.
> By Mr. R. Ronaldson—The noble art of Printing—a *full case* of health, happiness and prosperity to all who are engaged in the profession.
> By a Guest—The Art of Printing—that healing Art, which has made the blind see, the dumb speak, and set millions of slaves free.[66]

Their claims about the "art preservative of all arts" aside, the hundreds of toasts that typographical societies printed during the early nineteenth century reminded readers that the print medium was manned by workers—virtuous, self-educated men who took their calling seriously. Such documents reinforced the instrumental role of the workforce responsible for reproducing the ideas of Washington, Franklin, and other American notables. They showed reading audiences again that printing those words depended on the honest labor of innumerable men who vitally intervened—either by faithfully reproducing Franklin's words or by smoothing out the rough sentences of a less-practiced writer. The typographical societies' celebration of print as a democratic medium drew attention not just to their products but to their labor.

The self-representation printers cultivated, then, sought to assert their right to belong to the center of the American public and declared them fully deserving participants in public culture. These publications demonstrate that they assumed their right to participation based as much on their self-education in oratory and written language, patriotism, and virtuous labor as on their vital role in transmitting public knowledge via printed materials. By reciting again and again the narrative of print's contribution to democracy, they reminded the reading public of their own role in that story and thereby reinforced claims to civic engagement. Using the figure of Franklin as a model for journeymen printers even allowed them to represent themselves as stand-ins for the American public—examples of self-taught, hardworking citizens who, like Franklin, demonstrated their political virtue through their very dedication to work, democracy, and self-improvement. Still, the aspirational nature of these claims implied that the printers were striving for inclusion, much more so than groups like the Calliopeans. And the journeymen's most confident self-characterizations proved even more difficult to uphold with the dual pressures of a rapidly changing economy during the 1820s and new tensions in the master-journeyman relationship, particularly when they were challenged outright.

DUFF GREEN AND THE DENIGRATION OF JOURNEYMEN PRINTERS

During its first fifteen years of existence, the Columbia Typographical Society faced not even a hint of labor strife in Washington, DC, and it dedicated virtually every one of its monthly meetings to reading minutes, distributing money to sick members or the families of the deceased, and planning for anniversary celebrations. Its members went out of their way to include masters in their public events and celebratory dinners. The one conflict in those years was a minor controversy about how much the society spent on its annual celebrations and expensive parade banners—money some felt should have gone toward supporting the ill or burying the dead.[67] On the whole, journeymen in this city seemed to have no reason to worry about their public position and labor status. This changed when Duff Green, a prominent master printer, announced a new plan that, the Typographical Society believed, would eliminate most journeymen's jobs and transform the small remainder into mere overseers for poorly trained cheap labor. Even worse, he promoted the plan by using the journeymen's own rhetoric against them, questioning whether they could truly claim to be virtuous, hardworking members of the public whose labor deserved protection. What resulted was a protracted struggle by the society to plead its case to the broader public so as to pressure Green into changing his mind. This challenge reveals with particular clarity the journeymen's views of themselves as workers and members of the public.

By 1834 Duff Green controlled a formidable operation at the *United States Telegraph*. He employed approximately seventy-five journeymen printers, a large number of women, and at least forty boys—an enormous operation comparable to only two other offices in the city. Its size was also exceptional in the nation at large, since District of Columbia printers gleaned lucrative work from the federal government. Green not only published the *Telegraph*, which had national distribution and was the organ of the Democratic Party in the district, but had recently been elected by Congress to serve as the official printer of the Senate and the House—an enormous job that could be taken on only by a print shop with a large staff and extensive equipment.[68]

Green was a controversial figure in the city. He was not a regular printer but represented a new kind of editor becoming more common during the era: a wealthy and educated man who had come to printing in midlife and managed, rather than emerged from, his ranks of pressmen. He had arrived in Washington in 1826 from Missouri, where by age thirty-five he had already been a schoolteacher, land speculator, lawyer, and member of both the Missouri House and Senate. Drawn to journalism and Democratic Party politics, he purchased the St. Louis *Enquirer* and edited it for two years. It did not take long for Green to become an important and vocal supporter of the Andrew Jackson wing of the party, which smoothed his way to Washington and into editing the *Telegraph*.[69] After Jackson's election, he won the coveted position of official printer to the government by 1829 and subsequently joined Jackson's "Kitchen Cabinet" of unofficial advisers. Far from being an acolyte of the president or the party, however, Green gradually came to oppose Jackson and by 1832 shifted the support of the *Telegraph* to John C. Calhoun's campaign for the presidency, a move that lost him an estimated one thousand newspaper subscribers. Even after Jackson's reelection, Green's public support of Calhoun's nullification ideas likely led to his losing the election for printer to the House in 1832, leading to an enormous loss of business.[70] Indeed, his support of nullification was so controversial that in 1832 a congressman brutally assaulted him with a walking stick in broad daylight on the street, breaking Green's arm, hip, and collarbone.[71] Despite his provocative political moves, Green made savvy economic decisions during his tenure as a printer in Washington. His many print jobs, particularly government contracts, brought in the bulk of his business income—estimated at $70,000 a year, comparable to nearly $1.5 million in 2007 dollars.[72]

Almost as soon as he had purchased the *Telegraph,* Green began a dogged campaign to bring down labor costs, which earned him a reputation as a dangerous maverick who disregarded "regular" custom as well as the wage scale. In 1828 he proposed to other masters in the city that Washington journeymen's wages were out of line with those in New York and Philadelphia, recommending that they join him in reducing weekly rates to $8 a week—a reduction of $1 to $2 depending on the time of year. His peers throughout the city rejected this attempt and questioned the truth of his claims of exorbitant pay, underscoring the unconventionality of his plan. Moreover, such a proposal was difficult and risky, since Green's cost-cutting measures unsettled the good relationship that the Columbia Typographical Society had sustained between employers and journeymen during its fifteen years.[73] Green quickly backed away from this proposal, but it was not the last time he would attempt to reduce wages; his boys and female employees would go on strike several times between 1829 and 1834, objecting that they received the brunt of Green's draconian efforts to slash wages. His aggressive moves to save money on labor costs became so infamous that rumors circulated in subsequent years about new schemes. In 1831 a rumor flew through East Coast newspapers that he had tried to replace some of his employees with English immigrants willing to work for wages far below scale. Although Green publicly dismissed the rumors as crude machinations by his political opposition, newspapermen like the editor of the *Pennsylvania Inquirer* found the idea particularly galling; asking whether "ENGLISH COMPOSITORS" would "do the PRINTING of the AMERICAN CONGRESS in a PROPER MANNER!"[74]

By 1834 Green ratcheted up his efforts to save on labor costs to a new level—and with new audacity. During the speechmaking at the anniversary dinner of the Columbia Typographical Society, at which he was an honorary guest, he announced a plan for what he called the "Washington Institute," a school where two hundred boys between eleven and fourteen would glean a dual education in academic topics and the practice of printing. In describing the school, Green drew together many of the most popular ideas of the day about education and pedagogy. The children would attend school for five hours daily, learning an array of advanced topics—French, Spanish, Latin, and Greek as well as natural and moral philosophy, rhetoric, history, algebra, mathematics, and geography; some would also study art and music. Each of these, he explained, were valuable accoutrements for a printer but would serve well a young citizen who sought work in any number of professions. Further, Green promised to install strict regulations forbidding bad language and lax behavior and assured the public that the school would refrain from assigning menial labor and corporal punishment "to protect [the students'] feelings."[75] It would operate according to a modified monitorial system, requiring older students to oversee and teach the younger ones, a method other cities had begun to use in public education for large numbers of (usually poor) students. In each of these aspects, Green sought to align his school with progressive educational methods of the day.

The crucial difference between the Washington Institute and a public school, however, was Green's insistence that the students' daily school attendance be sandwiched between two four-hour shifts of work in Green's printing office. Adopting a Franklinesque penchant for precise scheduling, Green explained that each student's school and work hours would be balanced out by the remaining eleven hours dedicated to "refreshment, recreation, and sleep." Unlike some other manual labor schools, the students at this one would earn wages for their labor (minus the cost of food, clothing, and lodging, which Green promised would be minimal) that would accrue in trust until each boy reached age twenty-one, for an estimated total of $728 (or nearly $14,000 in 2007 dollars). As much as Green touted the boys' fine education and practical knowledge, however, he insisted that the real benefit of the school would consist of its messages of self-reliance and character. The boy who learned to "educate, feed, and clothe himself" would develop "a lofty spirit of independence" and internalize "a proper sense of what is due to others" as well as to "his own honor and character."[76] That independence of mind, advanced education, and savings would allow each individual to pursue the career of his choice. Green waxed eloquent about the possibilities of boys' using this education to become doctors, lawyers, and diplomats—not necessarily journeymen printers.[77] It was, in sum, a school that Green believed would advance the public good.

His emphasis on "independence" was crucial to his plan and implied a serious criticism of current journeymen. Rather than discuss the money-saving prospects of replacing his journeymen with boys paid at minimal rates, he framed the Washington Institute as an answer to a serious problem inherent in the printing industry itself, with insidious implications for the public at large. "There is a radical disease in the press," Green asserted, "and he will be a public benefactor who contributes to its cure."[78] That "disease" consisted of political control of newspaper presses by moneyed interests. The expense of running a press required printers to rely on political parties for patronage, especially new masters who had just advanced from their days as wage-earning journeymen. As a result, he explained, wealthy men maintained a pernicious influence over the press, controlling the tenor and slant of much public information. "The press, in such hands, does not speak the language of the editor, but of an irresponsible cabal—by whom it is used, not for the purpose of enlightening public opinion, but for the advancement of their personal ends," he warned.[79] Moreover, he implied, this corruption stemmed from the long-standing practice of training boys along the regular apprentice-journeyman-master route. The hierarchical nature of labor advancement reinforced an unmanly deference and kept boys from gaining the education that would foster true independence. Green's depiction of a newspaper press under the influence of moneyed interests suggested that the very medium intended to secure democracy was so corrupted as to subvert freedom. Solving the press's problem required a revolution in its oversight, he said.

Inasmuch as Green described a "diseased" and corrupt press, his charges reaffirmed the central importance of print in a republic. Indeed, by the 1830s the notion that print was vital to the nation had become such a truism that claims of corruption appeared particularly alarming. Green questioned the idea that one of print's virtues was the labor of its hardworking craftsmen. In fact, he embraced the notion that self-made or wealthy men (like himself) unencumbered by the antiquated customs and hierarchies of the craft should run the printing trade. He evinced a strong distrust of the apprenticeship track and recommended replacing it with the morally neutral figure of the capitalist.

To portray himself as that "public benefactor" who would reinvigorate the press's democratic potential, Green altered the narrative of journeymen's Franklinesque progress. Whereas they had long represented themselves as uniquely well educated among artisans, Green played on stereotypes of wage workers as prone to drink and laziness, insisting that their lack of a formal education made them ignorant rubes, naturally dependent on their betters. Still more damning, he argued that "regular" journeymen were fundamentally unfit to direct newspapers. Only proper schooling, Green insisted, gave men the "intelligence to *think* for themselves." After singing the praises of truly independent men, he asked suggestively, "What would be the condition of the public mind, if the press of the United States was under the guidance of such men now?"[80]

Apparently fearless of charges of hypocrisy, Green followed up his accusations of corruption by seeking wealthy backers to establish the Institute. In March 1834 he published a "Prospectus" for the school to draw in approximately two hundred subscribers who together would provide $30,000 to get the Institute afloat; he proposed to put up the total value of his press and real estate holdings as collateral.[81] He promised to repay these loans once the school was operational because, as he implied from his estimates, he would save enormously in labor costs with this new force of "students." Whereas journeymen made between $9 and $15 a week, his students' food and lodging would cost him only $4, while they gave him eight hours of labor a day. The savings—an estimated $15,600 annually—would be used, he insisted somewhat improbably, for teachers' salaries. He did not discuss the number of journeymen he would replace with boys.

Listening to this proposal described at their own annual meeting, the members of the Columbia Typographical Society were appalled but declined to react publicly. Their hesitancy did not stem from controversy within their ranks about the value of Green's school, since they universally agreed that it would severely harm journeymen's labor. With a strong sense of outrage, they noted in their record book that Green "did declare that he intended to monopolize all the work that was possible" and that children would "take the place of the journeymen now employed by him." They described the plan as "visionary in its final results, subversive of our rights as journeymen printers, and destructive of the profession to which we belong"; in a subsequent special meeting they resolved to reject his ideas: "We have a right, as men, to participate in [the] profits" and to "preserve the respectability of the profession."[82] But after some consideration of the problem, they elected to work in private "to convince Mr. Green of the deep injury which [would] result to us" if the Institute should open. Instead, they confined their strong words to society meetings.

Why did the Typographical Society not react with public outrage to a plan its members saw as "subversive of our rights as journeymen printers"?[83] It appears that they rejected a public campaign against the Institute because they could not imagine Green might succeed. Not only did they see themselves as integral to the profession and possessing essentially the same interests as their masters, they believed their employers would protect their jobs and uphold the harmonious relationship between master and journeyman. As they explained it in a letter to Green in April 1834, they were "well assured that their own interests and those of the employing printers are inseparable; that whatever injures the one, must ultimately reach the other; and, under the influence of this conviction, they would be slow to sunder the band of union which unites them."[84] This statement suggests further that they expected their masters to block the school's opening. Thus, although the society clearly recognized the dangerous implications of Green's plan, it still believed that its goals and Green's could be reconciled. It saw Green's idea less as a battle between employers and employed than as an outrageous proposal, so threatening to the craft of printing that it would surely be nipped in the bud.

Green's publication of a prospectus for the school two months later, however, signaled the failure of the society's behind-the-scenes efforts to change his mind. In the wake of the pamphlet's appearance, the society began to correspond with him to reiterate the need for "mutual good feelings" between journeymen and employing printers while also strongly objecting to the school. Even though Green doubtless *"intended"* no "encroachment upon the rights or interests" of the society, they explained with exaggerated generosity, the school "certainly will . . . subvert our interests and annihilate our rights as effectually as any scheme which the imagination of man could have devised. Is it not enough to say . . . that the operation of this school *entirely excludes the journeyman from employment?* At a single blow, his occupation is gone!"[85] The letter begged Green to reconsider his plan in light of the society's firm opposition.

In response, Green willfully misinterpreted their concerns in a manner that allowed him to allege again that shadowy interests controlled the actions of workingmen. Rather than address the issue of the school's "students" usurping journeymen's jobs, he reassured the society that *graduates* of the Institute would likely find other vocations rather than competing with regular journeymen printers. Having avoided the initial question, he concluded the letter with the declaration that his aims were so consonant with those of the society that any opposition to his school must originate from "the malevolence of an individual" seeking to manipulate journeymen. "I apprehend your fears have been unnecessarily excited by those who have sinister objects," he stated, employing the sleight-of-hand he had mastered as an author of political attacks.[86] Moreover, if a malevolent conspirator was not behind it, he suggested, the opposition must result from the journeymen's ignorance and inability to see the widespread benefits to all "disciples of Faust." By declining to answer the society's queries (much less offer reassurance), Green's letter only intensified the acrimony. Finally, with especially terse language, he threatened that should they mobilize a strike, he would sue.[87]

With an almost audible sigh of resignation, the society's final publicly printed letter made a great show of abandoning its earlier cordial tone. Again, the wording showed the printers' eagerness to be seen by the reading public as worthy, reasonable men faced with an impossible dilemma. In place of collegiality, they employed a stern yet high-minded firmness that remained focused on the issues at hand—a presentation certainly intended to undermine Green's portrayal by displaying their clearheaded intelligence. "It is certainly with feelings of surprise and regret" that they realized that Green should "hold us so lightly" as to charge their characters with "weakness" and "ignorance," they wrote. "We are not instigated in this inquiry by any one of 'sinister' or 'malevolent' intentions . . . but are acting from the impulse of our own deliberate convictions, after calm and patient investigation."[88] With frequent references to such "calm" and learned understanding of the situation, the society's letter refuted each justification for supporting Green's school and demonstrated that the journeymen would not "listen for a moment to the voice of 'malevolence.'" By representing themselves as both judicious and even-tempered, the journeymen indicated that their letter had a broader audience than Green alone: they had begun to anticipate appeals to the public at large.

Foiled in its attempt "to convince Mr. Green of the deep injury" he might inflict upon journeymen, the society determined by June 1834 that it was time to go public. At that month's meeting members fretted about rumors that Green's prospectus had already gained subscription funds and the support of orphan asylums in cities to the north that, it was said, appeared likely to provide eager students.[89] To quell this support for Green, the journeymen agreed to publish an exposé of the Washington Institute's darker purposes together with copies of all the Columbia Typographical Society's correspondence with him, believing this would persuade the public of Green's greed. In the months to come, the journeymen and Green published numerous "protests," "replies," "addresses to the people of the United States," and newspaper editorials as they battled for public opinion over "improving" or "protecting" the democratic nature of the public print media.[90]

Green's most potent arguments to the public characterized journeymen as corruptors of democracy and touted his Institute as democracy's protector. He soon took to inserting into the *Telegraph* letters to the editor from supporters that did his work for him.[91] "It does appear, as if you were determined to wield the press for the benefit of man, to its utmost power," wrote "K." in a September issue of the *Telegraph*. Striking a firm tone, K. termed the journeymen's objections mere "selfishness." "The argument used, is that it will 'cheapen wages,' if so is it not an important concern to the *people*, that your institution should be sustained, because, it will render *books, pamphlets,* and *newspapers, cheaper*—and is not the *general good paramount* to all other considerations?"[92] Above all, K. argued in a subsequent letter, Green's school would benefit *"the general welfare,"* and since "the public good is a pervading and paramount principle," journeymen should abandon their self-interestedness to uphold it.[93]

Journeymen had a different view of the problem and of the best means of protecting the public good. When they addressed "the public," they also spoke directly to other masters in the city. In their formal "Address to the People of the United States," they warned their readers in stirring, patriotic prose that the Institute threatened "the freedom of the people" as well as "the liberty of the press." Although they would suffer the immediate consequences of Green's plan, they insisted that it would injure "the whole community," for it would provide Green with "an entire monopoly of the business" in the capital city, allowing him to outbid other employers on contracts. This might force other printers to establish identical schools to compete. "Had we been satisfied that his motive in establishing this school was either patriotic or philanthropic, not one opposing word would have escaped our lips," they insisted. "But we cannot shut our eyes to the fact, that this institution calls for no personal or pecuniary sacrifice" but would actually enhance Green's already considerable wealth and influence. Owing to Green's duplicity, the Typographical Society returned several times in its "Address" to the true freedom of the press and the protection of democracy. "Next to liberty, we value the profession which we have adopted; and we shall do our best endeavors to maintain it in its purity and in its freedom. Never, we hope, will it be under the control of any *one* man, however great and wealthy he may be," they claimed, hoping to contradict Green's self-portrayal in the *Telegraph*.[94] Referring to themselves as "American citizens" and appealing to a broad public of the same, the journeymen hoped to persuade readers of Green's perfidy.

Yet if their talk of "liberty" and citizenship represented them as independent and clearheaded, they also reiterated their long-standing reliance on their masters by the end of their "Address," which they concluded with a special appeal. They specifically requested their masters' help in protecting their rights as laborers—a move that pictured them as requiring defense. "We call upon you as printers, as freemen, to rally round the shield of our liberties, to protect it in its *republican* form, its PURITY, its PRIVILEGES," they stated. "The Rubicon is passed, and we now proceed to the object we have in view—to protect our rights.... To you we look for an approval, and friendly co-operation in our exertions in resisting the encroachments of power."[95] The Columbia Typographical Society used such words to show that it viewed Green's attempts as highly exceptional, not indicative of broader, insidious changes within the industry or requiring a new form of organized labor designed to confront them. Thus, even when they claimed to be independent, journeymen printers situated themselves in a dependent position when they directly addressed their masters.

Ironically, this organization so dedicated to promoting print as the most American and democratic medium ultimately determined that its publications had failed to rouse adequate public objection to Green's Institute plans and that striking was the only solution. The Typographical Society concluded that allowing the public to decide the matter left too much to chance. Just before the United States Senate sat down to elect a printer for the year, the journeymen in Green's office turned out—a move that proved far more effective than their months-long war of words. Likely fearing that this news would ruin his chances at his lucrative government contract, Green relented. Promising to abandon all plans for the Washington Institute and to avoid firing the strikers or seeking legal action against them, he got reelected for the Senate printing job. The Columbia Typographical Society could take pride in having eliminated the greatest threat to journeymen's livelihood that they had yet encountered.

But even with the Washington Institute permanently behind them, Green's journeymen faced a series of ever more acrimonious labor battles throughout 1835. As William Pretzer has shown, Green hired a pair of draconian overseers whose harsh new rules produced a strike; even when the conflict was resolved, he refused to hire back the strikers. He subsequently attempted to replace a group of compositors with "two-thirders"; and when the Typographical Society announced another strike against Green's office, he hired approximately fifty men and boys from out of town. By this time the society's public lists of "rats" were insufficient to calm its members' anger at being replaced. Numerous public fights and riots took place in the streets and taverns near the *Telegraph* office during May and June 1835 between "regular" journeymen and the "rats" who had replaced them; some journeymen even threatened to attack the newspaper office directly, though this never took place.[96] And though Green lost the next election for Senate printer (a shift that forced him to abandon editorial control of the *Telegraph* and eventually to sell it), the society's members were threatened with prosecution and its leaders were arrested.[97] Clearly, resolving the Washington Institute matter could not return the Columbia Typographical Society to its earlier state of contentment.

The Washington Institute controversy reveals the shortcomings of the typographical societies' attempts to portray themselves as inheritors of Benjamin Franklin's legacy of honorable work and self-education. They retained such a fundamental connection to master printers that their claims to independent civic status appeared stretched. Even when many of the employing printers in the District of Columbia disapproved of Duff Green's actions, they left it to the Typographical Society to resolve those matters on its own. By the 1830s, Green's plans for the Washington Institute were only the tip of the iceberg of difficulties facing wage laborers. Employing printers in all cities increasingly sought to circumvent pay scales and the customary rules for working conditions, flying in the face of journeymen's ideals of mutual responsibility and harmony with their masters.

Despite it all, journeymen printers continued to present themselves, as they long had, as citizens essential to the nation as a whole; indeed, it is striking that they retained the same vision so completely. In 1836, shortly after the resolution of labor struggles in Green's office, the Columbia Typographical Society hosted a national convention of journeymen printers to establish a National Typographical Society, an organization intended to be more vigilant than the local societies. They suggested new rules to buttress wage rates and strengthen the apprentice system; moreover, they proposed that all local societies recognize only two classes of printers: masters and journeymen. Like earlier groups, they specifically targeted masters as their primary audience. The printed conference proceedings contained an "Address to the Printers throughout the United States" that explained the main difference between the national society and earlier typographical societies: the national society would dedicate more time to the outright protection of journeymen's jobs. "The property of the working man consists in the knowledge of his calling, and any infringement of that *right* is at once subversive of all civil institutions," they explained.[98] Still, the new typographical society reiterated the long-standing view that the interests of employer and employed were fully commensurate. The real enemies of the press were "speculators and partisans," men (like Green) whose actions "corrupt the morals of the community, and destroy our free institutions." Such a self-portrayal allowed printers to depict American society as knit together by harmonious ties between employers and workers, ties requiring mutual responsibility. That typographical societies dedicated only a relatively small portion of their time to direct negotiations with masters over wages reflects their view that harmony was more important.

In each of these ways—developing wage scales and policing labor, celebrating their "art," and battling with Duff Green—journeymen printers advanced their causes by asserting their value to the public: they claimed to be more than mere laborers, men whose skill, knowledge, and access to print made them essential figures in the republic. Yet journeymen found it difficult to reconcile their craft pride with their claims of manly independence. They might participate in their masters' artisan republicanism and liken themselves to Benjamin Franklin, representing themselves as crucial figures to the nation; their voluminous writings and speeches imagined an ideal public sphere in which laborers and employers felt mutual respect. But the very apprentice system that they so frequently defended still characterized them as dependents in a hierarchical society rather than as independent men worthy of public regard rather than protection. Indeed, their position was so tenuous that Green felt free to dismiss it—and faced little public reaction when he did.

Comparisons are valuable at this juncture, for yet again this chapter displays not just how a group might articulate its public worth, but a particular vision of the American public as a whole. Like the Calliopeans, journeymen printers wanted to use a confident style of self-representation that characterized them as fully engaged members of the public rather than as a counterpublic requesting acceptance or approbation. By depicting themselves as central to the public good, journeymen evoked an expansive, inclusive version of the public akin to the harmonious craft workshop that they celebrated. And even more vividly than the female orators and the Calliopeans, the case of the journeymen demonstrates how fragile such a self-characterization might be when challenged. Moreover, although journeymen printers were hardly representative of workingmen as a whole, their conflicts between loyalty to craft and touting themselves as independent likely resembled those faced by journeymen of all kinds. In fact, journeymen were only a small portion of the many nonelites in the 1820s and 1830s to debate conditions for public participation. During those decades contests over the definition of the public, control of public opinion, and the role of the nation's print and oral media would emerge at the forefront of political discourse—leading to radically altered visions of public participation.

CHAPTER 6

"Who's Afraid" of Frances Wright?
MEDIA DEBATES ABOUT THE
PUBLIC AND ITS SPOKESMEN

"I won't let Miss Wright alone, though you recommend it—who's afraid?" wrote "Q. in a Corner" in a letter to the editor of the *New York Statesman* after he attended one of Frances Wright's lectures at New York's Masonic Hall.[1] Q. assumed the persona of one who easily swallowed Wright's radical messages about women's place in society, education for the working classes, and the stifling effects of the Christian church on American society and culture. "I do pronounce her a great woman; and what's more, I like her doctrines, although I can't say that I exactly understand them." The *Statesman*'s editor introduced this letter by announcing to his readers, "The writer has adopted a proper mode of treating a subject, which is too ludicrous for grave argument, and too visionary to require serious opposition." Despite asserting that Wright deserved only mockery, this editor and dozens of others relentlessly attacked her with ad hominem insults, declaring angrily that she was "no woman," "masculine," and "a female monster."[2] Taken together, they represent a widespread effort by editors across the East Coast to ridicule and dismiss her and to curtail public attendance at her lectures during 1829, when she first appeared as a public speaker.

This mockery of Wright only accelerated after she left the stage in 1830—and the most exaggerated statements about her have become famous on their own. Almira Phelps, the principal of the Troy Female Seminary, argued in 1833 that Wright and her intellectual twin, Mary Wollstonecraft, had "thrown off the female character, and deserve no longer to be recognized as women; they are monsters, a kind of lusus naturae, who have amused the world to the great injury of that sex whom they have pretended to defend."[3] Indeed, by the early 1830s the very term "Fanny Wright" emerged as an epithet hurled at social reformers of all stripes, especially female reformers, as Lori Ginzberg has shown.[4] Such hyperbole led historians to assume that Wright was vilified for breaking an unspoken law of the 1820s: that women must not speak in public, particularly before "promiscuous," or mixed-sex, audiences.[5] In other words, the strongly gendered elements of antebellum criticism have continued to set the terms for historians' understandings of the furor over Wright's speeches. Yet as the following close examination of her lectures will show, not only was there no preexisting restriction on women's public speech, but most contemporaries only gradually came to attack her by focusing on her sex and asserting the impropriety of a woman's speaking in public.

Concentrating less on Wright herself as a controversial figure allows us to see that gender has cloaked the crucial conflict of the debate: the makeup of the public and the proper means of forming public opinion. When the *Statesman*'s editor declared Wright's social reform topics "too ludicrous for grave argument" and Q. announced that he found Wright to be "a great woman" even though he couldn't "exactly understand" her ideas, together they criticized both the *kind of argument* and the *kind of auditor* that came together in lecture halls. In doing so, newspapers puffed themselves when they addressed their readers as exemplars of an educated, rational public; they portrayed the dissemination of information through print as the appropriate means of producing considered public opinion. They also anchored class differences to the two mediums: crowd images filled their reports, alternately mocking and expressing distaste for the "throng" of bodies crowding into lecture halls.[6] In sum, the intense focus on Wright's gender came to stand in for, and ultimately to obscure, this debate over the nature of American society and legitimate public opinion. Thus, with this chapter we come full circle: to see how contentious and fraught was the definition of the American public, illustrated here by the battle between Wright' oratory and the editors' printed opinion.

This chapter follows up the previous case studies of editorial practices by the Calliopeans and print battles between the journeymen and Duff Green. As in those cases, the editors who criticized Wright used gendered topics and language to assert their authority. Newspaper editors in particular had much to gain in this era of increasing competition between papers. By addressing their readers as if they shared a sensibility superior to that of the "throng" that attended public lectures, editors sought an intimacy with them, potentially adding to their papers' readership. Even in these years before the advent of the penny press, newspaper editors innovated with new rhetorical forms to garner loyal readers and place themselves at the center of public opinion making.

Focusing on the topic of creating a public in the Wright case allows us to examine the gendered components of the debate in a new light. I argue that the dialectic between new thinking about the press and the public, on the one hand, and the press's increasingly rigid view of women in public on the other produced new gender norms.[7] Though efforts to dampen Wright's popularity were largely unsuccessful during 1829 the demonizing view of her as an ugly, boorish, masculine figure was nearly universal in the years after she had left the United States. This transformation was so complete that by the mid-1830s, when female abolitionists and reformers began delivering public addresses, they were attacked as "Fanny Wrightists" simply for engaging in oratory. This chapter repositions gender and grotesque images of Frances Wright as only one aspect of a complex debate about appropriate modes of public interaction between speakers, writers, and their reading and listening audiences.

AMERICAN FANTASIES AND VISIONS OF REFORM

Frances Wright's vision of the United States changed radically between 1818, when she first arrived, and 1828, when she delivered her first public lectures in Cincinnati and other midwestern cities. Inspired by the liberal Scottish intellectuals among whom she had come of age, Wright initially believed America was an egalitarian, republican haven, "a country consecrated to freedom," as she remembered later.[8] By the mid-1820s, deeply disappointed by Americans' lack of interest in her plans for changing the status quo, she determined to embark on a lecture tour to persuade the public to reinvigorate political reform and public engagement.

Wright's education encouraged her scholarship and her freethinking inclinations. Orphans raised by a series of relatives throughout Britain, Wright and her younger sister, Camilla, moved to Glasgow in 1813 to live with a great-uncle who taught moral philosophy at the university. There, at age eighteen, she joined a group of male and female intellectuals and reformers to discuss philosophy, literature, and social reform. Sympathetic to the original principles of the French Revolution, these philosophic radicals also denounced the slave trade and the exploitation of the working classes.[9] Wright's intellectual aspirations flourished in this environment: she wrote poetry, several plays, and a treatise on Epicurean philosophy. When she was twenty-three, she and her sister completed their educations by traveling not on a grand tour of Europe, as was common for wealthy youths of the era, but to the United States.

As she later explained the experience, she "seemed to hear and see [the] declaration of independence every where" in the United States—to a large degree, perhaps, because she was so disillusioned with the corruption of British politics.[10] In a series of self-consciously literary letters that she published as *Views of Society and Manners in America* (1821), she marveled at what she perceived to be the unique political engagement of all Americans. She painted a romantic portrait of democracy in America and particularly noted the high level of knowledge among the populace. "I have never yet conversed with the man who could not inform you upon any fact regarding the past history and existing institutions of his nation," she wrote admiringly.[11] Her criticism of British society and politics doubtless fostered her appreciation for the Americans, although, as Gail Bederman has noted, hers was an "anachronistic, 1790s version of Anglo-American republicanism" rather than a clearheaded assessment of 1820s American society.[12]

Her optimism was transformed on her second visit to the United States, when she began to recognize how much Americans took for granted the institution of slavery. Yet Wright maintained her essential faith in Americans as enlightened republicans. Slavery, she believed, was merely a vestige of the nation's British colonial past; Americans would cast it off when they could afford to.[13] In 1825 she formulated a plan to gradually abolish slavery and colonize the freed slaves using state-run farms, where enslaved men and women would work until they had accrued enough in "wages" to pay for their emancipation and colonization.[14] For her, the genius of this plan lay in its economic efficiency; slavery could be abolished and universal colonization achieved through such self-supporting farms. She was so confident of the plan that, when she received only lukewarm support from national leaders, she attempted it on her own. She established a model farm outside Memphis that she called Nashoba, using about a quarter of her small inherited fortune.

The project quickly failed, largely for economic reasons. Not only had Wright sorely miscalculated the project's expenses, but slaveholders were unwilling to sell her slaves at the rock-bottom price of $50 each, making it impossible to conceive of finding the funds for colonizing them in Liberia or Haiti. In addition, no financial backers stepped forward to assist with the plan. Within a few months conditions at Nashoba deteriorated as overseers began to enact grimly punitive measures to get more labor out of the slaves. To make matters worse, in her absence an overseer allowed his journal to be published in Baltimore's *Genius of Universal Emancipation*, describing the draconian punishments and a permissive sexual environment between blacks and whites—thus losing public sympathy and support. One correspondent to the paper called Nashoba "one great brothel" and asked, "Who can read without disgust, that an accomplished young English woman . . . [apparently gave] sanction to the formation of illicit sexual connections, without the obligations of marriage!"[15]

Disinclined to admit failure, Wright now altered her interpretation of America's social problems. The nation was not full of "citizen philosophers" but was controlled by entrenched pro-slavery, antiegalitarian interests.[16] She published an essay in the *Genius of Universal Emancipation* that encapsulated these new expansive and radical social views on segregation, organized religion, interracial sex, and marriage.[17] In it she wrote hopefully of the effects of interracial union on American attitudes toward racial equality—stunning her readers and associating her community with the taint of miscegenation. Going further, she condemned the effects of industrialization on workers and rejected marriage as destructive of women's individual rights.[18] Shortly after its publication and the subsequent collapse of Nashoba, some editors began to refer scornfully to Wright's radicalism in the newspaper and periodical press, since it seemed to smack of sexual libertinism. She especially raised editors' eyebrows when she moved to the utopian community at New Harmony to join Robert Owen's son, Robert Dale Owen, as coeditor of the free-thought *New Harmony Gazette*. At least one eastern newspaper reported this move, unsubtly suggesting that theirs was a sexual liaison. "Whether 'for better or worse,' 'until death do part them,' or whether it be mere platonic association, to be dissolved when no longer convenient or agreeable, is more than we can say," wrote the editor of the New York *Chronicle of the Times*, tongue firmly in cheek.[19]

Meanwhile, with only a small circulation drawn to the *New Harmony Gazette*'s reform messages, Wright and Owen took to criticizing the mainstream periodical press for its hostile views on social reform. "If Error have all the talking and Truth none, Error may walk over the course triumphant and unchallenged. It behoves Truth's advocates, therefore, as they would prosper her cause, to obtain for her a hearing," Owen explained in 1828.[20] They understood that their journal's small circulation was due in part to its "almost frontier" location, but they also blamed the mainstream press for the "prejudice and indifference of the world" to heterodox ideas. Their solution was to send Wright on a lecture tour, beginning in Cincinnati and Louisville and progressing to northeastern cities, including Philadelphia, New York, and Boston. "I have long doubted whether there was any effectual method of changing public opinion," Owen wrote, "except this one of public lectures."[21] Together they articulated a dichotomy between print and oratory that privileged oratory as the ideal forum for the freethinking reformer. In doing so, they joined scores of evangelicals, reformers, and politicians who made personal appearances as traveling speakers to garner support for their causes during the late 1820s.[22]

Even if most reformers and lay speakers did not explicitly denounce the mainstream press, many shared the belief that direct public speech bypassed entrenched, hierarchical power structures. In this respect the proliferation of lay public speaking implicitly reflected an antiauthoritarian stance. Indeed, social conservatives frequently voiced their discomfort with this upstart style of public persuasion. During the election of 1828, for example, when Jacksonian politicians ever more aggressively utilized stump speaking, John Quincy Adams bemoaned the state of politics that sent hopefuls into the countryside because they could no longer rely on the restrained political process of an earlier generation. Likewise, the elite New Yorker and former mayor Philip Hone regretted that the Jacksonians would "sell their souls" on the campaign trail for political victory.[23] Many eyewitnesses also worried about the rapid progress and popularity of evangelicals through areas like Ohio and western New York. That perspective reflected tensions between the more hierarchical social ties and formal rhetorical styles of an earlier era—an exclusive style of political and social organization that seldom admitted the participation of middling-status orators or mass audiences—and new styles that emphasized the speaker's rapport with a distinctly nonelite audience. This "middling style" or "democratic idiom," as Kenneth Cmiel has characterized it, used regional dialects, bawdy jokes, slang, and vernacular expressions to claim kinship with even the most rustic backwoodsman.[24] By the 1820s, the most genteel and high-born reformers risked being tarred with the same brush as frontier evangelicals and stump speakers. When Wright and Owen announced that oratory would serve their cause by helping them address new audiences (for they continued to publish the *Gazette*), they joined a conflicted cultural discourse inflected with messages about class and power.

Print, especially the newspaper press, was not immune to controversy either, particularly in the wake of the election of 1828. Newspaper matter of the era was acutely partisan and could occasionally escalate into sensationalism.[25] Wright and Owen argued that newspapers bred "Error" and promoted opinion and scandal over fair debate and discussion; but even those unsympathetic to free thought shared this view of newspapers in the late 1820s, particularly during the bitter electioneering of 1828. At the height of the election, in rural Newport, New Hampshire, a young law clerk named Benjamin Brown French captured in his diary his concerns about public discourse. "With what rancor the political war is carried on between the editorial corps! To what meanness vulgarity & abuse is that champion of liberty, in the proper hands, the press prostituted! With what lies and scandal does the columns of almost every political paper abound! I blush for my country when I see such things."[26] As different as they were, Wright and French shared the same concerns. Each of them idealized rational debate in the public sphere and decried the press's corruption of that aim. In sum, conflicts of opinion about the relative virtues of print and oratory bespoke broader concerns about public order in a democratic era, concerns that were heightened by electoral upheaval.

Wright emerged as a public speaker during the final months of 1828 when she toured eight midwestern cities. She immediately demonstrated her commitment to radical social ends by speaking on Sundays, hoping to shock the religious and, she said, provide the public with an alternative Sunday activity. One outraged newspaper writer denounced her in the *Louisville Focus* for breaking loose "from the restraints of decorum, which draw a circle round the life of women" and for leaping "over the boundary of female modesty, and [laying] hold upon the avocations of man, claiming a participation in them for herself and her sex."[27] His asserting the impropriety of women's public speech was unusual, however; most editors at this point expressed curiosity rather than distaste. The British traveler Frances Trollope reported that Cincinnatians were surprised "that a lady of fortune, family, and education, whose youth had been passed in the most refined circles of private life, should present herself to the people as a public lecturer."[28] For Trollope, such responses only accentuated the differences between British and American society.

News of Wright's tour did not appear in northeastern newspapers. Even though newspapers of the day were filled with news clipped from other papers—one scholar has found that 54 percent of all their content was borrowed—when she arrived in Baltimore the newspaper there simply identified her as being "from Mr. Owen's settlement" but did not rehash her Nashoba experience or discuss her views of marriage or miscegenation. Neither did her lectures garner notice outside the Baltimore and Annapolis newspapers. Most papers ignored the story entirely or mentioned it indifferently, as did the New York *National Advocate*, which reported that she was "delivering Lectures . . . [and that] her audiences are said to be large."[29] At no point in late 1828 did a New York newspaper report the controversy her talks aroused elsewhere—a far cry from the later treatment.

"A VOICE OF REMARKABLE SWEETNESS": ELOQUENCE AND GENDER

"The perfectly composed and self-confiding speaker began her address . . . [with] a voice of remarkable sweetness, distinctness, and power," wrote D. K. Minor of the *New-York American* after hearing Wright's first lecture in early January 1829.[30] Minor's admiration was representative of his editorial colleagues' initial response to Wright. Yet sometimes as quickly as her second lecture, editors' positive responses began shifting toward antagonism. If New York newspapers had ignored controversy in other cities, they compensated for that oversight once Wright's New York lectures began.[31] The evolution of their critique illustrates their attempt to articulate for their readers the danger posed by Wright's lectures. Over the course of the year they came to define her public address as a challenge to conventions of female behavior and a perversion of womanliness. Editors ceased to describe her "voice of remarkable sweetness" and instead called her "a bold lady-man" to capture her transgression of gender norms rather than criticize her reform message directly.[32]

During her first six months of lecturing, Wright delivered a five-evening series of lectures on "Knowledge" (for which she charged $3, a hefty sum) primarily in New York, with occasional visits to Philadelphia, Wilmington, Delaware, and New Jersey. In each ninety-minute lecture, she spoke on the importance of knowledge in a democracy, covering several controversial components. First, she downplayed religious faith as a source of human knowledge, arguing that one obtained knowledge solely by using one's senses and applying human reason. Second, employing enlightenment beliefs about the relation between education, liberty, and equality, she sought to convince her American auditors that their republic was doomed if the country's wealth, education, and power were held only by the few; she called especially for democratized education for both sexes and all classes. She railed against the Christian church because it opposed social reform and wrested philanthropic funds from organizations that would democratize education, reform labor practices, and improve institutions like penitentiaries, hospitals, and asylums.[33] Finally, she said, the church held women in a "debased" and "unenlightened" state that ultimately diminished both sexes.

Yet on first hearing, editors generally finessed her subject matter and instead acclaimed Wright's charisma and her gifts as an orator. Their praise clearly judged her speaking abilities within the context of prevailing elocutionary theory. William Leete Stone of the *Commercial Advertiser* enthusiastically praised her voice, emphasis, pauses, and gestures and announced that "so far as these qualifications constitute an orator, we believe she is unrivalled by any of the public speakers, of any description, in this city."[34] Likewise, when she first arrived in Boston in August 1829, editors acclaimed "the purity and elegance of her language, her correct pronunciation, and eloquent and fervid manner."[35] "Purity" of language, "fervid" manner, and perfect enunciation signaled achievement of the high standards that newspapers usually acknowledged only in the most celebrated orators. As she traveled to new cities to speak, writers continually expressed delight at her refinement and oratorical prowess.

These responses corresponded to Wright's privately expressed philosophy of reform rhetoric. As she wrote to a friend, her aim was "to persuade but certainly not to irritate." A reformer's opinions must be articulated in a manner "temperate" in language and "complete" in "reasoning," she explained.[36] In other words, Wright believed she could match her rhetorical style to her republican message—she presented her ideas about human reason and uplifting all Americans in a manner that anyone might understand and consider, without the overlay of rhetorical bluster, aggressive persuasion, or difficult logic. In doing so, she embraced a radically inclusive model of public discourse, one that imagined a reading or listening public of reasoning individuals who formed their opinions with care.

Only one New York critic initially claimed that Wright should not speak in public simply because she was a woman.[37] Nor should we be surprised by this. While it was rare to find a woman speaking in public in the 1820s, it was not unheard of. In addition to the still-prevalent practice of girls' delivering commencement orations, a large number of religious women became exhorters in this era, while still more women had performed with acclaim in American theaters since the 1780s.[38] Indeed, the advertisement for Wright's talks that appeared in the January 26th issue of the *New-York American* (fig. 16) is flanked by advertisements for Miss Rock and Miss Emery appearing on other stages. Most significant, as Granville Ganter and Rosemarie Zagarri have shown, a surprising number of women delivered deliberative speeches of their own composition.[39] Few argued flatly that women could not speak in public; editors only gradually developed complex gender codes to condemn Wright's views and counter her emerging popularity.

But increasingly, editors expressed a suspicion of Wright's powers of declamation that reflected a powerful sense of opposition between print and oral discourse. By mocking Wright's abilities, they urged their readers to distrust her oratorical manipulation. One correspondent to the *New-York*

PARK THEATRE.
First night of Miss ROCK'S Engagement.
THIS EVENING Jan. 26
Will be presented Shakspeare's comedy of AS YOU LIKE IT. Orlando, Simpson; Ameins, Richings; Jaques, Barry; Touchstone, Hilson; Rosalind, Miss Rock; Celia, Mrs. Sharpe; Phœbe, Wallack; Audrey, Wheatley.
After which, a new Medley Dance, by the Miss Parkers.
To conclude with the petit comedy of WINNING A HUSBAND: Or, Seven's the Main.—Sir Roderick Strangeways, Woodhull; Davy, Placide; Lucinda, Mrs. Wallack; Miss Jenny Transit, with six other characters, Miss Rock.
☞ Boxes 75 cents; Pit 37 1-2 cents; Gallery 25 cents
Doors open at 6, performance to commence at half past 6.

LA FAYETTE THEATRE.
☞ MISS EMERY'S BENEFIT. ☜
And her last appearance.
THIS EVENING, Jan. 26.
Will be presented the celebrated tragedy of EVADNE.—Colonna, Stevenson; Vicentio, Robertson; Ludovico, Scott; Evadne, Miss Emery; Olivia, Sibley.
To conclude with OUDALIM ARABS. Or, the Jew in Barbary.—Prince Selim, by a Gentleman of this City; Abdullah, Robertson; The Jew, Foster; Mammora, Miss Emery; The Princess Zelma, Sibley.
Tuesday, will be revived the grand melo-drama of EL HYDER. In which Two Elephants, Cæsar and Hanibal, direct from the Tower of London, and the entire Stud of Horses, formerly attached to this Theatre, will appear.
☞ The Box Office will be open from 10 to 4 o'clock.
Prices of Admission—Boxes 50 cents, Pit 25 cents.
Doors open at 1-2 past 5, performance to commence at 1-2 past 6

PEALE'S MUSEUM.
THE Public are respectfully informed, that the interest-

...weighed, to be measured and to be electrified.
Performance to commence at half past 7 o'clock precisely.

MISS FRANCES WRIGHT.—Has consented to re-deliver her Lectures on Knowledge, at the request of several respectable citizens, who stated, that they, and a number of others, had been prevented by the insufficiency of room in the Masonic Hall, from hearing her former course. Her friends, therefore, have engaged, for this purpose, the Park Theatre, and the first Lecture will be delivered on Tuesday evening next, 27th inst. at 7 o'clock. The proceeds of the house over the actual expenses will be appropriated to the erecting of a Hall of Science in this city. Tickets can be obtained at the Theatre—Boxes 50 cents, Pit 25, Gallery 12 1-2 cents. ja26 2t*

AUCTION NOTICE.—*Paintings*.—M. HENRY gives notice that the New York Gallery 100 Broadway will

FIGURE 16. A series of advertisements from the January 26, 1829, issue of the *New-York American*, featuring a notice for Wright's talks at the Park Theater. Notice the headlines for Miss Rock and Miss Emery, theater stars whose popularity clearly outshone that of their male peers. Courtesy of the American Antiquarian Society.

American, for example, described his initial sympathy for Wright as she emerged to face her auditors. "I was prepared to feel for her as she glanced around, and seemed to be making an ineffectual effort to speak. This sentiment was, however, soon put to flight by her breaking silence, in a clear, strong voice, and uttering [her ideas] coldly, and with scrupulously accurate enunciation."[40] The author contrasted his initial sympathy with his subsequent recoil from her "cold" oratory, implying that Wright's eloquence was calculating and insincere. Other writers fostered the same suspicion of Wright's eloquence by ridiculing her perfect articulation.[41] These disparaging representations of how she manipulated her audiences sought to discredit her oratorical skill as mere window dressing. Her reviewers' depiction of her eloquence as dangerous implicitly questioned the medium of public speech in relation to print. This criticism was selective: editors continued to admire other forms of public oratory, such as congressional debate, as appropriate, gentlemanly modes of public discourse. Their emerging hostility to Wright reflected a long-standing antitheatrical bias that questioned the sincerity of speech capable of moving large crowds; her undeniable skill was no longer praiseworthy but "cool" and artful calculation.[42]

Editors also responded to Wright's outspoken criticism of newspapers and her direct attacks on editors in her lectures as well as her writings in the *Free Enquirer*. She argued that editors stooped to pandering in order to please their readers. Her attacks on them increased in proportion to the criticism she received in the New York press and generated a shared antieditorial bias between Wright and her auditors. "I do not believe the citizens of New-York are hostile to me—excepting some of the editors," she slyly told her Masonic Hall audience on January 7, and was received with "cheers, 'bravos,' 'go on,' [and] 'here, here.'"[43] When one auditor cried, "Don't spare the rascally editors" at the beginning of Wright's Park Theater lecture series in late January, the editor of the *New-York Enquirer* noted that her attacks were "much relished by the audience, as good hits against the editors always are; probably on the principle of retributive justice."[44] Editorial distrust of oratory, then, coexisted with a popular antinewspaper sentiment that emerged in Wright's rapport with her lecture hall audiences. That the editors should reprint such slams is suggestive of their tactics. By making light of auditors' antinewspaper banter, they affected confidence and even a belittling indifference (for example, when noting that such attacks on newspapers were "always" relished by Wright's audiences). Wright and the newspapers jockeyed for position with the public by pitting one medium against the other.

Wright did not stop with lecture hall banter, however, for her antipathy toward the editors was exemplary of her larger criticism about the nature of public discourse. When her second New York lecture series concluded with a barrage of hostile newspaper reports, she attacked newspaper editors' anonymity as the singularly untrustworthy and irresponsible practice of a degraded public press. "Not satisfied with presenting no opinions, it is sold to party; not content to withhold truths, it propagates falsehoods; not satisfied with dullness, it aims at depravity," she wrote in the *Free Enquirer*. She also argued that behind the curtain of anonymity lay a bevy of interests and allegiances that surreptitiously colored the opinions expressed—much like Duff Green's efforts to discredit journeyman printers. If writers acknowledged their own authorship, responsible public discourse would surely follow, she argued. "Let all men set their names to their writings, and they will cease to write falsehoods and to offend the rules of good breeding."[45] The conservatively tinged reference to "good breeding" sought to one-up the editors who disparaged the occasionally raucous behavior of lecture hall audiences. It was not oratorical eloquence that misled the public, she argued, but printed vitriol that verged on libel. Wright thus implicitly praised the orator for being fully accountable to the public.

Editors hastened to make Wright responsible for *her* words as well, typically by dismissing them as absurd. They also increasingly reminded the public of Wright's radical views on miscegenation and marriage, though she did not discuss them in her New York talks.[46] William Cullen Bryant, editor of the *New-York Evening Post*, stated obliquely that "we have heard no allusion" to the "offensive doctrines on the subject of marriage which she is said to have broached at New Harmony," thus introducing the topic of those "doctrines" by alluding to them himself.[47] Several other editors leaped at the opportunity to discredit her as a legitimate public speaker. *Niles' Weekly Register* reported that "she would abolish marriages ... give a free range to inclination, and do away [with] all distinctions between natural and legitimate children, and the parents of such."[48] Wright angrily objected to these descriptions because editors failed to engage with the ideas she *did* discuss. "It appears so much the fashion to answer my observations on one subject by *imagining* my observations on another," she wrote in the *Free Enquirer*, asking New Yorkers to suspend judgment on her opinions of marriage until she actually addressed it.[49] In the meantime, editors began to regale their readers with salacious passages from Wright's early writings about marriage and gender that seemed to confirm her extremism.[50] They thus cast Wright as even more radical than she had thus far revealed to her New York audiences, giving their reports the tone of an exposé: their "discovery" of her sexual radicalism allowed editors to pigeonhole Wright and thereby dismiss her. By identifying her as a gender outsider, they opened up the possibility of criticizing her visage, her deportment, her clothing, and all other aspects of her feminine self-presentation in ways that impugned her character. This approach permitted editors to forefront gender and sideline her ideas without really debating them.[51]

Wright was not the only female public figure to be attacked on similar grounds in 1828 and 1829. The same newspapers that vilified her carried stories of the death of Rachel Jackson, the president's wife, who had suffered persistent newspaper criticism when irregularities in the Jacksons' marriage were revealed. Editors characterized her as immoral and caricatured her as an unmannered and coarse middle-aged woman, mocking her weight, lack of fashion, pipe smoking, and evangelical Presbyterianism. The scandal became particularly vicious during the election year of 1828 and ended only with her death in late December.[52] Following on the heels of Jackson's death and Wright's earliest lectures were newspaper stories about the trial of Anne Royall, an acerbic commentator on the hypocrisies of American society who had been brought to trial in Washington, DC, on the obsolete charge of being a "common scold" or public nuisance—a charge punishable by public dunking. Nationally circulated reports of the trial focused on Royall's sharp, unladylike wit and anticipated her public humiliation with a certain relish. Within the District, however, many journalists viewed the trial as an attack on freedom of the press.[53] Both cases revealed moments when women's behavior was amplified and scrutinized publicly in the course of elucidating larger political and moral tensions in American culture via the press.

Even when they were complimentary, editors' commentary was shot through with gendered assumptions about Wright's appearance and performance—assumptions that she appears to have anticipated and sought to forestall. The *Aurora and Pennsylvania Gazette* described her voice as "musical" and her declamation as "easy and agreeable," while the *Salem Observer* deemed her "altogether ladylike"—characterizations that doubtless reassured readers that the lectures were appropriate for refined audiences.[54] Wright appears to have sought this approval by always arriving with a male escort who remained on stage with her during her speeches.[55] Observing such proprieties directly countered the long-standing association between stage actresses and immorality.[56] By assuring her audiences of her decency from her first moment on stage, she encouraged them to view her as a cultivated as well as effective orator.

No slave to gender conventions, Wright also heightened the drama of her physical appearance onstage. Reports invariably noticed her short hair, her unusual height (she was at least five feet ten inches tall), and the simple empire-waisted New Harmony tunic of white muslin that she frequently wore (fig. 17). This distinctive dress "announced her contempt for contemporary female fashion and her immersion in the cult of neoclassical reason," as Sean Wilentz described it, and resembled the dress of iconographic representations of Liberty, Wisdom, and Columbia more than common clothing patterns of the 1820s (fig. 18).[57] Simple white clothing was idealized in several contexts, including religious literature and moral tales, as the ideal costume for the virtuous woman. Given Wright's well-known disdain for both piety and virginal purity, however, her dress may have given a slightly ironic twist to its up-front, theatrical neoclassicism rather than implying sexual innocence. Indeed, observers at the time often noted the classical referent in her appearance, which seemed to smack of allusions to Socratic dialogue and was considered especially apt for her lecture on "Knowledge." Indeed, her singular choice of dress may be seen as part of a larger intention to embody Knowledge on stage. The image in figure 18 depicts a classicized woman guiding children to knowledge.[58] This role combined the relative sexlessness of classical female figures with an unmistakable flair for the dramatic. That appearance was enhanced during some lectures when she arrived on stage with a group of young followers, whom editors described as a "dozen of female apostles," "Quaker ladies," or a "train of lovely nymphs."[59] Given the highly formal stages on which she spoke, in venues like the City Theater and the Park Theater (fig. 19) that ordinarily hosted conventional dramatic performances, Wright's simple white dress and her accompanying muses would have had a powerful impact in tandem with her subject material.

Rather than criticize Wright's theatricality, editors sometimes deplored the fact that she composed and delivered her own speeches. Such critics might compliment her elocutionary performance but suggested that she should not appear in public to transmit her own ideas. The *New-York Spectator* asserted disparagingly, for example, that Wright would be "worth going to hear" if she had only recited "Anthony's oration over the dead body of Caesar, or Cato's Soliloquy, or Brutus' address to the mob, or any sensible thing"—all tried-and-true elocutionary pieces intended to display a speaker's talent for passionate declamation and gesture.[60] The distinction is suggestive. Conventions of oratory demanded that speakers shun theatricality; yet their seeming to prefer it in Wright's case suggests they felt more at ease with acting and actresses than with broader forms of female public speech. Indeed, stage actresses during the late 1820s suffered little of the vitriol that Wright received and appear to have constituted an accepted category of female stage performer. Likewise, the newspaper columns that

FIGURE 17. Frances Wright at Nashoba, depicted in classicized New Harmony dress, in a ca. 1827 print by Auguste Hervieu. Courtesy of A. J. G. Perkins and Theresa Wolfson, *Frances Wright, Free Enquirer: The Study of a Temperament* (New York, 1939).

FIGURE 18. An image of a classically dressed woman in "Youth, Accompanied by Virtue, and Directed by Experience, Approaching the Temple of Happiness," from the *Sentimental and Literary Magazine* 1 (1797). Courtesy of the William L. Clements Library, University of Michigan.

FIGURE 19. Watercolor rendition of the Park Theater, New York, 1822, where Wright presented her series of talks on "Knowledge" in January 1829. This particular image includes actual portraits of eighty-four prominent New Yorkers, indicating how closely the theater was associated with elites. Courtesy of the New-York Historical Society.

promoted the performances of Mrs. Sharpe, Miss Rock, and other well-known actresses, as we saw in figure 16, imply that these women's popularity surpassed that of their male colleagues, at least judging from their domination of the advertisements.[61] Editors wished to channel Wright's public ambitions into the acceptable genre of dramatic elocution and defined her delivering self-composed lectures as a transgression.

Editors depicted that transgression in ways that allowed them to attack her person and her character. After admiring her first lecture, William Leete

Stone of the *Commercial Advertiser* focused on the "incongruity and impropriety" of her second performance by describing her physical presence on stage. Stone, a Federalist editor with a lifelong career in printing and editing, became one of Wright's most aggressive critics in the *Advertiser*, one of the most widely read New York newspapers. "When she delivered her first lecture, as we mentioned yesterday, Miss Wright stood behind a reading desk, and exhibited only the upper part of her person," Stone began. "Last evening she stood on the platform; presenting her whole person to the view of the audience, with the table to her left."[62] Stone's portrayal linked the presumption of her move out from behind the desk to insinuations of immorality and infidelity. By "presenting her whole person" to the audience, this passage implied, Wright displayed an unbecoming lack of female modesty. From the suggestion of immodesty, subsequent articles rapidly extrapolated that "her mind has run riot with the love of FAME," a distinctly unfeminine disposition. "While we may be disposed to admit her sincerity, we must most sincerely lament the aberrations of intellect, and the erratic course of a female genius," the same writer continued in a Philadelphia paper.[63] These accusations had a long history in conduct literature that warned "learned ladies" not to display their knowledge too proudly.[64] Words like *aberration* and *erratic* reveal a disdain for "female geniuses" and stigmatize them as social deviants. So identified, Wright became what scholar Mary Poovey has called a "border case": a woman who challenged prevailing gender norms.[65] And by defining her as a transgressor of gender codes, editors made her femininity susceptible to wide-ranging analysis and rebuke.

This analysis blossomed in a letter to the *New-York American* by a correspondent signed "X." who depicted Wright in freakish terms. Describing her gloveless right hand, for example, X. wrote that "it was neither very white, nor well-turned, nor lady-like, and . . . she would have done better to have left it covered like its mate." Likewise, he portrayed her first arrival on stage: "She seemed not embarrassed as a woman might feel, when gazed upon by the expecting eyes of hundreds of the less gentle sex, but stood up unmoved and self-dependent; either sustained by the importance of her mission, and the consciousness of honesty, or the utter absence of all sense of shame and womanly sensibility." X. clearly favored the latter interpretation, for in each aspect of his analysis he suggested improper gender behavior. Finally, after cataloging her personal lapses, X. concluded: "It may be thought that these remarks are harsh, and that there is a degree of generous courtesy which should never be withheld from woman. But when one thus shamefully obtrudes herself upon the public, waiving alike modesty, gentleness, and every amiable attribute of her sex, she also waives all claims to its privileges; she ceases to be a woman, and is no longer aught else than what we have taken the liberty of calling her—a female monster."[66]

X. positioned himself as the protector of the public, but he also showed he was aware of the dangers inherent in making antagonistic personal remarks about women. He termed Wright a "female monster" in part to legitimate his strong attack. These attacks were tenable and even necessary, he argued, because Wright had "waived all claims" to the protection due proper ladies. Like the word choices *aberrant* and *erratic,* his portrayal of a "female monster" identified Wright as abnormal: a hybrid, even unnatural being who was unclassifiable according to conventional gender criteria. Residually "female," she flouted the normative standards of womanhood. In his flamboyant description, Wright became a grotesque.[67]

X.'s aggressive attack on Wright *did* offend readers, however, and placed his editor in the position of defending his editorialist. On the day after X.'s column appeared the *American*'s editor, D. K. Minor, explained that one of its "old correspondents" had written to the newspaper in protest. Claiming to write on behalf of many readers' "wounded sensibilities," the old correspondent had asked the paper to publish a retraction for X.'s "unmanly attack upon a woman."[68] Minor resisted, however, upholding X.'s editorial in a lengthy explanation. "In throwing aside the decorum and restraints of her sex, and exhibiting herself as a coarse and vehement assailant of manners, institutions, and modes of belief, deemed essential to the prosperity of society, and dear to the great majority of its members," Minor insisted, she "must be considered as renouncing also the privileges of her sex, and all claims upon the courtesy which is so cheerfully extended to woman moving in her proper sphere." The tone of certainty belies the editor's defensive position. X.'s editorial was, after all, based on mockery of Wright's personal appearance and rhetorical style, not a considered analysis of her arguments: Minor avoided personal attack but still called Wright a "coarse and vehement assailant" of accepted social norms. More important, he upheld X.'s attack as a worthy and well-intentioned attempt to protect "society," even at the risk of offending a minority of its members. By hurrying to defend his editorialist, Minor reinforced his paper's patrolling stance on how to handle transgressive women and speakers.

Another conflict over such descriptions of Wright arose between William Leete Stone of the *Commercial Advertiser* and Robert Walsh, editor of the Philadelphia *National Gazette,* who publicly rebuked Stone for attacking a woman so forcefully. "Ridicule of her personal appearance [can] answer no good end," Walsh wrote. "Her personal appearance and condition should be spared. Some respect and kindness are still due to her sex."[69] "But surely Mr. Walsh forgets that she has unsexed herself, if we may be allowed the expression," Stone responded.[70] Of course Stone did not mean to suggest that Wright was a neutered or passionless figure, but rather that she had forfeited the privileges of normal womanhood. Indeed, Stone painted Wright as a dangerous woman and, using heated and erotic language, suggested that she threatened to sexualize society. "She comes amongst us in the character of a bold blasphemer, and a voluptuous preacher of licentiousness," Stone wrote in menacing tones. "Casting off all restraint, she would break down all the barriers to virtue, and reduce the world to one grand theatre of vice and sensuality in its most loathsome form.... It is iron equally in her head and heart; impervious to the voice of virtue, and case-hardened against shame!" Like X., Stone heightened the sexual element of Wright's public persona into an image of a grotesquely transgressive, even treacherous woman.

The image of Wright as a grotesque emerged most vividly in the Philadelphia cartoon captioned "A Down Wright Gabbler, or a goose that Deserves to be Hissed" (fig. 20), which pictured Wright in ladylike costume delivering a lecture at the Walnut Street Theater, but with a goose's head. The artist illustrated the scene realistically, including Wright's escort to her side with her hat in his hand, the tall spermaceti candles, reading table, pile of books, and Wright's bound lecture in her left hand—aspects of the stage scene reported in detail by numerous reviewers. Wright's right hand points to the audience in a gesture that might be interpreted as pedantic or dogmatic; her mouth is also emphatically open, with her goose's tongue in full motion. The open mouth and wagging tongue evoke the common character of the prattler, who frequently appeared in literature to warn of the dangers of unthinking speech. In this pose Wright is both foolish and "impervious," as Stone would have it; she is a gabbling goose-woman. Whereas she wished to appear as a classical Guide to Knowledge for her auditors, this cartoon positioned her as "a goose that deserves to be hissed"—or, better still, ignored.

The implicit message of the "Down Wright Gabbler" related to Wright's public auditors, the ones who did not ignore her. The image implies an audience, allowing Wright's escort to stand in for its own foolishness. This man gazes impassively forward, mildly and rather stupidly enjoying the proceedings. This is no rational auditor, but a dupe. He is emasculated by his passivity, depicted as obediently carrying Wright's hat, wearing a billowy jacket and cravat and standing in a feminine, Europeanized pose. The image conveys the sense that Wright as well as her escort and audience are all fools rather than dangerous. He also serves to caution men about

FIGURE 20. "A Down Wright Gabbler, or a goose that deserves to be hissed," an 1829 cartoon published in Philadelphia by J. Aikin. Courtesy of the Library Company of Philadelphia.

attending Wright's talks. If she "unsexed" herself by speaking in public, she also unsexed her auditors.

By characterizing Wright as dangerously or comically grotesque, editorialists opened for themselves a socially acceptable rhetorical space to vigorously denounce the sexual politics of her social philosophy without actually engaging with it. It granted them permission to use the flamboyant denunciations that would customarily be disallowed in printed discourse about a woman. When editors claimed that Wright had "unsexed" herself, they engaged in a cultural dialogue not only about the boundaries of acceptable *female* behavior, but also about *their own* proper behavior as journalists. Her "monstrousness" allowed editors to denounce with propriety every aspect of her person, philosophy, and character.

Editors found plenty to criticize in Wright's performances: her arguments against traditional marriage, women's place, and the church were deemed so radical as to tilt editorial analysis from aggressive to malevolent as editors sought ways to steer the public away from attending such a spectacle. But they seldom addressed the content of her arguments more than in passing. In their eagerness to serve as pivotal cultural mediators, they turned their coverage into a forum on feminine propriety, believing that their analysis of Wright's body and conduct would repel readers from such a scene. In this way, proscriptions for female conduct emerged during this event as an important means by which editors might bolster newspapers' significance in the public mind. In short, editors used their denunciations of Wright to grant themselves new license and the medium of print new authority in the public sphere. And as we shall see, they undertook these aims by means of both new modes of rhetoric and new characterizations of the public.

FEARS OF THE "THRONG": REPRESENTATIONS OF WRIGHT'S MALE AND FEMALE AUDITORS

Wright and New York newspaper editors struggled in print to control public opinion and especially to manage representations of her listening public. Editors used sarcastic and alarmist language to sway their readers and described theater audiences in terms laden with class implications. They frequently went so far as to raise fearful images of mobs and riots by using terms such as "crowd," "multitude," and "throng" to describe her listeners, thus producing a strong bias against the working classes whose rights Wright sought to uphold. Constructing a consistently negative depiction of these audiences allowed editors to position their readers, in contrast, as right-acting participants in condemning a moral outrage. Their apprehensions—especially about Wright's female auditors—reflected a widespread concern for the gap between prescriptions for women's conduct and actual female behavior. Such preoccupations indicated an interest in defining and regulating new mass public behavior.

To sway their readers, editors and writers of letters to the editor adopted one of three stances on the topic of Wright's lectures—outrage, alarmism, and sarcasm, using each to different effect. Outraged writers referred to the "pernicious" nature of Wright's ideas, to the "evil . . . that has already been done by her," and to their "astonishment" at the attendance of women at her lectures.[71] This language sought to envelop readers in the writer's sense of indignation at public scandal that might have larger implications. Even more broadly, it gave inflamed editors the chance to claim to represent the feelings of all right-thinking Americans. For example, when

Wright encountered opposition to her plan to speak in Philadelphia on a Sunday, the *New-York Spectator* reported:

> We shall be much surprised if the staid citizens of Philadelphia will allow the celebration of Beelzebub's worship in [a theater] on Sunday. If the law will prevent it, Miss W. is exactly the subject on whom its "searching operation" should be tried; her avowed object being to ride over not only the Gospel, but the law likewise. To say that she will thrive by persecution is well enough, while she keeps the peace; but it is absurd when she sets up her show-cart and does her jugglery on a day set apart for rest, and for piety.[72]

Here the writer's moral indignation and prescription for action called on readers to respond as a unified public: "we shall be much surprised if the staid citizens of Philadelphia will allow" and "the law . . . should be tried." Such strong moral language, combined with explicit counsel on treating the matter called forth the proper reaction to the situation.

Occasionally this language segued into a more extreme, alarmist style punctuating the need for readers to respond. Such alarmism specifically targeted an imagined middle-class reading public. At Wright's January 10 lecture, someone set fire to a barrel of turpentine and sent smoke billowing upstairs through Masonic Hall. Afterward the *New-York Evening Post* published a powerful letter by "Vindex" describing the scene. "The alarm spread amongst two thousand people at the sudden cries of Fire—the confusion consequent upon it—the stench of the gas, and the more pestilent doctrine I had just listened to, have made such an impression upon me, that I shall for ever associate them as proper concomitants."[73] In this impressionistic rendering, the danger and chaos inherent in Wright's ideas and the crowd's confusion combined in a particularly horrific moment. The writer described recoiling from the crowd at the same time as he was caught up in the turmoil, addressing educated readers with his refined language. Thus, when he determined that he would "for ever associate" Wright's ideas and the crowd's chaos "as proper concomitants," he exemplified the fears of an assumed middle-class reader.

The alarmist stance mobilized anxieties about class interaction in public spaces. Whereas Vindex depicted an actual mob, other writers resorted to fantasy. Two weeks after Vindex's letter, the *Post*'s editor, William Cullen Bryant, magnified those middle-class fears. Responding to the news that Wright had leased the Park Theater for six nights in late January and early February 1829, Bryant spun out an elaborate imaginary scene. "Suppose the singular spectacle of a female, publicly and ostentatiously proclaiming doctrines of Atheistical fanaticism, and even the most abandoned lewdness, should draw a crowd from a prurient curiosity, and that a riot should ensue, which should end in the demolition of the interior of the building, or even in burning it down, on whom would the loss fall?"[74] Premised entirely on conjecture, this fantasy combined mob activity, arson, and destruction in a vivid and elaborate slippery slope argument. Bryant anchored this passage in a defense of the economic concerns of the theater's stockholders, who would bear the burden of the imagined destruction of the theater. Yet he clearly appealed to a broader audience. He constructed a dichotomy between the propertied and those who potentially destroyed property, a class distinction that might also represent the reading public versus Wright's auditors. Bryant sought to mobilize a middle-class phobia of class mixing in order to rid public sites of dangerous performances. Similar desires to sanitize the theater of the lower orders or to establish alternative, exclusive venues had a long history, but associating arson with theaters was new.[75]

While such alarmism was a potent means of producing fear in middle-class readers, pieces like Bryant's were in the minority. With surprising rapidity, most writers adopted a sarcastic treatment of Wright, following the lead of the *Commercial Advertiser*'s William Leete Stone. This style allowed them to engage their readers in a shared joke at Wright's expense. With amused perspicuity, Stone dismissed her lectures as eloquent but unintelligible nonsense, elbowing his readers into joining his drollery. For example, after her second lecture in early January Stone commented that "those who went to learn how they might get knowledge, returned, we believe, like Ponce de Leon from his voyage after the waters of immortality."[76] Throughout the year, Stone characterized Wright as "a mind all confused in wandering mazes."[77] Following her progress through New England that summer, Stone noted that "solemn Editors have gravely undertaken to refute—they know not what; unless the oratrix made herself more intelligible than she did here."[78] And of her arrival in Philadelphia in the fall of 1829, he asserted that "we have no earthly objection to Miss W's spinning her rigmarole to the crack of her own doom, provided the laws are not infringed. It is perfectly harmless, and particularly nonsensical."[79] Such sarcasm proved infectious, judging by how often Stone's editorials were reprinted by other editors and his style mimicked by numerous writers. He asserted that his "satires" were "not only justifiable weapons, but those which are unquestionably to be wielded with the most effect."[80] That effect aimed to persuade readers to forgo Wright's public appearances. Sarcasm affected readers differently than the fear-mongering of Bryant's *New-York Evening Post*. It produced a sense of ironic distance that they could apply to Wright as well as to her low followers. Rather than dwelling on the contaminating aspects of class mixing, sarcasm promised to give readers a mental armor, a set of categories by which to dismiss and mock the world outside newspaper discourse. Constructing this sarcastic in-crowd was a form of resistance to Wright and her enthusiasts by contrasting them with the knowing universe of the newspaper-reading public.

But when neither alarmism nor sarcasm appeared to diminish Wright's popularity, editors soon began to blame Stone for *inciting* interest in Wright's lectures through his mockery of her. The *Chronicle of the Times* felt that Stone "ought to have known" that his excessive ridicule would "induce" readers, "especially those who prefer judging for themselves, to attend the lectures." Stone petulantly responded by claiming that good citizens *ought* to go hear her in order to feel the "unqualified disgust," "loathing and abhorrence" that he believed naturally followed from hearing her ideas, arguing that "judging for themselves" would accomplish that end.[81] Bryant's *New-York Evening Post* went so far as to suggest that she had schemed to receive precisely this hostile editorial response, "an ingenious stroke of policy on her part." "If therefore Miss Wright could induce the newspapers to attack her with some acrimony, she doubtless had the sagacity to see that she might be the gainer."[82] The disagreement between the *Chronicle* and the *Commercial Advertiser* hinged on whether a single prose style—the sarcastic invective—might permit editors to regulate readers' behavior. As editors grasped for explanations of Wright's continued popularity, they persistently sought to position the newspapers at the center of public discourse and to credit themselves with great influence on public behavior. This conception could figure the public as a singularly malleable body: sarcasm *induced* readers to see Wright themselves. Defending his position, Stone argued that the mental armor he provided for his readers would create revulsion should they be exposed directly to Wright's ideas. This debate also reveals the editors' frustration with their inability to hit on the right formula for controlling readers' responses. Even as they accused Wright of wooing the public through sophisticated propaganda, their discussion of effective writing styles sought the same result. They aspired to discipline and regulate public behavior through their embellished writing. Their much discussed concern about the relation between their own writing style and Wright's popularity exposed conflicting editorial opinions about the most appropriate and effective ways for newspapers to intervene in forming public opinion.

These issues grew so heated by mid-January that several editors resolved to stop reporting on Wright's lectures altogether to end the publicity they had inadvertently provided for her. At first Stone defended his continued reports by explaining that the public demanded information about "the Lioness of the day." After her fifth lecture, however, Stone determined that "it is time we should have done with Miss Wright," because "too much is just enough."[83] Since his constant criticism and mockery of Wright seemed to produce the wrong public response, he decided that silence was now the best policy. The *Chronicle of the Times* approved of Stone's self-imposed silence and told its readers that Stone had previously "demeaned himself very ungallantly indeed" and was "severely rebuked by several editors . . . but he has found out his mistake, and on Monday evening he 'cut Miss Fanny Wright adrift.'"[84] But because his articles continued to be reprinted in northeastern newspapers through mid-February, Stone's resolve to "have done" with Wright had limited effect. Many editors continued to ridicule Wright throughout the spring and summer of 1829 on their own account.[85] As a result, Stone's silence on the topic did not last long. By midsummer of 1829 he resumed frequent columns about her lectures in New England and Philadelphia, perhaps because stories about her were too good to copy from other papers.

Editorialists' representations of Wright's auditors were contradictory, reflecting the writers' uncertainty as they sought to be cultural mediators for a diverse American public. Writers' frequent allusions to the "novelty" of Wright's appearances seemed to reassure readers that the auditors who flocked to her lectures were in no danger of susceptibility. Thus the editor of *Niles' Weekly Register* told his subscribers that "in Baltimore she had many auditors, we learn, but made no converts."[86] In contrast, other writers tried to resolve their bewilderment at Wright's popularity by depicting her auditors as unthinking dupes easily charmed by her eloquence. At times alarmist writers went so far as to describe a menacing environment in which an audience dangerously moved by her words resembled an unruly mob.

Yet even the most hostile reports suggest that Wright attracted auditors of all classes and both sexes. These revelations imply that Wright gained a broad support that defies easy explanation. From the beginning, editors estimated the number of auditors and attempted to typify Wright's audiences. "Many of our most respectable citizens" attended her first lecture, according to Stone; the free-thought *Correspondent* uncharacteristically agreed with him, stating that "judges, lawyers, merchants—in fact the most respectable portion of our citizens, accompanied by their wives and daughters, have vied with each other in the constancy of their attendance."[87]

That "respectable" citizens should patronize Wright's talks granted them legitimacy and even an air of fashion. Once editors began to demonize her, they struggled to explain the continued presence of respectable auditors, frequently by attributing her popularity to novelty. "After the novelty of the thing has subsided, the world will probably go on in pretty much the same way as it did before," the *New York Statesman* assured its readers.[88] The *Evening Post* also foresaw that "as soon as this curiosity is gratified, her audience will be confined to the few free thinkers who have sufficient zeal for their doctrines to attend a regular public exposition and defense of them."[89] Such speculations satisfied editors during her lecture series in early January, but when she announced a second series late in the month, many formulated much more forbidding images of those who continued to confer such remarkable popularity on Wright.

The expanding popularity of her talks led writers to express exasperation with the public. When the managers of the Park Theater agreed to let its stage to Wright for six evening lectures, editors disparaged the theater's potential patrons. "What sort of a public may attend these exhibitions, we are not curious to inquire," the editor of the *New-York American* wrote skeptically, "but we cannot be mistaken in regard to the opinion which will be formed, by the sound public, of the manifest impropriety" of allowing Wright to use the theater.[90] In this writer's formulation, the actual lecture attendees were dismissively contrasted with the right-thinking "sound public" who were aligned with the editor and his readers ("we cannot be mistaken"). Disdainful depictions of Wright's auditors permitted editors to display condescension toward them for the benefit of their presumably middle-class readers. They represented members of her audiences as fools. "What a *select* auditory she must have; and how much good she is calculated to do the rising generation!" asked an article in the Utica, New York, *Western Recorder*, supplying its own answer to this rhetorical question.[91] Editors littered their columns with oblique references to "a certain class of people," and "the multitude [drawn] to see any other wonderment," and they regularly referred to her admirers as dupes.[92] "Our citizens again poured forth by thousands, all agape to swallow the contents of her ladyship's knowledge box," Stone wrote.[93] The letter from "Q. in a Corner," with which this chapter began, contributed to the stereotypical construction of a Fanny Wrightist in the press. Informally written and designed to humor readers with his coarse, unthinking allegiance to Wright, Q.'s letter professed great delight with Wright's antiestablishment ideas, though he also admitted, "I can't say that I exactly understand them."[94] Such letters constructed a divide between newspaper readers and lecture audiences based on allusions to education, intelligence, and class standing. Indeed, their ubiquitous use of terms like "the multitude" and "the throng" conspicuously contrasted Wright's auditors with the "perusal and reflection of the sober-minded citizens" who made up a *reading* public.[95]

Editors' mockery of and distaste for these duped, lower-class auditors built on long-standing class tensions about crowds and the mixed nature of theater audiences. These strains particularly emerged in publications where writers had articulated a classed distinction between themselves as refined observers of the social scene and the "lower sorts" who made theaters, carnivals, and the streets so unruly, as Peter Stallybrass and Allon White have described.[96] Those who purported to represent the "refined" classes had long recoiled from theater events at which they rubbed shoulders with those considered beneath them. The elite New York diarist Philip Hone, for example, expressed his aversion to Wright's lecture by using, even in a brief entry, the expressions "crowded to excess," "fools," and "I found the room so full that I remained but a short time."[97] Frances Trollope agreed to attend Wright's Cincinnati lecture only after being assured that she would be flanked by a number of other "ladies" and "gentlemen" of her acquaintance, considering "the immense crowd that was expected." "We congratulated ourselves that we had had the courage to be among the number" for such an enjoyable performance, she wrote.[98]

Editors' antitheatrical bias could also equate immorality with lower-class auditors and mobilize the old association between immorality and the stage. To do so, they stressed Wright's unorthodox opinions on Christianity, marriage, and race. "We cannot conceive of a more appropriate place than [the Park Theater] for a *female* to lecture on morality, whose system of morals, among other things, teaches that marriage is an *unnatural* restraint," the *Rochester Observer* declared in March 1829. "Who will not hereafter subscribe to the sentiment that 'the stage is a school of morals.'"[99] Portrayals like these, which tied together concerns about class difference and bodily intermingling, thus participated in a discourse that distinguished the refined, observant spectator-writer from the crowd at the site of the disorderly theater.

Usually these disdainful representations of the dupes who thronged Wright's lectures suggested that those auditors were willing to believe virtually anything if the orator packaged those arguments attractively enough. But occasionally editors acknowledged the presence of a small, radical segment of free-thought devotees within her listening audiences. Stone, for example, described periodic bursts of applause from the "Infidel Club" or a cheer from the "Free Enquirers." M. M. Noah, editor of the *New-York*

Enquirer, furthered this portrait with his description of her devotees as "a sort of hard boys, who call themselves philosophers, and 'free enquirers,' ... [who enjoyed] every hit against fashion, female education, editors, lawyers, clergy, &c. &c. &c."[100] Even when editors recognized the "free enquirers," they rarely permitted support of Wright or her followers to appear in their newspapers. "W.," a correspondent to Wright's *Free Enquirer,* claimed that out of a "host of *communications"* written by her supporters that had "inundated" the offices of local newspapers, only M. M. Noah's *Enquirer* and the free-thought *Correspondent* had published any of them. "Such is the real state of the press in this city at the moment," W. informed the *Free Enquirer*'s readers.[101] Indeed, editors occasionally admitted to ignoring their readers' letters about Wright for the larger purpose of discouraging public interest on the topic. And ignore them they did. Only three times did I find supportive letters published on her behalf;[102] clearly, editors avoided sending mixed messages.

Unsurprisingly, the *Free Enquirer* presented far more positive views of Wright's listening audiences, views that dovetailed with that periodical's criticism of mainstream newspaper journalism. When the *Free Enquirer* noticed that Philadelphia newspapers had been "very quiet on the subject of Frances Wright's lectures" in May 1829, it published the effusive report of "A Spectator":

> I have been present at many public meetings, and heard many popular orators; but an orator who could for an hour and a half enchain the attention of an audience, so that a whisper might have been heard all over the spacious building, I never before heard. At times, as the speaker advanced some more daring truth, her mild yet most impressive manner created such a breathless stillness, that one might have imagined that the house contained not a living being. ... You could see that the sentiment sunk into the hearts of her audience, impressing at once by its boldness, and, I incline to believe, by its importance and truth.[103]

The *Free Enquirer* continued to print such flattering reports of audience response during Wright's tour through Wilmington, Boston, Providence, and upstate and western New York. These audiences were "intelligent," "more than usually respectable," and "well-behaved" and never exhibited the characteristics of the crowd or the throng.[104] They also demonstrated a genteel capacity for composition in the letters they sent, representing a far different group of auditors than the mainstream press would allow.

Most important, the *Free Enquirer*'s reports and letters showed that those auditors included large numbers of women. From the beginning of her tour, virtually all editors exhibited enormous concern about the number of women who attended her lectures. "We are glad to state," the *New-York American* told its readers after Wright's first New York address, that the lecture hall was crowded "almost exclusively with men, not more than fifty females being present."[105] By her fourth lecture, however, the *Commercial Advertiser* told its readers melodramatically that "truth demands us to say—and our cheeks burn while we record it—that there were ladies there without disguises" in the audience at her City Hotel address.[106] It is difficult to generalize about female attendance figures, given the political volatility of the question and the few "impartial" observers. The overall impression from the reports, however, is that more and more women attended over the course of her tour. Wright apparently announced that she sought more female auditors, since several editors pointedly noted her wishes in their columns.[107] It was one thing for Wright to expound her radical message about women's place in American society, but quite another for women to attend her lectures and, possibly, to embrace that message. Editors' haste to disapprove of Wright both personally and intellectually very frequently reflected explicit concerns about the susceptibility of her female auditors.

Newspaper editorials demonstrated their writers' concerns about the presence of women in the very extremity of their tone. Vindex's letter to the *New-York Evening Post,* for example, concluded decisively, "My real design in writing this paper, was to bring under the consideration of the numerous females who attend her lectures, that having now avowed her pernicious principles in their full extent, no woman who entertains a decent share of respect for herself or her sex, can do other than absent themselves from her exhibitions."[108] The letter to the *Evening Post* from "A Mother" similarly culminated with a fearful appeal to "ye mothers of respectability, who yet feel concern for the future welfare of your daughters." "On you I call—by all that is valuable in society I conjure you to stem, while it is in your power, this torrent of vice, ere it break down the last barrier of female honour, and sweep away before it every domestic virtue!"[109] When Wright traveled to Utica, New York, the *Western Recorder* published a letter by "P.Q.T." that asked, "*Can* she have *any female* hearers? Can there be a *husband*, or *father*, that *loves* his *wife*, his *daughter*; a *brother*, that *loves* his *sister*; a *son*, that *loves* his *mother*; can there be a single *professing* Christian, among her hearers?"[110] Editors' evident discomfort at Wright's popularity with female auditors suggests how deeply they disapproved of this female behavior.

Newspaper editorialists manifested overweening concerns about the public that led them to draw sharp distinctions between Wright's listeners and their own readers. Eager to shape public opinion, they also imagined that their words—properly expressed—had an immediate effect on public behavior. When forced to acknowledge that they might inadvertently steer the public in the wrong direction, they invited their readers to join in as they sniffed at the theater's throng or expressed dismay at growing numbers of female attendees. Each of these turns in their response to Wright reveals editors' muscular efforts to enhance their own importance in public discourse and to characterize print as the most appropriate medium for public discussion by right-minded individuals. These contests reveal with particular clarity that editors' preoccupation with female oratory and women in public served to forward their goals of buttressing print and newspaper editorials in forming public opinion.

In March 1831—long after Wright's 1829 tour had ended—a nineteen-year-old clerk named Bradley Cumings noted in his diary that, according to newspaper reports, Frances Wright was to arrive in Boston by ship that day. His entry revealed how eagerly the newspapers resuscitated old stories—and how appealing was their sarcastic sense of superiority for impressionable readers like the teenage Cumings. "By several papers which I have late read, it seems the principal object of her party is, to break all marriage contracts: thus striking at the root, all chastity and sense of decorum among people: but, she will doubtless find, ere long, but little desire, to hear constantly, her doctrines and those of her party, among the New Englanders." In other words, Cumings happily joined the newspaper writers in expressing skepticism about Wright's ideas. But the following day he noted with a sense of anticlimax, "The papers of to day say, that the Miss Frances Wright who arrived here yesterday is not the lecturer."[111] Indeed, Wright was long gone from the American scene—she had left for Europe in June 1830 to aid her ailing sister and constant companion, Camilla, and she did not return to the United States until 1835.[112] Yet as Cumings's diary indicates, her absence only accelerated writers' comic portrayals of her, generating even more the sense that a unified reading public shared an aversion to Wright's "doctrines." As embarrassing as it might seem that the newspapers had mistakenly identified the ship's passenger, they gained more ground than they lost with these caricatures of Wright's absurdity.

Now that Wright was not there to defend herself or to win over urban lecture audiences, writers depicted her as a female monster with impunity.

By the mid-1830s, "Fanny Wrightism" had become an epithet applied to social reformers of all stripes. The power of the phrase lay in its ambiguity. When Wright's actual arguments about religion, marriage, education, and the uplift of the working classes were no longer discussed in lecture halls, writers could allude to her as the sole representative of a dangerous but unspecified heterodoxy. Although this epithet was not exclusively directed at women, when it was it signaled a particularly poisonous transgression. Catharine Beecher, for example, accused her of "attacking the safeguards of all that is venerable and sacred in religion, all that is safe and wise in law, all that is pure and lovely in domestic virtue" and continued with a flourish: "Who can look without disgust and abhorrence upon such an one as Fanny Wright, with her great masculine person, her loud voice, her untasteful attire, going about unprotected, and feeling no need of protection, mingling with men in stormy debate, and standing up with bare-faced impudence, to lecture a public assembly.... I cannot perceive any thing in the shape of woman, more intolerably offensive and disgusting."[113] "Fanny Wrightism" had become, as Lori Ginzberg has observed, "not so much what respectable Americans were but what they were not."[114]

The intense focus on Wright as a gendered body has distracted attention from some of the crucial issues at stake during the controversy over her public appearances—most important, from conflicting visions of a properly constituted American public and a clash over the appropriate methods of addressing that public. On one hand, Wright sought to elicit from her auditors a new vision of a reformed, egalitarian American society. She did so by using a rhetoric that, she believed, exemplified the rational discourse suitable to republics—and by locating that discourse within halls and theaters, where she might reach a broad audience. When she contested newspaper portrayals of her, she claimed to represent the thoughtful and reasoned public discussion that she accused them of betraying; newspapers, she charged, had become instruments in the defense of the status quo. Editors, on the other hand, acknowledged her oratorical gifts but termed her a demagogue. They used caricatures of her as a means of fretting about broader public behavior. Her talks were bad enough, they insisted; but even worse, those who attended were dupes, hardly the rational public Wright claimed to represent. In other words, Wright and the editors did more than seek to define appropriate public conduct and offer themselves as makers of public opinion: they called forth two different versions of an idealized public—publics that were at odds with each other.

Although Wright was not initially despised because she offended gender orthodoxy about female public speech, during the early 1830s few women followed her to the podium without becoming the objects of explicit hostility based on sex—or, more specifically, without becoming termed "Fanny Wrightists." Wright's tour played an important role in making coherent a far more restrictive ideology about female oratory that profoundly affected ordinary women's lives. Of course, women hardly shied away from public speaking after Wright had become a symbol of perverted womanhood. From women abolitionists to advocates of female education like Catharine Beecher and Almira Phelps, more women than ever spoke in public during the 1830s and later. For Beecher and Phelps, condemning Wright was often strategic—they could advocate an expanded education for girls by reassuring their auditors that their schools would never produce "learned ladies" as dangerous as Wright.[115]

Even if women reformers spoke in public more in the 1830s, the nature of their rhetoric and oratorical self-presentation differed sharply from Wright's. Whereas Wright sought to exemplify the "civic rhetor" whose persuasive discourse was based on reason, Maria Stewart, Sarah and Angelina Grimké, and their peers used a religious and even self-effacing style. In their oratorical self-presentation they were women first, Christians second, and orators a distant third, and they proved it by using an "eloquence of humility," a style that proclaimed "virtuous intent and submission to proper authority," as Granville Ganter has shown.[116] Thus women learned by the 1830s that "respectability" hinged on newly exaggerated notions of feminine modesty and piety, even for those whose eagerness for social change led them to public action.

Focusing on Wright's sole year of public lecturing rather than the one-sided backlash of subsequent years allows us to reposition the place of gender in the story. Gender constituted one vivid element of a larger and complex debate about appropriate public interaction between speakers, writers, and their reading and listening audiences. This different view of the Wright case also highlights the importance to this story of print and oratory and, more broadly, shows how deeply implicated they were in forming a national public. Her story reminds us that print and oratory were crucial *topics* within—not just mediums for—a broader, and ongoing, conversation about the nature of American public debate.

Conclusion

THE ONGOING PROCESS OF MAKING AN AMERICAN PUBLIC

In their first debate in January 1835, the young male clerks of the Northern Debating Society in Boston considered whether oratory or writing should be regarded as more valuable to the public. After debating the topic all evening, they held a vote that decided the question (sixteen to twelve) in favor of writing over speaking. "Though I made a few remarks in favor of extemporaneous speaking, my vote was on the other side," admitted Bradley Cumings in his diary.[1] The irony of a debating society celebrating writing over public speaking did not perturb the young men. Like the Calliopeans nearly fifty years earlier, the members of this society viewed good speech and good writing as conjoined skills necessary for young men who planned to impress their social superiors. Even as they discussed the distinctive characteristics and virtues of print and oratory, the very context in which they highlighted these differences underscores the way these two mediums remained inextricably linked during the 1830s and throughout the nineteenth century.

If we began with the messy beginnings of a disconnected new nation in the 1780s, we conclude in the early antebellum era, by which time a whole array of institutions existed to undergird a shared national identity. Although they were still far from universal, public education programs and print distribution networks had become far more widespread, diffusing knowledge to unprecedented numbers of people even in the most remote locales. New networks of roads, railroads, and canals, as well as an increasingly effective postal system, helped to foster those changes. Printing technologies also permitted large-scale publishers to sell their products for less—as little as a penny for daily urban newspapers early in the 1830s—making them available to vastly more readers. For the first time in the 1830s, some local school committees asked the schools in their jurisdiction to use identical schoolbooks rather than allowing children to bring whatever books they happened to own.[2] Furthermore, the locally based lyceums that began to appear during the late 1820s gradually became the locus for traveling speakers and "star" lecturers by the 1850s, setting the stage for the Chautauqua movement of the later nineteenth century; both of these developments encouraged attending lectures as an important component of lifelong self-education. It was still rare for a single text to be read by citizens across the nation or for a large percentage of people to have heard a popular speaker, but innovations in technology and transportation had begun to create "an unprecedented constancy of communications throughout the country"[3]—and the American media eagerly spread this optimistic news. As the Hutchinson Family sang in 1850:

> For the nations must remember
> That Uncle Sam is not a fool,
> For the people do the voting
> And the children go to school.[4]

Patriotic statements like this one closely associated fantasies of universal school attendance and rational voting practices with the image that Americans hoped to project abroad—for much of the song touted the nation's promise for new migrants. Like the patriotic Americans who sang such tunes, the historiography of the antebellum era often associates technological transformation with the democratization of society. Many scholars have coupled the spread of public education and print with the expansion of the franchise, which accelerated so markedly for white male voters before the Civil War. Of course, historians recognize the political exclusion of women, Indians, and African Americans that accompanied white men's increasing access to the vote. Yet these accounts still assert a form of technological determinism when they imply that the material and technological changes in American life gave the disenfranchised greater access to public participation.

But as *A Nation of Speechifiers* has shown, the antebellum expansion of education, print and oral media, and democratic politics represented a *continuation* and reinterpretation of public participation by ordinary people after the Revolution. These newly vibrant institutions added to and enhanced the numerous ad hoc practices of fostering a shared identity that had existed since the republic's founding. Nonelite men and women had long found descriptions of themselves in the print and oratory they consumed, which signaled to their readers or listeners that they already constituted a public to be courted, persuaded, or excoriated. Indeed, this book has sought to depict the transformation of "the public" into a specifically *American* public. When magazine editors used Indian eloquence to promote shared identification among their readers, or when newspaper editors made Frances Wright a foil against which proper Americans might imagine themselves, these media prompted men and women to participate in a public that had clear boundaries. Yet these media were not exclusively controlled by powerful editors or political leaders. Nonelites actively produced speech and writing, often to articulate their own roles as cultural arbiters or to envision an alternative view of the public sphere. Boys who delivered speeches at school exhibitions, or Calliopeans who adopted refined and knowing voices in the *New-York Magazine*, can be viewed as youths rehearsing public roles that they rightly assumed would eventually be theirs. In contrast, young female orators who teasingly challenged gender conventions, or journeymen printers who emphasized their vital labor, sought to criticize the exclusionary qualities of the public or expand its boundaries. In sum, the processes by which ordinary men and women came to consider themselves members of a public and participants in a national culture may have been uneven and gradual during the early republic, but they were sufficiently widespread to foster a sense of American identity long before institutions codified them.

The account of the Northern Debating Society also shows the long-lasting significance of print and oratory to nonelites' understanding of themselves within the public, since these media were intrinsically tied to larger questions about individuals' relation to the public at large. The members of the debating society educated and debated each other because they believed those efforts benefited the nation at the same time as they were improving one another; the wording of their weekly debates specifically invoked "the public" and "the community." Engaging as active participants in print and oral media allowed individuals like Cumings to imagine their place in public life and to exercise it. And delving more deeply into such organizations as the Calliopeans or typographical societies demonstrates that print and oratory gave men and women the means to assert their place as public actors by redefining the public. The remarkable antebellum growth of urban schools, newspapers, and literary societies run by and for African Americans and Native Americans reflected not so much a break from earlier practices as the expansion of institutions established earlier.

Americans in the antebellum era celebrated print and oratory in the same terms as their Revolutionary predecessors, claiming that these media fostered a dynamic interaction between the people and democratic institutions that was vital in a republic. A Massachusetts educator named Nehemiah Cleaveland, for example, waxed lyrical about the use of lyceums in fostering a participatory public culture. "A great amount of information may be imparted by oral lessons. They are aided by the tones of the living voice; and who knows how effective they *may be* to enlighten, impress, and persuade," he explained. Such lectures roused "the public mind; by creating a new taste,—the love and industrious pursuit of knowledge, where now all is apathy and indolence; by prompting men, in fine, to mould and educate themselves."[5] With these words, Cleaveland reiterated a long-standing theme of public discourse: he reminded his readers that their self-improvement would benefit the country as a whole. Such depictions of public culture continued to imagine a unified nation of right-minded citizens actively contributing to its welfare.

What *was* different by the antebellum era was the growing tendency by ordinary people to adopt an oppositional stance with regard to the public at large. In the preceding pages we have seen that even during the most bitter disputes, discussions of "the public" perpetually returned to the notion that there might be a *single* public. By the 1830s, however, the individuals who actively opposed Indian removal, slavery, prostitution, and irreligion embraced new, often abrasive rhetorics that articulated many conflicting publics. These men and women demanded public attention and eschewed the earlier inclusive persuasive styles. Such forms of self-positioning could have profound meaning for the individuals who embraced them. For women's rights reformers, gaining the confidence to speak in public became a crucial component of feminist narratives by the 1848 women's rights convention in Seneca Falls, New York. There women like Elizabeth Cady Stanton told a story of their "trembling voices" growing into vocal strength—a story that worked well as a metaphor for personal and group advancement. Advocates for the rights of woman capitalized on the notion that they had overcome a tradition of silence and subservience, the "seven-fold shield of habitual insignificance," as the British traveler Frances Trollope called it.[6] Likewise, abolitionists and moral reformers found meaning in staking out political positions that placed them severely at odds with the vast majority of the public, for it allowed them to imagine themselves involved in a fervent Christian project of changing the American public for the better. Such forms of an American counterpublic differed profoundly from the persuasive styles of the young female orators of the 1790s, who used playful gambits to prod reluctant auditors to alter their views of women in public. Indeed, it is not surprising that Frances Wright would find the aggressive rhetoric of William Lloyd Garrison so distasteful. Upon her return to the United States in 1835 she vocally opposed Garrison's tactics, arguing that he misled the public and sidestepped true reason. She embraced a mode of argument more typical of the early republic: one that sought social change, to be sure, but did so by imagining that the public as a whole could be moved by persuasion rather than condemnation. By this time, however, her banishment from public life was nearly complete, while Garrison's star was rising.

The shift for some reformers or politicians toward using combative discourse invoked new views of the public and incited heated arguments about public opinion—leading to profound political outcomes. These were not altogether unprecedented during the early republic: as we have seen, the debates between journeymen printers and Duff Green, and between Frances Wright and the newspaper editors, likewise disputed the nature of the public and sought to manipulate public opinion. By the antebellum period, however, reformers and politicians gradually created a pervasive and infectious alternative mode of argument and self-presentation that could be customized to one's cause. This style was based fundamentally on contrasting oneself with carefully chosen opponents—for reformers, these could include drunks, the sexually profligate, or advocates of African colonization—an opposition that provided a useful means for advancing a new vision of the public and the nation. Social reform took on a sense of urgency when it articulated such demons; it also granted the reformer a righteous persona that channeled Christian fervor in order to demand change, as Garrison famously did in the first issue of the *Liberator* in 1831:

> I am aware, that many object to the severity of my language; but is there not cause for severity? I *will* be as harsh as truth, and as uncompromising as justice. On this subject, I do not wish to think, or speak, or write, with moderation. No! no! Tell a man whose house is on fire, to give a moderate alarm; tell him to moderately rescue his wife from the hand of the ravisher; tell the mother to gradually extricate her babe from the fire into which it has fallen;—but urge me not to use moderation in a cause like the present. I am in earnest—I will not equivocate—I will not excuse—I will not retreat a single inch—AND I WILL BE HEARD.

Whereas the journeymen printers and earlier newspaper editors had struggled to arrive at an appropriate and successful means of fighting their battles, antebellum reformers coined a fervent language and corresponding self-fashioning that was gradually adopted by political advocates representing many causes—from anti-immigration protesters to partisans on both sides of the political battles of the 1850s, including the Kansas and Nebraska controversy, the appropriate applications of "popular sovereignty," and the Dred Scott decision. In each case, political advocates painted their opponents in stark contrast to themselves and warned of the impending collapse of American democracy as they fought to portray themselves as the true defenders of citizenship, self-determination, and the rights of the public.

In contrast, while political opponents in the early republic may have advanced conflicting views of the public and the nation's future, even in their most bitter disputes they shared a rhetorical tactic of calling forth an audience of like-minded members of a single public. In doing so, speakers and writers took on personae carefully crafted to appear to employ logic, display disinterested consideration, and bring to bear knowledge and educated experience: all qualities viewed as necessary for one who sought to address the whole public, as children learned from their schoolbooks. This deliberative style appealed to the reading or listening public as the final arbiters of the question at hand. Painstakingly described in elocution manuals and practiced exhaustively in schools, public addresses, and debating societies, this mode of self-presentation and rhetoric was used by ordinary men and women in their own writing and speech.

Let me be clear: I seek not to romanticize the early republic or to lament the eventual passing of such a mode of public discourse, but to demonstrate that this rhetorical style was well suited to match the cultural desire that Americans might attain national cohesion. The frequent refrain of so many published works in the postrevolutionary decades—that the United States sorely lacked skilled orator-leaders whose eloquence might galvanize a unified public and impress the rest of the world—figured public disunity as a fundamental problem. Print and oral media sought to resolve it by encouraging ordinary men and women to demand more from their leaders as well as themselves. Showing that many more nonelites participated than has been previously recognized, as *A Nation of Speechifiers* has done, still recognizes the significant class, racial, and gender boundaries and exclusions of the era. Indeed, the very nature of the American public invoked in print and oratory presumed and reproduced those exclusions, as we have seen.

The significant changes in the manner and matter of public discourse that took place especially during the 1810s and 1820s signaled the limitations of this vision of the national public as a unified body. The widespread diffusion of information permitted by technological and transportation improvements revealed imperfections in American society, generating unprecedented conflict.[7] Whereas the messy beginnings of the 1780s had fostered fantasies of public unity, during the 1830s many Americans questioned whether unity was the best model for the public, the best ideal for social improvement, or the best means of modulating public opinion.

Abbreviations

The archives housing the various collections of documents cited here are identified by the following abbreviations.

AAS	Manuscript Collections, American Antiquarian Society, Worcester, MA
BAT	Boston Athenaeum Manuscript Collections, Boston
COL	Special Collections, Butler Library, Columbia University, New York
HSP	Manuscript Collections, Historical Society of Pennsylvania, Philadelphia
JHU	Special Collections, Milton S. Eisenhower Library, Johns Hopkins University, Baltimore
LCP	Library Company of Philadelphia
LoC	Manuscript Division, Library of Congress, Washington, DC
MaHS	Manuscript Collections, Massachusetts Historical Society, Boston
MdHS	Manuscripts Division, Maryland Historical Society, Baltimore
NYHS	Manuscript Department, New-York Historical Society, New York
NYPL	Rare Books and Manuscripts Division, New York Public Library, New York
REU	Walter P. Reuther Library and Archives of Labor and Urban Affairs, Wayne State University, Detroit

In addition, I have abbreviated the following:

IEAHC	Institute of Early American History and Culture
OIEAHC	Omohundro Institute of Early American History and Culture
WMQ	*William and Mary Quarterly*, 3rd ser.

Notes

INTRODUCTION

1. Christopher Looby, *Voicing America: Language, Literary Form, and the Origins of the United States* (Chicago: University of Chicago Press, 1996); Edmund S. Morgan, *Inventing the People: The Rise of Popular Sovereignty in England and America* (New York: W. W. Norton, 1988); and Alfred F. Young and Terry J. Fife with Mary E. Janzen, *We The People: Voices and Images of the New Nation* (Philadelphia: Temple University Press, 1993). I have taken my title for this introduction from Malini Johar Schueller and Edward Watts, eds., *Messy Beginnings: Postcoloniality and Early American Studies* (New Brunswick, NJ: Rutgers University Press, 2003).

2. Linda Colley, *Britons: Forging the Nation, 1707–1837* (New Haven, CT: Yale University Press, 1992), 5–8; see also David A. Bell, *The Cult of the Nation in France: Inventing Nationalism, 1680–1800* (Cambridge, MA: Harvard University Press, 2001); Prasenjit Duara, "Historicizing National Identity, or Who Imagines What and When," in *Becoming National: A Reader,* ed. Geoff Eley and Ronald Grigor Suny (New York: Oxford University Press, 1996), 151–77; and Peter Sahlins, *Boundaries: The Making of France and Spain in the Pyrenees* (Berkeley: University of California Press, 1989), 8–9.

3. Joseph Galloway to [Samuel Verplanck?], Dec. 30, 1774, in *Letters of Delegates to Congress, 1774–1789,* ed. Paul H. Smith, et al. (Washington, DC: U.S. Government Printing Office for the Library of Congress, 1976), 1:288. Galloway ultimately opposed American independence and worked to arrive at a compromise during the prewar crisis. Long after the war, political leaders continued to worry about geographical divisions, as in George Washington's 1796 Farewell Address.

4. Rogers Smith, *Civic Ideals: Conflicting Visions of Citizenship in U.S. History* (New Haven, CT: Yale University Press, 1997), 122–23, 138. Contemporary United States censuses defined "urban" as those areas with populations over 2,500.

5. William Charvat, *Literary Publishing in America, 1790–1850* (Philadelphia: University of Pennsylvania Press, 1959); Trish Loughran, *The Republic in Print: Print*

Culture in the Age of U.S. Nation Building (New York: Columbia University Press, 2007); Meredith McGill, *American Literature and the Culture of Reprinting, 1834–1853* (Philadelphia: University of Pennsylvania Press, 2003); and Rosalind Remer, *Printers and Men of Capital: Philadelphia Book Publishers in the New Republic* (Philadelphia: University of Pennsylvania Press, 1996).

    6. Trish Loughran, "Disseminating *Common Sense*: Thomas Paine and the Problem of the Early National Bestseller," *American Literature* 78 (2006): 1–28, and Rollo Silver, *The American Printer, 1787–1825* (Charlottesville: Bibliographical Society of the University of Virginia, 1967), 173–74.

    7. See, for example, James Buchanan, *The British Grammar, or An Essay, in Four Parts, towards Speaking and Writing the English Language Grammatically, and Inditing Elegantly, for the Use of Schools, and of Private Young Gentlemen and Ladies* (Boston: Nathaniel Coverly for John Norman, 1784), and the two American editions of Hannah Neale's *Amusement Hall* (Philadelphia: Lang and Ustick, 1796; Elizabethtown, NJ: Shepperd Kollock for Cornelius Davis, 1797).

    8. Smith, *Civic Ideals*, 2. See also Douglas M. Bradburn, "Revolutionary Politics, Nationhood, and the Problems of American Citizenship, 1787–1804" (PhD diss., University of Chicago, 2003); James Kettner, *The Development of American Citizenship, 1609–1870* (Chapel Hill: University of North Carolina Press for the IEAHC, 1978); and Alexander Keyssar, *The Right to Vote: The Contested History of Democracy in the United States* (New York: Basic Books, 2000).

    9. Anthony LaVopa, "Conceiving a Public: Ideas and Society in Eighteenth-Century Europe," *Journal of Modern History* 64 (1992): 79.

    10. Jürgen Habermas, *The Structural Transformation of the Public Sphere: An Inquiry into a Category of Bourgeois Society*, trans. Thomas Burger (1992; Cambridge: MIT Press, 1989).

    11. This literature is vast. See, for example, Richard R. Beeman, *The Varieties of Political Experience in Eighteenth-Century America* (Philadelphia: University of Pennsylvania Press, 2004); Jeffrey Pasley, Andrew Robertson, and David Waldstreicher, eds., *Beyond the Founders: New Approaches to the Political History of the Early American Republic* (Chapel Hill: University of North Carolina Press, 2004); John Brewer, "This, That, and the Other: Public, Social and Private in the Seventeenth and Eighteenth Centuries," in *Shifting the Boundaries: Transformations of the Languages of Public and Private in the Eighteenth Century*, ed. Dario Castaglione and Lesley Sharpe (Exeter: University of Exeter Press, 1995); Dena Goodman, "Public Sphere and Private Life: Toward a Synthesis of Current Historiographical Approaches to the Old Regime," *History and Theory* 31 (1992): 1–20; Mary Kelley, *Learning to Stand and Speak: Women, Education, and Public Life in America's Republic* (Chapel Hill: University of North Carolina Press for OIEAHC, 2006); Lawrence Klein, "Gender and the Public/Private Distinction in the Eighteenth Century: Some Questions about Evidence and Analytic Procedure," *Eighteenth-Century Studies* 29 (1995): 97–109; John M. Murrin, "A Roof without Walls: The Dilemma of American National Identity," in *Beyond Confederation: Origins of the Constitution and American National Identity*, ed. Richard Beeman, Stephen Botein, and

Edward C. Carter II (Chapel Hill: University of North Carolina Press for IEAHC, 1987), 333–48; Andrew W. Robertson, "'Look on This Picture . . . and on This!' Nationalism, Localism, and Partisan Images of Otherness in the United States, 1787–1820," *American Historical Review* 106 (2001): 1263–80; Joan W. Scott, *Gender and the Politics of History* (New York: Columbia University Press, 1996); David Waldstreicher, *In the Midst of Perpetual Fetes: The Making of American Nationalism, 1776–1820* (Chapel Hill: University of North Carolina Press for IEAHC, 1997); Sean Wilentz, *The Rise of American Democracy: Jefferson to Lincoln* (New York: W. W. Norton, 2005); and Rosemarie Zagarri, *Revolutionary Backlash: Women and Politics in the Early American Republic* (Philadelphia: University of Pennsylvania Press, 2007).

12. Richard D. Brown, *Knowledge Is Power: The Diffusion of Information in Early America, 1700–1865* (New York: Oxford University Press, 1989); Kenneth Cmiel, *Democratic Eloquence: The Fight over Popular Speech in Nineteenth-Century America* (Berkeley: University of California Press, 1990); Cathy N. Davidson, *Revolution and the Word: The Rise of the Novel in America* (1986; New York: Oxford University Press, 2004); Jay Fliegelman, *Declaring Independence: Jefferson, Natural Language, and the Culture of Performance* (Stanford, CA: Stanford University Press, 1993); William J. Gilmore, *Reading Becomes a Necessity of Life: Material and Cultural Life in Rural New England, 1780–1835* (Knoxville: University of Tennessee Press, 1989); Sandra M. Gustafson, *Eloquence Is Power: Oratory and Performance in Early America* (Chapel Hill: University of North Carolina Press for OIEAHC, 2000); Looby, *Voicing America*; Loughran, *Republic in Print*; and Michael Warner, *The Letters of the Republic: Publication and the Public Sphere in Eighteenth-Century America* (Cambridge, MA: Harvard University Press, 1990).

13. Davidson, *Revolution and the Word*, chap. 4, esp. 68–69; see also Mary Kupiec Cayton, "The Making of an American Prophet: Emerson, His Audiences, and the Rise of the Culture Industry in Nineteenth-Century America," *American Historical Review* 92 (1987): 597–620; Roger Chartier, *Forms and Meanings: Texts, Performances, and Audiences from Codex to Computer* (Philadelphia: University of Pennsylvania Press, 1995), 43–97; Jonathan Rose, "Rereading the English Common Reader: A Preface to a History of Audiences," *Journal of the History of Ideas* 53 (1992): 47–70; Mary P. Ryan, *Civic Wars: Democracy and Public Life in the American City during the Nineteenth Century* (Berkeley: University of California Press, 1997); and Donald M. Scott, "The Popular Lecture and the Creation of a Public in Mid-Nineteenth-Century America," *Journal of American History* 66 (1980): 791–809.

14. Literacy rates are notoriously difficult to determine and highly dependent on sex, race, class, urban or rural locale, and region (New England apparently achieved the highest literacy rates). Still, most studies assert that the vast majority of white men and women in the Northeast were literate by the second half of the eighteenth century and that the youngest generation in particular achieved nearly complete literacy. This is confirmed by the 1850 U.S. Census, which recorded near-universal literacy for whites throughout the nation. I have assumed that literacy rates, particularly among youth, were very high during the era covered by this book. In coming

to these conclusions I have been most influenced by Ross W. Beales and E. Jennifer Monaghan, "Literacy and Schoolbooks," in *A History of the Book in America*, vol. 1, *The Colonial Book in the Atlantic World*, ed. David D. Hall (New York: Cambridge University Press, 2000), 380–81; Davidson, *Revolution and the Word*, 55–61; David D. Hall, "On Native Ground: From the History of Printing to the History of the Book," in his *Cultures of Print: Essays in the History of the Book* (Amherst: University of Massachusetts Press, 1996), 30; and Alan Tully, "Literacy Levels and Educational Development in Rural Pennsylvania, 1729–1775," *Pennsylvania History* 39 (1972): 301–12.

15. William Howard Gardiner, *An Address, Delivered before the Phi Beta Kappa Society of Harvard University, 28 August 1834, on Classical Learning and Eloquence* (Cambridge: James Munroe, 1834), 27.

16. Gardiner, *Address*, 29.

17. Charles Taylor, *Sources of the Self: The Making of Modern Identity* (Cambridge, MA: Harvard University Press, 1989), 27–36; see also Seyla Benhabib, "Sexual Difference and Collective Identities: The New Global Constellation," *Signs: The Journal of Women in Culture and Society* 24 (1999): 335–61, at 347. Unlike Taylor and especially Benhabib, however, I am less concerned with the interior or psychological experience of "becoming American" than with tracing the forms and sites of communication in the early republic. In this regard I have been influenced by what Dror Wahrman calls "historical epistemology." See Wahrman, *The Making of the Modern Self: Identity and Culture in Eighteenth-Century England* (New Haven, CT: Yale University Press, 2004), esp. xiii–xvii.

18. Schools were more prevalent and inexpensive in the American colonies than in Britain, which also correlated with higher rates of literacy. Carl Kaestle and other scholars have argued that most late eighteenth-century children went to school for at least some time, but because universal, state-funded education was not a legislative goal until the 1820s, some attended brief annual sessions for only a few years or less. More advanced Latin grammar schools and colleges remained available mostly to elites. Carl F. Kaestle, *Pillars of the Republic: Common Schools and American Society, 1780–1860* (New York: McGraw-Hill, 1983), 4, 28–29. See also Bernard Bailyn, "Education as a Discipline: Some Historical Notes," in *The Discipline of Education*, ed. John Walton and James C. Keuthe (Madison: University of Wisconsin Press, 1963); Lawrence A. Cremin, *American Education: The Colonial Experience, 1607–1783* (New York: Harper and Row, 1970), 524–31; and David D. Hall, *Cultures of Print: Essays in the History of the Book* (Amherst: University of Massachusetts Press, 1996), 30.

19. Gilmore, *Reading Becomes a Necessity of Life*, 146, 152, 172, 198–99, 201.

20. Lindley Murray's *English Reader* (1799) and Noah Webster's three-volume *Grammatical Institute* (1783–85) sold, respectively, an estimated 12.5 million and 10.6 million copies by 1840. These numbers are all the more remarkable alongside United States population statistics of the period, since there were 3.9 million inhabitants in 1790, 7.2 million in 1810, and 12.9 million in 1830. According to Frank Luther Mott's criteria, a book had to sell at least 25,000 copies during the 1780s to be considered a top seller, and at least 100,000 copies during the 1820s. Mott,

Golden Multitudes: The Story of Best Sellers in the United States (New York: Macmillan, 1947), 6, 299–301, 304–5. I examined approximately 220 schoolbook titles in undertaking this study.

21. Joseph Kett, *The Pursuit of Knowledge under Difficulties: From Self-Improvement to Adult Education in America, 1750–1990* (Stanford, CA: Stanford University Press, 1994).

22. Mark E. Kann, *On the Man Question: Gender and Civic Virtue in America* (Philadelphia: Temple University Press, 1991); Dana D. Nelson, *National Manhood: Capitalist Citizenship and the Imagined Fraternity of White Men* (Durham, NC: Duke University Press, 1998); and Carroll Smith-Rosenberg, "Dis-covering the Subject of the 'Great Constitutional Discussion,' 1786–1789," *Journal of American History* 79 (1992): 841–73.

23. Joanna Brooks, "The Early American Public Sphere and the Emergence of a Black Print Counterpublic," *WMQ* 62 (2005): 67–92. See also Joanna Brooks, *American Lazarus: Religion and the Rise of African-American and Native American Literatures* (New York: Oxford University Press, 2003); Susan Juster, *Doomsayers: Anglo-American Prophecy in the Age of Revolution* (Philadelphia: University of Pennsylvania Press, 2006), esp. 134–77; Elizabeth McHenry, *Forgotten Readers: Recovering the Lost History of African American Literary Societies* (Durham, NC: Duke University Press, 2002); and Michael Warner, *Publics and Counterpublics* (New York: Zone Books, 2002), 65–124. Other scholars have brilliantly analyzed the religious elements of nation making in this era, including Jon Butler, *Awash in a Sea of Faith: Christianizing the American People* (Cambridge, MA: Harvard University Press, 1990); François Furstenberg, *In the Name of the Father: Washington's Legacy, Slavery, and the Making of a Nation* (New York: Penguin, 2006); Nathan O. Hatch, *The Democratization of American Christianity* (New Haven, CT: Yale University Press, 1989); David Paul Nord, *Faith in Reading: Religious Publishing and the Birth of the Mass Media in America* (New York: Oxford University Press, 2004); and Waldstreicher, *In the Midst of Perpetual Fetes*.

24. Philip Deloria, *Playing Indian* (New Haven, CT: Yale University Press, 1998), 36.

25. I occasionally use "mediums" rather than "media" because, from the vantage of the twenty-first century, the media are so interwoven, global, and immediate that it has become common to refer to them as a singular entity—"the media." Thus my somewhat jarring usage is a reminder of the gulf between our time and the early republic, as well as of the fact that this book specifically examines *two* media.

26. Montgomery Bartlett, *The Practical Reader in Five Books: Good Reading Implies the Exercise of Good Sense, an Improved Taste, and Fine Feeling* (New York: Myers and Smith, 1822), 13.

27. Cited in Michael P. Johnson, ed., *Abraham Lincoln, Slavery, and the Civil War: Selected Writings and Speeches* (Boston: Bedford/St. Martin's, 2000), 5. The tendency to depict a switch from oral to silent reading by the Renaissance thus overstates the many sites, long afterward, in which the two were used simultaneously. Alberto Manguel, *A History of Reading* (New York: Viking, 1996), chap. 2; Paul Saenger,

The Space between Words: The Origins of Silent Reading (Stanford: Stanford University Press, 1997).

28. Some of the most influential texts on this topic are Robert Darnton, *The Kiss of Lamourette: Reflections in Cultural History* (New York: W. W. Norton, 1990), 107–35, 155–87; Elizabeth Eisenstein, *The Printing Press as an Agent of Change: Communication and Cultural Transformation in Early Modern Europe*, 2 vols. (Cambridge: Cambridge University Press, 1979); and Walter Ong, *Orality and Literacy: The Technologizing of the Word* (London: Methuen, 1982). This perspective associates oral culture with the "folk" (as opposed to learned or elite groups), especially when describing the persistence of orality into the modern era. Historians of early American print culture and reading practices have likewise contributed to the sense that print and writing were increasingly privileged over speaking. See Gilmore, *Reading Becomes a Necessity of Life*; Warner, *Letters of the Republic*, 82; and Ronald J. Zboray, *A Fictive People: Antebellum Economic Development and the American Reading Public* (New York: Oxford University Press, 1993), xvi.

29. On this topic I have been strongly influenced by Elizabeth Maddock Dillon, *The Gender of Freedom: Fictions of Liberalism and the Literary Public Sphere* (Stanford, CA: Stanford University Press, 2004), chap. 1.

30. John L. Brooke, "Consent, Civil Society, and the Public Sphere in the Age of Revolution and the Early American Republic," in Pasley, Robertson, and Waldstreicher, *Beyond the Founders*, 207–50; Craig Calhoun, ed., *Habermas and the Public Sphere* (Cambridge, MA: MIT Press, 1992); Thomas A. Gustafson, *Representative Words: Politics, Literature, and the American Language, 1776-1865* (Cambridge: Cambridge University Press, 1992); Habermas, *Structural Transformation of the Public Sphere*; Catherine E. Kelly, *In the New England Fashion: Reshaping Women's Lives in the Nineteenth Century* (Ithaca, NY: Cornell University Press, 1999); Klein, "Gender and the Public/Private Distinction"; Looby, *Voicing America*; and Larzer Ziff, *Writing in the New Nation: Prose, Print, and Politics in the Early United States* (New Haven, CT: Yale University Press, 1991).

31. Brooke, "Consent, Civil Society, and the Public Sphere"; Kelley, *Learning to Stand and Speak*, 5; Mary Catherine Moran, "'The Commerce of the Sexes': Gender and the Social Sphere in Scottish Enlightenment Accounts of Civil Society," in *Paradoxes of Civil Society: New Perspectives on Modern German and British History*, ed. Frank Trentmann (New York: Berghahn Books, 2000), 61–84.

32. Klein, "Gender and the Public/Private Distinction," 104–5. See also Dillon, *Gender of Freedom*, 6–7 and chap. 1; Goodman, "Public Sphere and Private Life," and Dena Goodman, *The Republic of Letters: A Cultural History of the French Enlightenment* (Ithaca, NY: Cornell University Press, 1994), 5–11, 54–89; Linda K. Kerber, "Separate Spheres, Female Worlds, Woman's Place: The Rhetoric of Women's History," *Journal of American History* 75 (1988): 9–39; Jan Lewis, "Politics and the Ambivalence of the Private Sphere: Women in Early Washington, D.C.," in *A Republic for the Ages: The United States Capitol and the Political Culture of the Early Republic*, ed. Donald R. Kennon (Charlottesville: University Press of Virginia for the United States Capitol Historical Society, 1999), 122-51; and Sarah Maza, "Women,

the Bourgeoisie, and the Public Sphere: Response to Daniel Gordon and David Bell," *French Historical Studies* 17 (1992): 935–50.

CHAPTER ONE

1. Daniel Staniford, *The Art of Reading: Containing a Number of Useful Rules, Exemplified by a Variety of Selected and Original Pieces, Calculated to Improve the Scholar in Reading and Speaking with Propriety and Elegance*, 2nd ed. (Boston: John West, 1802), 41–43. Approximately one-third of schoolbooks published before 1810 contained either a version of Demosthenes' life or one of his speeches. American schoolbooks borrowed these tales from the writings of the Greek historian Plutarch, who in turn lifted them from Demetrius Phalereus, an Athenian philosopher and statesman who composed a variety of texts including history, moral treatises, and fables—only fragments of which are extant. It is not known whether these stories were true.

2. Gustafson, *Eloquence Is Power*, 223–24, 230. Jefferson was a reticent public speaker at best, delivering his inaugural address in such a low voice that few heard it—and afterward refusing to deliver his State of the Union addresses orally. Madison mumbled his words; Elbridge Gerry stammered; and Rufus King had the unfortunate habit of freezing before an audience—all of which might be seen, as Jay Fliegelman has suggested, as reasonable responses to the impossible pressures and expectations of public oratory in the era. Fliegelman, *Declaring Independence*, 4–5, 104.

3. Increase Cooke, *The American Orator, or Elegant Extracts in Prose and Poetry: Comprehending the Diversity of Oratorical Specimens; Principally Intended for the Use of Schools and Academies* (New Haven, CT: Sidney's Press, 1811), 21.

4. "On the Importance of a Genteel Address," *Universal Asylum and Columbian Magazine* 5 (1791): 41–42.

5. Bernard Bailyn was the first historian to show convincingly that previous research had been anachronistic, in his *Education and the Forming of American Society* (New York: Random House, 1960); see also Bailyn, "Education as a Discipline," 125–39. His insights were supplemented by Lawrence Cremin's three-volume *American Education* (New York: Harper and Row, 1970, 1980, 1988), which provided vast empirical research on education in American history.

6. Benjamin Rush, "Of the Mode of Education Proper in a Republic," in his *Essays, Literary, Moral and Philosophical* (Philadelphia: Thomas and Samuel F. Bradford, 1798), 6, 14.

7. [Noah Webster], "Education," *American Magazine* 1 (1787): 23. See also V. P. Bynack, "Noah Webster's Linguistic Thought and the Idea of an American National Culture," *Journal of the History of Ideas* 45 (1984): 99–114, and Martin Brückner, *The Geographic Revolution in Early America: Maps, Literacy, and National Identity* (Chapel Hill: University of North Carolina Press for the OIEAHC, 2006), 98–107.

8. Merle M. Odgers, "Education and the American Philosophical Society," *Proceedings of the American Philosophical Society* 87 (1943): 13–14. At 172 and 93 pages,

respectively, the two published essays were among the most weighty texts on education in the era. Samuel Knox, *An Essay on the Best System of Liberal Education, Adapted to the Genius of the Government of the United States* (Baltimore: Warner and Hanna, 1799), and Samuel Harrison Smith, *Remarks on Education: Illustrating the Close Connection between Virtue and Wisdom. To Which Is Annexed, a System of Liberal Education* (Philadelphia: John Ormrod, 1798).

9. Siobhan Moroney, "Birth of a Canon: The Historiography of Early Republican Educational Thought," *History of Education Quarterly* 39 (1999): 486–87.

10. Lawrence A. Cremin, *American Education: The National Experience, 1783–1876* (New York: Harper and Row, 1980), 103.

11. Carl Kaestle, "'Between the Scylla of Brutal Ignorance and the Charybdis of a Literary Education': Elite Attitudes toward Mass Schooling in Early Industrial England and America," in *Schooling and Society: Studies in the History of Education*, ed. Lawrence Stone (Baltimore: Johns Hopkins University Press, 1976), 177–91. Almost no writings objecting to educating the poor appeared after 1800. See also Siobhan Moroney, "Latin, Greek, and the American Schoolboy: Ancient Languages and Class Determinism in the Early Republic," *Classical Journal* 96 (2001): 295–307, and Elaine Weber Pascu, "From the Philanthropic Tradition to the Common School Ideal: Schooling in New York City, 1815–1832" (PhD diss., Northern Illinois University, 1980), 1–9.

12. Cremin, *American Education: The National Experience*; Kaestle, *Pillars of the Republic*, 8–12; Lorraine Smith Pangle and Thomas L. Pangle, *The Learning of Liberty: The Educational Ideas of the American Founders* (Lawrence: University Press of Kansas, 1993), 106–45; Keith Whitescarver, "Creating Citizens for the Republic: Education in Georgia, 1776–1810," *Journal of the Early Republic* 13 (1993): 460, 470.

13. Bailyn, "Education as a Discipline," 135–37. Most colleges and many academies received state assistance during the early republic.

14. Anonymous, "My School-Boy Days in New York City Forty Years Ago," *New York Teacher, and American Educational Monthly* 6 (1869): 93.

15. Of the 220 schoolbooks I examined, I have cited approximately half.

16. An additional 3 million copies of *The English Reader* sold in Great Britain. That the United States had only 12.9 million total inhabitants in 1830 makes these numbers all the more extraordinary. Charles Monaghan points out that Murray allowed his volume to be reprinted without threat of copyright infringement, whereas Webster fought those who pirated his text. Charles Monaghan, *The Murrays of Murray Hill* (Brooklyn, NY: Urban History Press, 1998), 130–37; E. Jennifer Monaghan, *A Common Heritage: Noah Webster's Blue-Back Speller* (Hamden, CT: Archon Books, 1983), 227–29.

17. John Hubbard, *The American Reader: Containing a Selection of Narration, Harangues, Addresses, Orations, Dialogues, Odes, Hymns, Poems, &c. Designed for the Use of Schools* (Walpole, NH: Thomas and Thomas, 1804). Hubbard, an academy preceptor and eventually a professor at Dartmouth, wrote the similarly successful *Rudiments of Geography* (eight editions between 1803 and 1817).

Schoolbooks varied greatly in price and but would have been affordable to most families, particularly because of the flourishing secondhand book market. The least expensive sold for the same rock-bottom price as almanacs (less than a shilling in the late eighteenth century and twelve or fifteen cents by the 1810s). Lindley Murray's *English Grammar* cost $.25 in 1804, the *Juvenile Mentor* cost $.37½ in 1809, and Frederick Douglass paid $.50 for a used copy of *The Columbian Orator* in 1830. Earl L. Bradsher, "Early American Book Prices," *Publishers' Weekly* 83 (Mar. 8, 1913): 862–66; Elizabeth Carroll Reilly and David D. Hall, "Customers and the Market for Books," and Russell L. Martin, "A Note on Book Prices," both in *History of the Book in America*, vol. 1, *Colonial Book in the Atlantic World*, ed. Hall, 387–99, 522–23. David W. Blight, introduction to *The Columbian Orator,* Bicentennial ed. (New York: New York University Press, 1998), xiii.

18. Robert Finley, "National Uniformity in Textbooks and Curricula" (1815?), in *The Annals of America* (Chicago: Encyclopaedia Britannica, 1968), 4:393–97.

19. The New England states had the highest literacy rates and the greatest number of schools per capita during this era, although these statistics seldom take into account rural and remote parts of Vermont, New Hampshire, and Maine.

20. Daniel Adams, *The Understanding Reader, or Knowledge Before Oratory. Being a New Selection of Lessons, Suited to the Understanding and the Capacities of Youth*, 3rd ed. (1803; reprint, Leominster, MA: Salmon Wilder, 1805), iii. This volume appeared in at least thirteen editions in Massachusetts and Maine between 1803 and 1821. Adams was a young doctor who suspended his practice of medicine for approximately ten years to publish a newspaper, teach school, and edit a medical journal; much later, in the late 1830s, he served in the New Hampshire state senate. Emphasis in the original.

21. On elocution, see Fliegelman, *Declaring Independence*; Jay Fliegelman, "Introduction" to Charles Brockden Brown, *Wieland; and Memoirs of Carwin the Biloquist,* ed. Jay Fliegelman (New York: Penguin, 1991), xxvii–xxxvi; Wilbur Samuel Howell, *Eighteenth-Century British Logic and Rhetoric* (Princeton, NJ: Princeton University Press, 1971); and Frederick W. Haberman, "English Sources of American Elocution," in *History of Speech Education in America: Background Studies,* ed. Karl R. Wallace (New York: Appleton-Century-Crofts, 1954), 106–8.

22. Seventeenth-century American Puritan ministers in particular marked a clear distinction between style and substance when it came to oratory. They gleaned their plain, unadorned styles of delivery from the theories of Petrus Ramus of the University of Paris, who considered logic the central characteristic of a good sermon and rhetoric only so much verbal display. By the early eighteenth century, American styles of public speaking came more into line with contemporary European and especially British fashions, which idealized the classical styles described by such Roman theorists as Quintilian and Cicero. Carolyn Eastman, "Rhetoric," in *Encyclopedia of the New American Nation: The Emergence of the United States, 1754–1829,* ed. Paul Finkleman (New York: Charles Scribner's Sons, 2005), 3:142–44.

23. "The art of delivery with emphasis on accent, pitch, voice modulation, pause, timing, and gesture became, for many people in the eighteenth century, the whole

of rhetoric." Winifred Bryan Homer and Kerri Morris Barton, "The Eighteenth Century," in *The Present State of Scholarship in Historical and Contemporary Rhetoric*, ed. Winifred Bryan Homer (Columbia: University of Missouri Press, 1990), 126.

24. James Burgh, *The Art of Speaking*, 4th ed. (Philadelphia: R. Aitken, 1775), 3; emphasis in the original. American printers reprinted Burgh's book at least thirteen times before 1804. In addition, during the early republic editors frequently excerpted it in schoolbooks and magazines.

25. LaVopa, "Conceiving a Public," 79.

26. Nancy Armstrong, *Desire and Domestic Fiction: A Political History of the Novel* (New York: Oxford University Press, 1987); Richard L. Bushman, *The Refinement of America: Persons, Houses, Cities* (New York: Alfred A. Knopf, 1992), 11–203.

27. *Norwich (CT) Courier*, July 8, 1829.

28. "Mr. Turner, Lecturer on Elocution and Belles-Lettres, to the Public" (Boston, 1821), AAS Broadsides Collections. See also Ziff, *Writing in the New Nation*, 69–70.

29. This term also distinguishes the sources used here from the smaller percentage of schoolbooks that addressed other concerns, such as rudimentary alphabet books and more advanced geographies or Latin grammars.

30. Nathaniel Heaton Jr., *The Columbian Preceptor: Containing a Variety of New Pieces in Prose, Poetry, and Dialogues with Rules for Reading* (Wrentham, MA: Nathaniel Heaton Jr., 1801). Heaton published two other schoolbooks within a year of the appearance of this one. Several years earlier he had edited and published a newspaper, the *Minerva* (1796–98), in Dedham, MA.

31. Schoolbooks had much in common with other print genres of the period. As with magazines, their editors clipped most of their material from other sources, seeking to present the "best" anthologized array of literary information. Both genres participated fully in the "culture of sensibility," calling forth a refined perspective from their readers in the vein of Vicesimus Knox's wildly popular *Elegant Extracts* (London: Charles Dilly, 1783), reprinted many times in England and the United States through the 1820s. In doing so, they helped to make the larger literary culture accessible and manageable to readers. Barbara M. Benedict, *Making the Modern Reader: Cultural Mediation in Early Modern Literary Anthologies* (Princeton, NJ: Princeton University Press, 1996), 3–4.

32. Asa Lyman, *The American Reader: Containing Elegant Sketches in Prose and Poetry; Designed for the Improvement of Youth in the Art of Reading and Speaking with Propriety and Beauty*, 2nd ed. (Portland, ME: A. Lyman, 1811), xi.

33. *The Forum Orator, or The American Public Speaker: Consisting of Examples and Models of Eloquence, both That of the Bar and Popular Assembly, of Orations and Speeches* (Boston: David Carlisle for Joseph Nancrede, 1804), 21.

34. Joseph P. Roach, *The Player's Passion: Studies in the Science of Acting* (Ann Arbor: University of Michigan Press, 1993), 58–92.

35. Thomas E. Birch, *The Virginian Orator: Being a Variety of Original and Selected Poems, Orations, and Dramatic Scenes; to Improve the American Youth in the Ornamental and Useful Art of Eloquence and Gesture* (Richmond, VA: Samuel Pleasants Jr., 1808), xiv. Birch lifted these directives from Burgh's *Art of Speaking*, which cataloged the

"choreography of countenances" that purported to identify the "natural" expressions and gestures suited to particular emotions.

36. "On the Importance of a Genteel Address," *Universal Asylum and Columbian Magazine* 5 (July 1790): 42.

37. "That boys should stand motionless, while they are pronouncing the most impassioned language, is extremely absurd and unnatural, and that they should sprawl into an awkward, ungain[ly], and desultory action, is still more offensive and disgusting," the author explained. *The Elements of Gesture, Illustrated by Four Elegant Copper-Plates: Together with Rules for Expressing, with Propriety, the Various Passions and Emotions of the Mind* (Philadelphia: William Young, 1790), 6–8.

38. Joseph Richardson, *The American Reader: A Selection of Lessons for Reading and Speaking; Wholly from American Authors* (Boston: Lincoln and Edmands, 1810), 9. See also his *Clear and Practical System of Punctuation* (Boston: I. Thomas and E. T. Andrews, 1792).

39. And indeed, a substantial minority of authors so conflated outward appearances and "emotions of the heart" that they jeopardized the distinction between sincere and deceptive speech. For example, Seth Leonard informed readers that true eloquence emerged "with sincerity from the heart" while simultaneously instructing them to take on "an appearance of sincerity." Likewise, Henry Lemoine declared that eloquent ideas that "seem to come from the heart" would move listeners. Moments like these hinted that the distinction between artifice and true eloquence was not so clear and that auditors might be mistakenly satisfied with the pretense of sincerity. Seth Leonard, *The American Grammar: To Which Is Added, Elements of Reading and Oratory*, 3rd ed. (New York: M'Duffee and Farrand, 1819), 94; Henry Lemoine, *The Art of Speaking upon an Entire New Plan, and in Which the Operations and Emotions of the Mind Are Particularly Considered* (London: Lee and Hurst, 1797), 33.

40. *Lessons for Youth, Selected for the Youth of Schools*, 2nd Philadelphia ed. (1799; reprint, Philadelphia: Benjamin and Jacob Johnson, 1801), 106–7.

41. Caleb Bingham, *The American Preceptor Improved: Being a New Selection of Lessons for Reading and Speaking*, 11th ed. (1819; reprint, New York: Evert Duyckinck, 1820), 203; *The American Orator: Containing Rules and Directions, Which Are Calculated to Improve Youth and Others in the Ornamental and Useful Art of Eloquence* (Lexington, KY: Joseph Charless, 1807), 50. On duplicity and the theatrical sensibility in the eighteenth century, see Jean-Christophe Agnew, *Worlds Apart: The Market and the Theater in Anglo-American Thought, 1550–1750* (Cambridge: Cambridge University Press, 1986), 101–4, 135–48; Toby L. Ditz, "Secret Selves, Credible Personas: The Problematics of Trust and Public Display in the Writing of Eighteenth-Century Philadelphia Merchants," in *Possible Pasts: Becoming Colonial in Early America*, ed. Robert Blair St. George (Ithaca, NY: Cornell University Press, 2000), 219–42; Fliegelman, *Declaring Independence*, 31 and passim.

42. Undated memoir of Charles D. Deshler, a New Jersey judge, transcribed in David Murray, *History of Education in New Jersey* (Washington, DC: Government Printing Office, 1899), 33, 35. Spalding used Murray's *English Reader* for recitations and a variety of books for other subjects.

43. Many schools in New Hampshire (like other rural areas) were housed in decidedly modest surroundings. The town of Concord voted in 1790 to use the "pest house" (formerly used to isolate the sick) as a school by moving the building into town from the outskirts. Francestown and Hampton held local schools in barns and suspended school for the winter. Harriet Webster Marr, *Atkinson Academy: The Early Years* (Springfield, MA: John E. Stewart, 1940), 8–9. Because exhibitions required substantial room for auditors and a space for performers, they often took place in meetinghouses; if the schoolhouse did have sufficient space, they frequently constructed a stage at the front to give the audience a better view. See, for example, the description of an exhibition in Marietta, Georgia, in a letter from Hannah Gilman to her son in February 1819, where the stage was four feet high and separated from the audience by a curtain that the students could open and close as scenes began and ended. Emily Hoffman Gilman Noyes, *A Family History in Letters and Documents, 1667–1837* (St. Paul, MN: privately printed, 1919), 364.

44. Stephen Peabody diary, Oct. 15, 1787, transcribed in Marr, *Atkinson Academy*, 31–33 (the original is held at the AAS).

45. Scholars who have made passing reference to exhibitions include Gladys L. Borchers and Lillian R. Wagner, "Speech Education in Nineteenth-Century Schools," in Wallace, *History of Speech Education in America*, 277-300; Cremin, *American Education: The National Experience*; Barbara Finkelstein, "Reading, Writing, and the Acquisition of Identity in the United States, 1790–1860," in *Regulated Children, Liberated Children,* ed. Barbara Finkelstein (New York: Psychohistory Press, 1979), 114–39; Kaestle, *Pillars of the Republic*, 23; and William R. Johnson, "'Chanting Choristers': Simultaneous Recitation in Baltimore's Nineteenth-Century Primary Schools," *History of Education Quarterly* 34 (1994): 1-23. On earlier methods of teaching reading, see E. Jennifer Monaghan, *Learning to Read and Write in Colonial America* (Amherst: University of Massachusetts Press, 2005), 19–45, 197–212.

46. William Sewell, *Diary of William Sewell, 1797–1846, Formerly of Augusta, Maine, Maryland, Virginia, and Pioneer in Illinois*, ed. John Goodell (Beardstown, IL: John Goodell, 1930), 32, 94.

47. Bathsheba Whitman to Hannah Cushing, Aug. 3–24, 1806, Nathaniel Cushing Papers, MaHS; Charles Stearns, *Dramatic Dialogues for the Use of Schools* (Leominster, MA: John Prentiss, 1798), 18. Stearns was a Congregational minister who also ran the coeducational Liberal School in Lincoln, Massachusetts, from 1793 to 1808.

48. William Bentley Fowle, MS Autobiography, 1855, William Bentley Fowle Deposit, MaHS. Fowle later became a prominent educational reformer and schoolbook editor.

49. Heman Humphrey to Henry Barnard, Pittsfield, MA, Dec. 12, 1860, cited in Kaestle, *Pillars of the Republic*, 23.

50. Bathsheba Whitman to Hannah Cushing, Aug. 3–24, 1806, MaHS. Whitman's sense of "dread" was well founded, for some teachers lost their jobs as a result of a poor exhibition, as did Ethan Allen Greenwood in western Massachusetts in 1802. When his students displayed that they had "forgotten much of their

spelling &c." he reported in his diary cryptically that "the weasels began to attack my school & the exhibition was given over &c. &c. &c." Ethan Allen Greenwood, Diaries (1801–10), Feb. 24, 1802, AAS.

51. Sally Ripley, Diary, May 7, 1800, AAS.

52. Sarah Ayer, *Diary of Sarah Connell Ayer, Andover and Newburyport, Massachusetts, Concord and Bow, New Hampshire, Portland and Eastport, Maine* (Portland, ME: Lefavor-Tower, 1910), 404.

53. Hannah Syng Bunting, June 4, 1827, in *Memoir, Diary, and Letters of Miss Hannah Syng Bunting, of Philadelphia* (New York: T. Mason and G. Lane for the Sunday School Union of the Methodist Episcopal Church, 1837), 199. See also comments by Benjamin Shaw about the New York African Free School in 1817, quoted in Kaestle, *Pillars of the Republic*, 38.

54. "Local: Grammar School Exhibition," *Pastime: A Literary Paper* 1 (Schenectady, NY: Jan. 16, 1808): 241–42. Other newspaper reports were more circumspect in their assessments, as when a Utica, New York, paper pronounced that the common school's exhibition had been "perfectly satisfactory, and did great honour to the teacher and scholars" in 1826. "Common School Examination," *Western Recorder*, Feb. 28, 1826. Other students remembered the terror of forgetting their lines or laughing nervously.

55. Samuel Emerson to George Barrell Emerson, July 27, 1817, George Barrell Emerson Papers, MaHS; spelling as in the original.

56. *Elements of Gesture*, 15; this essay was reprinted in Increase Cooke, *Sequel to the American Orator, or Dialogues for Schools; to Which Are Prefixed, Elements of Elocution* (New Haven, CT: Sidney's Press, 1813), v.

57. "On the Evil Consequences of Public Examinations and Acting Plays in Elementary Schools," *Juvenile Mirror, or Educational Magazine* 1 (March 1812): 266, 269; emphasis in the original.

58. Stearns, *Dramatic Dialogues*, 25.

59. Matthias B. Roberts, *The Juvenile Reader, or Miscellaneous Selections, in Prose and Verse: Compiled for the Use of Schools in the U. States*, 2nd ed. (Baltimore: M. B. Roberts, 1823), 58–60. This title appeared in at least five editions in Baltimore and Pittsburgh by 1828.

60. William Osborne Payne, Apr. 24, 1796, transcribed in *An Unconscious Autobiography: William Osborne Payne's Diary and Letters*, ed. Thatcher T. P. Luquer (New York: privately printed, 1938), 9–10.

61. In a subsequent entry, however, the writer struggled to find enough praise for a competing minister. "It was the most pure, noble, dignified, eloquent, charming, lovely, solid, sound, & virtuous discourse that I ever heard, and delivd in a most engaging manner, and a man who could seet and not feel his heart throb & bosm glow to be virtuous, must be swalowed up in sensuality or sunk in ignorance." James Homer, Diary, 1821–23, MaHS; spelling as in the original.

62. Anna Eliza Heath, Commonplace Book, ca. 1824, Heath Family Papers, MaHS.

63. Fliegelman, *Declaring Independence*, 115.

64. Thomas Coffin Amory, Diary, Dec. 9, 1832, Amory Family Papers, MaHS. Amory was training to be a lawyer in Suffolk County; after passing the bar in 1834, at age twenty-four, he dedicated many years to public service with the Boston city government, particularly in its educational departments.

65. *The Memoirs of John Quincy Adams*, ed. Charles Francis Adams (Philadelphia: J. B. Lippincott, 1874), 1:445. I am grateful to James E. Lewis Jr. for this reference.

66. John Gallison, Diary, Nov. 1, 1809, Feb. 20, 1810, Apr. 14, 1810, Apr. 23, 1810, and May 1, 1810, MaHS. Ogilvie was a Scottish teacher and lecturer based in Milton, Virginia, whose skill in oratory earned him the praise of Thomas Jefferson, among others. He embarked on a public speaking tour in 1809 to promote the creation of professorships of rhetoric and oratory in all American colleges and the building of public halls for the exhibition of oratory in all American cities. Josiah Morse, "James Ogilvie," *Dictionary of American Biography on CD-ROM* (1931; New York: Charles Scribner's Sons, 1997).

67. In the 1760s and 1770s, the Massachusetts House of Representatives and the Pennsylvania Assembly created formal public seating in their attempts to turn government into a "School of Public Learning." Robert Blair St. George, "Massacred Language: Courtroom Performance in Eighteenth-Century Boston," in St. George, *Possible Pasts*, 339–43; Lewis, "Politics and the Ambivalence of the Private Sphere," 123–24.

68. Rhys Isaac, *The Transformation of Virginia, 1740–1790* (1982; New York: W. W. Norton, 1988), 88–94, 92.

69. Noah Webster, *An American Selection of Lessons in Reading and Speaking. Calculated to Improve the Minds and Refine the Taste of Youth. . . . Being the Third Part of a Grammatical Institute of the English Language* (Philadelphia: Young and McCulloch, 1787); Caleb Bingham, *The American Preceptor; Being a New Selection of Lessons for Reading and Speaking, Designed for the Use of Schools*, 3rd ed. (1794; reprint, Boston: Manning and Loring, 1796); and Caleb Bingham, *The Columbian Orator: Containing a Variety of Original and Selected Pieces; Together with Rules, Calculated to Improve Youth and Others in the Ornamental and Useful Art of Eloquence*, 6th Troy ed. (1797; reprint, Troy, NY: Parker and Bliss, 1815).

70. Ruth Miller Elson, *Guardians of Tradition: American Schoolbooks of the Nineteenth Century* (Lincoln: University of Nebraska Press, 1964); Furstenberg, *In the Name of the Father*; Ripley, Diary, July 30, 1799, AAS; punctuation and spelling as in the original.

71. These titles also conveyed ideas that held particular meanings during the early republic, of course: the distinction between art and artifice, the importance of companionate bonds, and so on.

72. Donald Fraser, *The Columbian Monitor: Being a Pleasant & Easy Guide to Useful Knowledge* (New York: Loudon and Brower for Donald Fraser, 1794), iii. Fraser was a New York schoolteacher and the author of several schoolbooks, including *History of All Nations* (1807).

73. Mathew Carey, *The School of Wisdom, or American Monitor: Containing a Copious Collection of Sublime and Elegant Extracts, from the Most Eminent Writers, on Mor-*

als, Religion and Government, 2nd ed. (Philadelphia: Mathew Carey, 1800), iv. Carey was an Irish-born printer and publisher with a terrifically successful Philadelphia business.

74. Warner, *Letters of the Republic,* 118–50.

75. Joseph Dana, *A New American Selection of Lessons, in Reading and Speaking,* 3rd ed. (1792; reprint, Exeter, NH: H. H. Ranlet for Thomas and Andrews, 1799), 290–93.

76. Richardson, *American Reader,* iii.

77. *The American Lady's Preceptor: A Compilation of Observations, Essays and Poetical Effusions, Designed to Direct the Female Mind in a Course of Pleasing and Instructive Reading,* 2nd ed., rev., corr., and enl. (Baltimore: Edward J. Coale, 1811), 48.

78. *Dialogues for Schools, Selected, with Alterations, from the Works of Various Dramatic Writers; to Which Is Added, an Appendix, Containing a Selection of Pieces for Declamation* (Hartford, CT: Hudson and Goodwin, 1800), 185.

79. Lyman, *American Reader,* 60.

80. Furstenberg, *In the Name of the Father,* 30–34.

81. John Jay, "The Importance and Blessings of Union," in Cooke, *American Orator,* 341.

82. John Quincy Adams, *An Inaugural Oration, Delivered at the Author's Installation, as Boylston Professor of Rhetorick and Oratory, at Harvard University, in Cambridge, Massachusetts, on Thursday, 12 June, 1806* (Boston: Monroe and Francis, 1806), 16, 26–27. It was reprinted and excerpted in numerous schoolbooks, including Richardson, *American Reader,* and B. R. Evans, *The Republican Compiler, Comprising a Series of Scientific, Descriptive, Narrative, Popular, Biographical, Epistolary, and Miscellaneous Pieces* (Pittsburgh: Cramer and Spear, 1818). See also Adam S. Potkay, "Theorizing Civic Eloquence in the Early Republic: The Road from David Hume to John Quincy Adams," *Early American Literature* 34 (1999): 147–70.

83. "Review," *Emerald, or Miscellany of Literature* 1 (July 5, 1806): 114. See also the review of the spoken address in the *Repertory,* June 17, 1806.

84. Rodolphus Dickinson, *The Columbian Reader: Comprising a New and Various Selection of Elegant Extracts in Prose and Poetry, for the Use of Schools in the United States,* 2nd ed. (Boston: R. P. and C. Williams, 1818), 115. When this was published, Dickinson was a twenty-one-year-old schoolteacher in Massachusetts and had not yet attended Williams College, from which he graduated in 1821. He ultimately practiced law and served as a Democratic United States congressman from Ohio in the 1840s.

85. William Wirt, "John Marshall," in Dickinson, *Columbian Reader,* 118–19.

86. Cooke, *American Orator,* 15.

87. Kaestle, *Pillars of the Republic,* 35.

88. By 1796, New York had six church charity schools; Philadelphia had at least twelve by 1810. Kaestle, *Pillars of the Republic,* 30–61; Pascu, "From the Philanthropic Tradition to the Common School Ideal," 1–49, 143–209. These schools did not appear in smaller towns and rural areas. In Lancaster, Pennsylvania, in the early nineteenth century, for example, "there was *not one free* [school] to the average

boy or girl whose parents could not afford to pay for their education," as William Riddle put it in an affronted tone in his *One Hundred and Fifty Years of School History in Lancaster, Pennsylvania* (Lancaster, PA: privately printed, 1905), 16; emphasis in the original.

89. By 1812 the Philadelphia Society for the Establishment and Support of Charity Schools had about 400 students in its schools; the New York Female Association had 750 students by 1823. Kaestle, *Pillars of the Republic*, 40. In 1826 New York's Free School Society was renamed the Public School Society, initiating the tendency to call free, inclusive schools "public."

90. Carl F. Kaestle, *Joseph Lancaster and the Monitorial School Movement: A Documentary History* (New York: Teachers College Press, 1973); Pascu, "From the Philanthropic Tradition to the Common School Ideal," 443–95. By 1804 American printers had begun to reprint Lancaster's *Improvements in Education* (London: Darton and Harvey, 1803) touting his accomplishments with large numbers of poor students.

91. Finkelstein, "Reading, Writing, and the Acquisition of Identity," 114–39.

92. "A Description of the Picture and Mezzotinto of Mr. Pitt, Done by Charles Willson Peale, of Maryland," broadside. Pitt died in November 1768, just as the portrait was completed. In addition to the version hung in Lee's home (and eventually transferred to the Virginia State House), Peale presented a nearly identical copy to the Maryland Assembly in 1775 for display in the new statehouse in Annapolis.

93. *Virginia Gazette*, Apr. 20, 1769, cited in Charles Coleman Sellers, "Virginia's Great Allegory of William Pitt," *WMQ* 9 (1952): 64. The mezzotint copies measured approximately fourteen by twenty inches.

94. On this subject see Patricia A. Anderson, *Promoted to Glory: The Apotheosis of George Washington*. Exhibition catalog, Smith College Museum of Art, Northampton, Massachusetts, February 22–April 6, 1980 (Northampton, MA: Museum, 1980); Gustafson, *Eloquence Is Power*, 213–32; Paul K. Longmore, *The Invention of George Washington* (Berkeley: University of California Press, 1988); Barry Schwartz, *George Washington: The Making of an American Symbol* (New York: Free Press, 1987); and Wendy C. Wick, *George Washington, an American Icon: The Eighteenth-Century Graphic Portraits* (Washington, DC: Smithsonian Institution Traveling Exhibition Services, 1982).

95. Newspapers throughout the country quickly reprinted it, and it appeared in schoolbooks within a year, rapidly becoming the first canonical piece of American oratory. Schoolbooks never mentioned that the address had not been orally delivered; in fact, they sometimes implied that it *had* by flanking it with descriptions of Washington as an orator. Bingham, *Columbian Orator;* Alexander Thomas Jr., *The Orator's Assistant: Being a Selection of Dialogues for Schools and Academies, Taken from Many of the Best Dramatic Writings in the English Language* (Worcester, MA: Isaiah Thomas, 1797). On the speech's initial publication see Furstenberg, *In the Name of the Father*, 1–6.

96. Anderson described the painting as "masterfully done," reiterating some of the ecstatic newspaper descriptions. John Anderson Jr., Diary (1794–98), Feb. 22 and Mar. 12, 1798, NYHS. Newspaper entries that described the portrait in-

clude "Anniversary Birth-Day of Gen. Washington," *Time-Piece* (New York), Feb. 10, 1798, and "Among the Various Exhibitions for Public Gratification," *Spectator* (New York), Feb. 24, 1798. See also Gustafson, *Eloquence Is Power*, 219–21.

CHAPTER TWO

1. "Messrs. Printers," *Guardian of Freedom* (Haverhill, MA), Nov. 4, 1793.
2. Aurelia, "For the Guardian," *Guardian of Freedom*, Nov. 25, 1793; spelling as in the original. The local minister's diary reveals that his daughter wrote the letter. Marr, *Atkinson Academy*, 41.
3. Almira, "For the Guardian," *Guardian of Freedom*, Dec. 5, 1793.
4. "For the Guardian," *Guardian of Freedom*, Dec. 5, 1793.
5. Most scholars have presumed that until the late 1820s women were prohibited from speaking in public. See, for example, Cmiel, *Democratic Eloquence*, 29–30; Karlyn Kohrs Campbell, *Man Cannot Speak for Her*, vol. 1, *A Critical Study of Early Feminist Rhetoric* (New York: Greenwood Press, 1989); and Fliegelman, *Declaring Independence*, 130. Several recent works have examined women's oratory, primarily in religious settings. Catherine A. Brekus, *Strangers and Pilgrims: Female Preaching in America, 1740–1845* (Chapel Hill: University of North Carolina Press, 1998); Sandra Gustafson, "The Genders of Nationalism: Patriotic Violence, Patriotic Sentiment in the Performances of Deborah Sampson Gannett," in St. George, *Possible Pasts*, 380–99; Rebecca Mountford, *The Gendered Pulpit: Preaching in American Protestant Spaces* (Carbondale: Southern Illinois University Press, 2003); and Juster, *Doomsayers*, chap. 6.
6. Lindal Buchanan, *Regendering Delivery: The Fifth Canon and Antebellum Women Rhetors* (Carbondale: Southern Illinois University Press, 2005); Kelley, *Learning to Stand and Speak*; Zagarri, *Revolutionary Backlash*.
7. I have identified approximately three dozen girls' speeches published in newspapers, magazines, and promotional literature by academies. These speeches were mostly delivered by students at elite female academies, primarily in Pennsylvania, New York, and Massachusetts during the 1790s and early 1800s.
8. A new literature has sought to specify the evolving meanings of women's public and political activities in the early republic and antebellum eras of American history. See, for example, Jeanne Boydston, "Making Gender in the Early Republic: Judith Sargent Murray and the Revolution of 1800," in *The Revolution of 1800: Democracy, Race, and the New Republic*, ed. James Horn, Jan Ellen Lewis, and Peter S. Onuf (Charlottesville: University of Virginia Press, 2002), 240–66; Kerber, "Separate Spheres, Female Worlds, Woman's Place," 9–39; Lewis, "Politics and the Ambivalence of the Private Sphere," 122–51; Marion Rust, "'Into the House of an Entire Stranger': Why Sentimental Doesn't Equal Domestic in Early American Fiction," *Early American Literature* 37 (2002): 281–309; Mary P. Ryan, *Women in Public: Between Banners and Ballots, 1825–1880* (Baltimore: Johns Hopkins University Press, 1990).

9. Nancy Fraser, "Rethinking the Public Sphere: A Contribution to the Critique of Actually Existing Democracy," in Calhoun, *Habermas and the Public Sphere*, 123; see also Brooks, "Early American Public Sphere and the Emergence of a Black Print Counterpublic," 67–92; and Warner, *Publics and Counterpublics*, 65–124.

10. Anna Harrington, "An Apology for Studious Ladies," in Stearns, *Dramatic Dialogues*, 499.

11. William Edmond letter to Polly Edmond, dated at Philadelphia, Dec. 7, 1799, transcribed in his *Letters and Journals*, ed. Elizabeth Curtis (New York: Case, Lockwood, and Brainard, 1926), 27–28. Edmond was a legislator in Connecticut, so they were likely of elite status.

12. Arnauld Berquin, *The Beauties of the Children's Friend: Being a Selection of Interesting Pieces... Intended to Promote a Love of Truth and Virtue; for the Use of Schools* (Boston: Manning and Loring and Lemuel Blake, 1808), 273–78. His *L'ami des enfans* was originally published in 1782–83 and translated into English the following year. Berquin avoided fairy tales, preferring to fill his stories with ordinary child protagonists and small family dramas. The book also contains a story titled "The Pleasures and Advantages of Sociability" about Leonora's opposite: a laconic, unsociable little boy named Harold. Like Leonora's, Harold's family teaches him to contribute appropriately to the sociability of the household. Prattling was not necessarily viewed as a female failing; other stories associated it with boys, as in Heaton's *Columbian Preceptor*. Still, the chattering woman was seen as a particular kind of problem.

13. Joan M. Jensen, "Not Only Ours but Others: The Quaker Teaching Daughters of the Mid-Atlantic, 1790–1850," *History of Education Quarterly* 24 (1989): 4–5. Black women's literacy rates were much lower; even by the 1850 U.S. Census, only 50 percent of adult black women in the Northeast were recorded as literate. Jensen speculates that their lower literacy rates may have resulted from black migration from the South, where black literacy was extremely low because of slave laws.

14. Monaghan, *Learning to Read and Write in Colonial America*, 237; Kathryn Kish Sklar, "The Schooling of Girls and Changing Community Values in Massachusetts Towns, 1750–1820," *History of Education Quarterly* 33 (1993): 517, 525. Because of the overwhelming localism of schools in this era, there are no estimates of girls' school attendance rates in the Northeast overall.

15. Ruth Bloch, *Gender and Morality in Anglo-American Culture, 1650–1800* (Berkeley: University of California Press, 2003), chap. 8; Nancy F. Cott, *The Bonds of Womanhood: "Women's Sphere" in New England, 1780–1835* (New Haven, CT: Yale University Press, 1977), 101–25; Davidson, *Revolution and the Word*, 62–70; Linda K. Kerber, *Women of the Republic: Intellect and Ideology in Revolutionary America* (Chapel Hill: University of North Carolina Press for the IEAHC, 1980), 189–231; and Thomas Laqueur, *Making Sex: Body and Gender from the Greeks to Freud* (Cambridge, MA: Harvard University Press, 1990).

16. John Bennett, *Strictures on Female Education; Chiefly as It Relates to the Culture of the Heart* (Philadelphia: W. Spotswood and H. and P. Rice, 1793), 2; and Rosemarie Zagarri, "The Rights of Man and Woman in Post-revolutionary America," *WMQ* 55 (1998): 205–6.

17. John Hamilton Moore, *The Young Gentleman and Lady's Monitor, and English Teacher's Assistant; Being a Collection of Select Pieces from Our Best Modern Writers*, 5th ed. (New York: Hugh Gaine, 1787), 122.

18. Kerber, *Women of the Republic*, 228. The book appeared in three Philadelphia editions and one Boston edition by 1794. David Lundberg and Henry F. May have estimated that 18 percent of American private libraries contained a copy—significantly more than included Thomas Paine's *Common Sense*. David Lundberg and Henry F. May, "The Enlightened Reader in America," *American Quarterly* 28 (1976): 262–71. See also Marcelle Thiébaux, "Mary Wollstonecraft in Federalist America, 1791–1802," in *The Evidence of the Imagination: Studies of Interactions between Life and Art in English Romantic Literature,* ed. Donald H. Reiman, Michael C. Jaye, and Betty T. Bennett (New York: New York University Press, 1978), 195–235; and Zagarri, "Rights of Man and Woman in Post-revolutionary America," 205–11.

19. Mary Wollstonecraft, *A Vindication of the Rights of Woman*, ed. Carol H. Poston, 2nd ed. (New York: W. W. Norton, 1988), 4.

20. Ann Harker, "The Salutatory Oration," in *An Essay on the Education and Genius of the Female Sex,* ed. James A. Neal (Philadelphia: Jacob Johnson, 1795), 17; spelling as in the original. See also Miss C. Hutchings's speech, "Influence of the Female Character on Society in General," *Boston Weekly Magazine*, October 30, 1802, 2–3; and the testimonials to female education in *American Lady's Preceptor*, 9.

21. Zagarri, "Rights of Man and Woman," 205; see also Bloch, *Gender and Morality;* Dillon, *Gender of Freedom*; Mary Catherine Moran, "From Rudeness to Refinement: Gender, Genre, and Scottish Enlightenment Discourse" (PhD diss., Johns Hopkins University, 1999), 6, 33–74. See also Margaret Nash, *Women's Education in the United States, 1780–1840* (New York: Palgrave Macmillan, 2005), 17, and Rosemarie Zagarri, "Morals, Manners, and the Republican Mother," *American Quarterly* 44 (1992): 192–215. On notions of women and civil society in the nineteenth century, see Kelley, *Learning to Stand and Speak*, 5–10.

22. See, for example, Michèle Cohen, "Gender and the Private/Public Debate on Education in the Long Eighteenth Century," in *Public or Private Education? Lessons from History,* ed. Richard Aldrich (London: Woburn Press, 2004), 15–35; Goodman, *Republic of Letters,* esp. chaps. 3 and 6; Moran, "'Commerce of the Sexes,'" 61–84; and Anne-Charlott Trepp, "The Emotional Side of Men in Late Eighteenth-Century Germany: Theory and Example," *Central European History* 27 (1994): 127–52.

23. *American Lady's Preceptor*, 20–21; Albert Picket, *The Juvenile Mentor: Being the Second Part of the Juvenile Spelling Book* (New York: Smith and Forman, 1813), 172–73. See also H. P. Powers, *Female Education: An Address, Delivered in Trinity Church, Newark, N.J. on the Anniversary of the Newark Institute for Young Ladies, July 21, 1826* (Newark, NJ: M. Lyon, 1826), 11.

24. Stearns, *Dramatic Dialogues*, 38.

25. Susannah Rowson, *A Present for Young Ladies: Containing Poems, Dialogues, Addresses, &c. &c. &c. as Recited by the Pupils of Mrs. Rowson's Academy, at the Annual Exhibitions* (Boston: John West, 1811), 10.

26. The same was true even at more advanced academies, where both sexes were taught rhetoric and oratory. When James Neal proposed to add this subject to the curriculum of his prestigious Young Ladies' Academy in Philadelphia, he assured them that it would "make you real ornaments of society, and bright examples to your sex" and "stimulate your exertions in the pursuit of virtuous knowledge," among other benefits. "Address delivered by James A. Neal, Principal of the Young Ladies' Academy, to His Pupils, on Saturday, June 27, 1801," *Philadelphia Repository and Weekly Register* 1 (July 4, 1801): 269.

27. Samuel Magaw, "An Address Delivered in the Young Ladies' Academy, at Philadelphia," *American Museum, or Repository of Ancient and Modern Fugitive Pieces* 3 (1788): 25.

28. Sally Ripley diary, July 27, 1799 (see also June 28, 1800, and Apr. 26, 1801), AAS; William Bentley Fowle, Manuscript Autobiography, 1855, 7, Fowle Deposit, MaHS; Donald Fraser, *The Mental Flower Garden, or An Instructive and Entertaining Companion for the Fair Sex* (New York: Southwick and Hardcastle, 1807), Library of Congress copy. For scholarship on gendered reading patterns, see Davidson, *Revolution and the Word*, 6–10.

29. C. Dallett Hemphill, *Bowing to Necessities: A History of Manners in America, 1620–1860* (New York: Oxford University Press, 1999), 104–5, 114, 116, 216–17.

30. Molly Wallace in *The Rise and Progress of the Young-Ladies' Academy* (Philadelphia: Stewart and Cochran, 1794), 73–74.

31. Nathan Webb, Diary, June 25, 1790, MaHS.

32. T. Knox, *Hints to Public Speakers; Intended for Young Barristers, Students at Law, and All Others Who May Wish to Improve Their Delivery, and Attain a Just and Graceful Elocution* (London: J. Murray and S. Highley, 1797), 9; emphasis in the original. This book, which was reprinted in Boston in 1803, likely took its cue from Lord Chesterfield's *Letters to His Son* (1774) in heralding women's talents in conversation. See also Adolph von Knigge, *Practical Philosophy of Social Life, or The Art of Conversing with Men* (Lansingburgh, NY: Penniman and Bliss, 1805), and H. L. Ewbank, "The Rhetoric of Conversation in America: 1775–1828," *Southern Speech Communication Journal* 53 (1987): 49–64. Carroll Smith-Rosenberg has shown that the "carefully choreographed heterosociability" of postrevolutionary American culture was organized by and around well-spoken, genteel women; its devotees saw it as "critical to the practice of virtuous citizenship." Carroll Smith-Rosenberg, "The Republican Gentleman: The Race to Rhetorical Stability in the New United States," in *Masculinities in Politics and War: Gendering Modern History*, ed. Stefan Dudink, Karen Hagemann, and John Tosh (Manchester, Eng.: Manchester University Press, 2004), 64. Admiring descriptions of George Washington's "open and free" conversation with women appear, for example, in John Kingston, *The Reader's Cabinet: Consisting of More Than a Hundred Papers, Original and Extract, in Prose and Verse Calculated to Instruct the Mind* (Baltimore: John Kingston, 1809), 131. Several books published as late as the 1830s continue to press this theme, such as Joseph Emerson, *The Poetic Reader, Containing Selections from the Most Approved Authors* (Wethersfield, CT, 1832), 7.

33. Goodman, "Public Sphere and Private Life," 14; see also Kerber, "Separate Spheres, Female Worlds, Woman's Place."

34. John Walker sternly recommended to boys that "a prudent orator, therefore, will behave himself with modesty, that he may not seem to insult his hearers; and will set things before them in such an engaging manner as may remove all prejudice, either from his person, or what he asserts." John Walker, *A Rhetorical Grammar: In Which the Common Improprieties in Reading and Speaking Are Detected, and the True Sources of Elegant Pronunciation Are Pointed Out*, 2nd American ed. (Boston: Cummings and Hilliard, 1822), 366.

35. Jonathan Barber, *A Practical Treatise on Gesture, Chiefly Abstracted from Austin's Chironomia; Adapted to the Use of Students* (Cambridge, MA: Hilliard and Brown, 1831). Barber, a medical doctor, left his practice to teach elocution on a lecture circuit and eventually earned a position teaching rhetoric at Harvard.

36. Barber, *Practical Treatise on Gesture*, 108, 112.

37. I suspect that the women's costumes are an indication of the growing discomfort with female orators that became typical of the 1830s; as such, the costumes may have indicated to readers that women should use oratorical gestures only in theatrical parts rather than other forms of speechmaking. As a result, costumes likely would not have appeared in books published thirty or forty years earlier. This discomfort became more pronounced after Frances Wright's lectures in 1829 (Barber's book was published in 1831), as we shall see in chapter 6.

38. Occasionally an author discussed the kinds of "action" that girls should avoid. Charles Stearns felt that "a lady should never extend her arms at full length, or strike her bosom with her hands, or raise her hand aloft, above her head—a lady in any violent passion should not give it full vent; but appear to be endeavoring to suppress it." Such opinions were rare, however. Stearns, *Dramatic Dialogues*, 21.

39. See, for example, John Pickering's letter to Joseph Stevens Buckminster, Apr. 22, 1802, Joseph Stevens Buckminster Papers, box 1, folder 3; and James T. Kirkland to R. H. Gardiner, printed circular letter, Dec. 22, 1814, William Tudor Papers, box 1, folder 7, both at the BAT).

40. *Lady's Magazine,* January 1793, 68–71, cited in Kerber, *Women of the Republic*, 198–99.

41. John Swanwick, "Thoughts on Education, Addressed to the Visitors of the Young Ladies' Academy in Philadelphia, October 31, 1787," *Universal Asylum and Columbian Magazine* 5 (1790): 150.

42. "The Following Address was Delivered at a Late Public Examination, by Miss——," *New-York Magazine, or Literary Repository* 2 (February 1791): 92–94.

43. Susannah Hoar, "Prologue to the Exhibition of the Liberal School, Sept. 27, 1793," in Stearns, *Dramatic Dialogues*, 481. Occasionally Stearns listed the age of the orator, which was usually between twelve and fourteen.

44. Molly Wallace in *Rise and Progress of the Young-Ladies' Academy*, 73–74. For a nearly identical articulation see "On Female Education: By a Young Lady, a Student in a Seminary in Beekman-Street," *New-York Magazine* 5 (1794): 569.

45. Ripley diary, Aug. 20, 1800, AAS. This dialogue was published in Stearns, *Dramatic Dialogues*, 219–30; spelling as in the original.

46. Rowson, *Present for Young Ladies*, 84.

47. The celebration of learned women was a distinct subset of biographies in early nineteenth-century schoolbooks. These biographies included sketches of women in seventeenth-century Venice who attained academic and medical degrees; Queen Christina of Sweden, who boasted a masterful education and intellect; and any number of female authors.

48. Bingham, *American Preceptor*, 48; emphasis in the original.

49. Rush's biography originally appeared in *Port Folio* (Philadelphia), new ser., 1 (June 1809): 520–27; spelling as in the original. It was reprinted in the *American Lady's Preceptor*, 172–80, and in each of that volume's subsequent nine editions. On Ferguson, see Susan Stabile, "Salons and Power in the Era of Revolution: From Literary Coteries to Epistolary Enlightenment," in *Benjamin Franklin and Women*, ed. Larry E. Tise (University Park: Pennsylvania State University Press, 2000), 141–42.

50. According to David S. Shields and Fredrika Teute, salons sought a somewhat paradoxical marriage between "the manners of European gentility" and "the morals of post-revolutionary American republicanism," since postrevolutionary republicanism condemned European courts for their luxury and corruption. David S. Shields and Fredrika Teute, "The Republican Court and the Historiography of a Woman's Domain in the Public Sphere," unpublished paper presented to the Sixteenth Annual Meeting of the Society for Historians of the Early American Republic, Boston, MA, July 15, 1994, 3–7. Cited with the permission of the authors. See also Catherine Allgor, *Parlor Politics: In Which the Ladies of Washington Help Build a City and a Nation* (Charlottesville: University Press of Virginia, 2000); Susan Branson, *These Fiery Frenchified Dames: Women and Political Culture in Early National Philadelphia* (Philadelphia: University of Pennsylvania Press, 2001), 133–34; and David S. Shields, *Civil Tongues and Polite Letters in British America* (Chapel Hill: University of North Carolina Press for the IEAHC, 1997), 314–23.

51. Martha Vicinus, "What Makes a Heroine? Nineteenth-Century Girls' Biographies," *Genre* 20 (1987): 171–88, at 175, 183. See also Alison Booth, *How to Make It as a Woman: Collective Biographical History from Victoria to the Present* (Chicago: University of Chicago Press, 2004); Barbara Cutter, *Domestic Devils, Battlefield Angels: The Radicalism of American Womanhood, 1830–1865* (DeKalb: Northern Illinois University Press, 2003), 133–41; Barbara Sicherman, "Reading and Ambition: M. Carey Thomas and Female Heroism," *American Quarterly* 45 (1993): 73–103.

52. *The Ladies' Literary Companion, or A Collection of Essays, Adapted for the Instruction and Amusement of the Female Sex* (Burlington, NJ: Isaac Neale, 1792), 44; emphasis in the original.

53. Harker, "Salutatory Oration," 17–18.

54. Joan Jacobs Brumberg, *Mission for Life: The Story of the Family of Adoniram Judson, the Dramatic Events of the First American Foreign Mission, and the Course of Evangelical Religion in the Nineteenth Century* (New York: Free Press, 1980), 68–70,

cited in Vicinus, "What Makes a Heroine?" 183; Booth, *How to Make It as a Woman*, chap. 1; and Scott E. Casper, *Constructing American Lives: Biography and Culture in Nineteenth-Century America* (Chapel Hill: University of North Carolina Press, 1999), 14–15, 85–86, 123–34.

55. Aurelia, "For the Guardian," *Guardian of Freedom*, Nov. 25, 1793.

56. Susanna Stearns, "Prologue; at the Young Ladies' Exhibition, Oct. 5th, 1796," in Stearns, *Dramatic Dialogues*, 492–93. Her reference to "honest" fame might have been a direct contrast to sexual infamy.

57. See, for example, Darlene Gay Levy and Harriet B. Applewhite, "Women and Militant Citizenship in Revolutionary Paris," in *Rebel Daughters: Women and the French Revolution*, ed. Sara E. Melzer and Leslie W. Rabine (New York: Oxford University Press, 1992), 97.

58. Margaret A. Nash, "'Cultivating the Powers of *Human Beings*': Gendered Perspectives on Curricula and Pedagogy in Academies of the New Republic," *History of Education Quarterly* 41 (2001): 241. The primary exception was a small number of courses related to vocation. For the antebellum era, see Kim Tolley, "Science for Ladies, Classics for Gentlemen: A Comparative Analysis of Scientific Subjects in the Curricula of Boys' and Girls' Secondary Schools in the United States, 1794–1850," *History of Education Quarterly* 36 (1996): 129–53. Not all academies were sex-specific; between 1783 and 1805 thirty-four coeducational academies existed in New Hampshire, Massachusetts, and Maine. The term "seminary" was apparently also used interchangeably with "academy," particularly during the antebellum era.

59. Henry Barnard, cited in Kim Tolley, "The Rise of the Academies: Continuity or Change?" *History of Education Quarterly* 41 (2001): 229–30.

60. Kim Tolley and Nancy Beadie, "Reappraisals of the Academy Movement: Introduction," *History of Education Quarterly* 41 (2001): 217.

61. Caroline Winterer, *The Mirror of Antiquity: American Women and the Classical Tradition, 1750–1900* (Ithaca, NY: Cornell University Press, 2007).

62. Lynne Templeton Brickley, "Sarah Pierce's Litchfield Female Academy, 1792–1833" (PhD diss., Harvard University, 1985), 54–55, 57.

63. Ann D. Gordon, "The Young Ladies' Academy of Philadelphia," in *Women of America: A History*, ed. Carol Ruth Berkin and Mary Beth Norton (Boston: Houghton Mifflin, 1979), 72–80.

64. John Poor, "The Following Address Was Delivered to the Graduates, by the Principal," in Neal, *Essay on the Education and Genius of the Female Sex*, 27–28.

65. Susanna Stearns, "Intermediate, at the Ladies' Exhibition, Sept. 1794. Spoken by a Miss of 12 Years Old," in Stearns, *Dramatic Dialogues*, 500–501.

66. Eliza Shrupp, "Valedictory Address," in *Rise and Progress of the Young-Ladies' Academy*, 51.

67. Priscilla Mason, in *Rise and Progress of the Young-Ladies' Academy*, 91; emphasis in the original. See also Branson, *These Fiery Frenchified Dames*, 45–46.

68. Zagarri, "Morals, Manners, and the Republican Mother," 201; Mason, in *Rise and Progress of the Young-Ladies' Academy*, 92–93. See also J. G. A. Pocock, *Virtue, Commerce, and History: Essays on Political Thought and History, Chiefly in the Eighteenth*

Century (Cambridge: Cambridge University Press, 1985), 48–50. It was common for writers to address the concern that, as Ann Negus put it, American manners "be contaminated by the contagion of foreign example." Ann Negus speech in Neal, *Essay on the Education and Genius of the Female Sex*, 34; see also Catherine Anna Haulman, "The Empire's New Clothes: The Politics of Fashion in Eighteenth-Century British North America" (PhD diss., Cornell University, 2002), 7–16, and Moran, "From Rudeness to Refinement," 33–74. These passages have further benefited from scholarship on slightly later eras, including Paula Baker, "The Domestication of Politics: Women and American Political Society, 1780–1920," *American Historical Review* 89 (1984): 620–47; Elizabeth R. Varon, "Tippecanoe and the Ladies, Too: White Women and Party Politics in Antebellum Virginia," *Journal of American History* 82 (1995): 494–521; and Anthony F. C. Wallace, *Rockdale: The Growth of an American Village in the Early Industrial Revolution* (New York: Alfred A. Knopf, 1978), 22–32, 110–13, 312–17.

69. James Tilton, "An Oration," *Columbian Magazine, or Monthly Miscellany* 5 (1790): 372, quoted in Mary Beth Norton, *Liberty's Daughters: The Revolutionary Experience of American Women, 1750–1800* (Boston: Little, Brown, 1980), 245.

70. Priscilla Mason, in *Rise and Progress of the Young-Ladies' Academy*, 95.

71. Flowery writing was not limited to female writers, as Wollstonecraft well knew; she condemned Burke for using a deceptively elaborate style, especially because she recognized how much it appealed to readers and auditors. Elizabeth Wingrove, "Getting Intimate with Wollstonecraft in the Republic of Letters," *Political Theory* 33 (2005): 344–69. Similar complaints about "dazzling" yet insubstantial writing emerged in the schoolgirl diary of the Boston schoolgirl Amelia Russell: "I do not myself like Miss Owensons stile she dazzles you for a moment but can charm you no longer. Her writings are all outside glitter but no substance; they put me in mind of what I heard my father say after he had attended one of Oglevie's speakings I asked him how he was pleased? he replied that the oration appeared 'like a whip sillybub in an egg shell' I think this observation applicable to both for they both speak too much to the passions & not enough to the reason." A whipped syllabub was a frothy drink made with cream and wine. Russell, Diary, Dec. 1, 1814, MaHS; spelling and punctuation as in the original. Russell was writing of the Owenson novel *The Novice of St. Dominick*, published in London in 1806.

72. Boydston, "Making Gender in the Early Republic;" Zagarri, "Rights of Man and Woman in Post-revolutionary America," 210.

73. Amelia E. Russell diary, Nov. 17, 1814, Jonathan Russell Papers, box 5, folder 2, MaHS.

74. Zagarri, *Revolutionary Backlash*, chaps. 4–5.

75. Almira Hart Lincoln Phelps, *Lectures to Young Ladies, Comprising Outlines and Applications to the Different Branches of Female Education, for the Use of Female Schools, and Public Libraries* (Boston: Carter, Hendee, 1833), 86–87; Lydia Sigourney, *Letters to Young Ladies by a Lady* (Hartford, CT: P. Canfield, 1833), 55. See also Dorothea Dix, *Conversations on Common Things, or Guide to Knowledge: With Questions; for the Use of Schools* (Boston: Munroe and Francis, 1824), 249; Abigail Field Mott, *Observations*

on the Importance of Female Education, and Maternal Instruction, with Their Beneficial Influence on Society*, 2nd ed. (New York: Mahlon Day, 1827), 9; and the anonymous satirical view of female orators in "Female Orators," *Juvenile Port-Folio, and Literary Miscellany*, June 11, 1814, 91.

76. Boydston, "Making Gender in the Early Republic," 250–52; Branson, *These Fiery Frenchified Dames*, 4, 125–42; R. M. Janes, "On the Reception of Mary Wollstonecraft's *A Vindication of the Rights of Woman*," *Journal of the History of Ideas* 39 (1978): 293–302, esp. 297–98, 302; Judith Apter Klinghoffer and Lois Elkis, "'The Petticoat Electors': Women's Suffrage in New Jersey, 1776–1807," *Journal of the Early Republic* 12 (1992): 159–93.

77. See Bloch, *Gender and Morality*, chap. 7, and Leonore Davidoff and Catherine Hall, *Family Fortunes: Men and Women of the English Middle Class, 1780–1850* (London: Hutchinson, 1987).

78. Kelley, *Learning to Stand and Speak*, chap. 4.

79. See also Rosemarie Zagarri's discovery of the speech by "Miss Cole" in Marlborough, Vermont, in 1822 in *Revolutionary Backlash*, 72–73.

80. Granville Ganter, "The Unexceptional Eloquence of Sarah Josepha Hale's Lecturess," *Proceedings of the American Antiquarian Society* 112 (2002): 274. Ganter also notes the number of women before 1830 who spoke in public outside the educational context without losing their claims to respectability.

81. Catharine Maria Sedgwick, *A New-England Tale, or Sketches of New-England Character and Manners*, ed. Victoria Clements and Cathy N. Davidson (1822; New York: Oxford University Press, 1995), 51.

82. Sedgwick, *New-England Tale*, 53–55.

83. Sedgwick, *New-England Tale*, 54.

84. Sedgwick, *New-England Tale*, 54–55.

CHAPTER THREE

1. Thomas Jefferson, *Notes on the State of Virginia*, ed. William Peden (1787; Chapel Hill: University of North Carolina Press for the IEAHC, 1972), 62–63. On earlier versions of the speech, see James H. O'Donnell, "Logan's Oration: A Case Study in Ethnographic Authentication," *Quarterly Journal of Speech* 65 (1979): 150–56. Several analyses of Logan's speech have influenced this chapter, including Robert A. Ferguson, *The American Enlightenment, 1750–1820* (Cambridge, MA: Harvard University Press, 1993), 164–65; Edward G. Gray, "The Making of Logan, the Mingo Orator," in *The Language Encounter in the Americas, 1492–1800*, ed. Edward G. Gray and Norman Fiering (New York: Berghahn Books, 2000), 258–77; and Gordon M. Sayre, *The Indian Chief as Tragic Hero: Native Resistance and the Literatures of America, from Moctezuma to Tecumseh* (Chapel Hill: University of North Carolina Press for the OIEAHC, 2005), 162–202.

2. On the trope of Indian eloquence, see Edward G. Gray, *New World Babel: Languages and Nations in Early America* (Princeton, NJ: Princeton University Press,

1999), and Gray, "Making of Logan, the Mingo Orator"; Gustafson, *Eloquence Is Power*, 75–139; Mark L. Kamrath, "American Indian Oration and Discourses of the Republic in Eighteenth-Century American Periodicals," in *Periodical Literature in Eighteenth-Century America*, ed. Mark L. Kamrath and Sharon M. Harris (Knoxville: University of Tennessee Press, 2005), 143–178; Matthew Lauzon, "Savage Eloquence in America and the Linguistic Construction of a British Identity in the 18th Century," *Historiographica Linguistica* 23 (1996): 123–58; David Murray, *Forked Tongues: Speech, Writing and Representation in North American Indian Texts* (London: Pinter Publishers, 1991); and Anthony Pagden, *European Encounters with the New World: From Renaissance to Romanticism* (New Haven, CT: Yale University Press, 1993). On the vanishing Indian, see Brian W. Dippie, *The Vanishing American: White Attitudes and U.S. Indian Policy* (1982; reprint, Lawrence: University Press of Kansas, 1991), 3–44; Roy Harvey Pearce, *Savagism and Civilization: A Study of the Indian and the American Mind* (1965; reprint, Berkeley: University of California Press, 1988); and Richard Slotkin, *Regeneration through Violence: The Mythology of the American Frontier, 1600–1800* (Middletown, CT: Wesleyan University Press, 1973).

3. I alternate between the terms "Americans," "Anglo-Americans," and "whites," a practice that reflects the oscillating way the sources themselves referred to their subjects. My sources are almost entirely American imprints, though many were anthologized from British or French texts. Some sources were written by British colonials before the Revolution, before "American" was commonly used as a designation for white colonists. Ultimately, whiteness and Americanness became bound together in a discourse about national identity targeted to American readers in the early republic.

4. Editors displayed little interest in authenticating speeches and at times seemed to consider the matter irrelevant. Magazines tended to present more claims about their speeches' authenticity than schoolbooks did; still, such comments appeared less than half the time, and it appears likely that many of the remaining speeches were invented by editors or other writers. For these reasons I leave aside the question of the authenticity of speeches or accounts, choosing instead to analyze the ways this trope of Indian eloquence worked in the cultural environment of the early republic. On unreliable transcriptions of Indian speeches, see James H. Merrell, "'I Desire All That I Have Said ... May Be Taken Down Aright': Revisiting Teedyuscung's 1756 Treaty Council Speeches," *WMQ* 63 (2006): 777–826.

5. Deloria, *Playing Indian*, 36; see also Roger D. Abrahams, "Making Faces in the Mirror: Playing Indian in Early America," *Southern Folklore* 52 (1995): 121–35. My ideas about the triangulation of identity have been influenced as well by Michelle Burnham, "The Periphery Within: Internal Colonialism and the Rhetoric of U.S. Nation Building," in Schueller and Watts, *Messy Beginnings*, 139–54; Eve Kornfeld, "Encountering 'the Other': American Intellectuals and Indians in the 1790s," *WMQ* 52 (1995): 287–314; Christopher James Looby, "The Utterance of America" (PhD diss., Columbia University, 1999), chap. 5; Smith-Rosenberg, "Dis-covering the Subject," 841–73; and Mary E. Stuckey, *Defining*

Americans: The Presidency and National Identity (Lawrence: University Press of Kansas, 2004), chap. 1.

6. Doris Sommer, *Foundational Fictions: The National Romances of Latin America* (Berkeley: University of California Press, 1991), 7; see also Lauren Berlant, *The Anatomy of National Fantasy: Hawthorne, Utopia, and Everyday Life* (Chicago: University of Chicago Press, 1991), and Lora Romero, "Vanishing Americans: Gender, Empire and New Historicism," in *Subjects and Citizens: Nation, Race and Gender from Oroonoko to Anita Hill*, ed. Michael Moon and Cathy N. Davidson (Durham, NC: Duke University Press, 1995), 87–105.

7. Rayna Green, "Poor Lo and Dusky Ramona: Scenes from an Album of Indian America," in *Folk Roots, New Roots: Folklore in American Life*, ed. Jane S. Becker and Barbara Franco (Lexington, KY: Museum of Our National Heritage, 1988), 79.

8. Deloria, *Playing Indian*, 71–92; Pearce, *Savagism and Civilization*, 169–236; and Sayre, *Indian Chief as Tragic Hero*, 1–41.

9. Robert G. Parkinson, "From Indian Killer to Worthy Citizen: The Revolutionary Transformation of Michael Cresap," *WMQ* 63 (2006): 97–122.

10. Jefferson, *Notes on the State of Virginia*, 227; Parkinson, "From Indian Killer to Worthy Citizen," 104.

11. Jefferson, *Notes on the State of Virginia*, 227. Edward Gray has verified Jefferson's claim about the dissemination of Logan's speech, finding it reprinted in at least seven newspapers between February and May 1775. Gray, "Making of Logan, the Mingo Orator," 260 n. 6.

12. David Blight has estimated that *The American Preceptor*, which appeared in at least seventy editions from presses throughout the country, sold 640,000 copies between 1794 and 1824, making it one of the runaway best sellers of the era. David Blight, introduction to *The Columbian Orator,* Bicentennial ed. (New York: New York University Press Press, 1998), xvii. It also appeared in many schoolbooks, including *The American Orator*; William Darby, *The United States Reader, or Juvenile Instructor*, 2nd ed. (Baltimore: Plaskitt, 1830–31); A[braham] T. Lowe, *The Columbian Class Book, Consisting of Geographical, Historical, and Biographical Extracts, Compiled from Authentic Sources* (Worcester, MA: Dorr and Howland, 1824); and William H. McGuffey, *Eclectic Fourth Reader*, 6th ed. (Cincinnati: Truman and Smith, 1839).

13. *American Pioneer* 1 (1842): 7, quoted in Gray, "Making of Logan, the Mingo Orator," 273.

14. By the late eighteenth century, white leaders followed Indian conventions of treaty speech (conventions that predated European contact and that were quite different from other forms of Indian oratory) because they believed the Indians demanded this treaty style. Transcripts of treaty speeches circulated relatively widely, although printed transcripts did not explain the uniqueness of this style to readers; thus it seems likely that most readers perceived this to be an ordinary manner of speaking. See, for example, the ceremonial greeting of Governor Thomas Mifflin of Pennsylvania to a visiting group of chiefs of the Five Nations, including Farmer's Brother, in *Pennsylvania Gazette*, Mar. 28, 1792. For examples of this style of speech

being circulated in other popular texts, see Birch, *Virginian Orator*, 1-6; "Miscellany: Indian Talk from the President of the U. States to the Creek Indians, through Col. Crowell," *New Hampshire Gazette*, June 30, 1829, 1; J. Long, *Voyages and Travels of an Indian Interpreter and Trader, Describing the Manners and Customs of the North American Indians* (London: Privately printed, 1791), 68-69; and John Sergeant, "Extracts from the Journal of John Sergeant, Missionary to the Stockbridge Indians from the Society in Scotland, from the First of July, 1803, to the First of January, 1804," *Panoplist* {Boston} 1 (November 1805): 268-70.

15. Deloria, *Playing Indian*, chap. 1; see also Roger D. Abrahams, "White Indians in Penn's City: The Loyal Sons of St. Tammany," in *Riot and Revelry in Early America*, ed. William Pencak, Matthew Dennis, and Simon P. Newman (University Park: Pennsylvania State University Press, 2002), 179–204; Rayna Green, "The Tribe Called Wannabee: Playing Indian in America and Europe," *Folklore* 99 (1988): 30–55; and Carroll Smith-Rosenberg, "Surrogate Americans: Masculinity, Masquerade, and the Formation of a National Identity," *PMLA: Publications of the Modern Language Association of America* 119 (2004): 1325-35.

16. Adams cited in Fliegelman, *Declaring Independence*, 180.

17. Benjamin Franklin, *The Autobiography of Benjamin Franklin: A Genetic Text*, ed. J. A. Leo Lemay and P. M. Zall (Knoxville: University of Tennessee Press, 1981), 13–14.

18. Fliegelman, *Declaring Independence*, 181.

19. Calliopean Society, Record Books, Jan. 17, Mar. 13, and Aug. 14, 1792, Manuscript Department, NYHS. Debating society records are a particularly valuable source for determining the kinds of texts the young memorized and recited (as well as the frequency), since teachers in common schools seldom kept such records. In addition, Julie Ellison has shown that eighteenth-century plays such as Addison's *Cato*—as well as "Indian" plays such as *Liberty Asserted* (1711) and *Ponteach, or The Savages of America, a Tragedy*—performed a version of stoicism and eloquence that idealized manly sensibility. Julie Ellison, *Cato's Tears and the Making of Anglo-American Emotion* (Chicago: University of Chicago Press, 1999), chap. 3.

20. "Caroline Chester—Her Diary—Extracts from Her Commonplace Book" (1815–16), in Emily Noyes Vanderpoel, comp., and Elizabeth C. Barney Buel, ed., *Chronicles of a Pioneer School from 1792 to 1833: Being the History of Miss Sarah Pierce and Her Litchfield School* (Cambridge, MA: University Press, 1903), 150–60.

21. Rufus Anderson, *Memoir of Catharine Brown, a Christian Indian of the Cherokee Nation* (Boston: Crocker and Brewster, 1828), 138–39. The speech was by a chief of the Stockbridge (Massachusetts) tribe, originally delivered in 1775, and concerned the tribe's participation in the Revolution. I am grateful to Pat Crain for sharing this source with me.

22. Indian speeches had circulated in print and manuscript form since the seventeenth century, from Captain John Smith's works to John Eliot's 1685 *The Dying Speeches of Several Indians*. See Edna C. Sorber, "The Noble Eloquent Savage," *Ethnohistory* 19 (1972): 227–36; see also Gustafson, *Eloquence Is Power*, 33–39.

23. Hugh Blair, *Lectures on Rhetoric and Belles Letters* (1783; Philadelphia: Troutman and Hayes, 1853), 72. Blair's writings frequently appeared in American schoolbooks to guide students' declamation. See, for example, Dana, *New American Selection of Lessons.*

24. "Specimen of Indian Eloquence," *South Carolina Weekly Museum* 1 (1797): 273–75.

25. Benjamin Franklin, "Remarks concerning the Savages of North America," *Monthly Miscellany* 1 (1794): 14–16.

26. "Aboriginal Traits: General Character of the Indians," *Massachusetts Magazine* 5 (1793): 160–62.

27. "Indian Oratory," *Universal Asylum and Columbian Magazine* 5 (1790): 367. Michael Warner, "Savage Franklin," in *Benjamin Franklin: An American Genius,* ed. Gianfranca Balestra and Luigi Sampietro (Rome: Bulzione, 1993), 75–87, makes a similar point about Franklin's concern with politeness. See also Murray, *Forked Tongues,* 35–36.

28. "Aboriginal Traits: General Character of the Indians," 160–61.

29. James Adair, *The History of the American Indians; Particularly Those Nations Adjoining to the Mississippi, East and West Florida, Georgia, South and North Carolina, and Virginia* (London: Edward and Charles Dilly, 1775), 434. Gordon Sayre notes that this literary figure of the Indian chief "knows the wide spectrum of social class and virtues" but uses that knowledge to "enforce a higher law of honor" with his words. In doing so, this figure reprised classical and Renaissance theater that often featured such a character. Sayre, *Indian Chief as Tragic Hero,* 9.

30. Bingham, *Columbian Orator,* 52. See also "Indian Eloquence: Speech of the Chief of the Mickmakis or Maricheets Savages," *Impartial Gazetteer and Saturday Evening's Post,* May 24 and 31, 1788, and Kornfeld, "Encountering 'the Other,'" 291.

31. Bingham, *Columbian Orator,* 269. This volume was known for its pointedly antiracist material.

32. *Native Eloquence, Being Public Speeches Delivered by Two Distinguished Chiefs of the Seneca Tribe of Indians* (Canandaigua, NY: J. D. Bemis, 1811), 16–17.

33. Bingham, *Columbian Orator,* 269. See also "William Cocke, of Mulbery Grove," *New-Hampshire Gazette and General Advertiser,* Dec. 19, 1792.

34. John Smith, *The Generall Historie of Virginia, New England, and the Summer Isles* (1624; Glasgow: James MacLehose, 1907), 1:238–39.

35. "The Following Is an Exact Copy of a Letter from Capt. John Smith," *American Magazine* 1 (1787): 776–78. See also Heaton, *Columbian Preceptor.*

36. "The Indians," *Christian Register,* July 25, 1829, 120.

37. Christopher Leslie Brown, *Moral Capital: Foundations of British Abolitionism* (Chapel Hill: University of North Carolina Press for the OIEAHC, 2006), and Colley, *Britons,* 350–61.

38. "Remarks," *American Magazine* 1 (1788): 107–8.

39. "For the Anthology (an Indian Speech)," *Monthly Anthology* 6 (1809): 158.

40. Deloria, *Playing Indian,* 36.

41. "The Anecdotist,—no. VIII," *American Museum, or Universal Magazine* 10 (1791): 27. It is noteworthy that such comments about "removing" the Indians may acknowledge the prevailing belief that the Indians truly did "own" their land, as Stuart Banner has shown. *How the Indians Lost Their Land: Law and Power on the Frontier* (Cambridge, MA: Harvard University Press, 2005), esp. chap. 5.

42. "An Indian's Account of the Reception Which His Countrymen Gave the White Colonists," *Weekly Magazine* 2 (1798): 410. Brian Dippie makes a similar point about the Indians as American history in *Vanishing American*, 24. Writing about seventeenth-century accounts of the speeches of dying Christian Indians, Kristina Bross shows that these were likewise manipulated to unify colonial communities of faith. Bross, "Dying Saints, Vanishing Savages: 'Dying Indian Speeches' in Colonial New England Literature," *Early American Literature* 36 (2001): 325–52.

43. [Red Jacket], "Indian Speech II," *Monthly Anthology, and Boston Review* 6 (April 1809): 222–23; emphasis in the original. This account was reprinted as a broadside in Boston between 1810 and 1814 and appeared in *Native Eloquence* in 1811. Christopher Densmore, *Red Jacket: Iroquois Diplomat and Orator* (Syracuse: Syracuse University Press, 1999), 7–70, 141–42.

44. According to Craig Calhoun, such assertions of inheritance constituted a part of many ideologies of nationality. Calhoun, "Nationalism and Civil Society: Democracy, Diversity, and Self-Determination," in *Social Theory and the Politics of Identity*, ed. Craig Calhoun (Cambridge, MA: Blackwell, 1994), 312.

45. Sacvan Bercovitch, *The Rites of Assent: Transformations in the Symbolic Construction of America* (New York: Routledge, 1993), chap. 2. See also Bercovitch, *American Jeremiad* (Madison: University of Wisconsin Press, 1978).

46. Brown, *Moral Capital*, 2.

47. John Sergeant, Diary, Sept. 19, 1791, Society for Propagating the Gospel Records, 1752–1948, MaHS; spelling as in the original.

48. Gen. Henry Knox to Timothy Pickering, May 2, 1791, Timothy Pickering Papers, MaHS; spelling in as the original. See also Sylvester Churchill, Journal, 1836–37, LoC-M).

49. Brown, *Moral Capital*, 451–62; see also Thomas Haskell, "Capitalism and the Origins of Humanitarian Sensibility," *American Historical Review* 90 (1985): 339–61, 547–66. Elizabeth B. Clark ties the full-blown sympathy for enslaved peoples in the 1830s to the emphasis on their physical pain above and beyond emotional suffering; this was not emphasized in the case of Indians. Clark, "The Sacred Rights of the Weak: Pain, Sympathy, and the Culture of Individual Rights in Antebellum America," *Journal of American History* 82 (1995): 463–93.

50. Outalissa, "Fragments from the Woods," *New Monthly Magazine and Literary Journal, American Edition* 2 (1821): 60.

51. See, for example, "Indian Oratory" (a 1690 speech), *Universal Asylum and Columbian Magazine* 5 (1790): 365–67, and "An Indian's Account of the Reception Which His Countrymen Gave the White Colonists" (a 1754 speech), *Weekly Magazine* 2 (1798): 410.

52. James H. Merrell, "Declarations of Independence: Indian-White Relations in the New Nation," in *The American Revolution: Its Character and Limits*, ed. Jack P. Greene (New York: New York University Press, 1987), 197–223; Dippie, *Vanishing American*, 3–11; Michael D. Green, *The Politics of Indian Removal: Creek Government and Society in Crisis* (Lincoln: University of Nebraska Press, 1982); and Richard White, *The Middle Ground: Indians, Empires, and Republics in the Great Lakes Region, 1650–1815* (Cambridge: Cambridge University Press, 1991), 493–517.

53. Remer, *Printers and Men of Capital*, 2–3, 6–8, 69–99; Silver, *American Printer*, 106–7.

54. Silver, *American Printer*, 105–10.

55. "For the Anthology (an Indian Speech)," *Monthly Anthology, and Boston Review* 6 (1809): 158–59, 221–24.

56. This account was reprinted as a broadside in Boston between 1810 and 1814 and in *Native Eloquence* in 1811. Densmore, *Red Jacket*, 67–70, 141–42.

57. "For the Anthology (an Indian Speech)," 152.

58. Michael T. Gilmore, "Letters of the Early Republic," in *The Cambridge History of American Literature*, vol. 1, *1590–1820*, ed. Sacvan Bercovitch and Cyrus R. K. Patell (Cambridge: Cambridge University Press, 1994), 541–57; Warner, *Letters of the Republic*, 124–27, 132–38; and Smith-Rosenberg, "Discovering the Subject."

59. François Jean Chastellux first published his *Essays on Historic Subjects* in Amsterdam in 1772. His version of the Pocahontas story appeared in 1796 in Caleb Bingham's schoolbook *The American Preceptor*, 148–51, and was rapidly adopted in at least five other schoolbooks and magazines during the first decade of the nineteenth century.

60. Reportedly first published in the *Monthly Anthology*, it was reprinted in the *Literary Tablet* 1 (1804): 94; *Philadelphia Repository and Weekly Register* 5 (1805): 5–6; *Tickler* 2 (1809): 4; *Visitor* 1 (1809): 89–90; and numerous other magazines and schoolbooks.

61. The story of Pocahontas was also romanticized shortly thereafter in other media, beginning with James Nelson Barker's stage play *The Indian Princess, or La Belle Sauvage, an Operatic Melodrama in Three Acts* (1808), and succeeded by John Gadsby Chapman's painting "The Baptism of Pocahontas" (1836–40) and Lydia Sigourney's 1841 poem "Pocahontas."

62. Henry Clay, Jan. 20, 1819, in *Annals of Congress,* House of Representatives, 15th Cong., 2nd sess., 639–40. See also William Clark to James Barbour, Mar. 1, 1826, in which Clark notes that before 1815 "The tribes nearest our settlements were a formidable and terrible enemy; since then their power has been broken, their warlike spirit subdued, and themselves sunk into objects of pity and commiseration." *American State Papers, 2, Indian Affairs,* 2:653.

63. See also Lewis Cass, "Removal of the Indians," transcribed in *The Cherokee Removal: A Brief History with Documents,* 2nd ed., ed. Theda Perdue and Michael D. Green (Boston: Bedford/St. Martin's Press, 2005), 115–21; Andrew Jackson, "Second Annual Message," Dec. 6, 1830, reprinted in *A Compilation of the Messages and Papers*

of the Presidents, 1789–1897, ed. James D. Richardson (Washington, DC: Bureau of National Literature, 1897), 500–529.

64. John T. Frederick, "Cooper's Eloquent Indians," *PMLA: Proceedings of the Modern Language Association* 71 (1956): 1014, and Harry Liebersohn, "Discovering Indigenous Nobility: Tocqueville, Chamisso, and Romantic Travel Writing," *American Historical Review* 99 (1994): 746–66. See also [Lydia Maria Child], *Hobomok: A Tale of Early Times, by an American* (Boston: Cummings, Hilliard, 1824); Scott C. Martin, "Interpreting 'Metamora': Nationalism, Theater, and Jacksonian Indian Policy," *Journal of the Early Republic* 19 (1999): 73–101; and Jeffrey D. Mason, "The Politics of *Metamora*," in *The Performance of Power: Theatrical Discourse and Politics*, ed. Sue-Ellen Case and Janelle Reinelt (Iowa City: University of Iowa Press, 1991). *Metamora*, the most famous Indian drama, was first performed in December 1829.

65. Joseph Doddridge, *Logan: The Last of the Race of Shikellemus, Chief of the Cayoga Nation* (Buffalo Creek, VA: Solomon Sala, 1823); Sayre, *Indian Chief as Tragic Hero*, 182–91.

66. As Mary Hershberger has shown, popular opposition to Indian removal helped prompt many antislavery sympathizers to reject colonization plans, which seemed to resemble the offensive nature of Indian removal. And at least at first, abolitionists tied the Indians' cause to that of the enslaved. Hershberger, "Mobilizing Women, Anticipating Abolition: The Struggle against Indian Removal in the 1830s," *Journal of American History* 86 (1999): 15–40; see also Linda K. Kerber, "The Abolitionist Perception of the Indian," *Journal of American History* 62 (1975): 271–95.

67. William Apess, "Eulogy on King Philip," in *"A Son of the Forest" and Other Writings*, ed. Barry O'Connell (Amherst: University of Massachusetts Press, 1997), 103–38; Granville Ganter, ed., *The Collected Speeches of Sagoyewatha, or Red Jacket* (Syracuse: Syracuse University Press, 2006), xxi–xxxvii.

68. "Indian Eloquence," *Manuscript* 2 (Feb. 1, 1828): 93.

69. Samuel Willard, *Secondary Lessons, or The Improved Reader; Intended as a Sequel to the Franklin Primer, by a Friend of Youth* (Greenfield, MA: Phelps and Clark, 1827), 193–94.

70. [Sarah Everett Preston Hale], *Boston Reading Lessons for Primary Schools* (Boston: Richardson and Lord, 1828), 37–39.

71. Loughran, *Republic in Print*, xix.

CHAPTER FOUR

1. Joseph P. Hornor, Notebook, "Poetry Consisting of Detached Pieces Written . . . for My Own Amusement," 1801–4, HSP; spelling as in the original.

2. See, for example, Mark C. Carnes, *Secret Ritual and Manhood in Victorian America* (New Haven, CT: Yale University Press, 1989); Howard P. Chudacoff, *The Age of the Bachelor: Creating an American Subculture* (Princeton, NJ: Princeton University Press, 1999).

3. Young men's literary societies also differ from some of the most renowned Anglo-American clubs of the mid-eighteenth century, whose members tended to be wealthy, established married men. Robert Micklus, Introduction to *The Tuesday Club: A Shorter Edition of "The History of the Ancient and Honorable Tuesday Club" by Dr. Alexander Hamilton*, ed. Robert Micklus (Chapel Hill: University of North Carolina Press for the IEAHC, 1995), xi–xxix; David S. Shields, "Anglo-American Clubs: Their Wit, Their Heterodoxy, Their Sedition," *WMQ* 51 (1994): 293–304; Shields, "The Tuesday Club Writings and the Literature of Sociability," *Early American Literature* 26 (1991): 276–90; and Shields, *Civil Tongues and Polite Letters in British America* (Chapel Hill: University of North Carolina Press for the IEAHC, 1997).

4. Not only were self-improvement and literary societies enormously popular during the early republic, but their members displayed exceptional resourcefulness in saving their associational records; archival repositories throughout the eastern seaboard hold the records of over one hundred such societies. See, for example, Eleanor Bryce Scott, "Early Literary Clubs in New York City," *American Literature* 5 (1933): 6.

5. "The Club," *New-York Magazine, or Literary Repository* (hereafter *NYM*) 1 (1790): 318.

6. In addition to "The Drone" and "The Club," Calliopeans published poetry in the column "The American Muse" and additional essays either individually or in periodic columns such as "The Friend" and "The Miscellanist." On the *Magazine*, see Sharon M. Harris, "The *New-York Magazine*: Cultural Repository," in Kamrath and Harris, *Periodical Literature in Eighteenth-Century America*, 339–52; and David Paul Nord, "A Republican Literature: A Study of Magazine Readers and Reading in Late Eighteenth-Century New York," *American Quarterly* 40 (1988): 42–64. Both these scholars describe the magazine's content as more mainstream than I have found it to be. On associations, see Peter S. Field, "The Birth of Secular High Culture: *The Monthly Anthology and Boston Review* and Its Critics," *Journal of the Early Republic* 17 (1997): 575–609; Gilmore, "Literature of the Revolutionary and Early National Periods," 1:558–72; Eve Kornfeld, "Making an American Culture, 1775–1815" (PhD diss., Harvard University, 1982), 95–99; Albrecht Koschnik, *"Let a Common Interest Bind Us Together": Associations, Partisanship, and Culture in Philadelphia, 1775–1840* (Charlottesville: University of Virginia Press, 2007); and Bryan Waterman, *Republic of Intellect: The Friendly Club of New York City and the Making of American Literature* (Baltimore: Johns Hopkins University Press, 2007).

7. John Barent Johnson, Diary, vol. 8, September 1794, MS Columbiana, COL. The diary reveals that, in addition to attending events in Manhattan, Johnson traveled as far as Princeton to hear speeches. In 1796 he moved to Albany to take a position in the Reformed Protestant Dutch Church. "John Barent Johnson," in *Appletons' Cyclopedia of American Biography*, ed. James Grant Wilson, John Fiske, and Stanley L. Klos (New York: D. Appleton, 1887–89) 3:444; Teunis Van Vechten, "John Barent Johnson," in *Annals of the American Pulpit*, ed. William B. Sprague (New

York: Robert Carter, 1869), 9:116–17. The society at Columbia had been formed in 1784 by college trustees, who sought to bring students together with other young men in the city for "improving themselves in polite literature." Helen P. Roach, *History of Speech Education at Columbia College, 1754–1949* (New York: Teachers College, 1950), 34.

8. Peter Clark, *British Clubs and Societies, 1580–1800: An Associational World* (Oxford: Clarendon Press, 2000); Waterman, *Republic of Intellect*, chap. 1.

9. Society for the Attainment of Useful Knowledge, Record Book, 1797–1800, MS 767, MdHS.

10. On this transformation see Koschnik, *"Let a Common Interest Bind Us Together,"* 48–53.

11. In its first five years, the Uranian Society of New York amassed 148 titles; at the same time, in 1794, the Calliopeans reported that their library contained 249 volumes. John F. Roche, "The Uranian Society: Gentlemen and Scholars in Federal New York," *New York History* 52 (1971): 130; Calliopean Society, Record Book (1792–95), Dec. 16, 1794, NYHS.

12. For a sunnier view of the clubs' ability to offer their members "relaxation and happiness," see Clark, *British Clubs and Societies*, 490–91.

13. Considering that the brothers John and Alexander Anderson reported being teased that "Mama kept my brother & me cheeping about her, instead of letting us stir abroad," it may have been customary for middling men to find rooms of their own during their early twenties. Alexander (who was twenty-one at the time) was studying medicine; John (twenty-three) was studying the law. Alexander Anderson Diary (1793–1799), Jan. 11, 1796, COL.

The city's population had doubled from 12,000 to 24,000 between 1783 and 1785 alone, and it more than doubled again (to 60,000) by 1800. By 1805 New York had surpassed Philadelphia as the largest city in the nation—even more remarkable considering the crippling yellow fever epidemics of 1795 and 1798 that killed thousands of residents. Some of this expansion came from locating the new federal government in this city in 1789, but the vast majority resulted from the attractions of the New York harbor—a far more navigable port than Philadelphia's, allowing New York merchants to cut in on the wealth to be made in both domestic and international trade. Edwin G. Burrows and Mike Wallace, *Gotham: A History of New York City to 1898* (New York: Oxford University Press, 1999), 270, and Sean Wilentz, *Chants Democratic: New York City and the Rise of the American Working Class* (New York: Oxford University Press, 1984), 24–25.

14. John Barent Johnson letter to Elbert Herring (typescript), Nov. 10, 1794, Johnson Family Papers, box 13, folder 7, AAS; Thomas Foster, *Sex and the Eighteenth-Century Man: Massachusetts and the History of Sexuality in America* (Boston: Beacon Press, 2006), chap. 1.

15. Daniel A. Cohen, "Arthur Mervyn and His Elders: The Ambivalence of Youth in the Early Republic," *WMQ* 43 (1986): 367, 378.

16. Calliopean Society, Record Book (1788–92), Nov. 20, 1788, NYHS. Their extant records do not extend past 1799; some anecdotal sources indicate that the

club remained in existence until 1831, although these may refer to a new club with the same name, since other Calliopean societies existed throughout the country. Scott, "Early Literary Clubs in New York City," 12–13.

17. Joseph Addison, *Cato, a Tragedy* (1713), depicted the last days of the prominent Roman republican leader Marcus Portius Cato Uticensis (Cato the Younger) and addressed more broadly the themes of individual liberty and government tyranny. The play was enormously influential in the American colonies and reportedly influenced revolutionary leaders' determination to hew to their beliefs in the name of liberty.

18. Calliopean Society, Record Book of the Committee of Examination (1793–99), Oct. 19, 1793, NYPL.

19. "Report of the Committee of Examination," Calliopean Society, Record Book (1792–95), July 3, 1792, NYHS. When they received an essay denouncing a fellow member "whose manner of debating has given considerable offense," they reproved its author. "The stile is correct and the execution plainly evinces that the writer is not a novice at composition. The remarks are probably just yet their undisguised severity and pointed personality favor an opinion that they do not proceed from the pen of friendly criticism, but are the reprehensions of one smarting from the lash he so keenly reprobates." Record Book of the Committee of Examination (1793–99), July 3, 1795, Sept. 11, 1795, and Feb. 24, 1797.

20. Calliopean Society, Record Book (1788–92), Nov. 27, 1788, Feb. 19, 1789, and June 2, 1789, NYHS; spelling as in the original. The topics they chose for debate were deeply unoriginal, lifted from lists of topics used by debating societies in American colleges or public debating societies in London. They often used exactly the same wording that had been used by another society; in fact the same questions appear in the meeting minutes of American debating societies throughout the nineteenth century. This tendency shifted after 1791 as the questions they debated became increasingly relevant politically, as the next section will show. See, for example, a list of nearly identical questions for debate in the papers of the Society for the Attainment of Useful Knowledge, MdHS, and the Morris Literary Society of Morristown, New Jersey, during 1802 and 1803 in Charles Horton Morrell Papers, Morrell Family Papers, box 2, NYHS.

21. On this topic see Patricia Meyer Spacks, *Privacy: Concealing the Eighteenth-Century Self* (Chicago: University of Chicago Press, 2003).

22. By the Revolution, virtually every American college hosted at least one society that aimed to make its members "more illustrious, learned, and mannerly." Most of the earliest debates were conducted in Latin and adhered to a programmatic format that relied heavily on the oversight of a tutor or professor. As James McLachlan has noted, these groups played an enormous role in students' lives during an era when colleges suffered strong criticism for their rigidity and resistance to change. James McLachlan, "The *Choice of Hercules*: American Student Societies in the Early 19th Century," in *The University in Society*, vol. 2, *Europe, Scotland, and the United States from the 16th to the 20th Century*, ed. Lawrence Stone (Princeton, NJ: Princeton University Press, 1979), 472; Kornfeld, "Making an American Culture,

1775–1815," 97–98; David Potter, "The Literary Society," in Wallace, *History of Speech Education in America*, 238–58; and Shields, *Civil Tongues and Polite Letters in British America*, 210–13. McLachlan has found literary and debating societies at Brown, Dartmouth, Dickinson, Harvard, New Jersey (Princeton), Queen's (Rutgers), William and Mary, and Yale colleges before 1790. In 1784 the trustees of Columbia College approved a society consisting of both students and other young men in the city for "improving themselves in polite literature." Postrevolutionary college societies usually conducted debates in English and without oversight. See also Christopher Grasso, *A Speaking Aristocracy: Transforming Public Discourse in Eighteenth-Century Connecticut* (Chapel Hill: University of North Carolina Press for the OIEAHC, 1998), 394–97.

23. See, for example, Koschnik, *"Let a Common Interest Bind Us Together,"* 19. Society records of vote tallies reveal that few decisions were unanimous and many were quite close.

24. Record book of the Society for the Attainment of Useful Knowledge (Baltimore), 1797–1800, MS 767, MdHS.

25. These had been a vibrant aspect of city life since the 1750s and attracted huge audiences in part by advertising their debate topics widely in the newspapers. Some even set aside evenings during which only women could speak. Donna T. Andrew, "Popular Culture and Public Debate: London 1780," *Historical Journal* 39 (1996): 405–23; Mary Thale, "The Case of the British Inquisition: Money and Women in Mid-Eighteenth-Century London Debating Societies," *Albion* 31 (1999): 31–48; and Thale, "London Debating Societies in the 1790s," *Historical Journal* 32 (1989): 57–86.

26. George L. Craik, *The Pursuit of Knowledge under Difficulties* (1830; reprint, London: Nattali and Bond, 1846). The *North American Review* called this volume "a favorite food of a generation of young Americans." It consisted of hundreds of brief biographies of people who had persevered in their quest for knowledge. Craik followed it up with a similar volume of female biography. Kett, *Pursuit of Knowledge under Difficulties*, 86. See also Allan Silver, "'Two Different Sorts of Commerce'—Friendship and Strangership in Civil Society," in *Public and Private in Thought and Practice: Perspectives on a Grand Dichotomy*, ed. Jeff Weintraub and Krishan Kumar (Chicago: University of Chicago Press, 1997), 43–68.

27. The Calliopeans had few college-educated members. Only one of the group's original twenty-one members had college experience; this changed only after 1792, when a larger number of Columbia College students joined. In all, twenty-five of the society's approximately one hundred members attended college at some point, mostly as medical students (which did not require prior college education).

28. Of the approximately one hundred names listed in the club's extant record books for 1788–95, I found some material for eighty-seven members covering their family background, education, and subsequent careers. Four members died before assuming a career. Because the remaining thirteen were listed without first names and had common last names, it is virtually impossible to identify them. I ascertained vocations for forty members' fathers.

29. These consist of seventeen merchants, fifteen physicians/druggists, and thirteen attorneys, as well as a smattering of high-ranking military officers, diplomats, iron merchants, state auditors, brokers, politicians, judges, and ministers. Of the eighty-three members whose careers I identified, fifty fell into this category. The category "unskilled" includes low-ranking members of the army and carmen.

30. The category "artisans" consists of ironmongers, butchers, carvers/gilders, distillers, grocers, weavers, blacksmiths, tailors, chairmakers, dry-goods store owners, glovemakers, watchmakers, fringe and stocking manufacturers, tavern owners, coachmakers, jewelers, silversmiths, starch manufacturers, and hair powder manufacturers. At least some of the members who became artisans followed in their families' business. The category "low white-collar" also includes printers and surveyors. Only one Calliopean appears to have taken an unskilled job (as a carman).

31. For more on this topic, and for a more precise definition of "merchant," see Thomas Doerflinger, *A Vigorous Spirit of Enterprise: Merchants and Economic Development in Revolutionary Philadelphia* (Chapel Hill: University of North Carolina Press for the IEAHC, 1986), and Cathy Matson, *Merchants and Empire: Trading in Colonial New York* (Baltimore: Johns Hopkins University Press, 1998). The number of merchants in New York grew exponentially during this period as economic opportunities opened in a variety of markets (such as the southern cotton trade): from 1790 to 1800 alone, the number listed in city directories quadrupled, from 248 to over 1,100.

32. The literature on middle-class formation is vast, but several of the most significant works include Stuart M. Blumin, *The Emergence of the Middle Class: Social Experience in the American City, 1760–1900* (Cambridge: Cambridge University Press, 1989); Bushman, *Refinement of America*; and Mary P. Ryan, *Cradle of the Middle Class: The Family in Oneida County, New York, 1790–1865* (Cambridge: Cambridge University Press, 1981).

33. Evidence shows that members frequently turned to one another for assistance in beginning their careers. At least twenty-two members formed business partnerships with one another, including the physicians Matthew Coe and Edward Carroll, the schoolteachers John Campbell and B. Payne, and the grocers Robert Wardell and Daniel White. Other kinds of connections developed as well: William Irving Jr. married the sister of fellow member William Paulding; three members took turns editing the newspaper *The Diary* in the late 1790s; and the printer James Swords published the writings of at least seven fellow members. Because scholars have not analyzed the demographic paths of men in debating societies, I cannot provide comparative data. Bryan Waterman's *Republic of Intellect* analyzes the nearly contemporaneous New York Friendly Club, a society consisting of enormously talented and influential men in New York and Connecticut; but because this was a much smaller group of older men (most were at least in their later twenties) who were more markedly dedicated to literary and cultural accomplishments (rather than to assisting one another in the establishment of their careers), it makes a poor comparison.

34. Carolyn Eastman, "Reading Aloud: 'Societies of Gentlemen' and the Editing of Magazines in the Early Republic," forthcoming in the *Journal of the Early Republic*.

35. Anthology Society, Record Book (1805–11), Feb. 26, 1807, Dec. 13, 1808, Jan. 16, 1806; MaHS; spelling as in the original. The members of the Anthology Society differed significantly from the Calliopeans: composed largely of elite Congregational ministers, the Anthologists were significantly older and more established in their professions. Field, "Birth of Secular High Culture," 595.

36. "The Club," *NYM* 1 (1790): 318.

37. The magazine appears to have reached a comparatively broad readership. In his analysis of the *NYM*'s subscription list, David Paul Nord concludes that reading magazines was a far more democratic pursuit than scholars have usually acknowledged. Not only did a surprising number of artisans, workingmen, and women subscribe to the magazine, he shows, but the magazine's varied content welcomed those readers as partners in creating a republican society. Nord, "A Republican Literature." At the subscription cost of $2.25 a year, however, the *NYM* surely would have been viewed as a luxury.

38. Koschnik, *"Let a Common Interest Bind Us Together,"* 11–19.

39. "The Club, VI," *NYM* 1 (1790): 680.

40. The club took seriously the need to protect the anonymity of outside contributors. They built a special box for anonymous submissions and established a rule that "all persons concerned in reading or examining the Compositions shall be obliged to keep secret whatever conjectures or discoveries they make with respect to the names of the authors." Calliopean Society, Record Book (1792–95), Sept. 17, 1793.

41. Jefferson, *Notes on the State of Virginia*, 161.

42. These passages have been influenced by Seth Cotlar, "Reading the Foreign News, Imagining an American Public Sphere: Radical and Conservative Visions of 'The Public' in Mid-1790s Newspapers," in Kamrath and Harris, *Periodical Literature in Eighteenth-Century America*, 307–38; and David Waldstreicher, Jeffrey L. Pasley, and Andrew W. Robertson, "Introduction: Beyond the Founders," in Pasley, Robertson, and Waldstreicher, *Beyond the Founders*, 1–28.

43. Calliopean Society, Record Book (1788–92), Mar. 5, 1789, June 30, 1789, and Mar. 9, 1790; spelling as in original.

44. Calliopean Society, Record Book (1788–92), Dec. 22, 1789, Jan. 12, 1790.

45. In this regard the men appear to have been willing Constitutionalists, as Albrecht Koschnik describes them in *"Let a Common Interest Bind Us Together,"* a term that distinguishes them from Federalists, which by the early to mid-1790s represented a highly specific political position.

46. These societies of Americans disillusioned with the policies of the Washington administration appeared in approximately forty areas throughout the nation (predominately, though not exclusively, urban). They included a variety of ethnic groups as well as a wide spectrum of economic and vocational backgrounds, from laborers to elite and merchants. Cotlar, "Reading the Foreign News";

Albrecht Koschnik, "The Democratic Societies of Philadelphia and the Limits of the American Public Sphere, circa 1793–1795," *WMQ* 58 (2001): 615–36; Philip S. Foner, *Democratic-Republican Societies, 1790–1800: A Documentary Sourcebook* (Westport, CT: Greenwood Press, 1976); and Alfred F. Young, *The Democratic Republicans of New York: The Origins, 1763–1797* (Chapel Hill: University of North Carolina Press for the IEAHC, 1967).

47. Calliopean Society, Record Book (1788–92), Mar. 2, 1790, July 13, 1790, Jan. 21, 1791, NYHS; spelling as in the original. Abraham Morehouse was to have been executed along with two accomplices for "forged obligation" but was released by Governor George Clinton. *New-York Daily Gazette*, June 6, 1789.

48. These Belfast-area radicals often referred to Paine's *Rights of Man* as "the Koran of Belfast." This subject matter further confirms Cotlar's argument that democratic politics became a broad transatlantic conversation appealing to men of many backgrounds. Cotlar, "Reading the Foreign News."

49. "Introductory Essay," *NYM* 1 (1790): 195–98.

50. Waterman, *Republic of Intellect*, passim.

51. They also determined that the president should be elected annually and that there should be limitations on the amount of property owned by each individual. Calliopean Society, Record Book (1792–95), May 20, 1794, Dec. 23, 1794, NYHS.

52. "Perdition seize that Democratic Society," *General Advertiser* (Philadelphia), May 16, 1794; Cotlar, "Reading the Foreign News," led me to this quotation. This mocking essay is written in the voice of an aristocrat offended by the people's desire to analyze "governmental doctrines and measures." "Oh! horrid to relate, an analysis of this sort," he laments, clearly indicating the writer's sympathy for the radical people. See also Foner, *Democratic-Republican Societies*, 10, and Koschnik, *"Let a Common Interest Bind Us Together,"* 25.

53. One of the most active members during this period was Tunis Wortman, a youth training to be an attorney, who became involved in the New York Democratic Society and delivered the Tammany Society's 1796 oration. "The charms of wealth, the allurements of luxury, the thirst of gain and the ruinous system of speculation, have borne down like the irresistible flood upon us," he warned his auditors; they had "nearly banished from our minds the sentiment of public virtue, destroyed the ardor of liberty, and diminished our attachment to the sacred interests of our country." Cited in Foner, *Democratic-Republican Societies*, 9.

54. Harris, *"New-York Magazine,"* 341–42.

55. "Petition of Madame Guillon," *NYM* 2 (1791): 637–41; "Address of the Proscribed Deputies of the National Convention," *NYM* 5 (1793): 80–83.

56. Simon P. Newman, *Parades and the Politics of the Street: Festive Culture in the Early American Republic* (Philadelphia: University of Pennsylvania Press, 1997), 121. Contemporary letters and diaries confirm New Yorkers' enthusiasm for the French. The Calliopean Jotham Post woke up to the sound of bells ringing on December 27, 1792, and heard about "the happy turn of affairs in France ... Go On France in the noble cause of freedom," he wrote. Jotham Post Diary (1792–93), NYHS. John Anderson Jr. describes dancing the carmagnole around the American and French

flags in March 1794 and speaks of painting both flags on silk for a friend on the Fourth of July 1795. Anderson, Diary (1794–98), Mar. 7, 1794, July 4, 1795, NYHS.

57. Cited in Harris, "*New-York Magazine*," 344.

58. Cited in Foner, *Democratic-Republican Societies,* 31; Waterman, *Republic of Intellect,* chap. 2. Contrary to Washington's claim, the Democratic-Republicans had not played a role in the rebellion.

59. As Margaret Jacob and David Shields have argued, this distinction obtained among radical clubs in Europe and colonial American societies as well. Margaret Jacob, *The Radical Enlightenment: Pantheists, Freemasons, and Republicans* (London: Allen and Unwin, 1981), passim; Shields, *Civil Tongues and Polite Letters in British America,* 176–77.

60. "The Drone," *NYM* 5 (1794): 67–70. This piece expanded on an earlier column that acclaimed that "ornament of rhetoric, that useful and beautiful figure, Swearing" and traced its history back to the eloquence of the Greeks and Romans. "The Drone: The Advantages of Swearing," *NYM* 3 (1792): 323–35.

61. David S. Shields, "The Science of Lying," in Schueller and Watts, *Messy Beginnings,* 223–36; clearly, I disagree with Shields's contention that the Calliopeans' satirical columns marked them as Federalists. See also Shields, *Civil Tongues and Polite Letters,* 324–25.

62. "The Drone," *NYM,* n.s., 1 (1796): 226–27.

63. The Free Thinker, "On Debating Societies," *Philadelphia Repository and Weekly Register* 1 (1800): 262.

64. John Gallison, Diary B (1808–10), Jan. 9, 1810, MaHS.

65. Koschnik, *"Let a Common Interest Bind Us Together."*

66. For a take on a different group of intellectuals during the late 1790s, see Waterman, *Republic of Intellect.*

67. "The Drone," *NYM* 4 (1793): 643–46.

68. Mary Wollstonecraft, "A Vindication of the Rights of Woman, with Strictures on Political and Moral Subjects," *NYM* 4 (1793): 77–81.

69. The *New-York Magazine* published a variety of poetry and reviews by women, including the writings and speeches of female academy students. "To the Editors of the New-York Magazine, &c.," *NYM* 1 (1790): 9–10; see also Sharon M. Harris's analysis of their treatment of women in *"New-York Magazine,"* 345–48.

70. Calliopean Society, Record Book (1788–92), May 21, 1789, May 17, 1791, Mar. 20, 1792, and Dec. 7, 1790, NYHS. In these cases matrimony and wit won out over celibacy and beauty; children were deemed capable of marrying without consent, and bachelors were taxed. They also rehashed these questions in subsequent years, asking again about the benefits of matrimony in 1790 and about bachelors in 1793; they debated variations on questions about beauty and dissimulation in women six times throughout the 1790s.

71. Contemporaneous London debating clubs used the same questions (the wording is sometimes identical) as American college societies, as Donna Andrew has shown in "Popular Culture and Public Debate," 412–14. In several cases specific questions had been popular for decades. A 1742 newspaper article on the fictitious

"Petticoat Club," for example, explained that the ladies not only supported a tax on bachelors but argued that "if any of the aforesaid Drones shall presume in their Obstinacy till the Age of 40," the tax should rise sharply as a *"Badge of Disgrace." Boston Evening-Post*, Apr. 17, 1742. Foster, *Sex and the Eighteenth-Century Man*, 103.

72. Debate is mentioned in Calliopean Society, Record Book (1788–92), July 14, 1789, NYHS. On this topic, see Foster, *Sex and the Eighteenth-Century Man,* 102. The bachelor resembled the contemporary literary figure of the hermit, who likewise used his isolation from social norms to speak with special authority on the flaws and foibles of society, as Eric Slauter shows in "Being Alone in the Age of the Social Contract," *WMQ* 62 (2005): 31–66.

73. "The Drone," *NYM* 4 (1793): 645–46.

74. Carroll Smith-Rosenberg demonstrates that the vocabulary of republican political theory and that of seduction novels were "remarkably similar. In both corruption undermines 'independence'; the vicious, nonproductive elegance of the aristocracy threatens 'virtue'; reason and restraint serve the common good while passion promotes self-interest and civic disorder." Smith-Rosenberg, "Domesticating 'Virtue': Coquettes and Revolutionaries in Young America," in *Literature and the Body: Essays on Populations and Persons,* ed. Elaine Scarry (Baltimore: Johns Hopkins University Press, 1988), 160–84, at 160; see also Cathy N. Davidson, Introduction to Hannah Webster Foster, *The Coquette* (New York: Oxford University Press, 1986), vii–xx, and Karin Wulf, *Not All Wives: Women of Colonial Philadelphia* (Ithaca, NY: Cornell University Press, 2000), 25–52, 201. As Wulf shows, there was a growing number of unmarried women in Philadelphia (and possibly other cities as well) during this era, even as print representations tied women ever more firmly to marriage and dependence.

75. The argument begins with a formal address to "Mr. President" and is peppered with oratorical flourishes, such as periodic references to the presiding officer for the debate—as in, "Sir, I will be so bold as to affirm" and "I believe, Sir."

76. "An Oration on the Question, 'Which Is the More Eligible for a Wife, a *Widow* or an *Old Maid?*'" *NYM* 4 (1793): 494–99.

77. Toby L. Ditz, "Shipwrecked, or Masculinity Imperiled: Mercantile Representations of Failure and the Gendered Self in Eighteenth-Century Philadelphia," *Journal of American History* 81 (1994): 53. All these passages have been influenced by Ditz's analyses and commentaries on masculinity in history, particularly in "The New Men's History and the Peculiar Absence of Gendered Power: Some Remedies from Early American Gender History," *Gender and History* 16 (2004): 1–35.

78. Homi K. Bhabha, "Are You a Man or a Mouse?" in *Constructing Masculinity*, ed. Maurice Berger, Brian Wallis, and Simon Watson (New York: Routledge, 1995), 58.

79. Smith-Rosenberg, "Domesticating 'Virtue,'" 161.

80. "Oration on the Question, 'Which Is the More Eligible for a Wife, a *Widow* or an *Old Maid?*'" 495–96.

81. Clare A. Lyons, *Sex among the Rabble: An Intimate History of Gender and Power in the Age of Revolution, Philadelphia, 1730–1830* (Chapel Hill: University of North Carolina Press for the OIEAHC, 2006); see also Rodney Hessinger, *Seduced, Abandoned, and Reborn: Visions of Youth in Middle-Class America, 1780–1850* (Philadelphia: University of Pennsylvania Press, 2005). The diary of Alexander Anderson, a doctor in training, comments extensively on the manifestations of this pleasure culture in his everyday life. He treated one Calliopean Society member several times for gonorrhea, for example, and frequently described city "scenes" on his evening walks: "As I was returning with two others, a Prostitute, gaily dress'd, appear'd at the window of a house opposite the Brick Meeting, and display'd her Breast to our view, with a most artful smile, affording an idea of a scene often described." Anderson Diary (1793–99), Jan. 17, 1793, Sept. 26, 1793, COL.

82. Their skepticism of male tendencies also appeared in their weekly debates, as when in 1792 they asked whether "conjugal infidelity proceed[s] more from improper behavior in the man or the woman" (man).

83. See her essays, including Smith-Rosenberg, "Dis-covering the Subject," 841–73, and "Republican Gentleman," 64. Smith-Rosenberg also demonstrates that these early published writings constructed bourgeois manliness by portraying blacks, poor whites, and Indians as well as women as antitypes.

84. "The Drone.—No. XXI," *NYM* 5 (1794): 196.

85. Epistolary novels allowed the various voices of letter writers to articulate different perspectives without the presiding voice of an omniscient narrator. This form can be traced to the fifteenth century; for the English language, it was used most famously in Samuel Richardson's *Pamela* (1740) and *Clarissa* (1748)—to be copied by numerous American novelists, including William Hill Brown in *The Power of Sympathy* (1789) and Hannah Foster in *The Coquette* (1797). On this subject see Davidson, *Revolution and the Word*, chap. 6, and Davidson, Introduction to *The Coquette*.

86. The Marquis de Chastellux, "Portrait of George Washington," *NYM*, n.s., 2 (1797): 98–99; "Speech," *NYM*, n.s., 2 (1797): 158–63.

87. *Poems by Richard B. Davis: With a Sketch of His Life* (New York: T. and J. Swords, 1807). Davis died in 1799 at his father's home in New Brunswick, New Jersey. Subsequent references to the pamphlet indicate that it was written by his fellow Calliopeans immediately after Davis's death but published when they obtained access to his poems. When his father, an auctioneer, died shortly afterward, the newspaper noted that his son had been "the eccentric poet."

88. Davis wrote "The Eloquence of the Counter" (on the brilliance of salesmanship discussed above) and the poem "Elegy to an Old Wig," as well as several "Drone" columns; he also had a longtime position on the club's Committee of Examination. A manuscript volume of his poetry is now held at the New Jersey Historical Society.

89. "The Drone," *NYM* 3 (1792): 579–83.

90. Member Jotham Post noted in his diary in 1792 that four members had already died since the club's founding. Post Diary (1792–93), Oct. 15, 1792, NYHS.

Many died during the smallpox outbreaks during the era, particularly in 1795 and 1798.

91. Michael T. Gilmore, *American Romanticism and the Marketplace* (Chicago: University of Chicago Press, 1985).

92. *Poems by Richard B. Davis*, vii–x.

CHAPTER FIVE

1. Adoniram Chandler, *An Oration, Delivered before the New-York Typographical Society, on Their Seventh Anniversary, July 4, 1816* (New York: J. Seymour for the Society, 1816), 11.

2. Jefferson Clark, *Address Delivered at the Anniversary Celebration of the Franklin Typographical Society, January 17th, 1826* (Boston: Dutton and Wentworth, 1826), 17.

3. Alfred F. Young, *Liberty Tree: Ordinary People and the American Revolution* (New York: New York University Press, 2006), 33.

4. My sources in this chapter include the collection of transcriptions of records of journeymen printers' associations that were compiled and copied during the early twentieth century by social scientists at Johns Hopkins University; the originals appear to have been lost since that time. The first scholar to use the Hopkins material was George E. Barnett in "The Printers: A Study in American Trade Unionism," *American Economic Association Quarterly* 10 (1909): 1–809. In addition, I use Ethelbert Stewart, "A Documentary History of the Early Organizations of Printers," *Bulletin of the Bureau of Labor* 11, 61 (1905): 857–1033, a comprehensive work that quotes liberally from typographical societies' original records, some of which were not transcribed in the Hopkins collection.

5. Wilentz, *Chants Democratic*, 102; Bruce Laurie, *Working People of Philadelphia, 1800–1850* (Philadelphia: Temple University Press, 1980); Ronald Schultz, *The Republic of Labor: Philadelphia Artisans and the Politics of Class, 1720–1830* (New York: Oxford University Press, 1993). See also Mark L. Lause, *Some Degree of Power: From Hired Hand to Union Craftsman in the Preindustrial American Printing Trades, 1778–1815* (Fayetteville: University of Arkansas Press, 1991); William S. Pretzer, "The Printers of Washington, D.C., 1800–1880: Work Culture, Technology, and Trade Unionism" (PhD diss., Northern Illinois University, 1986); Howard B. Rock, *Artisans of the New Republic: The Tradesmen of New York City in the Age of Jefferson* (New York: New York University Press, 1979); and Charles G. Steffen, *The Mechanics of Baltimore: Workers and Politics in the Age of Revolution, 1763–1812* (Urbana: University of Illinois Press, 1984).

6. Michael Warner views printers' celebrations of their "art" less as patriotic expressions of pure craft pride than as early protectionist efforts to advance American imprints over English ones and as exemplary of businessmen's tendency to associate consumption of domestic products with nationalism. Warner, *Letters of the Republic*, chap. 5. See also Remer, *Printers and Men of Capital*, 41–44, and Jeffrey L. Pasley, *"The Tyranny of Printers": Newspaper Politics*

in the Early American Republic (Charlottesville: University Press of Virginia, 2001).

7. "S. W. Andrews," *Commercial Advertiser* (New York), May 5, 1802; see also identical wording in P. Heard's 1801 advertisement cited in Rita Susswein Gottesman, *The Arts and Crafts in New York, 1800–1804: Advertisements and News Items from New York City Newspapers* (New York: New York Historical Society, 1965), 302.

8. For more on this topic see Lause, *Some Degree of Power*; Silver, *American Printer*, chap. 1; Sharon V. Salinger, "Artisans, Journeymen, and the Transformation of Labor in Late Eighteenth-Century Philadelphia," *WMQ* 40 (1983): 62–84; Michael Sonenscher, *Work and Wages: Natural Law, Politics and the Eighteenth-Century French Trades* (Cambridge: Cambridge University Press, 1989), chap. 6; and Donald Woodward, "The Determination of Wage Rates in the Early Modern North of England," *Economic History Review* 47 (1994): 36–38.

9. For more on class and labor during this era, see Seth Rockman, "The Contours of Class in the Early Republic City," *Labor: Studies in Working-Class History of the Americas* 1 (2004): 91–107.

10. Evidence suggests that these established scales had existed at least as early as 1754 in Philadelphia. Henry P. Rosemont, "Benjamin Franklin and the Philadelphia Typographical Strikers of 1798," *Labor History* 22 (1981): 404–7. George A. Stevens also notes that the journeymen who worked for James Rivington's *Gazette* had turned out in 1776 to demand better wages from their employer, but this was apparently an isolated case and did not lead immediately to forming a society. Stevens, *New York Typographical Union No. 6: Study of a Modern Trade Union and Its Predecessors* (Albany: J. B. Lyon, 1913), 34–35.

11. Robert Aitken to John Nicholson, Nov. 16, 1797, Typographic Library and Museum Papers, COL.

12. John M. Burnside to Benjamin and Thomas Kite, Oct. 23, 1810, Typographic Library and Museum Papers, COL.

13. Rosemont, "Benjamin Franklin," 398–429. The journeymen fought for their pay to be set at $6 a week, equivalent to the 45 shilling rate.

14. Stewart, "Documentary History," 864; see also Stevens, *New York Typographical Union No. 6*, 35–41. By 1810 the New York organization had grown to 120. For a full list of organizations as they emerged (and were replaced) in each city, see Lause, *Some Degree of Power*, 60–61. The Philadelphia Typographical Society paid $1 a month to use a schoolhouse in Church Alley. Philadelphia Typographical Society (hereafter PTS), typescript copy of Record Book of Proceedings (1802–4, 1806–10), June 11, 1803, JHU. Historians have traced craftsmen's attempts to organize work rules and set wages as early as the medieval period. Journeymen's organizations were often called "brotherhoods" or "friendly societies" in Europe and sometimes extended across regions and nations. These groups strongly asserted journeymen's rights, even to the point of striking for better wages. Mary Roys Baker, "Anglo-Massachusetts Trade Roots, 1130–1790," *Labor History* 14 (1973): 352–96; Catharina Lis and Hugo Soly, "An Irresistible Phalanx: Journeyman Associations in Western Europe, 1300–1800," trans. Lee Mitzman, *International Review of Social History* 39

(1994): 11–52; and Michael J. Neufeld, "German Artisans and Political Repression: The Fall of the Journeymen's Associations in Nuremberg, 1806–1868," *Journal of Social History* 19 (1986): 491–502. In his study of journeymen printers, Mark Lause compiled a list of 590 men known to have belonged to at least one typographical society on the eastern seaboard before 1816. Lause, *Some Degree of Power*, app. B, 155–71.

15. The societies prohibited interruptions, required that men remove their hats before speaking, and indicated that no member should speak a third time on a subject without permission from the president. See, for example, New-York Typographical Society (hereafter NYTS), typescript copy of Record Book of Proceedings (1809–16), Aug. 17, 1811, JHU; PTS Record Book, May 2, 1807, JHU; and Columbia Typographical Society (hereafter CTS), Record Book of Proceedings (1814–34), Aug. 2, 1828, Columbia Typographical Union Archive, Apr. 15, 1815, REU.

16. By 1814, organizations in New Orleans and Washington, DC, had been added to the list.

17. New members arrived from various points in Pennsylvania, including Pittsburgh; from numerous states, including Delaware, North Carolina, New Jersey, Rhode Island, and Massachusetts; and from Germany, Ireland, and London. PTS Record Book, June 28, 1803, JHU.

18. NYTS Record Book (1809–16), July 13, 1811 (copy of a circular letter "To the Master-Printers of the city of New York"), JHU. See also David Waldstreicher, *Runaway America: Benjamin Franklin, Slavery, and the American Revolution* (New York: Hill and Wang, 2004), chaps. 1–2.

19. Among journeymen in all the crafts, the total number had multiplied nearly tenfold at the turn of the century, while the number of masters remained approximately the same—something many workingmen clearly recognized, as Joshua R. Greenberg notes in "Advocating 'the Man': Masculinity, Organized Labor, and the Market Revolution in New York, 1800–1840" (PhD diss., American University, 2003), 33–34.

20. "TO PRINTERS," *Gazette of the United States*, Aug. 19, 1803.

21. PTS Record Book, Apr. 23, 1803, JHU.

22. NYTS Record Book (1809–16), Sept. 30, 1809, JHU; see also John Clough, *An Address, Delivered on the Fourth of July, 1801, before the Franklin Typographical Association of New-York, and a Select Company* (New York: George F. Hopkins, 1801), 12–13.

23. PTS, printed circular letter, Feb. 22, 1802, transcribed in Stewart, "Documentary History," 865.

24. NYTS Record Book (1809–16), Oct. 28 and 30, 1809, JHU.

25. See, for example, Clough, *Address*, 12.

26. NYTS Record Book (1809–16), circular letter "To the Master-Printers of the city of New York," July 13, 1811, JHU. This letter was subsequently published in September 1811 in the *Independent Mechanic*, a weekly newspaper edited by two of the society's members.

27. PTS Record Book, Aug. 22, 1803, JHU.

28. NYTS Record Book (1809–16), Sept. 9, 1809, JHU; spelling as in the original.

29. Letter from the Albany Typographical Society (hereafter ATS) to the Washington City Typographical Society [sic], Oct. 4, 1816, transcribed in Stewart, "Documentary History," 889–90.

30. CTS Record Book, Feb. 16, 1819, REU.

31. Letter from the ATS to the Washington City Typographical Society [sic], no date listed, transcribed in Stewart, "Documentary History," 890.

32. Remer, *Printers and Men of Capital*, 94–99; Silver, *American Printer*, 59–62.

33. NYTS Record Book (1809–16), circular letter "To the Master-Printers of the City of New York," July 13, 1811, JHU. For evidence that masters often acceded to these efforts, see the Society of Printers of Boston and its Vicinity/Faustus Association, typescript copy of Constitution and Records (1805–15), July 16, 1805, JHU.

34. Ava Baron, "Questions of Gender: Deskilling and Demasculinization in the U.S. Printing Industry, 1830–1915," *Gender and History* 1 (1989): 181, 186. Baron rightly notes that while some journeymen articulated the concern that women were being hired at lower rates to replace them, just as much gendered anxiety circulated around the hiring of boys and "half-way journeymen." See also Greenberg, "Advocating 'the Man'"; Gay L. Gullickson, "Commentary: New Labor History from the Perspective of a Women's Historian," in *Rethinking Labor History*, ed. Lenard R. Berlanstein (Urbana: University of Illinois Press, 1993), 200–213; and Gregory L. Kaster, "Labour's True Man: Organised Workingmen and the Language of Manliness in the USA, 1827–1877," *Gender and History* 13 (2001): 24–64.

35. PTS to Mathew Carey, December 1826, transcribed in "Historical Sketch of the Philadelphia Typographical Society," *Printers' Circular*, no. 5 (July 1867): 251. The letter also announces that the other person to whom they had awarded an honorary membership was Isaiah Thomas, the Revolutionary patriot-printer whose *History of Printing in America* (1810) described the careers of prominent printers in each region of the nation. The *ars artium* referred to print's being the "art of all arts."

36. Stevens, *New-York Typographical Union No. 6*, 76. It is not clear that they passed this resolution.

37. NYTS Record Book (1816–18), Mar. 7, 1818, JHU; spelling as in the original.

38. George Churchill, *An Address, Pronounced before the Albany Typographical Society, November 6, 1813; On the Advantages Resulting to Mankind from the Invention of the Art of Printing* (Albany, 1813), 5.

39. Churchill, *Address*, 5.

40. Clough, *Address*, 10.

41. William Burdick, *An Oration on the Nature and Effects of the Art of Printing, Delivered in Franklin-Hall, July 5, 1802, before the Boston Franklin Association* (Boston: Munroe and Francis, 1802), 10.

42. Chandler, *Oration*, 10–11. For a description of a later celebration of the "art of printing," see Ronald J. Zboray, *A Fictive People: Antebellum Economic Development and the American Reading Public* (New York: Oxford University Press, 1993), 3–9.

43. Ebenezer Mack, *An Oration, Delivered before the New-York Typographical Society, on the Fifth of July, 1813 in Celebration of the Thirty-Seventh Anniversary of American Independence, and Fourth of the Society* (New York: S. Woodworth, 1813), 14. For more on this subject see Remer, *Printers and Men of Capital*, 65.

44. Master printers and publishers sought a greater cooperation with each other—and made a concerted effort to tout domestic imprints over imported ones—by forming cooperative groups like the Philadelphia Company of Printers and Booksellers (1791) and the American Company of Booksellers (1801), which sought to regulate book prices as the renowned Leipzig Fair had done earlier. Remer, *Printers and Men of Capital*, 57–62. A different group of printers formed the short-lived New York Association of Text Book Sellers (1802) to puff "correct American editions" of schoolbooks. Charlotte E. Morgan, *The Origin and History of the New York Employing Printers' Association: The Evolution of a Trade Association* (New York: Oxford University Press, 1930), 32. Between 1800 and 1802 masters also urged the federal government to pass a protectionist tax on imported printed materials. Rollo G. Silver, "The Book Trade and the Protective Tariff: 1800–1804," *Papers of the Bibliographical Society of America* 46 (1952): 33–44.

45. Thomas G. Fessenden, "Hymn: The Art of Printing," *Address Delivered at the Anniversary Celebration of the Franklin Typographical Society, January 17th, 1826*, ed. Jefferson Clark (Boston: Dutton and Wentworth, 1826), 19.

46. Stephen Botein, "'Meer Mechanics' and an Open Press: The Business and Political Strategies of Colonial American Printers," *Perspectives in American History* 9 (1975): 127–225; Botein, "Printers and the American Revolution," in *The Press and the American Revolution*, ed. Bernard Bailyn and John B. Hench (Worcester, MA: American Antiquarian Society, 1980), 11–57.

47. Clough, *Address*, 6–10.

48. George Asbridge, *An Oration, Delivered before the New-York Typographical Society, at Their Second Anniversary, on the Fourth of July, 1811* (New York: C. S. Van Winkle, 1811), 7–8.

49. The sum of $83.60 would be nearly $1,100 in 2007 dollars.

50. PTS Record Book, Sept. 17, 1803, JHU; "The Philadelphia Typographical Society," *Poulson's American Daily Advertiser* (Philadelphia), Sept. 24, 1803.

51. "Philadelphia Typographical Society," *Saturday Evening Post* 2 (Nov. 8, 1823): 2.

52. Clough, *Address*, 14. This toast-poem was repeated by several other societies over time, including some in Philadelphia; see "Philadelphia Typographical Society. Twenty-Second Anniversary," *New England Galaxy* (Boston) 7 (Nov. 19, 1824): 371. For other examples of puns embedded in the toasts they drank, see "Philadelphia Typographical Society," *Saturday Evening Post*, 2, 45 (Nov. 8, 1823): 2. Even when they toasted the Constitution, the army, manufactures, or the fair sex, journeymen found ways of embedding puns with printers' terms. In this regard they drew on

Franklin's *Autobiography*, which used such words as "errata" to describe events in his life; Franklin also described himself as a "pretty good *riggite*, that is, a jocular verbal satirist." *Autobiography of Benjamin Franklin*, 47.

53. "Philadelphia Typographical Society."

54. NYTS Record Book (1809–16), Apr. 11, 1811, JHU.

55. NYTS Record Book (1809–16), Sept. 4, 1813, JHU.

56. NYTS Record Book (1816–18), June 15, 1816, JHU; see also Chandler's reference to a society library of books in *Oration*, 4.

57. Society of Printers of Boston and Its Vicinity/Faustus Association, typescript copy of Constitution and Records (1805–15), JHU. See also *The Constitution of the Company of Printers, of Philadelphia* (Philadelphia: William W. Woodward, 1794), and Samuel Hamilton, *Typographical Association, or Society for the Promotion of Literature and the Fine Arts* (Boston: [Hilliard, Gray], 1827).

58. Kett, *Pursuit of Knowledge under Difficulties*, 45–52, 63–73.

59. NYTS Record Book (1809–16), July 18, 1810, JHU; spelling as in the original.

60. NYTS Record Book (1809–16), July 23, 1810, JHU.

61. "Journeymen Printers," *Boston Recorder and Religious Telegraph*, July 18, 1828. Other jokes about journeymen's ignorance or lack of education appeared regularly; see, for example, "Typographical," *Ladies Literary Cabinet* (New York) 4 (Sept. 8, 1821): 142. The Columbia Typographical Society expressed outrage at the *Recorder*'s representation of them, noting that the Franklin Typographical Society had drawn up "a series of resolutions, denying its truth, and deprecating in mild and forbearing language, the existence of that spirit of calumny." CTS Record Book, Aug. 2, 1828, REU.

62. "From the Port-folio of a Journeyman Printer," *Emerald, or Miscellany of Literature* (Boston) 2 (Mar. 28, 1807): 150. See also Chandler, *Oration*, 4.

63. D. C., "The Proof-Sheet," *New Monthly Magazine and Literary Journal*, American ed. (Philadelphia) 1 (1821): 233–34. The quotation is from Horace: "To give light from smoke." The essay was reprinted in the *New-York Literary Journal, and Belles-Lettres Repository* shortly thereafter in April 1821. Such references were not limited to published writings. Journeymen also appealed to masters to insist on full apprenticeships for boys by insisting that without that education, boys would "make but sorry printers." NYTS Record Book (1809–16), July 13, 1811, JHU.

64. Such statements were reinforced in public notices about the typographers' annual celebrations, as in 1834, when the Columbia Typographical Society quoted a guest's oration: "It was in a printing office, said Mr. Davis, that my mind was formed. It was there that I learned the importance of reading and of thinking.... I have found no class of men, that, as a whole, possessed so much intelligence, or so much practical knowledge, as the journeymen printers." Pleased, the writer commented that Davis "will never consent to kick away the ladder by which he climbed." *United States Telegraph*, Jan. 12, 1834.

65. D. C., "Proof Sheet," 233; emphasis in the original.

66. "Philadelphia Typographical Society," *Saturday Evening Post* 3 (Nov. 13, 1824): 3.

67. CTS Record Book, July 3, 1824, REU. For the following passages I am indebted to William S. Pretzer, "The British, Duff Green, the Rats and the Devil," *Labor History* 27 (1985–86): 5–30, and William Stephen Belko, "Duff Green: A Public Life, 1791–1840" (PhD diss., Mississippi State University, 2002).

68. In addition to the elected printer for the House and Senate, private printers contracted to print and bind publications by each of the government offices until 1860, when the Government Printing Office was established.

69. During the 1828 campaign, Green did not hesitate to attack and counterattack Jackson's opposition. Outraged by the allegations of irregularity in Jackson's marriage, for example, Green invented vicious rumors about John Quincy Adams's wife — suggesting that she was an illegitimate child and that she and Adams had engaged in premarital relations. Gretchen Garst Ewing, "Duff Green: Independent Editor of a Party Press," *Journalism Quarterly* 54 (1977): 733–39.

70. Green relinquished his role as editor of the *Telegraph* in 1836, though he remained as publisher. He later gave up printing entirely to focus on political and diplomatic concerns.

71. This was one of Green's many physical duels, brawls, and other confrontations. Belko, "Duff Green," 1.

72. By 1832 he had lost three thousand subscribers, and the paper was operating at a $5,000 annual loss. Joel H. Silbey, "Duff Green," in *American National Biography*, ed. John A. Garraty and Mark C. Carnes (New York: Oxford University Press, 1999), 9:484–85; Belko, "Duff Green," 338, 441.

73. When the society was founded in 1815 and created its first list of prices, it mostly codified rather than increased the weekly rates that journeymen received throughout the city. Congress dictated that journeymen working on government-related print jobs would be paid by the week — $10 if Congress was in session, and $9 if not — rather than by the piece as was common for all other work. In 1819 Congress passed legislation confirming this scale. Pretzer, "British, Duff Green, the Rats and the Devil," 11–12; Stewart, "Documentary History," 989. Compared with the more acrimonious relations that typographical societies in New York and elsewhere had with their employers, the Columbia Typographical Society had had no problems by 1834.

74. "The Congressional Printer," *Workingmen's Advocate* 2 (Feb. 5, 1831): 1. This article proudly announced that even the alleged scabs were unwilling to work on Green's terms.

75. Duff Green, "Prospectus of the Washington Institute," reprinted in *Protest of the Columbia Typographical Society, Addressed to the Public Generally, and Particularly to the Printers of the United States, against the Washington Institute* (Washington, DC: Francis Preston Blair, 1834), 18–19. The pedagogical desire to avoid corporal punishment was in vogue among certain groups in the 1830s. Philip Greven, *Spare the Child: The Religious Roots of Punishment and the Psychological Impact of Physical Abuse* (New York: Knopf, 1991). Like certain prison reformers of the day, Green proposed the punishment of solitary confinement for boys who behaved badly, a notion the CTS described as "so ridiculous, that we deem it unworthy of serious consideration." *Pro-*

ceedings of the Meetings of Printers of the District of Columbia, relative to the Washington Institute (Washington, DC: William W. Moore, 1834), 13.

76. Green, "Prospectus," 18.

77. Green, "Prospectus," 17.

78. Green, "Prospectus," 18.

79. Green, "Prospectus," 18.

80. Green, "Prospectus," 19.

81. In lieu of paying interest on these loans, Green would provide each subscriber with copies of one of his publications.

82. CTS Record Book, Jan. 11, 1834, REU; A. McGrath to Duff Green, Apr. 3, 1834, transcribed in *Protest of the Columbia Typographical Society*, 15.

83. CTS Record Book, Jan. 11, 1834, REU; see also Pretzer, "British, Duff Green, the Rats and the Devil," 14–15.

84. William Walters to Duff Green, Apr. 17, 1834, transcribed in *Protest of the Columbia Typographical Society*, 17.

85. A. McGrath to Duff Green, Apr. 3, 1834, transcribed in *Protest of the Columbia Typographical Society*, 15; emphasis in the original.

86. Duff Green to Messrs. McGrath and others, Apr. 7, 1834, transcribed in *Protest of the Columbia Typographical Society,* 16. See similar language in "The Washington Institute," *United States Telegraph*, Sept. 10, 1834.

87. He reminded the society that beyond the rates of pay, they had no right to complain about a master's employment practices. So if the society were to interfere with a decision to "find it in my interest to employ but ten" journeymen rather than fifty, he would take it to court.

88. Walters to Green, transcribed in *Protest of the Columbia Typographical Society*, 16–17.

89. CTS Record Book, June 7, 1834, REU.

90. In August the members of the CTS published *Protest of the Columbia Typographical Society*, a twenty-one-page pamphlet that combined a long narrative explaining the negotiations with Green and transcriptions of seven letters between the two parties, as well as a copy of Green's "Prospectus." By early September they published *Proceedings of the Meetings of Printers*, a sixteen-page pamphlet displaying in transparent detail the journeymen's meetings and their formal "Address to the People of the United States" that described, in exposé format, the facts behind the Institute as they saw them. Later that month they followed it with an eight-page pamphlet, *Reply of the Columbia Typographical Society to the Strictures of Gen. Duff Green, upon the Protest of That Body against the Washington Institute* (Washington, DC: Francis Preston Blair, 1834). This last document responded to a series of editorials Green published in his *United States Telegraph* during August and September. Green continued to publish editorials throughout October. Meanwhile other East Coast societies joined in denouncing Green, most prominently the Baltimore Typographical Society (which published editorials in newspapers throughout the District of Columbia) and the newly reorganized New York Typographical Association. See typescript of the latter's Record Book (1831–40), Aug. 16, 1834, June 13, 1835 (hereafter NYTA Record Book), JHU.

91. The CTS immediately dismissed these letters as Green's own work. "From the style and manner, we are tempted to believe, [this letter] was dictated or written by the Editor himself," they explained in *Reply of the Columbia Typographical Society*, 8.

92. K., "Washington, 11th September, 1834," *United States Telegraph*, Sept. 13, 1834.

93. K., "For the United States Telegraph," *United States Telegraph*, Sept. 25, 1834; emphasis in the original. See also the anonymous, strongly supportive "Washington Institute," *United States Telegraph*, Oct. 3, 1834, purportedly written by a former "mechanic" who had risen to be "one of the most highly respected citizens of the west," according to Green's prefatory note. In addition, Green's foreman, William W. Moore, published an apologia for Green that told a far more sympathetic version of the dispute. *United States Telegraph Extra: To the Public, and Especially to the Printers of the United States* (Washington, DC: Duff Green, 1835).

94. *Proceedings of the Meetings of Printers*, 7, 11–12; emphasis in the original.

95. *Proceedings of the Meetings of Printers*, 14–15; emphasis in the original. See similar wording in the response by the NYTA to the Washington Institute scandal in the NYTA Record Book, Sept. 15, 1832, JHU.

96. Pretzer, "British, Duff Green, the Rats and the Devil," 16–17. After strongly opposing Martin Van Buren's candidacy for president in 1836—and putting his public reputation on the line to support Calhoun—when the election failed to go his way Green determined to leave public life. He sold the paper in 1837 and set off to make money in land in Mississippi and then Texas.

97. Shortly afterward, the CTS attempted to develop a uniform plan for addressing the problem of apprentices. This included taking boys as apprentices only up to age fifteen and extending their apprenticeship until age twenty-one—excessively long in this era—and asking for proof of a man's full apprenticeship before hiring. *Apprentices to the Printing Business* (Washington, DC: Columbia Typographical Society, 1835).

98. *Proceedings of the National Typographical Convention: Held at the City of Washington, from the Seventh to the Eleventh November, 1836* (Washington, DC: National Typographical Society, 1836), 14–16. Perhaps because it offered little more protection than had been provided by local societies, the National Typographical Society dissolved in 1838.

CHAPTER SIX

1. Q. in a Corner, "From the N.Y. Statesman," *Norwich* [CT] *Courier*, Jan. 21, 1829.

2. "Wrightiana," *New-York American*, Jan. 29, 1829; "From the Boston Gazette," *Free Enquirer*, 2nd ser., 1 (July 22, 1829); X., "The Female Monster," *New-York American*, Jan. 8, 1829. Of the thirty northeastern newspapers I systematically studied, I have yet to find one that fails to mention Wright's lectures during 1829. Moreover, aside from the New York–based free-thought periodicals the *Correspon-*

dent and Wright's own *Free Enquirer,* virtually all take a dim view of her work and lectures.

3. Phelps, *Lectures to Young Ladies,* 40.

4. Lori D. Ginzberg, "'The Hearts of Your Readers Will Shudder': Fanny Wright, Infidelity, and American Freethought," *American Quarterly* 46 (1994): 195-226.

5. See, for example, Cmiel, *Democratic Eloquence,* 70-71; Celia Morris Eckhardt, *Fanny Wright: Rebel in America* (Cambridge, MA: Harvard University Press, 1984), 171; and Christine Stansell, *City of Women: Sex and Class in New York, 1789-1860* (Urbana: University of Illinois Press, 1986). In contrast, see Susan Zaeske, "The 'Promiscuous Audience' Controversy and the Emergence of the Early Woman's Rights Movement," *Quarterly Journal of Speech* 81 (1995): 191-207. On Wright's life and work, see Elizabeth Ann Bartlett, *Liberty, Equality, Sorority: The Origins and Interpretation of American Feminist Thought; Frances Wright, Sarah Grimké, and Margaret Fuller* (Brooklyn, NY: Carlson, 1994); Susan S. Kissel, *In Common Cause: The "Conservative" Frances Trollope and the "Radical" Frances Wright* (Bowling Green, OH: Bowling Green State University Popular Press, 1993); A. J. G. Perkins and Theresa Wolfson, *Frances Wright, Free Enquirer: The Study of a Temperament* (New York: Harper and Brothers, 1939); Molly Abel Travis, "Frances Wright: The Other Woman of Early American Feminism," *Women's Studies* 22 (1993): 389-97; and Wallace, *Rockdale,* 246–55, 275–95.

6. Peter Stallybrass and Allon White, *The Politics and Poetics of Transgression* (Ithaca, NY: Cornell University Press, 1986), 80–124, 93. Questions of class are important to these conflicting images of the theater "crowd" and the reading public for specific reasons: Wright explicitly supported workingmen's groups and equal education for the poor. Some of her most visible supporters came from the lower-class community of freethinkers.

7. On the reconstruction of the gender system in antebellum America, see Nancy Isenberg, *Sex and Citizenship in Antebellum America* (Chapel Hill: University of North Carolina Press, 1998); Varon, "Tippecanoe and the Ladies, Too"; Mary P. Ryan, "Gender and Public Access: Women's Politics in Nineteenth-Century America," in Calhoun, *Habermas and the Public Sphere,* 259–88.

8. Frances Wright D'Arusmont, "Biography and Notes," in her *Life, Letters, and Lectures, 1834-1844* (1844; New York: Arno Press, 1972), 11.

9. Born in Dundee in 1795, Wright was orphaned at age two and raised by relatives in London, Devonshire, and Glasgow. Eckhardt, *Fanny Wright,* 10, 180-83; Kathleen Edgerton Kendall and Jeanne Y. Fisher, "Frances Wright on Women's Rights: Eloquence versus Ethos," *Quarterly Journal of Speech* 60 (1974): 60; Lillian O'Connor, *Pioneer Women Orators: Rhetoric in the Ante-bellum Reform Movement* (New York: Columbia University Press, 1954), 51–52; and Virginia A. Rutherford, "A Study of the Speaking Career of Frances Wright in America" (PhD diss., Northwestern University, 1960), 166–77.

10. "When I was but a child, my friends, my enthusiasm was fired with admiration of your glorious political revolution of 1776, and my earliest essays in literature

were a eulogium upon your nation," she told a Boston audience in August 1829. "Miss Wright," *Boston Galaxy*, reprinted in the *Springfield* [MA] *Republican*, Aug. 19, 1829. Eckhardt, *Fanny Wright*, 16. See also Robert J. Connors, "Frances Wright: First Female Civic Rhetor in America," *College English* 62 (1999): 30–57, at 33–38. Gail Bederman, "Revisiting Nashoba: Slavery, Utopia, and Frances Wright in America, 1818–1826," *American Literary History* 17 (2005): 438–59, at 439–40; D'Arusmont, *Life, Letters, and Lectures*, v–vi.

11. Frances Wright, *Views of Society and Manners in America in a Series of Letters from That Country to a Friend in England, during the Years 1818, 1819, and 1820* (New York: E. Bliss and E. White, 1821), 19–20. British reviewers condemned the book, but Wright gained many international admirers, including Jeremy Bentham, the Marquis de Lafayette, and Albert Gallatin. Eckhardt, *Fanny Wright*, 49–54.

12. Bederman, "Revisiting Nashoba," 440.

13. Bederman, "Revisiting Nashoba," 453.

14. Frances Wright, "A Plan," *Genius of Universal Emancipation* (Baltimore), Oct. 15, 1825.

15. *Genius of Universal Emancipation* (Baltimore), Aug. 18, 1827; quoted in Eckhardt, *Fanny Wright*, 143.

16. Bederman, "Revisiting Nashoba," 451.

17. Wright, "Nashoba: Explanatory Notes Respecting the Nature and Objects of the Institution of Nashoba," *Genius of Universal Emancipation* (Baltimore), Feb. 23, 1828.

18. Eckhardt, *Fanny Wright*, 155-57, 163–65. I have found no evidence that the "Explanatory Notes" was published in northeastern newspapers during 1828. Several did, however, republish key parts of that essay during 1829 when they sought to discredit Wright during her New York lecture tour.

19. "Miss Wright," *Chronicle of the Times*, Aug. 16, 1828; "Miss Frances Wright," *Niles' Weekly Register* (Baltimore) 34 (Aug. 2, 1828): 376. See also "Miss Frances Wright Has Taken Charge," *National Advocate* (New York), July 15, 1828. These articles imply that readers would already have known something of Wright's views of marriage and sexuality.

20. "Frances Wright's Lectures," *Free Enquirer*, 2nd ser., 1 (Dec. 10, 1828): 54.

21. And it worked. Within months, about fifty freethinking "men of wealth and influence" in the Midwest had subscribed $1,300 to establish a "Temple of Reason" to advance the ideas she had proposed in her talks. Eckhardt, *Fanny Wright*, 183.

22. Barnet Baskerville, *The People's Voice: The Orator in American Society* (Lexington: University Press of Kentucky, 1979), and Hatch, *Democratization of American Christianity*.

23. Philip Hone cited in Cmiel, *Democratic Eloquence*, 72.

24. Critics of this style believed that such strenuous efforts to demonstrate affinity with one's auditors perilously overemphasized role-playing at the expense of expressing one's true virtue and sentiment. Cmiel, *Democratic Eloquence*, 25–27, 55–93, and Christine Oravec, "The Democratic Critics: An Alternative American Rhetorical Tradition of the Nineteenth Century," *Rhetorica* 4 (1986): 395-421.

25. Not until the 1840s and 1850s did newspapers begin to consign partisan opinion to editorial commentary pages, and it took far longer—until nearly the turn of the century—for any newspaper to establish the "objective" journalistic ideal. The conception of objective reporting began to emerge only after severe critique of editorial license in the 1830s. Gerald Baldasty, *The Commercialization of News in the Nineteenth Century* (Madison: University of Wisconsin Press, 1992); Hazel Dicken-Garcia, *Journalistic Standards in Nineteenth-Century America* (Madison: University of Wisconsin Press, 1989); Pasley, *"Tyranny of Printers"*; Michael Schudson, *Discovering the News: A Social History of American Newspapers* (New York: Basic Books, 1978).

26. Benjamin Brown French, *Witness to the Young Republic: A Yankee's Journal, 1828–1870* (Hanover, NH: University Press of New England, 1989), 15–16, dated Sept. 15, 1828. Newspapers of this era remained small and were the highly personal products of their editors or publishers. In general the same man wrote, edited, managed, and printed a newspaper. Schudson, *Discovering the News,* 16.

27. "Fideles," *Louisville Focus,* cited in the *Free Enquirer,* 2nd ser., 1 (Dec. 10, 1828): 54–55.

28. Frances Trollope, *Domestic Manners of the Americans* (1832; New York: Dodd, Mead, 1927), 57.

29. "Miss Frances Wright, from Mr. Owen's Settlement," *National Advocate* (New York), Dec. 24, 1828.

30. "Miss Wright's Lecture upon Knowledge," *New-York American,* Jan. 5, 1829.

31. Of the nine New York newspapers I examined, six included firsthand reports of her earliest appearances. All together, forty-four papers were published in New York in 1829, making it the newspaper capital of a country well known for having the most in the world. New York's teeming newspaper market reflected its rapidly growing population—which by 1830 was equal to the populations of Boston, Philadelphia, and Baltimore combined. In the country as a whole between 1790 and 1830, the number of newspapers published increased almost sixfold. Frank Luther Mott, *American Journalism: A History of Newspapers in the United States through 260 Years: 1690 to 1950,* rev. ed. (New York: Macmillan, 1950), 167–68, 181.

32. "Doleful Ditty" from a New York newspaper, cited in Kendall and Fisher, "Frances Wright on Women's Rights," 66.

33. D'Arusmont, *Life, Letters, and Lectures,* 18, 31–34.

34. "Miss Frances Wright," *New-York Spectator,* Jan. 9, 1829, reprinted from the *New-York Commercial Advertiser.*

35. Editorials in the *Boston Courier* and *Boston Statesman,* reprinted in the *Free Enquirer,* 2nd ser., 1 (Aug. 12, 1829): 329–30.

36. Frances Wright's letter to James Richardson, Aug. 18, 1827, cited in William Randall Waterman, *Frances Wright* (New York: Columbia University, 1925), 120–21.

37. M. M. Noah, the Jacksonian editor of the *New-York Evening Post,* objected to "female expounders" and insisted on the "incongruity of the practice with our

notions of the proper sphere of their sex." "Miss Wright's Lectures," *New-York Evening Post*, Jan. 10, 1829. In contrast, the radical free-thought *Correspondent* asserted that female oratory "is not a circumstance attended with much novelty either in this country or in Europe." "Miss Wright's Lectures," *Correspondent* 4 (Jan. 10, 1829).

38. Nor did they dismiss her for speaking in front of promiscuous audiences, a charge that would later be leveled against Angelina and Sarah Grimké and other female abolitionists. As Susan Zaeske has suggested, not until the early 1830s did religious leaders construct a firm notion of promiscuous audiences, a concept that bound together conceptions of separate spheres with religiously inspired views of women's sexual morality. Zaeske, "'Promiscuous Audience' Controversy," 191–97.

39. Ganter, "Unexceptional Eloquence," 270; Zagarri, *Revolutionary Backlash*.

40. X., "The Female Monster," *New-York American*, Jan. 8, 1829.

41. "Miss Fanny Wright," *Springfield* [MA] *Republican*, Jan. 21, 1829, reprinted from the *New-York Commercial Advertiser*, Jan. 12, 1829.

42. Agnew, *Worlds Apart*, esp. 125–48; Ditz, "Shipwrecked," 51–80; and Ziff, *Writing in the New Nation*, 54–106.

43. "Frances Wright," *Christian Intelligencer and Eastern Chronicle* (Gardiner, ME), Jan. 30, 1829.

44. "Miss Wright," *Richmond* [VA] *Enquirer*, Feb. 7, 1829, reprinted from the *New-York Enquirer*.

45. Frances Wright, "Anonymous Writing," *Free Enquirer*, 2nd ser., 1 (Feb. 15, 1829): 48.

46. Editors depicted Wright's ideas in rapid-fire inventories that gave readers little pause to consider them seriously. "She would abolish religion; rid the world of priest craft; destroy the Sabbath; sell the churches, and set the ministers to working," wrote X. in the *New-York American*, Jan. 8, 1829. In doing so, editors dismissed her arguments as so fanatically anti-Christian that they did not deserve consideration.

47. "Miss Wright's Lectures," *New-York Evening Post*, Jan. 10, 1829.

48. "Miss Frances Wright," *Niles' Weekly Register* (Baltimore) 35 (Jan. 14, 1829): 345.

49. Frances Wright, "To the New York Reader," *Free Enquirer*, 2nd ser., 1 (Jan. 28, 1829): 8.

50. See, for example, "Infidelity," *Boston Recorder and Religious Telegraph*, Jan. 29, 1829, reprinted from the *New York Journal of Commerce*; and "Miss Wright Again," *Springfield* [MA] *Republican*, Feb. 11, 1829, reprinted from the *New-York Enquirer*. Other papers referred to Wright's ideological affiliation with Mary Wollstonecraft and Thomas Paine. The elite and conservative Philip Hone described her as a "female Tom Paine" who sought to "unsettle the foundations of civil society, and subvert our fundamental principles of morality." Philip Hone, *The Diary of Philip Hone, 1828–1851*, ed. Allan Nevins (New York: Dodd, Mead, 1927), 1:9–10 (Jan. 7, 1829).

51. On this topic see Scott, *Gender and the Politics of History*, 49.

52. She married Jackson before her first marriage had officially ended in divorce, and though the mistake was apparently an honest one, it tarred her with the brush

of bigamy for the rest of her life. Norma Basch, "Marriage, Morals, and Politics in the Election of 1828," *Journal of American History* 80 (1993): 890–918.

53. Royall especially denounced the hypocrisy of religious evangelicals, including one religious leader who had fathered children with one of his very young female slaves. Her sarcastic rebuke of these figures led to the "common scold" charge. She was indicted and sentenced to pay a fine rather than be dunked—a fine that her colleagues from the *Washington National Intelligencer* paid in the name of journalistic camaraderie. See Bessie Rowland James, *Anne Royall's U.S.A.* (New Brunswick, NJ: Rutgers University Press, 1972).

54. "Last Evening, Miss Frances Wright," *Aurora and Pennsylvania Gazette*, Jan. 8, 1829; "Miss Wright," *Daily Albany Argus,* Nov. 7, 1829, reprinted from the *Salem Observer.*

55. See "Miss Fanny Wright," *Springfield* [MA] *Republican*, Jan. 21, 1829, reprinted from the *New-York Spectator,* and "Miss Wright," *Norwich* [CT] *Courier,* Feb. 4, 1829.

56. "Miss Frances Wright," *New-York Spectator,* Jan. 9, 1829, reprinted from the *New-York Commercial Advertiser* of Jan. 5, 1829. Since the seventeenth century, British actresses had battled a reputation for prostitution. On this topic see Ellen Donkin, "Mrs. Siddons Looks Back in Anger: Feminist Historiography for Eighteenth-Century British Theater," in *Critical Theory and Performance,* ed. Janelle G. Reinelt and Joseph R. Roach (Ann Arbor: University of Michigan Press, 1992), 276–90. It is notable that no reports suggested a sexual relationship between Wright and her escort, Timothy Jenkins (alternatively reported as Jennings).

57. Wilentz, *Chants Democratic,* 177.

58. As Linda Kerber has perceived, Columbia frequently appeared as an idealized republican mother. Kerber, *Women of the Republic,* passim; see also John Higham, "Indian Princess and Roman Goddess: The First Female Symbols of America," *Proceedings of the American Antiquarian Society* 100 (1990): 63, and Winterer, *Mirror of Antiquity,* chaps. 3–4. Higham and others have noted the sexual propriety of Columbia in contrast to her forebear, the Indian princess. On the increasingly constricting and elaborate contemporary dress of the 1820s, see Davidoff and Hall, *Family Fortunes,* 413–15. On the Christian implications of American dress, see Bushman, *Refinement of America,* 314–19. Frances Trollope, who heard Wright speak in Cincinnati, described the dress as hanging "around her in folds that recalled the drapery of a Grecian statue." Trollope, *Domestic Manners of the Americans,* quoted in Eckhardt, *Fanny Wright,* 172. For other classical references, see "Miss Frances Wright," *New-York Spectator,* Jan. 9, 1829, reprinted from the *New-York Commercial Advertiser* of Jan. 6, 1829, and "Frances Wright," *Aurora* (Philadelphia), Jan. 10, 1829.

59. When she delivered a Fourth of July address in Philadelphia, she entered the stage with "some thirty or forty friends." At other appearances, reporters described these supporters as "tradespeople." Kendall and Fisher, "Frances Wright on Women's Rights," 61.

60. "Miss Wright has finished her lectures," *New-York Spectator,* Aug. 11, 1829. In fact, Wright helped form a class in public speaking at the Hall of Science,

which she and her *Free Enquirer* compatriots founded in New York in April 1829. They also began holding public debates there in 1830. O'Connor, *Pioneer Women Orators*, 51.

61. Trollope, *Domestic Manners of the Americans*, 57. Indeed, actresses like Mrs. Siddons and Fanny Kemble were some of the most popular theatrical performers in Britain and America during the first half of the nineteenth century. William W. Clapp Jr., *A Record of the Boston Stage* (1853; New York: Greenwood Press, 1969), 5–10; Calvin Lee Pritner, "A Theater and Its Audience," *Pennsylvania Magazine of History and Biography* 91 (1961): 72–79; Richard Gooch, "America and Americans in 1833–4: New York Theatre in the 1830s," *Nineteenth-Century Theatre* 19 (1991): 45–51.

62. "Miss Frances Wright," *New-York Spectator,* Jan. 9, 1829, reprinted from the *New-York Commercial Advertiser* of Jan. 6, 1829.

63. W. Young, *Twelve Letters to Young Men on the Sentiments of Miss Frances Wright and Robert D. Owen* (Philadelphia: Thomas Kite, 1830), 9. These "letters" were originally published in a Philadelphia paper.

64. This advice had grown increasingly vehement among writers like Catharine Beecher, who wrote in 1829 that such women "cultivated certain powers of mind in a disproportionate extent, and destroyed that true balance of mind which is so necessary for a woman." Beecher, *Suggestions Respecting Improvements in Education, Presented to the Trustees of the Hartford Female Seminary, and Published at Their Request* (Hartford, CT: Packard and Butler, 1829), 42–43. For an earlier example of this advice, see T. Knox's "Cautionary Hints to Learned Ladies," in *The New Pleasing Instructor, or Young Lady's Guide to Virtue and Happiness* (Boston: I. Thomas and E. T. Andrews, 1799), 175, though Knox cautions women against *affecting* knowledge they do not have. Diatribes against the learned lady arose in particular as part of the backlash against Mary Wollstonecraft in the late 1790s and specifically warned women against ambition and the desire for fame. See Ann Douglas, *The Feminization of American Culture* (New York: Knopf, 1977), 259–88, and Mary Poovey, *The Proper Lady and the Woman Writer* (Chicago: University of Chicago Press, 1984), 35–47 and passim.

65. Mary Poovey, *Uneven Developments: The Ideological Work of Gender in Mid-Victorian England* (Chicago: University of Chicago Press, 1988), 12–15.

66. X., "The Female Monster," *New-York American,* Jan. 8, 1829.

67. On female monstrousness, see Marie-Hélène Huet, *Monstrous Imagination* (Cambridge, MA: Harvard University Press, 1993); Mary Poovey, "'My Hideous Progeny': The Lady and the Monster" (on Mary Shelley's *Frankenstein)*, in Poovey, *Proper Lady and the Woman Writer*, 114–71.

68. "We Were Called upon by an Old Correspondent," *New-York American*, Jan. 9, 1829.

69. "How Could Our Friend of the New York Commercial Advertiser," *National Gazette and Literary Register* (Philadelphia), Jan. 9, 1829; "We Can Admit That the Editor of the New York Gazette," *National Gazette and Literary Register*, Jan. 13, 1829.

70. "Miss Fanny Wright," *Springfield* [MA] *Republican*, Jan. 21, 1829, reprinted from the *New-York Commercial Advertiser*, Jan. 12, 1829.

71. A Mother, "To the Editors of the *Evening Post*," *New-York Evening Post*, Jan. 27, 1829; A Friend to Truth, "Letter to Messrs. Editors," *New England Palladium and Commercial Advertiser* (Boston), Aug. 7, 1829; "Infidelity," *Boston Recorder and Religious Telegraph*, Jan. 29, 1829, reprinted from the *New York Journal of Commerce*.

72. "Under the Head of *National Education*," *New-York Spectator*, Sept. 15, 1829. In fact, some "staid citizens of Philadelphia" did prevent Wright's Sunday speech. On the same day this article appeared, the Philadelphia papers the *Aurora* and the *National Gazette* reported that her request to use the Walnut Street Theater, or Washington Hall, had been refused. She then shifted the location to the Military Hall, but, dramatically, on the evening of her lecture the Hall and the street outside were so packed with people that Wright literally could not emerge from her carriage. She rescheduled the lecture for late September at the Arch Street Theater. "Miss Wright," *New-York Spectator*, Sept. 18, 1829.

73. Vindex, "From the New York Evening Post," *Maryland Gazette* (Annapolis), Jan. 29, 1829, reprinted from the *New-York Evening Post*, Jan. 12, 1829.

74. "Park Theatre," *New-York Evening Post*, Jan. 26, 1829. According to Eckhardt, *Fanny Wright*, Bryant was the author of these articles; but it appears from other sources that he was one of several editors of the *Post*.

75. Stallybrass and White, *Politics and Poetics of Transgression*, 80–124; Lawrence W. Levine, *Highbrow/Lowbrow: The Emergence of Cultural Hierarchy in America* (Cambridge, MA: Harvard University Press, 1988), 60–69. Famous theater fires occurred later, in the early 1830s and 1840s. See also David Grimsted, *American Mobbing, 1828–1861: Toward Civil War* (New York: Oxford University Press, 1998).

76. "Miss Frances Wright," *New-York Spectator*, Jan. 9, 1829.

77. "Frances Wright," *Aurora and Pennsylvania Gazette* (Philadelphia), Jan. 10, 1829, reprinted from the *New York-Commercial Advertiser*.

78. "Miss Wright Has Finished Her Lectures," *New-York Spectator*, Aug. 11, 1829.

79. "Under the Head of *National Education*," *New-York Spectator*, Sept. 15, 1829.

80. "Miss Fanny Wright," *New-York Commercial Advertiser*, Jan. 12, 1829. These editors' widespread sarcasm about Wright developed in tandem with Wright's own sarcastic representations of the newspaper press in her lectures. "Miss Frances Wright," *New-York Spectator*, Jan. 9, 1829, reprinted from the *New-York Commercial Advertiser*.

81. *New-York Commercial Advertiser*, Jan. 15, 1829, cited in Eckhardt, *Fanny Wright*, 187; "Mr. Stone of the Commercial," *Chronicle of the Times* (New York), Jan. 17, 1829.

82. "Miss Wright's Lectures," *New-York Evening Post*, Jan. 10, 1829.

83. *New-York Commercial Advertiser*, Jan. 10, 1829, cited in Eckhardt, *Fanny Wright*, 186; "Miss Fanny Wright," *Springfield* [MA] *Republican*, Jan. 21, 1829, reprinted from the *New-York Commercial Advertiser*.

84. "Mr. Stone of the Commercial," *Chronicle of the Times* (New York), Jan. 17, 1829. Philadelphia editors were more likely to remain silent during her lecture ap-

pearances than were editors in other cities. I have found very few mentions, for example, of her frequent speeches there in May, June, and July 1829, except in Wright's own *Free Enquirer*. She reported that some papers refused to publish the Walnut Street Theater's advertisement for her lectures. "Unnecessary Precaution," *Free Enquirer,* 2nd ser., 1 (May 20, 1829): 238.

85. To that effect, William Cullen Bryant of the *Evening Post* encapsulated the situation sarcastically in a poem addressed to Wright. In it, he enjoyed the fact that "Colonel Stone, the learn'd and brave ... Hangs on the words that leave thy mouth, / Slaking his intellectual drouth / In that rich stream of eloquence, / And notes thy teachings, to repeat / Their wisdom in his classic sheet." *New-York Evening Post,* Jan. 29, 1829, cited in Waterman, *Frances Wright,* 173.

86. "Miss Frances Wright," *Niles' Weekly Register* (Baltimore), 35 (Jan. 24, 1829): 345.

87. "Miss Frances Wright," *New-York Commercial Advertiser,* Jan. 5, 1829, reprinted in the *New-York Spectator;* "Miss Wright's Lectures," *Correspondent* (New York), 4 (1829): 414.

88. "From the N.Y. Statesman," *Norwich* [CT] *Courier,* Jan. 21, 1829.

89. "Miss Wright's Lectures," *New-York Evening Post,* Jan. 10, 1829.

90. "Park Theatre," *New-York American,* Jan. 26, 1829.

91. "A Female Preacher," *Boston Recorder and Religious Telegraph,* Mar. 19, 1829, reprinted from the *Western Recorder* (Utica, NY); see also "Park Theatre," ibid.

92. See, for example, "A Female Preacher," *Boston Recorder and Religious Telegraph,* Mar. 19, 1829; emphasis in the original; "Frances Wright," *New-York Evening Post,* Jan. 29, 1829; "Frances Wright," *Christian Intelligencer and Eastern Chronicle* (Gardiner, ME), Jan. 30, 1829. Philip Hone, the New York diarist mentioned above, also used these designations.

93. "Miss Fanny Wright," *Springfield* [MA] *Republican,* Jan. 21, 1829, reprinted from the *New-York Spectator.*

94. Q. in a Corner, "From the N.Y. Statesman," *Norwich* [CT] *Courier,* Jan. 21, 1829.

95. "Frances Wright," *New-York Evening Post,* Jan. 29, 1829.

96. They depict a new "urgent attempt to expel the lower sort altogether from the scene of reception, to homogenize the audience by refining and domesticating its energy, sublimating its diverse physical pleasures into a purely contemplative force, replacing a dispersed, heterodox, noisy participation in the *event* of the theatre by silent specular intensity." Stallybrass and White, *Politics and Poetics of Transgression,* 87.

97. Hone, *Diary of Philip Hone, 1828-1851,* 1:9-10. In 1802-3, Washington Irving employed a similar language of contempt for his fellow theatergoers when he likened the noise from the gallery "to that which prevailed in Noah's Ark; for we have an imitation of the whistles and yells of every kind of animal." Likewise, in 1832 Frances Trollope observed audience members in coarse dress, spitting, and reeking "of onions and whiskey." Cited in Levine, *Highbrow/Lowbrow,* 25.

Levine and other scholars have found that theatergoers of the nineteenth century were so heterogeneous as to be termed "a microcosm of American society."

Though audiences were divided by class within the theater by ticket prices (elites inhabited the boxes, the "middling sort" sat in the pit, and everyone else—apprentices, servants, poor workingmen, blacks, prostitutes—sat in the gallery), he has argued that this microcosm represented a "rich shared public culture" that was to disappear by the twentieth century. In doing so, he downplays the distaste for their fellow audience members expressed by Irving and others in order to stress the positive qualities of that shared public culture—an interpretation that rests on its contrast with twentieth-century public life. Levine, *Highbrow/Lowbrow*, 9, 24.

98. Trollope, *Domestic Manners of the Americans*, 149.

99. "Mistress Wright's Lectures," *Western Recorder* (Utica, NY), Mar. 10, 1829, reprinted from the *Rochester Observer*.

100. "Miss Wright Again," *Springfield* [MA] *Republican*, Feb. 11, 1829, reprinted from the *New-York Enquirer*.

101. W., "State of Public Feeling in New York," *Free Enquirer*, 2nd ser., 1 (1829): 147.

102. See, for example, "Wrightiana," *New-York American*, Jan. 29, 1829; An Amateur, *Daily Albany Argus*, Nov. 7, 1829; Philadelphus, "Priestcraft and Witchcraft," *Free Enquirer*, 2nd ser., 1 (Sept. 23, 1829): 380.

103. A Spectator, "To the Editors of the Free Enquirer," *Free Enquirer*, 2nd ser., 1 (May 20, 1829): 238.

104. "For the Free Enquirer," *Free Enquirer*, 2nd ser., 1 (June 10, 1829): 271; "News from Boston," and "Miss Frances Wright," *Free Enquirer*, 2nd ser., 1 (Aug. 12, 1829): 329–30.

105. "Miss Wright's Lecture upon Knowledge," *New-York American*, Jan. 5, 1829.

106. "Miss Wright," *New-York Commercial Advertiser*, Jan. 10, 1829. For more attention to the women in her audiences, see "Last Evening, Miss Frances Wright," *Aurora and Pennsylvania Gazette* (Philadelphia), Jan. 8, 1829; "Miss Frances Wright," *New-York Spectator*, Jan. 9, 1829; "Miss Wright," *Chronicle of the Times* (New York), Jan. 10, 1829; and "Infidelity," *Boston Recorder and Religious Telegraph*, Jan. 29, 1829, quoting from the *New York Journal of Commerce*.

107. Wright claimed that the number of women attending her talks increased steadily throughout the tour. D'Arusmont, *Life, Letters, and Lectures*, 20. Simon O'Ferrall, an English traveler who saw her speak at the Hall of Science in July 1829, reported that the sexes were equally distributed in the audience; and by June 1830 the *New York Courier and Enquirer* reported that her New York audience had more women than men. Simon A. O'Ferrall, *A Ramble of Six Thousand Miles through the United States of America* (London: E. Wilson, 1832), 15, 330. Frances Trollope believed more women attended Wright's farewell address in Philadelphia than she had ever seen in an American theater. Trollope, *Domestic Manners of the Americans*. Likewise, substantial evidence about Wright's relative success in making converts is lacking. Yet several observers, including Lyman Beecher, attested that women of all classes (most shockingly, for Beecher, elite women) "numbered among her votaries, and advocated her sentiments." Beecher, *Works*, 1:93. Each of these ob-

servers was surprised by such high female attendance. On her wish for more female auditors, see "Miss Wright's Lecture upon Knowledge," *New-York American,* Jan. 5, 1829.

108. Vindex, "For the Evening Post," *New-York Evening Post,* Jan. 12, 1829.

109. A Mother, "To the Editors of the Evening Post," *New-York Evening Post,* Jan. 27, 1829. The writer's tone of panic inspired the *Free Enquirer* to speculate that this was no "mother" but a nervous male minister hiding behind a pseudonym. A.Z., "For the Free Enquirer," *Free Enquirer,* 2nd ser., 1 (Mar. 11, 1829): 156.

110. P.Q.T., "Miss Mary Ann Wolstoncraft," *Western Recorder* (Utica, NY), Oct. 20, 1829.

111. Bradley N. Cumings diary, vol. 1, Mar. 17–18, 1831, MaHS.

112. Wright left the United States briefly for Haiti in early 1830, when she took Nashoba's former slaves there as part of her earlier promise to free them and transport them out of the country. Camilla became ill shortly after her return and died within months after they arrived in Paris. Wright returned to the United States in 1835 and settled in Cincinnati, accompanied by her daughter and her new husband, a French physician and reformer named Guillaume Philquepal D'Arusmont. She lectured again in 1836 and 1838 on behalf of the Democratic Party and began a new series of lectures on the evils of contemporary society. Her audiences were so scanty, however, that she abandoned her lecture career and returned to France in 1839. Thereafter she published one more work, *England, the Civilizer* (1848), but never returned to public speaking. She died in 1852 at age fifty-seven.

113. "Any thing in the shape of a woman" may have evoked the old phrase, "devil in the shape of a woman." Catharine Beecher, *Letters on the Difficulties of Religion* (Hartford, CT: Belknap and Hamersley, 1836), cited in Molly Abel Travis, "Frances Wright: The Other Woman of Early American Feminism," *Women's Studies* 22 (1993): 389-97.

114. Ginzberg, "'Hearts of Your Readers Will Shudder,'" 195–96.

115. See, for example, Emma Willard, "Address," read by Rev. Mr. Peck in St. John's Church, Troy, New York, Jan. 8, 1833 (cited in O'Connor, *Pioneer Women Orators,* 48 n. 20). Like Beecher and Phelps, Willard, an educator at the Troy Female Seminary, used her attack on Wright as a means of touting better education for girls. "When men forget in their legislative capacity, our rights—spend nothing on girls' education and millions on males—make oppressive laws on us, it is not strange some seek to break the lock which God has instituted and in which woman, in obedience to her nature and the express commands of God, acknowledges man as her head. Hence the ravings of Mary Wollstonecraft, of Frances Wright and Robert Owen, and hence the fanatic set." In other words, a better female education would not *produce* Wright-like, dangerous "learned ladies"; it would *prevent* their being made. With such statements Willard, Beecher, and others purported to defend their sex against such dangers, taking on the mantle of gender guardians—a powerful and authoritative role for female educators.

116. Ganter, "Unexceptional Eloquence of Sarah Josepha Hale's *Lecturess*," 274; see also Caroline Field Levander, "Bawdy Talk: The Politics of Women's Public

Speech in *The Lectures* and *The Bostonians*," *American Literature* 67 (1995): 467–85, esp. 475–76.

CONCLUSION

1. "From which does the community derive the greatest benefit, the talent of extemporaneous speaking or communicating ideas by writing?" Bradley N. Cumings, Diary, Jan. 16, 1835, MaHS.

2. See, for example, the Boston School Committee's endorsement of John Pierpont's *National Reader* in a printed circular advertisement of 1835. Carter, Hendee and Co. to Elias Nason, Apr. 16, 1835, Elias Nason Papers, AAS.

3. Zboray, *Fictive People*, 55.

4. Jesse Hutchinson Jr. (lyrics) and N. Barker (arrangement), "Uncle Sam's Farm: Song and Chorus" (Boston: Geo. P. Reed, 1850), Lester S. Levy Collection of Sheet Music, JHU.

5. Nehemiah Cleaveland, "On Lyceums and Societies for the Diffusion of Useful Knowledge," in *Annual Meeting of the American Institute of Instruction* (Boston: Hilliard, Gray, 1831), 150–51.

6. Trollope, *Domestic Manners of the Americans*, 57.

7. On this subject see Loughran, *Republic in Print*.

Index

Abeel, Garret, 129
abolition movement, 97–98, 181, 214–16
academies, 20–21, 68, 73–79, 132
actors and acting, 53–55, 187, 192. *See also* theatricality and theatrical scenes
Adair, James, 92
Adams, Daniel, 22
Adams, John, 87, 141
Adams, John Quincy, 36, 43–44, 48, 184
Addison, Joseph, 121
African Americans, 9, 160, 213
Age of Reason, 130
Aikin, John, 60
Aitken, Robert, 148
Albany Typographical Society, 153–57
Allan, Reverend, 89, 108–9
ambition, 54, 61, 65–67, 71–72, 74–77, 80, 129, 195
American Grammar, 26
American Lady's Preceptor, 41
American literature, 39–46, 65–66, 70, 73–75, 83, 85, 89, 102–3, 105–7, 127–28, 130–44
American Magazine, 94–95
American Museum, 96

American Orator, 18, 43, 46
American Philosophical Society, 20
American Preceptor, 87
American Preceptor Improved, 28
American Reader, 22, 41, 43
Ames, Fisher, 45, 105
Amory, Thomas, 36
Andrews, Sydney, 147
Anthology Society, 124–25
Apess, William, 106
artisan republicanism. *See* republicanism: artisan
Art of Speaking, 23
Asbridge, George, 160
associations. *See* societies and clubs
Atkinson Academy, 29–31
audiences, 14, 45–48, 91–92, 180, 197–98, 203; promiscuous audiences, 180, 203, 205–8
Aurora and Pennsylvania Gazette, 191

bachelors, 11, 134–44
Barber, Jonathan, 62–64
Barlow, Joel, 121
Baron, Ava, 155
Bartlett, Montgomery, 10
Bederman, Gail, 182
Beecher, Catharine, 79, 209–10

belles lettres, 103–5
Bemis, J. D., 93
Bercovitch, Sacvan, 97
Berquin, Arnauld, 56
Bhabha, Homi, 139
Bingham, Caleb, 39, 70, 87, 89, 93
biography, female, 69
Black Friars Society, 117–18
Blair, Hugh, 23–24, 40, 90
Blumin, Stuart, 124
Boston Latin School, 41–42
Boston Reading Lessons, 107
Boston Recorder, 165
Boston Tea Party, 87
Boston Typographical Society, 160
Botein, Stephen, 160
Boydston, Jeanne, 78
Britishness, 2–3, 39–40, 84–85, 95
Brown, Christopher Leslie, 98–99
Bryant, William Cullen, 190, 200–202
Burdick, William, 158
Burgh, James, 23
Burke, Edmund, 17
Bushman, Richard, 124

Calhoun, John C., 169
Calliopean Society, 116–48, 157, 167, 178, 180, 211, 213
Campbell, George, 23
Carey, Mathew, 96, 102, 155
Cass, Lewis, 106
Catherine II of Russia (the Great), 77
Cato, 121, 192
Chandler, Adoniram, 145, 159
Chastellux, François Jean (Marquis), 104
Chautauqua adult education movement, 212
Cherokee Indians, 89, 106, 108
Chester, Caroline, 89
Chesterfield, Philip Dormer Stanhope (Lord), 60
Christian Register, 94
Chronicle of the Times, 183, 202–3

Churchill, George, 156–57
Cicero, 44, 67, 71, 83–84
citizenship, 1, 3–4, 11, 129–30, 139, 170–71; for women, 75–77
City Hotel (New York), 207
civic virtue, 17
civil society, 12, 58–59
Clark, Jefferson, 145
class, 123–24, 151, 167–78, 180, 184, 202–6
classical languages (Latin and Greek), 20, 67, 166, 170
Clay, Henry, 19, 105
Cleaveland, Nehemiah, 214
Cliosophic Society, 117
Clough, John, 160–61
clubs. *See* societies and clubs
Cmiel, Kenneth, 5, 184
Cohen, Daniel, 120
college, 20–21
College of William and Mary, 21
colonization of freed slaves, 182–83
Columbia (iconic figure), 2
Columbia College, 117
Columbian Monitor, 40
Columbian Orator, 89, 93, 108
Columbian Preceptor, 24
Columbian Reader, 45
Columbian Society, 133
Columbia Typographical Society, 153, 155, 167–78
Commercial Advertiser, 186, 195–96, 201–2, 207
Common Sense, 110
conduct, 6, 13, 23–24, 34–35, 38–39, 41–43, 55–57, 60, 84, 87–88, 91–94, 116–21
conversation, 53–57, 61–65, 81, 115–21, 124–28
Cooke, Increase, 18
Cooper, James Fenimore, 106
coquettes, 59, 74, 79–81, 134
Cornplanter (Seneca Indian), 98
Correspondent, The, 203, 206

counterpublic, 55, 72, 214
courtship, 134–41
Cremin, Lawrence, 20
Cresap, Michael, 83, 86, 100
criticism (of writing and oratory), 6, 28–29, 31–38, 121, 124–26
Cumings, Bradley, 208, 211, 213

Dana, Joseph, 40
Davis, Richard Bingham, 141–44
debating societies, 9, 13, 79, 88, 115–44, 211, 213
Declaration of Independence, 39
Deloria, Philip, 9, 87, 95
Democracy in America, 144
Democratic Party, 168
Democratic-Republican Societies, 117–18, 129–31
democratization, 44–48, 77–81, 111
Demosthenes, 17–19, 45–46, 67, 83
Dennie, Joseph, 133
Depeyster, Gerard, 121
Diary, The, 142
Doddridge, Joseph, 106
Dorion, Stephen, 153–54
Dramatic Dialogues, 34
Dunmore, Lord (John Murray), 86
duplicity, 92–96, 98, 138–44. *See also* theatricality and theatrical scenes
Duryee, John, 129

editors, 8, 10, 84, 91, 93–96, 103, 130–44, 165–66, 179–210
Edmund, William and Polly, 56
education, 1, 8, 10–11, 13–14, 18–82, 86–90, 159, 170–72, 211–13; for African Americans, 33; centralization in, 20–21, 211–14; female, 11, 13, 53–82; for Indians, 89–90, 108–9; Lancastrian system, 47–48, 170; for the poor and working classes, 20, 46–48, 179; reform of, 21–22, 46–48. *See also* schoolbooks; schoolchildren; schoolteachers

Elements of Gesture, 25–26
elocution, 10, 13, 22–52, 54–55, 59–65, 67–69, 75, 79–82, 84–85, 87–89, 109–11, 116, 125, 132, 186, 192, 216. *See also* gesture
Emery, Miss, 187–88
emulation, 17, 25, 87–88
English Reader, 22, 40
Enquirer, The (St. Louis, MO), 168
Erskine, Thomas, 1st Baron (Lord), 100
exhibitions and examinations, 8, 11, 13, 19, 30–38, 51, 53, 79–81, 89, 110

fame. *See* ambition; modesty
Farmer's Brother (Seneca Indian), 84, 93
Faustus Association, 164
Federalist, The, 43, 127
Federalists, 3, 131, 133
female education. *See* education: female
female intellectual capacity, 58–61, 65, 70
female monsters, 179–81, 195–98, 208–9
female oratory. *See* oratory: female
Ferguson, Elizabeth Graeme, 70, 77
Fliegelman, Jay, 5, 36, 88
Foster, Hannah, 135
Founding Fathers, 1
Fowle, William Bentley, 60
Franklin, Benjamin, 39, 87, 91, 145–46, 148, 161–62, 164–65, 167, 170–71, 177–78
Franklin Typographical Society (Boston), 159
Franklin Typographical Society (New York), 148, 160–61
Fraser, Nancy, 55
Frederick, John, 106
Free Enquirer, 189–90, 206. *See also* *New Harmony Gazette*
Freemasons, 117–18

free thought, 184, 203, 205–6
French, Benjamin Brown, 185
French and Indian War, 83
French Revolution, 117, 130–31, 133, 181
friendship, 118–20, 123–24

Gallatin, Albert, 35
Gallison, John, 37, 133
Galloway, Joseph, 3
Ganter, Granville, 79, 187, 210
Gardiner, William Howard, 7
Garrison, William Lloyd, 215
Gazette of the United States, 150
gender, 10–14, 53–82, 117, 134–44, 154–55, 166, 179–81, 185–203, 205–10, 213
General Advertiser, 130
Genêt, Edmund-Charles (Citizen), 130
Genius of Universal Emancipation, 182–83
German society, 118
gesture, 25–27, 35, 37, 62–64
Ginzburg, Lori, 180, 209
Gleaner, The, 65–66
Gleason, Joseph, 164–65
Godwin, William, 78
Goodman, Dena, 5
Grammatical Institute, 22
Greek. *See* classical languages (Latin and Greek)
Green, Duff, 168–78, 180, 190, 215
Grimké, Angelina and Sarah, 210
Gustafson, Sandra, 5

Habermas, Jürgen, 4–5, 12, 61
halfway journeymen, 148, 152–55, 176
Hallet, Jeremiah, 123
Hamilton, Andrew, 128
Harker, Ann, 58, 71
Harrington, Anna, 55
Heaton, Nathaniel, Jr., 24
Hemphill, Dallett, 60
Henry, Patrick, 17–18

Hervieu, Auguste, 193
heterosociability, 12, 60
Hints to Public Speakers, 61
Hoar, Susannah, 66–68
homosociability, 118
Hone, Philip, 184, 205
Hornor, Joseph, 115
Hubbard, John, 22
humanitarianism, 91, 94, 97–98
Hunt, Henry, 123
Hutchinson Family, 212

illiteracy. *See* literacy
Indian oratory. *See* oratory: Indian
Indians, 1, 9, 83–111, 140; Indian princess (iconic figure), 2; interaction with whites, 84, 86; removal, 101, 214; "vanishing," 85, 99–109
Isaac, Rhys, 39

Jackson, Andrew, 106, 168, 184
Jackson, Rachel, 191
Jacobins, 131, 142
Jefferson, Thomas, 20, 83, 85–86, 90, 128
jeremiads, 97
Johnson, John Barent, 117–18, 120
journeymen, 116, 120, 145–47, 156–57, 165; journeymen printers (*see* printers, journeymen)
Juvenile Reader, 34

Kaestle, Carl, 47
Kelley, Mary, 5, 79
Klein, Lawrence, 5, 12, 61
Knox, Henry, 98
Knox, T., 61
Koschnik, Albrecht, 133

Ladies' Literary Companion, 71
Lancaster, Joseph, 47
Lancastrian system of education. *See* education: Lancastrian system

Latin. *See* classical languages (Latin and Greek)
Leonard, Seth, 26
Lessons for Youth, 28
letters, 10
Letters to His Son, 60
levees. *See* salons
Liberator, The, 215
libraries, 119
Lincoln, Abraham, 10
literacy, 7, 57–58; illiteracy, 85
localism, 3, 4
Locke, John, 58
Logan (Mingo Indian), 83, 85–87, 91, 95, 99–100, 106
Loughran, Trish, 5, 109
Louisville Focus, 185
lyceums, 212, 214

Mack, Ebenezer, 159
Madison, James, 128
Magaw, Samuel, 59
magazines, 13, 84–86, 90–105, 110, 116–17, 124–44
manners, 18, 75–76. *See also* conduct
Manuscript, The, 107
Marshall, John, 45–46
Mason, Priscilla, 75–77
Masonic Hall (New York), 179, 189, 200
Massachusetts Magazine, 91–92
Maxwell, Robert, 149
McGuffey's Readers, 87
Mental Flower Garden, 60
Merrell, James, 101
Metamora, 106
Minor, D. K., 186, 196
modesty, 61, 65–67, 72, 79–82. *See also* ambition
monitorial education. *See* education: Lancastrian system
Montesquieu, Charles-Louis de Secondat, 92
Monthly Anthology, 95, 102–3, 124

Monthly Miscellany, 91
Murray, Judith Sargent, 65, 135
Murray, Lindley, 22, 40

Nashoba, 182–83, 185
National Advocate, 185
National Gazette, 196–97
national identification, 1, 2, 4, 19–20, 38–52, 45–48, 80, 82, 84–85, 88, 95–99, 105–10, 127–32, 146–47, 158–60, 162–63, 166–67, 172, 212–17
National Typographical Society, 177–78
Native Eloquence, 102
New American Selection of Lessons, 40
New England Tale, A, 79–81
New Harmony, Indiana, 183, 190, 192–93
New Harmony Gazette, 183–84. *See also Free Enquirer*
Newman, Simon, 130
New York American, 186–89, 195, 204, 207
New York Enquirer, 189, 206
New-York Evening Post, 190, 200, 202, 204, 207
New York Free School Society, 47
New-York Magazine, 116, 124–44, 213
New York Spectator, 192, 200
New York Statesman, 179–80, 204
New-York Typographical Society, 145, 148–49, 151–52, 154–59, 162–64
Niles' Weekly Register, 190, 203
Noah, M. M., 205–6
Northern Debating Society, 211, 213
Notes on the State of Virginia, 83, 87, 128
novels, 79–81

Ogilvie, James, 37
old maids, 74, 134–41
Oneida Indians, 98
Ontario Repository, 102
oratory, 4, 6, 7, 10, 19; classical, 17, 30, 43, 46, 48, 83; female, 9, 11,

oratory (*cont.*)
13, 53–82, 179–210, 213; Indian, 9, 10, 13, 83–111, 213; male, 17, 35–37, 43–47. *See also* elocution
Owen, Robert Dale, 183–85

Paine, Thomas, 117, 129–30
Parkinson, Robert, 86
Park Theater, 189, 194, 200, 204–5
parlors, 35, 60–61
Payne, B., 121
Peabody, Stephen, 30
Peale, Charles Willson, 48–50
Pennsylvania Inquirer, 169
penny press, 180, 211
Persian Letters, 92
Phelps, Almira, 78–79, 179, 210
Philadelphia Repository, 133
Philadelphia Typographical Society, 148–50, 155, 161, 166
Philippa of Hainault (Queen), 71
Pitt, William, 17, 39, 48–50
plagiarism, 164–65
Pocahontas, 94, 103–5, 107
political participation, 4, 54, 72–78, 129–32, 137–41, 143–44, 182–83, 212–13
Poor, John, 73
Poovey, Mary, 195
Poulson's American Daily Advertiser, 161
Practical Reader, 10–11
Practical Treatise on Gesture, 62–64
prattling, 55–57
Present for Young Ladies, 59, 77
Pretzer, William, 176
Priestley, Joseph, 23
printers, journeymen, 9, 13–14, 145–78, 190, 213, 215; "rats" (journeymen working below rate), 152–55, 176; wage-setting campaigns, 146–56, 168–78
print media, 3–5, 13–14, 84–85, 95, 99–111, 146–47, 154–78, 180–81, 183–214

print/oratory interdependency, 10–11, 22, 27, 44–45, 85, 94–95, 124–26, 151–52, 162–64, 167, 183–85, 187–90, 209–13
promiscuous audiences. *See* audiences: promiscuous audiences
public, the, 1, 4–7, 9–10, 12, 14, 19, 28, 37–38, 43, 46–48, 51, 54, 61, 72, 78, 81, 84, 90–91, 94–99, 105–11, 116, 126–31, 146–47, 170–78, 180–81, 189, 197–217. *See also* audience; civil society; counterpublic
public opinion, 4, 116, 125–34, 171, 180–81, 199–210, 215–16
public participation, 4–6, 11, 13, 18–19, 35–38, 43–45, 54–55, 58–59, 72–78, 81–82, 84, 91–99, 105–11, 126–31, 137–44, 151–52, 159–68, 170–78; women's, 53–82
public personae, 121–22, 125, 132–44, 216
public/private distinction, 5, 10–12, 58–61, 117, 122
public sphere, 6, 9, 11–12, 54, 58–61, 115, 144, 151, 160, 185
punctuation, 27

Rafield, John, 60
rakes, 137
Randolph, John, 19
Red Jacket (Seneca Indian), 84, 96, 103, 106
regular training, 147–48, 151, 154, 168–69, 171–72, 177
Reins, David, 148
republicanism, 54, 77, 182, 187; artisan, 146, 178
republican motherhood, 54, 67, 69–72, 76–77
Republicans, 3, 78, 127, 130
rhetoric, 23, 65–68, 73, 76–77, 97, 125, 132–33, 161, 186–87, 209, 214–16
Richardson, Joseph, 27, 40
Rights of Man, 135

Ripley, Sally, 32, 39, 60, 68
Rochester Observer, 205
Rock, Miss, 187–88
Rose, Joseph, 123, 129
Rowson, Susannah, 59, 69, 77, 135
Royall, Anne, 191
Rush, Benjamin, 19, 21, 70
Russell, Amelia, 77
Ryan, Mary, 124

Salem Observer, 191
salons, 61, 70–71
school attendance, 22, 57–58
schoolbooks, 8–10, 17–19, 21–22, 24–28, 33–35, 39–41, 43–46, 51–52, 55–57, 59–65, 68–72, 84–88, 93, 100–101, 104, 107–10, 212; biographical sketches in, 17, 41–43, 45–46, 65, 69–72
schoolchildren, 8, 13, 84–85, 88–89
School of Wisdom, 40
schools. *See* education
schoolteachers, 8, 22, 30–31
Scott, Joan, 5
Scottish Enlightenment, 58–59, 76, 82, 181
Secondary Lessons, 107
Sedgwick, Catharine Maria, 79–81
self-improvement, 17, 22–25, 30–43, 55–58, 60, 68–69, 87–99, 116–17, 157–67, 211, 214
seminaries. *See* academies
Seneca Falls Convention, 214
Seneca Indians, 98
sensibility, 19, 24, 41–43, 75–76, 91, 94–95, 110, 118
Sewell, William, 31
Shakespeare's plays, 71, 121, 192
Sharpe, Mrs., 194
Shawnee Indians, 86
Shenandoah (an Indian orator, possibly fictional), 89
Shrupp, Eliza, 74
Sigourney, Lydia, 78–79

slavery, 182–83
Smith, John (Captain), 94, 103–4
Smith, Rogers, 4
Smith, Thomas, 88
Smith-Rosenberg, Carroll, 139–40
societies and clubs, 115–21, 126–27, 130–31, 133–34, 143–44, 148, 150–52, 164–65, 168
Society for the Attainment of Useful Knowledge, 118
Sommer, Doris, 85
South Carolina Weekly Museum, 91
Spalding, Mr., 28–29
Speckled Snake (Muscogee Indian), 84, 94
Spectator, The, 87–88
Stagg, Thomas, Jr., 123
Stallybrass, Peter, 205
Stanton, Elizabeth Cady, 214
Stearns, Charles, 34
Stearns, Susannah, 72, 74
stereotyping, 154
Stewart, Maria, 210
Stockbridge Indians, 96
Stone, William Leete, 186, 194–97, 201–4, 207
Stoutinburgh, Thomas, 123
strikes, 148, 169, 174, 176–77
Stuart, Gilbert, 51
Swanwick, John, 66

Tammany Society, 87, 117, 119
Taylor, Charles, 8
teachers. *See* schoolteachers
theatricality and theatrical scenes, 25, 27–28, 33, 53, 62–64, 187–89, 192, 205–6. *See also* actors and acting; duplicity
Theological Society, 117
Tilton, James, 76
toasts, 161–64, 66–67
Tocqueville, Alexis de, 144
Tontine City Tavern (New York), 51
Trollope, Frances, 185, 205, 214

Troy Female Academy, 78, 179
Tullian Society, 115
Turner, Mr. (elocution instructor), 24
typographical societies, 14, 147–78

Understanding Reader, 22
United Irishmen, 129
United States Telegraph, 168–69, 175–77
Universal Asylum, 18, 92
Uranian Society, 117
U.S.-Britain comparisons, 2–3, 17–18, 38–41, 84–85
U.S. Constitution, 1, 3, 39, 128
U.S. flag, 2
U.S.-Indian policy, 86, 97, 99–101, 105–7

Vicinus, Martha, 70
Views of Society and Manners in America, 182
Vindication of the Rights of Woman, 58, 68, 135
Virginian Orator, 25

Waldstreicher, David, 5
Wallace, Molly, 60, 67–68
Walsh, Robert, 196–97
Warner, Michael, 5, 40
Washington, George, 2, 10, 18, 40–41, 43, 51–52, 61, 69, 84, 131, 141, 167; Farewell Address, 10, 43, 51; Lansdowne Portrait, 51
Washington Institute, 170–78
Waterman, Bryan, 130
Webb, Nathan, 60
Webster, Daniel, 19, 105
Webster, Noah, 19, 22, 39, 94–95
Weekly Magazine, 96
Western Recorder, 204–7
Whigs, 127
Whiskey Rebellion, 131
White, Allon, 205
Whitman, Bathsheba, 31
Wilentz, Sean, 146, 192
Willard, Samuel, 107
Wingrove, Elizabeth, 77
Wirt, William, 105
Wollstonecraft, Mary, 55, 58–59, 68, 75–79, 81, 135, 179
women's rights, 58–59, 76–77, 214
Wright, Frances, 12–14, 179–210, 213–15; physical appearance, 191–92, 197–98; sister Camilla, 181, 208

Young Gentleman and Lady's Monitor, 58
Young Ladies' Academy of Philadelphia, 59, 66–67, 73, 75
Young Ladies' Accidence, 60

Zagarri, Rosemarie, 59, 76, 78, 187